D0853497

LaGrave Ave. CRC Media Center
107 LaGrave Ave. SE
Grand Rapids, MI 49503
(616) 454-7204
www.lagrave.org

FEB 1 4 2013

Reforming Hollywood

REFORMING HOLLYWOOD

How American Protestants Fought for Freedom at the Movies

WILLIAM D. ROMANOWSKI

OXFORD
UNIVERSITY PRESS

OXFORD

UNIVERSITY PRESS

Oxford University Press, Inc., publishes works that further
Oxford University's objective of excellence
in research, scholarship, and education.

Oxford   New York
Auckland   Cape Town   Dar es Salaam   Hong Kong   Karachi
Kuala Lumpur   Madrid   Melbourne   Mexico City   Nairobi
New Delhi   Shanghai   Taipei   Toronto

With offices in
Argentina   Austria   Brazil   Chile   Czech Republic   France   Greece
Guatemala   Hungary   Italy   Japan   Poland   Portugal   Singapore
South Korea   Switzerland   Thailand   Turkey   Ukraine   Vietnam

Published by Oxford University Press, Inc.
198 Madison Avenue, New York, New York 10016

www.oup.com

Oxford is a registered trademark of Oxford University Press

Library of Congress Cataloging-in-Publication Data
Romanowski, William D.
Reforming Hollywood: how American Protestants fought for freedom at the movies /
William D. Romanowski.
p.   cm.
Includes bibliographical references (p.) and index.
ISBN 978-0-19-538784-1
1. Motion pictures—Religious aspects—Protestant churches. 2. United States—
Church history—20th century. 3. United States—Church history—21st century. I. Title.
BR517.R56   2012
261.5'7—dc23   2011037884

1 3 5 7 9 8 6 4 2
Printed in the United States of America
on acid-free paper

For Donna, and Michael, and Tara,
and in loving memory of
Mary Sawchak Romanowski

The freedom of the screen in its creative processes is related to freedom of speech, freedom of assembly and freedom of the press. These rights are never unlimited but are always conditioned by public welfare and safety. The problem, as related to the commercial cinema, is to strike effectively at its deliberate degradation, to encourage the development of exceptional films and films for selected groups, to appreciate and applaud the finer achievements of producers, directors, writers, artists, technicians, and exhibitors, and to assist in elevating the public taste.
Federal Council of the Churches of Christ in America, 1933

Contents

Preface and Acknowledgments

IN 1933, ALMOST two decades before the Supreme Court granted free speech status to the movies, the Federal Council of Churches of Christ in America, a national Protestant organization, issued a statement succinctly summarizing its position on the cinema: "The freedom of the screen in its creative processes is related to freedom of speech, freedom of assembly and freedom of the press. These rights are never unlimited but are always conditioned by public welfare and safety." The following year, Roman Catholic bishops formed the Legion of Decency to coordinate boycotts of immoral movies. Within months, a lay Catholic was appointed head of the film industry's new Production Code Administration (PCA), whose task was to ensure that every movie exhibited in theaters adhered to the tenets of the 1930 Production Code—a document drawn up by Catholics and Hollywood personnel.

Protestant leaders expected to harness 1920s Hollywood through the person and agency of Will H. Hays, an eminent Presbyterian layman and a powerful leader in the national Republican Party. Hays had been instrumental in the election of Warren G. Harding to the presidency in 1920, and resigned as postmaster general to become the first president of the Motion Picture Producers and Distributors of America (MPPDA) in 1922. The prevailing view in histories of American film is that Protestants were determined to impose the rule of censorship on Hollywood, and for that reason they refused to cooperate with the Hays organization, as the MPPDA became known.

Hays's first major initiative was to set up a Committee on Public Relations as a point of contact between film producers and national civic and religious organizations. Noting that some of "America's most prestigious social organizations" were represented on the committee, Garth Jowett writes in his definitive social history, *Film: The Democratic Art,* "Organized religious bodies (especially Protestants) played a minor role in the work of this committee because their objectives still lay in the direction of censorship, and they saw this type of cooperation with the industry as a distraction created to draw attention away from their efforts." To the contrary, my research reveals that Protestants occupied *the* top leadership positions in both the MPPDA and the Committee on Public Relations. Moreover, throughout the 1920s, Hays eagerly pursued an ongoing cooperative arrangement with the Federal Council of Churches as central to his public relations campaign. This evidence also refutes Frank Walsh's contention in his thorough analysis of Catholic undertakings, *Sin and Censorship: The Catholic Church and the Motion Picture Industry*, that Hays failed "to draw any significant backing from the Protestant churches, which should have been the natural constituency of someone who was a Presbyterian elder, [and] made Catholic cooperation all the more necessary."

Hollywood's cooperation with Catholics in the early 1930s signaled a dramatic shift in cultural power and also marks an end to the Protestant thread in film histories. Little is known of ongoing Protestant-Hollywood relations after the advent of the Production Code Administration. Afterward, Protestant activities typically receive no more than a mention or are relegated to an "other" category. Two explanations stand out. First, Protestant actions have been situated within the discourse of *censorship*, when they were more centrally about industry *regulation*. For the most part, the strategies of church leaders who sought to establish government control have been categorized as "Protestant" and have been mistaken as the sum total of Protestant activity, whereas those of church officials who might have cooperated with the film industry toward self-regulation were somehow not identified as being religiously motivated.

A second, related explanation is that Hays's empowerment of a Catholic quality control over movie content in effect rendered Protestant initiatives moot, while also obscuring Protestant contributions for future historians. Even with an awareness of earlier Catholic involvement, most accounts take the studio alliance with Catholics as a sudden, surprising, and momentous—if also somewhat isolated—event that had little, if any, relation to the Protestant establishment. In any case, in the struggle for cinematic freedom Protestants have been cast as unrelentingly censorial and pitted against both movie "czar" Will Hays, a Presbyterian teetotaler who favored Prohibition no less, and Catholics who opposed government regulation but took up a stringent church-enforced censorship of movie content. This book tells an altogether different story.

Reforming Hollywood introduces extensive archival research, much of it based on previously unexamined primary material from Protestant, Catholic, and film industry sources. Along with articles from religious periodicals, industry trade publications, and the press, these archival findings offer a fresh perspective on pivotal moments in film history and highlight other events of importance that have long been overlooked.

Because of the sometimes bewildering array of characters and organizations that appear in these pages, a brief alphabetical listing labeled "The Cast" immediately precedes the notes.

This study builds on existing ones in film and religious history and benefits from the pioneering work of scholars like Richard Maltby, Francis G. Couvares, Garth S. Jowett, Lary May, and others who have given particular attention to Protestantism. Theirs and other valuable studies that focus on the Catholic narrative, women's organizations, or movie censorship are referenced throughout this work. Indeed, I owe special thanks to Richard Maltby for making available to me materials from the Motion Picture Producers and Distributors of America, Inc., Microfilm Archive.

So many people helped during the course of this project. Though I cannot list everyone, I will always be thankful for family, friends, and colleagues who in countless ways lent their support. Let me begin by expressing my appreciation to the many librarians, archivists, and support staff who showed kindness, patience, and skill in providing assistance with my research: Nancy Taylor, Susan Flacks, Kenneth Ross, Eileen Meyer Sklar, Bridget Clancy, Beth Bensman, Leah Gass, Art Baxter, Charlene Peacock, and David Koch (Presbyterian Historical Society); Marion Parkinson (Free Library of Philadelphia); Barbara Hall and staff (Margaret Herrick Library); Randi Hokett, Hayden Guest, Jonathon Auxier, and Laura LaPlaca (USC Warner Bros. Archives); Ned Comstock (USC Cinema TV Library); Kevin Feeney (Archival Center, Archdiocese of Los Angeles); Sister Marguerita Smith (Archival Center, Archdiocese of New York); Sharon Sumpter (The Archives, University of Notre Dame); Nicholas Scheetz, Chris Ulrich, Lynn Conway, Karen O'Connell, and Scott Taylor (Special Collections Division, Georgetown University Library); John Shepherd and Jane Stoeffler (American Catholic History Research Center, Catholic University of America); Matthew Turi and Robin Davies Chen (Manuscripts Department, University of North Carolina); Carol Leadenham and Ronald M. Bulatoff (Hoover Institution Archives, Stanford University); Mark Vopelak and Brent Abercrombie (Indiana State Library); Dagmar K. Getz and Ryan Bean (Kautz Family YMCA Archives, University of Minnesota);

Susan Wade (New York Public Library); Bertha L. Ihnat (The Ohio State University Archives); David Heim and Heidi Baumgaertner (*The Christian Century*).

Bill Fore, Tom Trotter, and Jim Wall made their personal papers available to me, graciously submitted to interviews, and took time to respond to additional queries. Ken Wales was kind enough to give me details on the behind-the-scenes activities in the operations of the Broadcasting and Film Commission's West Coast Office.

Special thanks to Jim Trammell for sending me articles from his dissertation research files, Chris Rifkin for a copy of Barbara Stones's interview with Julian Rifkin, Mark Rasbach for a copy of his father's unpublished manuscript, H. K. Rasbach, "Proclaiming Christianity on Celluloid" (1940), Read Hanmer for providing information on his grandfather, and Joan Graves and the late Jack Valenti for consenting to interviews. Judy Dickie, then Valenti's personal assistant, was most hospitable in arranging and ensuring that the interview happened on what turned out to be a very busy day at the office. My sister Kim Dunderdale and her family opened their home to me and provided transportation to the library at UNC.

It would have been impossible to carry out the archival research and manage the time to write this book without institutional support. I gratefully acknowledge a grant from the National Endowment for the Humanities. The NEH Fellowship and Faculty Research Award, combined with a sabbatical leave, afforded me the time to finish the manuscript. Substantial financial assistance for travel, project expenses, and release time, for which I owe a debt of gratitude, was provided by Calvin College, the Calvin Center for Christian Scholarship, and the Calvin College Alumni Association. Much appreciation to Lois Konyndyk, Joel Carpenter, Deans of Research Stephen Evans, Janel Curry, and Matt Walhout, and Provost Claudia Beversluis for their help and support.

My thanks to the librarians at the Hekman Library, especially Harry Boonstra, Glen Remelts, Kathleen Struck, Eugene Schemper, and Kathi DeMay. I salute Bill Vriesema, Nate Wallace, and the IT staff at Calvin College. My colleagues in the Communication Arts & Sciences Department were steadfast in their encouragement. Over the years, a number of Calvin College students were involved with the research legwork: Peter Clark, Gretchen Cooper, Lise Evans, Mieke Jones, Katie Kladder, Kate Landau, Sarah Lawrence, Jonathan Shaw, Drake Dominici, Matt Harris, Brent Smith, Megan Thomassen, and Jennifer Vander Heide.

I am most appreciative for the valuable feedback I received from Peggy Bendroth and Carl Plantinga, and for the helpful comments from Terry Lindvall and Richard Maltby in the publisher's evaluation. My deep gratitude to Jim Bratt, who read not only the manuscript, but just about everything I've written related to this project, and who was a constant conversation partner as I worked my way through this twentieth-century American narrative. While I benefited from the insights of these fine scholars, any errors in fact or interpretation are of course entirely my responsibility. At Oxford University Press, Theo Calderara shepherded this project from start to finish with professional care and the utmost in proficiency.

Finally, I treasure immensely the enduring and heartfelt love and support of my family, and dedicate this book to them.

Reforming Hollywood

Introduction

Amusement is not only a great fact and a great business interest, it is also a great factor in the development of the national character.
WASHINGTON GLADDEN, Congregational minister, 1885

WHILE I WAS researching this book, a production assistant working on a documentary about the movie rating system called me. It turned out he had no interest whatsoever in my research, but was only hoping that I could identify the church representatives on the Classification and Rating Administration's (CARA) appeals board. I put him in contact with James M. Wall, a United Methodist and former editor of the *Christian Century*, who has long been a non-voting member of the rating appeals board on behalf of the National Council of the Churches of Christ in the USA.

The documentarian's lack of inquisitiveness was perhaps a bit unfortunate. Critics faulted *This Film Is Not Yet Rated* (2006) for its lack of balance, nuance, and historical perspective. The segment on the church representatives does not even attempt to explain why a Protestant and Catholic official attend rating appeals hearings or to clarify their exact roles, and makes it seem as if they serve as censors. Wall's interview ends abruptly with the filmmaker cutting him off mid-sentence. "Make your picture, make it work, but realize that if you go down this road too far, you're cutting off a certain audience, and that's your choice," Wall explains. "We don't want to restrict the film artist. We want to give the artist freedom to make the films they want to make, but we do not want to make it totally free. . . ." According to Wall, what was cut from his statement was something like ". . . which is why the rating system has its different ratings that either prevent children from attending (NC-17), or restrict them from coming without a parent or adult guardian (R)."[1] Parental guidance apparently did not fit the producer's narrative and is mentioned in the film only in passing.

Nevertheless, when in the name of artistic freedom this "feisty, intellectually engaging" exposé, as one reviewer called it, made it known that church officials served on the rating appeals board, the revelation came as a shock to many. It also revealed crucial historical ignorance about a long-standing and complicated relationship between Protestant churches and the movie industry. In 1971, Jack Valenti, president of the Motion Picture Association of America (MPAA), invited church officials to attend CARA appeals hearings as public observers, monitoring the procedure "to bear witness to how the system works."[2] Nor was this the first time that eminent Protestants had, or sought, this sort of role. Indeed, for the better part of the twentieth century, Protestants—the reigning religious and cultural establishment at the dawn of the cinema—struggled to formulate a constructive approach to the movies. Protestants spearheaded movie reform in the early twentieth century, and studio owners in Hollywood employed Will H. Hays, a prominent Presbyterian, to head their trade organization in 1922. In 1930 they adopted a Production Code of standards drafted with the help of Roman Catholics, who were later empowered in movie regulation. These facts underscore the importance of religious groups for understanding the American cinema and dramatic shifts in the center of cultural power. Recovering the central and persistent role of Protestants in this story is especially important. Although Protestantism was close to America's cultural center well into the twentieth century, it is markedly absent in histories of American film. I aim to restore Protestants to American film history and tell a story that goes to the heart of the role of film and religion in a democratic society.

The Protestant Establishment and the Movies

At the dawn of what would come to be called "the American Century," the new ownership of the *Christian Oracle* magazine (which was in the process of renaming itself) speculated about the years ahead: "May not the coming century be known as the Christian century?"[3] At the time, the two notions would have been nearly synonymous, for it was hard to see the United States as anything other than a Christian nation. The *Christian Century* would serve as *the* voice of a Protestantism that saw itself as setting the tone and norms for American public life. Protestants relished their status as the established religion; their sense of inherited authority came with a God-given responsibility for the moral and religious character of the nation and a sacred duty to work toward its improvement.

Protestants identified their core values—a profound emphasis on the individual conscience, justice, and stewardship—with the democratic values of America. The preservation of these values and the institutions that supported them was crucial to ensure both faithful Christian living and the integrity of American liberty. Protestant leaders were confident that they could have it all; they wanted social control and individual freedom, progress and traditional moral purity, corporate profits and the common good—apparent tensions in the value system that they were determined to guard and promote. The organic unity of society and the basic motive of service guided Protestant thinking about industry, profit making, and competition. A key conviction was that individual freedom ought to be controlled in the interest of the public welfare. "We have been told now and again of the individual's right to go to the devil in his own way," one Protestant leader maintained. "Society recognizes no such right in the individual if going to the devil involves the welfare of anyone else." To profit from a business that was detrimental to people and society violated the scriptural command of love of neighbor and constituted "commercialized iniquity."[4] The same logic applied equally to liquor trafficking, food and drugs, banking and investment, and the movie industry.

The rise of the American cinema coincided with the transition from Protestant to pluralist America. Movies were a new visual mass communication that defied conventional notions of art and presented a fundamental challenge to word-based Protestant culture. The film industry was also a crucial site where non-Protestant and non-Christian players gained a new voice in the public arena. Church leaders responded variously with a set of strategies to block, co-opt, channel, or accommodate this challenge. But the guiding principle of Protestant approaches to film regulation was their proud claim to have custody of American civil liberties and a deep concern for the moral character of industry and society.

A different portrait of Protestants predominates among film historians, with church leaders often cast as intractable bluenose censors who, in the extreme, condemned all movies as evil. There were, of course, Protestant clergy whose fiery rhetoric confirmed the stereotype. The fundamentalist preacher John R. Rice, for example, condemned movies as "an unmitigated curse," and one denominational leader deplored Hollywood as the place "where Satan has his throne."[5] But only the most conservative

Christians condemned moviegoing per se, and then not simply because of entrenched Puritan suspicions about amusement and drama. Some were Protestant fundamentalists who wanted a unitary, homogenous culture that adhered to their values and beliefs. Certain ethno-religious immigrant groups, like the Dutch Reformed, also shunned the movies. Devoted to their religious traditions while also hungering for social respectability, they were determined to establish themselves in their new country without imitating its secular practices. With its godlike stars and opulent movie palaces "resembling cathedrals right down to the massive organ," Hollywood appeared a brazen symbol of consumerism and worldliness. These Protestant groups perceived the cinema as both a threat to moral purity and also a force that could completely homogenize and nationalize their ethno-religious traditions. The risk was too great; they branded movies "things of the world, the flesh, and the devil."[6]

Cultural separatism was not typical of most Protestants, however, even if they viewed the film industry on a sliding scale of skepticism. They perceived themselves as cultural caretakers responsible for securing a fitting place for movies in American life. The cinema was a vital agent of socialization, and there was a deep desire on the part of Protestant leaders for film producers to work in harmony with home, school, and church to promote a truly healthy Americanism. Moreover, even if they were not always frequent moviegoers themselves, the Protestant elite recognized that film contributed to the marketplace of ideas. They saw legal censorship as un-American, undemocratic, impractical, unnecessary, and prone to political graft and corruption. At the same time, they believed that a reasonable measure of self-restraint on the part of moviemakers was acceptable— even necessary—to protect the public welfare. And yet, it is common for Protestants to be dismissed collectively as moralistic crusaders or high-brows who were out of touch with the citizenry and determined to legislate morality (à la Prohibition). How is it that Protestants, by tradition defenders of American civil liberties, are seen primarily as ardent proponents of movie censorship?

Finding Protestants in the Crowd

This caricature of Protestants was established in the earliest accounts, some written by people who were themselves involved in these events. Historian and film executive Benjamin B. Hampton, for example, thinks of the "professional reformers and fanatics" agitating for "rigorous censorship" of movies in the late 1910s as Protestant; they are the same Prohibitionists whose "ancestors gave up the pleasant sport of burning witches." Likewise, Raymond Moley, who was an adviser to Will Hays, president of the Motion Picture Producers and Distributors Association (MPPDA), targets unnamed Protestant organizations as those who were "head-hunting for the movie makers" in the early 1920s. "Many of them had tasted blood when they successfully mobilized the country behind the prohibition amendment," he observes. "When that battle was done, they had needed a new campaign, a new crusade."[7] These pejorative observations obscure reality. Church leaders worked cooperatively with film executives, some of whom were Protestant churchgoers, to advance constructive initiatives.

This points to a persistent problem in film histories. The tendency is to treat religious faith primarily as a social identifier, with the result that scholars often overlook or minimize its distinct influence, and even miss important connections among various players. MPPDA executives Carl Milliken, Francis Harmon, and Arthur DeBra, for example, all had close church affiliations, but are not usually identified as being Protestant. Protestantism is laced with a bewildering array of sometimes conflicting and even contradictory beliefs and values. It is too easy to view this diverse religious community as homogenous, mistaking particular individuals or groups as representative of all Protestants. On the other hand, being mindful of the varieties of Protestantism can also make it difficult to generalize and draw clear conclusions; a measure of ambiguity is unavoidable.

To further complicate things, Protestantism has historically been identified so closely with American culture as to blur its internal distinctions and conflate the religious with the secular. Through most of the twentieth century, the Protestant establishment "must be understood as a personal network of Protestant leadership that extended across the churches, controlled most of the nation's political life, and managed virtually all of the major secular institutions and entities in American society," religious historian William R. Hutchison explains. Protestants not only served in churches, denominational and parachurch organizations, but on city, state, and federal legislatures and judiciaries, censor boards, civic organizations, newspaper and magazine staffs, university faculties, industry trade groups, film companies, and even the Motion Picture Association. As individuals, their religious faith might have been vital, irrelevant, or perhaps an "afterimage," an indelible imprint on their thinking whether or not they were conscious of it. Progressive activist Frederic Howe, for example, discarded "the evangelical religion" of his upbringing, but remained wed to its moral vision, sense of duty, and the value of personal sacrifice, which he believed were "the most characteristic influence of my generation."[8] As a category then, *Protestant* includes a wide range of people who can be grouped in different ways.

Formal denominational differences are not particularly helpful. Wilbur Crafts, who assailed movies as "schools of vice and crime" that offered children five-cent "trips to hell," migrated from Methodist to Congregationalist, and finally to the Presbyterian Church, the denominational home of Orrin G. Cocks of the National Board of Review, and MPPDA President Will Hays. How does the Presbyterian designation help explain their divergent attitudes toward the cinema? It doesn't. It is more profitable to chart the Protestant landscape along the lines of different *perspectives*. I use this term to refer to the way in which theological, cultural, and ideological factors crystallize into different mind-sets that hang together in thought, word, and deed.[9] Discourse about film played an important role in the articulation of various perspectives within the Protestant community.

I focus on the Federal (later National) Council of the Churches of Christ in America. Created in 1908, this national organization was the common front of not all, but certainly the foremost Protestant denominations of the day. Baptist, Congregational, Disciples of Christ, Methodist, Presbyterian, and Reformed, which were all known as "evangelical" churches at the time, belonged to the Federal Council. I use the term *Protestant* throughout to refer to these "mainline" denominations, until later chapters when it becomes necessary to distinguish them from fundamentalists and evangelicals. Churches like the Southern Baptist Convention and other denominations that emphasized a literal Biblical interpretation, personal salvation, and cultural separatism, refused to join, and were even critical of the Council's liberal theology and social reform agenda. In contrast to "the extreme individualism and sharp separation of religion from the rest of life" that marked the fundamentalist movement, the mission of the Federal Council was based on a recognition "that the churches are vitally interested in everything that concerns human welfare," as one Council official explained. The organization's strategy was to teach religion and develop a social conscience among young people who would in turn "powerfully influence the thinking and acting of the adult mind of the nation."[10] Federal Council leaders distinguished themselves from the conservative element in Protestantism while also hailing this unifying agency as a concrete illustration of democratic progress as distinguished from the uniformity and hierarchy of the Roman Catholic Church.

The Federal/National Council's activities are *the* central thread in the story of Christian negotiation with the film industry; around this thread all the others—dissenting Protestant and Catholic alike—are entwined. Yet these events have received scant treatment in film histories, even though they were covered in their time by the secular, religious, and trade press.

Protestant Strategies for Movie Reform

The story of Protestants and Hollywood involves a cast of characters with strong personalities, deep convictions, driving desires, and sharp differences. As expected, they were influenced by the prevailing notions, values, and assumptions of their time, and often enough worked by trial and error within existing social, political, and industrial realities. Human agency is complex; motives are usually mixed. This book investigates ways that religious views and commitments informed approaches to film as popular art, culture, industry, and social influence. My aim is to take religious identities and loyalties seriously, while understanding that these convictions are entangled with contemporary cultural or ideological forces, whether ethnic or class antagonisms, concerns over the debasement of high culture, social hegemony, or control over the means of communication. Indeed, I argue that religious context is essential to understanding the development of the American cinema. As a crucial medium of communication, movies were enmeshed in, and bear the marks of, religious, cultural, and class conflicts throughout the twentieth century.

Divergent Protestant strategies for reforming the movies are best understood in terms of *pietist* and *structural* motifs. The pietist tendency sees social problems as the result of personal shortcomings and failings, and not harmful social conditions. If the individual is the genesis of social change and religion the basis for virtue, then a healthy society depends on getting people "right with God," and then—through education and organization—right with each other. The *structural* motif finds the core problem in patterns of organization and emphasizes transforming the systems that influence and govern people's lives. Improving institutions and eliminating unjust, corrupt, or repressive policies and practices will free people to pursue opportunities and will advance the public welfare. Without generalizing too much, theological conservatives, foregrounding the human capacity for sin and the transcendence of God, can be associated with the pietist tendency; theological liberals, more optimistic about human nature and stressing God's immanence, the structural one. These are, of course, merely dominant themes, not necessarily mutually exclusive tactics. For example, people affirming either approach might submit proposals for government oversight of the film industry: one to the House Committee on Education and the other to the Committee on Interstate Commerce. These two directions for movie reform became more distinct over the course of the twentieth century in accord with divergent theological trends and related attitudes about the relation of Christianity and culture.[11]

Protestants should neither be caricatured as bluenose censors nor cast as Hollywood saviors, but understood as honestly attempting to deal with a complex situation by employing the best tools available. By the existing legal standard in the early twentieth century, a work could be judged obscene based on isolated parts and their potentially harmful effect on the most susceptible individuals—children and the immature. There was general agreement, even among film producers, that if movies were going to be exhibited to an audience of all ages, some mode of regulation was necessary—if only to keep producers and exhibitors out of the courts and jails. The real issue was the means of control: either some kind of prior restraint or "censoring" (meaning editing or approval by an accepted authority) or punishment after exhibition.[12]

Legal censorship was commonly understood to mean cuts made to the final print by some external agency, like a local or state board. Protestants typically favored persuasion and voluntary regulation, which were seen as being in accord with individual freedom and responsibility. They believed, moreover, that "no amount of snipping with the scissors or alteration of titles or obliteration of dialogue can ever make a good picture." They emphasized a film's overall perspective instead of nit-picking at perceived immoral incidents. "A good picture requires real dramatic materials, treated dramatically and honestly by sincere directors and actors," Protestant academics insisted. "Censorships are dangerous to the liberties of a free people. . . . We have purchased our liberties in this country at a great price. We must not sacrifice them or relinquish them, even when they are so grossly abused by the makers of unwholesome pictures."[13] The threat of legalized censorship might be used to rein in recalcitrant filmmakers, Protestant leaders believed, but only as a last resort, if producers failed to make good on their promise not to release movies judged detrimental to the common good.

Apprehension about the influence of the cinema was not simply based on conjecture, but on social science research. Sociologists used an "imitation-suggestion theory" to explain how people related to one another and developed character in a rapidly changing society; studies on crowd psychology showed how easily the masses were influenced by opinions imposed on them.[14] Nevertheless, Protestant movie reform was by no means singularly motivated; hegemonic control, racism, social duty, civil and religious liberty were all at play. But nearly all proposals can be interpreted to some degree as measures to prevent a domino effect that would result in a repressive official censorship. In short, Protestant strategies for movie regulation were informed by their distaste for censorship as well as existing circumstances and exigencies.

Profits and Public Welfare

This kind of historical analysis lends itself well to interdisciplinary investigation. I seek to understand and interpret historical events and also to identify patterns and developments that are shaped by, and emerge from, the dynamic interplay of cultural and intellectual developments, social and religious institutions, art and industry. This narrative traces major innovations, shifts, and conflicts in Protestant communions and examines their effect on, and confluence with, contemporary trends. It chronicles events that transpired within larger patterns in American religious and cultural life and the film industry; as much as space has allowed, I have tried to weave these different threads together. My intent is not to write a history of either Protestantism or the American cinema; nor is this an institutional history. I make no pretense of exhaustiveness. My aim is to trace key themes and events in the historical interaction of two dynamic American institutions engaged in a struggle over cultural power and the function of popular art.

It should be clear that, in presenting the Protestant story, one purpose of this book is to answer questions left unresolved by other studies and to provide a corrective to some of the oversimplification and misinterpretation that exists regarding the role of Protestants in film history. I also hope to establish the importance of the erosion of the Protestant hegemony for understanding the cinema, and to demonstrate that the film industry is an important catalyst for examining how this socio-religious group coped with a dramatic loss of power. These events are examined here in terms of enduring themes and significance to the evolution of the film industry and also the course of Protestantism across the twentieth century and into the next. By uncovering these forgotten but formative events and shedding new light on familiar accounts, I hope to expand the horizon of film history, to counter conventional interpretations, and ultimately to reframe the discourse on Protestants and movie regulation.

It is unfortunate that so much of the Protestant contribution to film history has been lost. The Protestant story is not nearly as sensational as that of Catholics, but it is at least as significant. Indeed, by way of institutional partnering, Protestant principles and strategies eventually prevailed in the film industry. If there is a tendency to think of movie regulation primarily in terms of artistic freedom versus censorship, or a hegemonic control over public morals and movie content, this inquiry emphasizes another dimension by revealing that Protestants characteristically sought a measure of harmony between individual liberty, artistic freedom, and the common good in their efforts to establish a fitting role for the cinema. Indeed, I cannot emphasize enough how much the tension between the film industry's interest in profit margins and the church's concern to protect civil liberties and the public welfare was at the crux of the struggle that Protestants waged over the movies. This dynamic is the key to understanding Protestant approaches, and it runs centrally through the narrative that follows.

I

Reforming the Movies

WHAT COULD POSSIBLY GO WRONG?

*Is a man at liberty to make money from the morals of
people? Is he to profit from the corruption of the minds of
children? The man who profits from such things is doomed
to double damnation.*

F. M. FOSTER, Presbyterian minister, 1908

THE AMERICA THAT took shape in the early twentieth century was an
uneasy entanglement of faith and science, altruism and self-sufficiency,
spiritual devotion and financial prosperity. Protestants were dominant,
but in a short time, from the 1890s to the 1930s, the forces of modernity
challenged the Victorian norms that, they believed, held the country together. The nation's ideals were put to the test by ethno-religious rivalries.

Catholic and Jewish immigrants funneled into the largest cities and
reshaped the nation's religious complexion. Modern intellectual trends
challenged the Christian concept of a universe created and ordered by God.
Liberal Protestants tended to accommodate modernist ideas within a theis-
tic framework; conservatives and Roman Catholics stood against these
trends and defended the Christian faith against both modernism and liberal theology. Biblical literalists disputed Darwin's theory of evolution and
worried that Freudian psychology would unleash sexual passions and
undercut moral restraint. The birth of mass consumer society, which would
both foster and benefit from movie culture, had an enormous impact on
Americans' conception of the self. *Character*—so central to the Victorian
worldview—encompassed a set of producer-oriented values derived from a
higher moral law: work, duty, sacrifice, and achievement. But character was
soon eclipsed by *personality*, a means of fulfillment that spotlighted self-
realization and the pursuit of meaning and pleasure through leisure and
consumption.[1] Character tended to deflate the self, personality to idolize it.

Large-scale industrial and economic growth, along with urbanization, brought corporate monopolies, a disparity of wealth, widespread poverty, and political corruption that deprived ordinary people of the equality of opportunity popularized in Horatio Alger's "rags to riches" novels. Protestants feared that their traditional emphasis on intrinsic human worth was being transformed into unrestrained freedom; in pursuit of greater wealth and power, the corporate and political elite were turning the modern world into "a soulless chaos."[2] From any number of vantage points, there was an alarming sense that the nation was in crisis.

The Progressive movement and its Protestant establishment branch, the Social Gospel, emerged to confront these problems. The two movements were nearly inseparable, really a diverse array of reform efforts animated by various moral, social, economic, or political issues, and involving mostly well-educated, middle-class Protestant professionals. Fearing that cultural heterogeneity and lack of moral cohesion would lead to a collapse of the social order, they sought to restore their vision of America as a place where individuals were free to pursue their dreams under a shared ethos of self-restraint and public responsibility. The continued dominance of Protestant culture and institutions was widely accepted as the means to this end.

To match the scope of the problem, Protestants emphasized denominational cooperation, founding the Federal Council of the Churches of Christ in America in 1908. Representing 30 denominations, its leaders were theologically liberal and committed to the Social Gospel. They believed that the church ought to be the nation's conscience and guide, and they stressed human welfare and the improvement of social conditions as manifestations of God's Kingdom on earth. Council officials thought their work was essential "for the moral and spiritual welfare of the nation and of the world." Globally, they sought the establishment of means for the arbitration of international differences to alleviate war and to prevent arms buildups. Nationally, they were determined to confront the problems of the emerging modern world—from vice and political corruption to industrial relations, the saloon, and commercial exploitation— by bringing together, in a display of "differentiation and coherence," church denominations with interdenominational and other agencies focused on such activities as missions, peace, and temperance. General Secretary Charles S. Macfarland proclaimed that when Protestants translated their "spiritual authority" into a united front, "the gates of hell shall no longer prevail against her [the church], and she will be no longer weak and helpless before the haggard, sullen, and defiant face of injustice, inhumanity, and heartless neglect, and she will be able to take care of all her children—and her children are humanity."[3] Such triumphalism presumed the superiority of "Protestant"—that is, democratic—values. The Federal Council was likened to the United States Congress and contrasted sharply with the hierarchy of the Roman Catholic Church. If Catholicism claimed divine authority, Protestantism was the voice of democratic reasoning and also the reservoir of "good character" that could maintain a sound society—and Protestant power—in the face of rising religious competition, especially from Roman Catholics.

A House of Dreams

In every way, the cinema embodied these incredible changes. It was art, entertainment, culture, industry, and a social institution of enormous appeal and growing power. This "first art child of democracy" seemed a world apart from the Victorian high-culture tradition that detached art from commerce. With the Victorian elite as the self-appointed guardians of the Protestant-European heritage—its art, etiquette, and collected learning—culture itself was a tool of control, an expression of symbolic power over subordinate groups. Though scorned as necessarily "lowbrow," movies originated as a highly commercialized urban folk art that appealed to a diverse audience and became regular recreation for typical wage-earning families. To cope with the monotony of industrial life and to escape small, crowded homes, people went out for fun, spending three times as much on amusements as on their churches, according to one estimate. These conditions—and not church sanction—justified their participation in the city's amusements.[4]

As both a cultural and social space, movie theaters represented a breakdown of traditional Victorian norms. More than mere entertainment, films reflected the realities of urban life by depicting, for example, men and women mingling together at work and play.[5] Without traditions to guide them in urban America, non-English-speaking immigrants and blue-collar families found silent films exciting, compelling, and user-friendly—they transcended constant language barriers.

For better or worse, movies played a role in the enculturation process, which was a source of irritation to both clergy and many first-generation immigrant parents who worried about their effect, not just on the young and impressionable, but also on the family and church. For young people struggling to find "a satisfactory code of morals," the well-known Protestant social worker Jane Addams observed, the movie theater became a "veritable house of dreams" that reflected the realities, hopes, and disappointments of their lives. Addams articulated a view developing among middle-class reformers: movies could satisfy working-class leisure needs, foster community and public discourse, and advance a reform agenda. The aim of Progressive and Social Gospel leaders was to counteract any negative influence and turn this mechanical marvel into an ally of home, school, and church. At the same time, Protestants had to play their trump card against the Catholics. Recognizing the humanizing value of the city's entertainment, church denominations replaced prohibitions with individual discretion; let Christian conscience decide "what is fit and proper."[6]

Cheap Amusements and the Commercialization of Sunday

Enthusiastic public reception to nickelodeons—small storefront theaters that started popping up in urban centers—put them on the radar of city officials and clergy. Within months after the Chicago Tribune condemned the city's 116 nickelodeons as "without a redeeming feature to warrant their existence," the Windy City became the first to pass an ordinance allowing police to inspect and license all movies prior to exhibition.[7] The issue was complicated. Safety and sanitary conditions—overcrowded aisles, poor ventilation, not enough fire exits—were major concerns. Another was that nickelodeons were darkened places filled with crowds of unsupervised children and young people of both sexes, with mostly foreign immigrants handing out tickets. Clergy wanted theaters closed on Sunday out of respect for the Sabbath, but public support was not strong and business went on as usual.

In New York City, the largest movie market and center of film production, two Progressive reform organizations—the People's Institute and the Woman's Municipal League—funded a pioneering study of Manhattan's amusements in 1908. John Collier, the People's Institute's field investigator, reported that, unlike the penny arcade and cheap vaudeville, nickelodeons were no longer "a carnival of vulgarity, suggestiveness and violence." Not a single "immoral or indecent picture" was uncovered in visits to more than 200 nickel theaters. The conclusion was that with proper supervision the considerable entertainment and educational value of movies could be harnessed for beneficial purposes. And Collier indicated that the People's Institute was developing a plan with the film industry to give "endorsement to the best of the shows and receiving in return the right to regulate their programs."[8]

After a deadly fire at a nickelodeon in Pennsylvania, George B. McClellan, mayor of New York, ordered an investigation of all places showing movies. Clergy meanwhile petitioned the mayor for stricter enforcement of Sunday observance, or "blue" laws, a strategy that linked moral "decency" with religious observance. Canon William Sheafe Chase, pastor of Brooklyn's Christ Episcopal Church, was dubbed "the ringleader of the crusaders" by the industry trade *Variety*. Renowned for his devoted campaign against vice and for moral purity, Chase was a veteran in the battle to protect the Sabbath. He cofounded the Interdenominational Committee for the Suppression of Sunday Vaudeville, which played a central role in fostering public sentiment against Sunday amusements. In January 1908, Chase addressed a group of about 100 people, mostly women, who gathered to pass a resolution "condemning Sunday desecration" and asking city officials to enforce Sunday laws. Movies were "particularly demoralizing because of the low price of admission, the small capital needed, and the way they spring up all over the city," Chase said. "They attract our Sunday school children with their 5 cents."[9]

As the situation stood, the New York State Supreme Court had ruled that laws prohibiting Sunday theatrical performances were constitutional. Mayor McClellan, however, over protests by Chase's committee, issued a regulation permitting Sunday performances of a "sacred or educational" nature. The theaters remained open, as did interpretation of the existing laws by police and judges. When several nickelodeon managers were arrested for violating Sunday laws and showing indecent pictures, a group of mostly Jewish and Italian theater owners organized to protect their financial interests. Ministers might have objected to any commercialization of the Sabbath, but on the exhibitor's weekly balance sheet, a seventh day of showings was sheer profit.[10]

At Canon Chase's urging, McClellan announced a public hearing two days before Christmas to decide whether movie theaters were safe and should be closed on Sundays. Catholic and Protestant clergy stated their opposition to Sunday movies and accused the film industry of promoting indecency for the sake of financial profit—a charge entangled with common Jewish stereotypes. "These men who run these shows have no moral scruples whatever," Chase declared, expressing classic Progressive sentiment. "They are simply in the business for the money there is in it." When Progressive activist Charles Sprague Smith, founder and managing director of the People's Institute, remarked to the effect that "there were things more rotten than moving picture shows," the gallery, packed with ethnic immigrants, mostly Jews, burst into applause, only to be rebuked by the mayor.[11]

The next day, McClellan revoked the licenses of all five-cent theaters in the city. The symbolism of shutting down some 550 mostly Jewish-owned movie houses on Christmas Eve cannot be missed; Protestant and Catholic clergy, usually adversarial, were temporarily united in protecting the Christian Sabbath. Afterward, Chase's Interdenominational Committee issued a patronizing call for Jews to subscribe to "American law and custom" and "in return for the generosity of our free institutions to unite with the Christian forces to secure one day of the week for the whole people, free from business and free for worship." Exhibitors quickly secured court injunctions to reopen their businesses, but the mayor's edict threw their business into chaos over how city officials would enforce the existing Sunday ordinance. Under the leadership of William Fox and Marcus Loew, both Jews, the exhibitors called for censorship as protection against the film manufacturers who, they alleged, "foisted improper pictures on them." Sensing an ally, they approached the People's Institute; regulating movies fit perfectly with its Progressive program for "the redemption of leisure."[12] Given the volatility of the New York situation, some kind of regulation was needed to guard against legal censorship. John Collier proposed to set up an independent, voluntary censorship board under the auspices of the People's Institute.

On the same day that McClellan announced the public hearing on the movies, Thomas Edison and the leading manufacturers of motion picture equipment held a dinner commemorating the formation of the Motion Pictures Patent Company (MPPC). The "Trust," as it was called, was a cartel designed to monopolize the business by controlling the patents for film and equipment. An ulterior motive was to prevent enterprising Jews from gaining too much control in the industry. Together, the Patent companies accounted for about two-thirds of the films produced in the United States.[13]

The impression shared by the People's Institute and MPPC was that only a small number of objectionable movies, usually from fringe producers, were ruining the industry's overall reputation. Whatever "censoring" was needed would be nominal and the Board's existence temporary. The producers agreed to submit their films for review as a quick fix to assuage overly zealous reformers and prevent reactionary measures. After a three-month experimental period, the Board's potential as a national clearinghouse became evident, and in June 1909 the People's Institute announced the formation of the National Board of Censorship of Motion Pictures. This cooperative venture between the producers, exhibitors, and the National Board represented the first attempt to resolve the problem between freedom and public morals in the cinema—the central concern of this book.[14]

Fundamental Wholesomeness

The National Board was mainly Protestant and saw itself as an "inspiring experiment in democracy." Though empowered and financed by the film interests, the Board had no legal or contractual power with the industry; its authority was derived solely from the film interests. Movies were free to deal with serious themes; the Board tried only to minimize sensationalism. To represent the public, a group of committees—made up mostly of women—did the reviewing based on accepted Victorian sentiments. The disproportionate number of women affirmed the Victorian notion that they were morally superior by nature and best qualified to judge a movie's influence. The general effect of a film on adults, who made up the bulk of the movie audience, and not youth, the most impressionable viewers, was the benchmark for evaluation. Films were approved or censored by majority vote.[15]

The rationale for voluntary censorship rested on a model of supply and demand grounded in an optimistic view of human nature and democratic progress that characterized the Progressive and Social Gospel movements. The assumption that industry profits and traditional Protestant morality were compatible was a recurrent theme throughout the century, and a lesson that reformers never seemed to remember. In each era, the dominant Protestant group, claiming to give voice to the indigenous American soul, declared that the majority of Americans were basically good, churchgoing, God-fearing people who desired clean and wholesome entertainment. Only the alien "Other," which would change from time to time, wanted immoral films.

Believing in the "fundamental wholesomeness of the people," Board officials were confident that the way to improve movies was not by curtailing expression, but by educating the public. With proper tastes and values, audiences would stimulate demand and, in turn, fuel production of high-quality films. They would also refuse to accept censorship. Making movies safe for the respectable middle class was the linchpin in the Board's voluntary censorship. An influx of middle-class patronage was supposed to kick-start the demand for worthwhile movies that would affirm Victorian culture and be exhibited to youth and immigrants. Such films would also supposedly reap greater financial rewards for the producers, which Collier made known was "the obvious and professed reason" for their co-operation with the Board.[16] What could possibly go wrong?

Nagging answers to that question would surface periodically in the press, pulpit, and government hearings for decades to come. If audiences desired wholesomeness, why were there so many indecent movies? If the Board opposed legal censorship on principle, wasn't it still in effect curbing expression and restricting audience choice? National Board officials cast themselves as moral interpreters for producers who "through being closely engaged in actual production and impelled by commercial instinct only, are apt to lose sight of public interest and welfare."[17] This would become stock-in-trade reasoning on both sides of the discourse on censorship. Reality, however, impinged soon enough to highlight these issues, question the prevailing assumptions, and set new and enduring terms of movie reform.

New York's nickelodeon managers, who regularly complained that their customers lacked "class," noticed a steady increase in middle-class patronage and were eager to exploit the middle-class family trade. As with vaudeville, women were especially important. They were vital to the consumer culture. They made up a significant portion of moviegoers, and their presence signaled respectability—by definition a mixed, not male-only, clientele. The most ambitious exhibitors, like William Fox, acquired more comfortable vaudeville houses and then legitimate theaters, starting a trend of building lavish movie palaces that brought a new level of respectability to moviegoing. This marked the beginning of an epochal shift in the corporate—and ethnic—control of the movie industry. In a fiercely competitive struggle, independent producers wrested control of production and distribution from Edison's Trust and paved the way into the middle-class market. The heads of the Patents companies misjudged audience interest in more sophisticated movies and balked at higher production budgets and salaries for "stars." The independents took risks on multi-reel "feature" films capable of adapting stories from magazines, novels, and stage plays with middle-class appeal. Also, partly as a result of the National Board's review, movies began to display a uniformity that made them more fitting for nationwide distribution. Weekly attendance figures nearly doubled, from 26 million in 1908 to some 49 million in 1914.[18]

In a relatively short time, these independent companies became financial powerhouses. The Protestant pioneers of motion pictures were wiped out. In their place were men like Adolph Zukor, Carl Laemmle, William Fox, and Marcus Loew, all Jewish immigrants of Eastern European origin with little formal education. They entered the business by operating penny arcades, nickelodeons, or vaudeville theaters. As their fortunes rose, they formed huge firms with a stable of "stars" centered on the production of feature films in Hollywood, and began expanding their power by merging companies. These Jewish entrepreneurs now ruled an entertainment empire with a potential audience that was overwhelmingly Protestant and Catholic. That fact was not lost upon the religious elite, who were reminded now and again that movies were "probably reaching more people day by day than the combined Protestant churches of the country."[19] Cultural authority and religious difference moved to the forefront of movie regulation, right alongside protecting children and the public welfare.

Trafficking in Souls

Ultimately, the National Board's success hinged on assuring that audiences would encounter nothing indecent and harmful in movies, while protecting the film industry from official censorship. This became an increasingly difficult course to navigate, especially as the popularity of moviegoing grew among the middle class. The Board's scheme was partly flawed by an idealism grounded in assumptions of a static universe and the supposed self-evident superiority of Victorian culture. Reviewers imagined an ideal spectator who had little basis in reality; actually, people harbored all sorts of prejudices that might inform their judgment of a film. The assumption that Victorian sentiments would provide a consensus on standards of acceptability proved faulty.

Film producers discovered that middle-class patrons were not all that interested in morality plays and adaptations of literary and historical works. Plans for a Bible-themed series with high production values aimed at "forging an alliance with organized religion and other 'respectable' elements of the community" ended in disappointment. An exhaustive marketing campaign drew large numbers of clergy and church groups who "padded" the attendance during the first week of Pathé's *The Life of Our Saviour* (1914). Afterward, box office was dismal and the film's commercial prospects "fell down with a thud." *Variety* estimated that the Pathé's financial forecast relied too heavily on small-town churchgoers, while the film's depiction of "the crucifixion in a repellant manner . . . also mitigated against the chances for success." The conclusion drawn was that "the big city bookings show one result—the people do not care for the big Biblical pictures."[20]

Meanwhile, audiences were flocking to white slavery films like *Traffic in Souls* (1913)—melodramas about innocent Anglo-American women forced into prostitution. Purporting to document a national problem, the white slavery pictures were defended by some for bringing sexual and social problems like prostitution into the public discourse, and disapproved by others for propagating sexual stereotypes and villainizing immigrants. That the Board passed these controversial movies raised questions about its viability as a national censor and rejuvenated city and state regulation—the very situation that the Board was meant to prevent. Ohio and Kansas passed censorship bills in 1913; the following year, the Pennsylvania governor revived a dormant law passed in 1911 and set up a state censorship board. Exhibitor associations filed suits to prevent enforcement of state censorship laws, contending that they were "legalized graft" and violated freedom of the press. Movies, they claimed, were "a newspaper in motion." An Ohio case was appealed to the U.S. Supreme Court.[21]

Rev. Wilbur F. Crafts, superintendent of the International Reform Bureau, which he had established in 1895, emerged, with Canon Chase, as an aggressive and relentless crusader against the movies. Crafts was a zealous reformer who made a career out of relentlessly attacking not just movies, but Sunday baseball, close dancing, and automobile rides, which "often proved a ride of lifelong shame and woe." His reform strategy relied on Progressive notions and typified the pietist impulse. Crafts believed that religion was the basis for personal virtue and a healthy society—a characteristically Victorian view. More than anything else, people had to have a sense of their own personal responsibility to God. The church's duty was to confront corruption, exploitation, and disorder. To that end, he declared, "The Church therefore has a right to appeal to the state to remove all unnecessary obstacles to the fundamental work which it is expected to do, the production of honesty and good morals."[22] His recourse was legislation that would eliminate immorality at the source of production.

Crafts thought that the National Board had duped the public and was actually working on behalf of the film interests (a charge that would recur years later with the Hays organization). A 1910 survey by the Humane Society of Cleveland, Ohio, determined that 40 percent of films viewed contained material inappropriate for children. *Variety* had a field day citing examples of the Board's lax standards—including titles by Patents Company members—and dismissed the Board as a "long standing picture trade joke." One Biograph film told of a drunkard who abandons his wife—she goes crazy—and years later almost marries his own daughter. The Pathé company presented an upended Good Samaritan story; a drunk becomes covered with blood while trying to help a robbery victim and goes insane after being falsely accused of the crime. A Selig picture featured a white woman "knocked senseless and left alone" in a den of Chinese drug smugglers and showed "how thieves drug a victim and dispose of his helpless body."[23] Convinced that profit-hungry producers were incapable of maintaining high moral standards, Crafts and Chase advocated federal regulation.

The two ministers were major players behind the Smith-Hughes Bill authorizing a federal commission that would, for all practical purposes, replace the National Board. The gist of their case was that industry cooperation with the Board was a tacit admission of the need for censorship; the continued existence of local censoring bodies was proof that this voluntary system was insufficient; and the national scope and influence of Hollywood now rendered city and state boards inadequate. Federal regulation of production was the only viable recourse. The crux of the matter was only whether an industry-funded board or government-appointed commission ought to be the arbiter of movie morality. The House Committee on Education passed the bill, but it never made it through Congress. Nevertheless, the spread of censor boards and negative publicity from the hearings cast doubt on the National Board's power to prevent legal censorship and drew even more public scrutiny of its judgments.[24]

The following week, on February 23, 1915, the Supreme Court issued a crucial and far-reaching decision in *Mutual Film Corp. v. Ohio Industrial Commission*. The Court rejected arguments that state censorship laws were an unlawful burden on interstate commerce and violated the First Amendment. Even more important, finding exhibition of movies to be "a business pure and simple," the court defined film as commerce and not as a medium for the communication of ideas. Movies thus were denied free speech protection and were made subject to legal prior restraint, a ruling justified in part because they were "capable of evil, having power for it, the greater because of their attractiveness and manner of exhibition."[25] If, in retrospect, the *Mutual* decision seems shortsighted, it fit with prevailing ideas of "commercialized iniquity" and Progressive beliefs about the need for government to act in the interest of the public welfare.

The *Mutual* decision exposed an emerging rift between the National Board and film companies, for whom the financial burden of censorship spoke "louder than a megaphone." The Ohio state tax, an estimated $11,000 per year, would be applied on top of the fees that producers were already paying to the Board—another $12,000.[26] What if other states followed suit? Latent fears that movies were only a stepping-stone to a wider censorship of literature, stage plays, and the visual arts suddenly seemed a real possibility.

The Birth of a Blockbuster

No sooner had the court categorized movies as unprotected speech than D. W. Griffith's *The Birth of a Nation* took the art of filmmaking to a new level and demonstrated beyond question the dramatic power of a motion picture to represent events and communicate ideas. Griffith's Civil War saga opened in New York on March 3, 1915, and was immediately heralded a cinematic tour de force. It also took the lid off the National Board, an agency founded out of Progressive ideals, and it exposed as false a common assumption about audience ethics and interests.

An evangelical Methodist, Griffith made films that demonstrated the potential for movies to propagate a Victorian idealism and advance a Progressive agenda. *The Birth of a Nation*'s conventional Southern view, however, idealized the Victorian woman and family, disparaged African Americans, and made heroes of the Ku Klux Klan for violently restoring order during Reconstruction. Under pressure from the NAACP (National Association for the Advancement of Colored People), the National Board's General Committee screened the film and required Griffith to modify certain scenes and eliminate others, including a lynching sequence. The film passed, but with a split vote. For the majority, it came down to consistency with the Board's ideals; it was not within the Board's purview to protect the "the pride or interests of any special faction, section or race."[27] The committee's struggle portended the fierce controversy that ensued.

Middle-class Victorians were at a loss over how to reconcile the film's artistic triumph with its warped history and blatant racism. Jane Addams, for example, denounced the film's "pernicious caricature" of African Americans as "both unjust and untrue" and its "glorification" of the Ku Klux Klan as "perfectly ridiculous." With others, she joined the NAACP in calling for the film's suppression.[28] To do so, however, was to deny the director's freedom of expression—just as Griffith claimed. But for many, the film's racist worldview and social influence outweighed its artistic value. Was Griffith's movie superb art or merely propaganda? Either way, it belonged arguably in the public discourse. But under what conditions? Without some kind of regulation the cinema could be awash in propaganda of all sorts. And under whose control? The film confirmed that movies were becoming more powerful in communicating ideas. This in turn heightened concerns about untutored audiences who might lack the ability to discern fact from fiction and reality from drama.

That *The Birth of a Nation* quickly became the first "blockbuster" hit and gave movies a new respectability and legitimacy with the middle class proved ironic. Progressives had pinned their hopes for an improved cinema on the notion of a market driven by fundamentally wholesome people. The incredible popularity of a movie denigrating a racial minority, despite NAACP-led public protests, rattled that assumption. And the fact that the Board had declared it fit for public consumption when many cities and some states denied exhibitors licenses to show it exposed the Board's ineffectiveness in representing the divergent values that existed across the country. The consensus undergirding the Board's authority started coming apart as criticism mounted, which in turn empowered the Board's opponents. The argument that voluntary regulation was not adequate to prevent the showing of objectionable films was gaining traction.

"Prolapsus of the Bankroll"

As the playing field shifted in the mid-1910s, the struggle for control over the movies became more intense, even as the basic issues remained the same. There were middle-class reformers who believed that the cinema was much more than commercial entertainment; movies were a popular art capable of shaping character, attitudes, and behavior, and therefore qualified as protected speech. Their aim was to harness film's artistic potential for education and international good will. Producers saw things differently. They wanted to make good pictures, but it was absolutely necessary to make profitable ones. The balance sheet, not art or education, mattered most.

Public opinion remained fragmented. Those who condemned movie-going as sinful were shrinking in number. A much larger group supported the elimination of specific elements or entire films on subjects they found offensive and not fit for public consumption. A third group advocated as much freedom as possible for movies, letting box office determine acceptability. As they saw it, and contrary to the *Mutual* decision, the fact that movies were "democracy's theater," a mass medium with broad appeal, had no affect on "the essential question of the right of freedom." The cinema was no different from art, literature, or journalism; curbing the freedom of any of these forms of communication set a dangerous precedent.[29]

Despite shared principles and a common outlook, efforts to reform the movies followed two divergent approaches. Women's organizations supported the National Board's voluntary regulation as a means of moral persuasion. They worked with the Board's network of Better Films Committees to improve public taste and promote exceptional movies as a way to exert influence on the producers via the box office. Finding the National Board's refusal to censor movies for children mind-boggling, clergy like Chase and Crafts resorted to federal regulation as the only viable solution to the perceived problem of Hollywood's corruption of youth. For more than a decade, Protestants would be divided over these two methods, which embodied a real tension between their principled opposition to censorship and their duty to protect the social good.

The Birth of a Nation debacle marked a shift in leadership in the National Board. Frederic Howe, the chair, and others left the Board around this time. Howe was replaced by Cranston Brenton, a Protestant Episcopalian minister and director of the American Red Cross. Brenton began working with Board secretaries W. D. McGuire and Orrin G. Cocks, a Presbyterian minister, to redefine the organization's mission. In December 1915, the Board called a meeting with film companies to set up a new payment arrangement. Only three representatives showed up, and they requested a full accounting of the financial cost of the Board's censorship. *Variety* took this as a strong indication that the Board would "soon die of the familiar disease known as prolapsus of the bankroll."[30]

2

The Federal Council of Churches Enters the Frame

But to control industry is one thing; to control art and per-
sonal taste is quite another thing.
EVERETT DEAN MARTIN, chairman of the National Board
of Review, 1920

THE BIRTH OF *a Nation* controversy brought a good deal of confusion
to the whole matter of movie regulation. The film industry, concerned
clergy, and social agencies banked on the National Board of Censorship
as an alternative to unpredictable city and state censor boards that applied
varying standards and were known to be quite provincial. The proprietor
of a theater in Little Rock, Arkansas, that catered exclusively to African
Americans was fined $1,000 for exhibiting a film that showed "a white
woman in the embrace of a colored man." The court found the movie
to be "obscene" and "a menace to white women." Police in Providence,
Rhode Island, banned *The Scarlet Letter*, calling the screen adaptation of
Nathaniel Hawthorne's classic novel "ungodly, immoral and wholly unfit
for Providence's picture houses." By the time the censors in Worcester,
Massachusetts, were finished with *The Cowboy's Schoolmate, Variety* reported, "there wasn't much left of the reel but scenery."[1] The unreliability
of local and state boards was frustrating—and costly—to producers. By establishing nationally accepted standards, producers believed, the National
Board would alleviate the fears of clergy, social workers, and educators by
ensuring the suitability of movies for an undifferentiated audience, and
would also reduce the cost of censorship. If the National Board proved
ineffective, what alternatives existed?

The right of state and federal governments to regulate business in the public interest was a basic tenet of the Progressive Era. Protestant leaders conceived of the "motion picture problem" in terms of existing models for industry regulation, like the Interstate Commerce Commission and the Federal Trade Commission. While they were mindful of the dangers of censorship, some kind of government supervision seemed the logical recourse. They reasoned that public scrutiny of a federal commission would reduce the political corruption and capricious judgments linked with city and state boards. A federal body, moreover, could provide a uniform opinion (democratically conceived) that would over time become "a sort of code for national morality," an accepted basis upon which "movies, like books and newspapers, would be largely immune from censorship through the establishment of a social morale."[2] While the plan was paternalistic, the intent nonetheless was to create suitable conditions for the film industry to develop artistically and responsibly, and implicitly to eschew its crass commercialism. Toward this end, two entirely different modes of government regulation were advanced. Rev. Wilbur Crafts and Canon William Sheafe Chase continued to advance the pietist case; the chaos and discord drew the Federal Council of Churches into the fray to represent the Protestant establishment with a structuralist approach.

Leveling the Playing Field

In 1916, committee hearings on a revised Smith-Hughes bill dramatically revealed the contours of movie regulation in the wake of the *Mutual* decision. To explain the apparent contradiction in opposing censorship, while submitting films to the National Board, an industry spokesman likened the Board's work to that of a newspaper copy editor whose final evaluation eliminated anything that might be cause for legal action because it was "libelous, immoral, or obscene." The analogy stuck and became part of the industry's jargon in fighting legal censorship. Striking testimony by a stated representative of several film companies silenced the room. The executives he spoke for favored federal regulation to safeguard reputable filmmakers from those who produced indecent movies. Rev. Wilbur Crafts saw this as a tacit admission that immoral films *were* being exhibited. But the industry had also produced a handy scapegoat—fly-by-night companies who were making quick profits from cheap and immoral movies. There is merit to the charge, as film historian Benjamin B. Hampton, who was a producer himself, explains: "This class of temporary manufacturers, usually deficient in both capital and morals, was willing to 'go the limit on sex stuff,' and there were exhibitors who would screen their cheaply made stories if the lobby photographs contained suggestive scenes."[3] The argument only went so far, however. Reputable companies were mining huge box-office returns from the same bread-and-butter movies that some clergy, and even the trade press, found objectionable.

Film producers hated censorship and wanted the freedom to follow their business instincts. Noting that at least half the exhibitors in a survey favored movies that were "risqué," Universal's Carl Laemmle admitted that it was easy enough to put out a movie that was "off-color now and then as a feeler." And that was precisely the problem, as Protestant clergy and many others saw it. In the interest of swift profits, irresponsible producers catered to the crude, unsophisticated, and depraved tastes of a minority of moviegoers. Competitors were quick to cash in on a commercial hit with a cycle of imitations, often less restrained than the original. Tracking the box office, everyone realized, might push the envelope too far and ignite a public backlash that would lead to more repressive measures. Such fears were widespread, and warnings to that effect were repeated by Protestant reformers whenever pressure mounted for state or national censorship, which was often.[4]

Some kind of regulation, the producers reasoned, was needed to level the playing field in a fiercely competitive business. "I believe in censorship," one director/screenwriter said. "All of us in the game know that it is needed. Without it some producers would go the limit, beyond the limit, and then some." The implication was that they were only responding to public demand. This would become the industry's mantra and a major point of contention with religious critics, who rejected the unspoken assumption that "the public mind itself is salacious." They would assert to no end that most people were wholesome and desired clean entertainment, meaning movies that contained action, emotional drama, and affirmed "evil overcome in themselves, in society and in the movie."[5] Box-office statistics lent themselves to a contrary reading of public tastes and would be—indeed, still are—an ongoing source of contention.

Nationwide film distribution had also made meddling city and state censorship increasingly problematic for film companies. Preferring to deal with a single agency, producers were willing to endorse the concept of federal regulation, even as they opposed specific pieces of legislation. The real issue had become the mode of regulation: either some form of prior restraint or punishment after exhibition. For different reasons, producers and reformers both favored the former. Producers would rather negotiate

during production to avoid legal defense fees and penalties. The way reformers saw it was simple enough: once an immoral movie reached its
audience, the harm was done, making ex post facto punishment moot.
And so there was general agreement that a reasonable measure of prior
restraint was acceptable to protect the public welfare.

A film industry delegation had to secure help from President Woodrow
Wilson in a last-ditch effort to prevent passage of the Smith-Hughes bill.
Afterward, the producers circled the wagons to protect their interests and
formed the National Association of the Motion Picture Industry (NAMPI),
headed by William A. Brady. The new trade organization marked a shift
toward industry autonomy and self-regulation. The National Board meanwhile charged that agitation for legal censorship was being hyped by
"well-meaning, but ill-informed, clergymen and others," no doubt a reference to Crafts and Canon William Sheafe Chase, which revealed a rift
between the Board and Protestant leadership. The American public, and
not Protestant clergy, Board officials insisted, should be the final arbiter of
motion pictures.[6]

Sparring with the National Board

The Federal Council of Churches had grown in importance, but Council
leaders had been too preoccupied with coordinating program initiatives
and establishing a solid financial footing for the agency to invest much in
the movie question. But complaints about the National Board and
mounting pressure for legal censorship increased the urgency of the
movie issue. To provide a unified Protestant voice on matters of common
interest, the Council took up denominational initiatives through investigation, and also by speaking and acting as a representative of its constituent
members. One of its studies revealed that only about 9 percent of all the
movies that the Board inspected in 1914 required changes; the vast majority of films were found to be "neither good nor bad, but are flat, negative and harmless." While critics attributed the small percentage to the
Board's low standards, the Federal Council took this as a mark of accomplishment. The Board's task, to function as a kind of "thermometer of
public opinion," was not an easy one and demanded a "liberal judgment."[7]
In short, the Board's review was adequate to the task.

The Protestant establishment was already exerting itself as cultural
custodian via its presence on the National Board. General Secretary
Charles S. Macfarland represented the Federal Council on the Board's

General Committee, which had administrative oversight of the review agency. Stoop-shouldered, square-jawed, limping a little, Macfarland was a powerhouse in the Federal Council, tirelessly devoted to the Social Gospel agenda, but his duties and frequent travel prevented him from being active on the National Board. Instead of resigning, he was represented on the General Committee by F. Ernest Johnson (already a member of the Board's Reviewing Committee). Johnson was a natural choice. He believed deeply that movies should not be censored any more than the press and favored "a liberal, voluntary censorship" over "the various proposals for legal control." As head of the Federal Council's Research Department, Johnson was directly responsible for developing the organization's policy on movies and making recommendations to church denominations.[8]

As the Federal Council was aware, the National Board's credibility with the public was waning. To redefine itself, it changed its name in 1916 to the National Board of *Review*, and to clarify its mission adopted a new slogan—"Selection, not Censorship"—that was the motto of the Board's National Committee for Better Films. This committee's task was to organize local groups into a national movement and to put resources into classifying and providing information about individual movies. Despite expressed public dissatisfaction, the Board would not compromise its established principles. Administrators reaffirmed the Board's standing commitment to "the free expression of ideas in the press, the theatre, and the motion pictures," and on that basis continued to approve films on contentious social issues. They also refused to slant reviews out of concern for youth; movies were essentially an adult form of entertainment, not to be subjected to the limitations of a juvenile mind-set.[9]

The purported strengths of the Board's system of voluntary regulation had become fodder for its critics. The Board had no legal power to enforce its rulings, failed to sufficiently represent public opinion, and approved too many objectionable films that had to be cut subsequently by city and state boards. A constant complaint was that it passed adult-oriented movies that were not appropriate for impressionable young people in the audience. The Federal Council received its share of complaints about specific rulings, along with accusations that its financial dependence on the industry rendered the Board powerless. The Board took a major hit when, after intense debate, the General Federation of Women's Clubs (GFWC) withdrew its long-term support in 1918. After issuing a damaging report the next year, it threw its weight behind state censorship. This marked a growing division among clubwomen over the viability of continued cooperation with the film industry. With the Board's clout declining, the Federal Council was also under considerable pressure, even from more liberal constituents, to endorse proposals for federal regulation.[10]

Ernest Johnson pressured National Board officials to make changes in an attempt to stop the bleeding. He pointed out drawbacks to its absolute financial dependence on the film industry and argued that failure to review films with youth in mind frustrated the Board's purpose and even threatened its existence. The immediate issue was the Board's decision to pass *The Solitary Sin*, one of a spate of sex hygiene films that, for assorted reasons, were being censored by state boards, sparking a hostile public reaction that together could lead to censorship legislation. Board Secretary Orrin G. Cocks thought Johnson was overreacting. He was confident that federal regulation would meet opposition from both political parties, and he had been approached by the GFWC chair about "constructive ways" of dealing with the youth situation.[11] Johnson nevertheless persisted.

Meanwhile, NAMPI, the film interests trade group, struck out on its own and announced plans to censor its own product based on a list of resolutions, "Thirteen Points," that were pretty much restatements of the Board's general standards. It was mostly a publicity stunt; no enforcement mechanism was established, and NAMPI lacked the political clout with producers to make it effective, anyway. At their third annual convention in August 1919, the producers declared their right to produce movies as they saw fit with public opinion alone as the judge of acceptability. According to *Variety*, legal censorship was "pummeled, derided, battered and kicked out of the window" in forceful speeches by industry leaders who resented the inference that they needed "a moral guide to tell them what is a naughty picture and what is not."[12]

By 1920, a number of Protestant denominational agencies had either registered protests against the condition of movies or passed resolutions in favor of state control. Delegates at the Southern Baptist Convention, which was not a member of the Federal Council, wrote off the National Board as a pawn of the film interests; its approval was no guarantee that a film was "void of evil." Independent church organizations sprung up to supplant the Board. It was "no news" when Catholics established an official review agency in New York, but since Catholic organizations had promoted boycotts in several cities, some suspected that the real purpose was to advise clergy on which films to ban and "so have their market value greatly mitigated against." Protestant denominations also started creating their own "white" lists of worthwhile movies, preferring that individuals decide for themselves what to see, rather than issue a "black" list of unapproved films. *Variety* warned that should Hollywood be confronted with "a really united Protestant control, a censorship greater than any legal one will have been established."[13] The nearly 18 million Roman Catholics far outnumbered any single Protestant denomination, but altogether there were around 46 million Protestants. Whether they could be galvanized in a move against the film industry was an entirely different matter.

On May 20, 1920, the Federal Council recommended that the National Board give its General Committee members more direct involvement in the review process, and do a better job of informing the public about its standards, program initiatives, and financial arrangement with the film industry. In the resolution was a verdict. On the same day, Johnson informed W. D. McGuire, the Board's executive secretary, that he would soon make a decision on "the future relation" of their organizations. McGuire had been trying to edge Johnson out, noting that his affiliation with the newly formed National Motion Picture League (a Board competitor) disqualified him from participation on the General Committee.[14] Shortly after the Council's resolution, Johnson tendered his resignation and, per McGuire's suggestion, was replaced by Samuel McCrea Cavert, who was no less confrontational. He questioned the logic of the Board's position against making judgments with youth in mind. There was no principled reason to censor movies for adults, Cavert insisted; the purpose of regulation was only "to get pictures that are decent for young people."[15] The Board did begin reevaluating its standards and review process, but for the most part remained intransigent. Despite reports indicating widespread outrage over the condition of movies, a 1920 Board survey showed that only 5 percent of moviegoers favored censorship. Why tinker with success?

National Board officials underestimated how crucial the concern for youth was in the politics of movie reform. Estimates of children's attendance varied, going as high as half of the movie audience, but most reports put the figure at around 25 percent.[16] People by and large did not want to see movies attuned to a child's aptitude, but still had deep reservations about the effects that movies were having on youth. This concern, which was probably *the* main motivation behind efforts for official censorship, simply could not be separated from the central issue of regulating motion pictures.

Not Censorship, More Comedies

Sparked by a sense of unity and idealism, Protestant zeal for social reform ran high in the years immediately after World War I and found concrete expression in the victory of Prohibition. Part of the momentum was generated by a nationwide demand for better movies and agitation for legal censorship. Gearing up for another crack at federal control in December 1920, Wilbur Crafts resolved "to rescue the motion pictures from the hands of the Devil and 500 un-Christian Jews." To get rid of "the menace of the movies," he announced a full-scale plan to enlist the aid of the Catholic Church and reform organizations in a massive congressional petition drive. Close to 100 movie-related measures were introduced in over 35 states in 1921, many with support from Protestant churches and organizations.[17]

Only four states—Pennsylvania, Ohio, Kansas, and Maryland—had censor boards, but the political climate had shifted. Republicans won majorities in both houses of Congress in 1918. Woodrow Wilson, having suffered a stroke, was an invalid in the White House, and Warren G. Harding easily defeated his Democratic opponent in the 1920 presidential election. Harding's campaign manager, Will H. Hays, quietly met with Adolph Zukor, William Fox, and other film executives to ensure that his candidate received favorable treatment in newsreels. A proliferation of state laws banning the sale of alcohol throughout the 1910s was one factor leading to national prohibition. The same course could just as easily result in federal regulation of the film industry.[18]

In January 1921, Federal Council executives asked Lee F. Hanmer to investigate the effectiveness of the existing state censorship operations. An elder in the Dutch Reformed Church, Hanmer was director of the Department of Recreation with the Russell Sage Foundation, a progressive organization dedicated to social science research, and had served on the National Board's General Committee. In conjunction with Hanmer's study, Ernest Johnson's Research Department coordinated church groups in a number of cities to assess the character of films in their communities. The aim was to gather reliable information to determine whether government action or voluntary public education was the better approach. The Federal Council was charting its own course.[19]

A censorship bill on the docket of the New York legislature brought the National Board under close scrutiny. An investigative series in the *Brooklyn Daily Eagle* disclosed, among other things, that the Federal Council's Charles Macfarland and Congregational minister S. Parkes Cadman were inactive members who had no clue about the kinds of movies the Board passed. Film executive Benjamin Hampton publicly blamed the preponderance of risqué movies on the people who "flock to see them," and to prove it, revealed that film companies might gross only $75,000 to $100,000 on a decent drama, compared with "sex-plays" that were pulling in $250,000 to $2.5 million. These sobering figures helped make the industry's case about public tastes. Even so, Hampton warned that excessive "sex-stuff" in movies would elicit "a hurricane of public wrath" and would lead to restrictive censorship measures. The flagship Protestant journal, the *Christian Century*, had already given notice that if film companies allowed "commercial interests to irritate public opinion into a reaction against the Board of Review as a sufficient monitor they will get official censorship for their pains."[20]

Hoping to buy some time, NAMPI president William Brady extended an olive branch to the industry's chief antagonist, Wilbur Crafts. At a March 14 meeting, Brady presented NAMPI's Thirteen Points and outlined plans to bar objectionable films, which Crafts took as an indirect admission that improper movies had been passed by the National Board. Still, the minister's objective was to clean up movie content; the means was a minor matter. Appearing satisfied, he agreed to hold off on his bid for federal action.[21] Crafts however, rightly understood NAMPI's initiative as a sign of vulnerability. He incorporated the Thirteen Points into his bill for a federal film commission and within days made the announcement, alleging incredibly that NAMPI actually supported some features of his plan. The *New York Times* editorialized, "The morality of this is no doubt apparent to reformers; among the worldly it excites wonder." Brady, who was both stunned and furious at the minister's about-face, repudiated Crafts's claim and blasted him for reneging on his pledge to give the industry time to improve. The *Times* marked Crafts's move as evidence that he wanted far-reaching regulation of public morals: "What is begun with the film will go on to the play, the picture and the book."[22]

To ameliorate the situation, Gabriel Hess, chair of NAMPI's censorship committee, arranged a conference with Crafts and members of the New York Civic League, Women's Christian Temperance Union (WCTU), Society for the Prevention of Crime, and City Federation of Women's Clubs. There was little consensus, however, among the "uplifters," as *Variety* dubbed them. In lieu of a definite plan, a tentative agreement was reached, allowing NAMPI to develop a means of control over producers by mandating adherence to the Thirteen Points.[23]

On March 15, the Federal Council issued a press release ostensibly addressing "The Crisis in the Motion Picture Industry." The Council affirmed the National Board's method of "unofficial reviewing" as the best alternative to legal censorship, while also acknowledging that there was a great deal of public dissatisfaction with the review agency. By airing its grievances, the Council distanced itself from the Board and soon began dealing directly with NAMPI. On the same day as the Council's press release, the Brooklyn Federation of Churches held a day-long conference on movie censorship. The 125 clergy present voted unanimously to denounce the work of the National Board as "a mere rubber-stamping of moving picture corporation interests" and pledged support for the New York censorship measure, the Lusk-Clayton bill.[24]

The Federal Council was in a difficult position. The National Board routinely cited the Council's cooperation to deflect criticism; by association, the Council was being accused of sanctioning the movies that the Board passed—movies that an influential benefactor deemed "definitely injurious to the young people of this country." Council executives Macfarland and Cavert tried to turn up the heat and insinuated that unless the situation improved, their connection with the Board was in jeopardy. Hearing this, National Board executive W. D. McGuire was incensed. "Sick and tired" of veiled threats, he was ready to let the Federal Council "go to the dogs." Working with them was futile "because they do not fundamentally believe in the wholesomeness of people generally," he contended. "We are dealing with the amusement of the mass of the people and the mass of the people are not going to church these days." McGuire thought the Council was bluffing; absent some other channel of influence, the Board was a "distinct asset."[25] But not for much longer.

At a hearing on the Lusk-Clayton bill in April, Canon Chase and other Protestant and Catholic clergy spoke in favor of the measure. No one, not even NAMPI executives, defended the state of the film industry's product. Hoping to defer action on the bill, NAMPI offered to cover the expense of a governor-appointed commission to make recommendations to the film industry, and proposed to establish its own internal review board—a new Editorial Committee. So much for the National Board of Review. An industry spokesperson guaranteed that a handful of studio executives who were responsible for 95 percent of the movies exhibited in the United States could "absolutely insure the quality of these pictures to any standard that might be agreed upon." The intent was to put the blame for salacious movies on fringe producers, but the astonishing admission that movie magnates like Adolph Zukor, Marcus Loew, and William Fox had the power to eliminate objectionable films was gold for certain reformers. New York governor Nathan L. Miller threw his weight behind the bill; it was estimated that fees collected by a board would boost the state's revenues by over $500,000. After intense debate and with some political shenanigans, the bill was passed. It was a major blow to both NAMPI and the National Board. The liberal Catholic journal *America* sarcastically remarked that the Board was "about as useful as a hole without a dough-nut around it."[26]

Despite the flurry of state proposals reportedly backed by "professional reformers," only New York and Massachusetts enacted measures. Florida passed a makeshift bill requiring National Board approval for all films exhibited in the state. In Federal Council circles, the sense was that the debates over state censorship had exposed its shortcomings and reversed public opinion. Most Americans considered censorship an undesirable limitation of American liberty. Moreover, as the *Christian Century* was astonished to discover, even with all the hoopla, most churches were largely indifferent to the issues involved with "better control of the movies." The observation tapped an important aspect of the controversy. The ongoing struggle was far from the lives of ordinary people. Eighty percent of children in a Parent-Teacher Association survey in Buffalo, New York, liked "blood and thunder" movies, "wild-west, Tarzan, and jungle films," although in other areas there was some preference for travel and educational films. As it was, from wild westerns and heart-wrenching melodramas to "sensational society films," the vast majority of people were quite satisfied with the entertainment that movies provided.[27] They just wished that Hollywood would make more Charlie Chaplin and Harold Lloyd comedies and melodramas starring Mary Pickford.

Two Proposals for Government Regulation

Film companies were caught in a bind. Box office remained solid: roughly one-fifth of the U.S. population went to the movies every week. But it was common knowledge that the more lurid the advertising, "the greater the throngs that flocked to the picture palaces." And for that reason the industry was under siege. In May 1921, the General Assembly of the Presbyterian Church in the United States resolved: "Since some of those engaged in the business are not amenable to the appeal for clean movies, we urge a nationwide campaign for legal censorship by the Federal Government."[28]

With movies being distributed nationally and the National Board a lame duck, Canon Chase, relying on pietist assumptions, drafted a bill to authorize a federal commission to license for exhibition every film produced in the United States or imported from abroad. The explicit purpose was to "free the new art form from the tyrannical control and influence of degrading, ignorant, greedy degenerates." Chase's tract was quite prejudicial. He might have preferred that the film industry regulate itself, but as he saw it, Jewish studio heads were incapable of doing so because they lacked character. Movie standards should be set and enforced by a nonpartisan federal film commission representing the people and not the likes of "Mr. Fox, Mr. Goldwyn, Mr. Griffith, Mr. Selznick, Mr. Laemmle and Mr. Lasky." The *Mutual* decision made any comparison of movies to the press moot, he maintained. Besides, artistic freedom in the hands of profiteers was only license to depart from "the fundamental laws of truth." Playing semantics, Chase defined censorship as decisions that were "arbitrary and based upon personal opinion" and without appeal, as distinguished from licensing, which enforced "a certain legal standard" with the licenser's decision subject to court appeal. The commission's task corresponded to that of the Food and Drug Administration: protecting consumers from harm.[29]

By contrast, Charles Lathrop drafted a report for the Federal Council based on the studies conducted by Lee Hanmer and Ernest Johnson. The Lathrop report, illustrating the structural approach, offered a realistic appraisal and developed a hybrid, comprehensive strategy to avert legal censorship, two enduring characteristics of the Federal Council's approach. The authors conceived the situation altogether differently from Chase, whose premise was that the producers were to blame for immoral movies. By contrast, Lathrop, Hanmer, and Johnson maintained that audience demand was "the dominant moral factor in the situation," and to some extent a reason for the "Philistine" mind-set among Hollywood producers. Insofar as producers and exhibitors (who feared that attendance would drop for movies approved by a censor board) were directed by box-office returns, they were only displaying good business sense. Art and morality were apparently of small concern to most moviegoers; even respectable folks treated moviegoing as a "moral holiday." Indeed, the report took a jab at "conventional moralists" for failing "to realize that realistic art is not necessarily immoral because of its frank and intimate treatment of elemental life situations." Though careful not to dismiss the efforts of state-church federations that were backing proposals for censorship legislation, especially in Ohio and Massachusetts, the Council's report was undoubtedly conceived as a workable alternative to legal censorship. It went on to highlight the failings of censor boards, the difficulty of reaching consensus on standards (even among "high-minded people"), and the need to recognize limits to legal censorship. The best that could be hoped for was to establish broad standards and try to get the producers to observe them as much as possible.[30]

In the estimation of the Federal Council's experts, Chase's licensing scheme constituted an objectionable prior censorship. They believed that putting the onus on producers and distributors to serve the public welfare was more consistent with the principles of individual liberty and social duty than relying on an external board. The centerpiece of the Lathrop Report, then, was the assignment of responsibility to different agencies best suited to carry out particular tasks toward improving the overall situation. Instead of state or national censorship of movies prior to exhibition, the Federal Council recommended a diffuse legislative authority to monitor films based on broad, widely accepted standards.

The plan began with government oversight of the film industry as a public service utility. Producers, distributors, and exhibitors would be licensed to conduct business through interstate commerce on the condition that these companies not ship movies considered "obscene, indecent and detrimental to the morals of the people," as Hanmer put it. Industry executives had long maintained that existing penal laws were sufficient to this end and made censorship unnecessary. Let states enact laws making it a misdemeanor to exhibit films judged by the courts to be obscene; a recent amendment to the federal Penal Code in July 1921 made interstate transport of "any obscene, lewd or lascivious . . . picture, motion picture film, papers, letter, writing, print or other matter of indecent nature" punishable by a fine and imprisonment. Local licensing and inspection would ensure that exhibitors adhered to the law. In addition, schools and churches ought to teach film appreciation. Boycotts of local theaters were firmly rejected. Religious and social agencies were also responsible for providing recreational alternatives and, with Better Films Committees, educational opportunities to improve public taste and demand for high-quality movies.[31] In sum, the emphasis was on persuasion and encouragement of the good rather than an ethic of compulsion or the suppression of evil.

The Federal Council issued its report as a four-part series in June 1922. The *New York Times* praised it as "the most intelligent and thorough study of its kind that has yet appeared." Coming from a religious organization, it defied expectations by carefully navigating "between the ballyhoos of the film business on one side and the professional reformers on the other." The report refrained from sensationalizing its subject, was informed and balanced, urged caution and restraint, admitted the complexity of the problem, and dealt with it comprehensively. The *Times* objected, however, to the licensing scheme as a "governmental paternalism" that marred the overall proposal by giving it "fundamentally the character of censorship." Any such commission, even with the right of court appeal, would still be too relativistic and prone to abuse, the *Times* contended. Better to keep the constructive emphasis on community education to raise the moral and intellectual level of the movies.[32]

The main impetus for the Chase and Lathrop reports was not to impose censorship on the film industry, but to construct an alternative to the floundering National Board of Review. Voluntary regulation appeared to have failed as a means of ensuring quality films for public consumption. Still, based on starkly different assessments of the situation, the Chase and Lathrop proposals for a mode of federal regulation were fundamentally at odds, even if the authors might have shared a view that legal censorship was a last resort in dealing with motion picture producers. These two divergent approaches—a commission to represent public tastes and supervise production versus voluntary industry regulation in conjunction with laws that would keep the market open to demands for better films— would persist for more than two decades. The underlying principles would remain, even as the strategies morphed into new forms.

Forging a New Alliance

With the great disillusionment that swept America after World War I, a reactionary patriotism erupted in prejudices against Catholics and Jews. Along with fears of a Communist threat, this would lead to legislative quotas restricting immigration in the 1920s. In this increasingly hostile climate, and with the passage of the Lusk-Clayton bill, it was clear that filmmakers' cooperation with the National Board was not enough to prevent the spread of city and state censor boards or to quiet calls for federal supervision. NAMPI needed a powerful Protestant ally. This is likely the reason NAMPI head William Brady intimated to Protestant leaders in May 1921 that producers were willing to make movies publicizing church humanitarian and missionary work, provided an overture come from an interdenominational church agency. NAMPI and the Federal Council were both looking to forge a new alliance among "the more progressive and forward-looking elements" in the churches and the film industry. The Federal Council appointed a special Motion Picture Committee to serve as a liaison. If successful, this cooperative venture would promote church work, provide more films for clergy use, and also perhaps give Protestant leaders "an indirect influence" toward improving the character of the cinema. These became the main objectives of church cooperation with the film industry. For a variety of reasons, Brady was unable to arrange a meeting until October. An initial plan was sketched, with another meeting scheduled for the following month, but by then NAMPI was in no position to act on it.[33]

Film executives quickly discovered that the in-house Editorial Committee they envisioned was simply unworkable. How could any one of them judge their own product and that of a rival company without bias? And where would busy producers and studio executives find the time to review the entire output of each company? After the loss in the New York legislature, Brady had recklessly bragged that the industry planned to become an influential factor in political elections. His remarks sparked a call for a Senate Judiciary Committee probe that included unfavorable mention of the National Board of Review. Nothing came of it, but all the publicity the industry was getting drew unwanted attention from both the government and Protestant churches to the concentration of power within the film industry. The Federal Trade Commission was also registering complaints from independent exhibitors and began an investigation of the industry's trade practices.[34]

Film companies had been consolidating their power through mergers and acquisitions. In a policy shift, President Wilson backed off from his initial preference for antitrust legislation and adopted the more Republican concept of establishing a trade commission. The Federal Trade Commission was created in 1914 to monitor and proscribe unfair business practices. A flurry of corporate mergers ensued, and the suspension of antitrust laws during World War I fueled the growth of monopolies that thrived during the 1920s. Though likely in violation of antitrust laws, the vertical integration of film companies was part of a flurry of corporate mergers.

The studios followed Adolph Zukor's Famous Players-Lasky Corporation (later Paramount) and instituted a distribution scheme to reduce the risk of production investments by controlling distribution. In brief, compulsory block booking forced exhibitors to contract for a company's entire yearly output in advance of production. If exhibitors wanted titles with big stars, they also had to lease the studio's lesser quality films, sight unseen (known as "blind selling"). It amounted to an all-or-nothing proposition. When a group of the most powerful exhibitors started their own production-distribution company to mount a challenge, the studios retaliated with an aggressive move to acquire first-run theaters and exhibition circuits. The vertical integration of the film industry was soon complete, leaving a small number of "major" Hollywood studios wielding control over the production, distribution, and now the exhibition of movies. The studio system was obviously more complex, and distribution more flexible than it would seem from this short description. For example, the producers-distributors leased movies to exhibitors on a revenue-sharing basis, and both benefited from adjusting a film's run to correspond with audience demand; exhibition contracts included a cancellation clause allowing theater owners to reject a certain percentage of a block. Also, from the distributor's vantage, block booking also ensured screen time for their releases, in part by preventing competitive exhibitors from overbooking their theaters just to keep their local rivals from getting movies they had no intention of screening. Suffice it to say that the industry's cutthroat trade practices highlighted the fact that the movie business was controlled by large syndicates headed by "Jewish capitalists" with "little feeling for either Christian or Jewish ideals," the *Christian Century* observed, wallowing in Jewish stereotypes: "Their motto is profits."[35] Block booking became a lightning rod for Protestant attacks on the studio system.

By December, the beleaguered NAMPI was finished and the National Board was in jeopardy. Jewish studio owners needed major political clout: a Protestant with Washington connections would have to be the industry's next leader. Speculating on rumors that Will Hays, postmaster general in the Harding administration, was on the short list to head a new industry trade organization, *Variety* remarked, "No one for a moment suggests that Hays would or could invoke the power of his political machine in the interests of a business, but his selection would suggest to the public mind an effort to secure to the industry the good will of one of the great parties."[36] The producers offered Hays an amazing $100,000 salary. It took some persuading, but the Republican Hays, a public relations man and a teetotalling Presbyterian elder, eventually accepted the job and took over as president of the new Motion Picture Producers and Distributors of America (MPPDA) in March 1922.

3

Presbyterian in Charge of Hollywood

the well to do, but pictures are for the
and their appeal is universal. And do
'e serve the leisure hours of the masses
is, so do we rivet the girders of society.
dress to the Men's Bible Class Annual
ier, Baptist Church, 1923

IN MARCH 1919, New York State legislators decided to settle the ongoing and often heated dispute over showing movies on the Sabbath by passing an ordinance allowing cities to decide for themselves. That May, the Oswego Common Council had "a red hot public hearing" over whether the city would permit Sunday movies and baseball. A member of the Trinity Methodist Evangelical Church claimed that local exhibitors opposed the ordinance and even named two of them. One theater manager, who coincidentally belonged to the same church, happened to be present and flatly denied the assertion. He told the council that "if he waited for sufficient patronage from his fellow church members, he wouldn't have money enough to buy salt," according to *Variety*. "All of which created some fun."[1] Over the strenuous objections of church folks, the ordinance passed 6 to 1; one alderman voted in favor of Sunday baseball, but not movies. America's favorite pastimes were getting more leeway, but would soon be in need of a major housecleaning; following the lead of baseball owners who hired Judge Kenesaw Mountain Landis to clean up the sport after the Black Sox scandal in 1919, studio heads put Will H. Hays in charge of the film industry's public relations.

By the 1920s, Hollywood had become a powerful and pervasive business that some Protestant leaders perceived as antagonistic to the faith. There were reports that the Catholic Church and national Jewish societies protected their interests in Hollywood. Under pressure from the B'nai B'rith and the Anti-Defamation League, D. W. Griffith changed the Christ crucifixion scene in *The Mother and the Law*, a film that was incorporated into Griffith's mammoth production, *Intolerance*. The Federation of Catholic Societies protested *Diana's Inspiration*, reportedly objecting to a scene in which "Acteon, the Greek hunter, surprises Diana at her bath in a stream," and threatened a theater boycott. Catholic officials apparently were successful in preventing the exhibition of *The Power of the Cross*, a movie featuring a scene with a young curate and a woman he loved prior to his ordination, which church officials deemed sacrilegious. The Federal Council was not so inclined, but did pass along complaints from rank-and-file Protestants. Presbyterians charged that Hollywood was "spreading a moral blight across America" with a flood of movies that made light of marriage, a woman's virtue, and the Sabbath, and contained "anti-prohibition propaganda." Too many films singled out Protestant ministers—and not Catholic priests or Jewish rabbis—for depiction as "weak-kneed, lady-like men."[2]

Cecil B. DeMille's scandalous—yet enormously profitable and trend-setting—bedroom melodramas were especially troublesome. Voyeuristic in style, while still cautionary in theme, films like *Old Wives for New* (1918) and *Don't Change Your Husband* (1919) featured the fashions and sex intrigues of the exceedingly rich and offered vicarious living for working- and middle-class moviegoers. As one scholar succinctly put it, DeMille's movies "gave voice to a crucial myth of modern culture: metamorphosis through consumption."[3] But the new morality and the accent on materialism did not play well with clergy and women's groups, especially in small towns and cities. Their Victorian sensibilities were jarred by scenes featuring heavy drinking, drug use, seduction, divorce, and lavish displays of wealth—all fodder for popular imaginings of Hollywood as a place of rampant decadence. A series of highly publicized scandals involving marquee celebrities elicited widespread attacks on Hollywood as morally bankrupt. Especially damaging was news that Roscoe "Fatty" Arbuckle, one of the most popular comedians of the Silent Era, allegedly raped and killed a young starlet at a hotel drinking party.

At the same time, as much as they feared the cinema's capacity for harm, Protestant clergy and educators were alerted to the incalculable possibilities that movies afforded home, school, and church for "visual-ized instruction, inspiration and entertainment." While fundamentalists denounced the idea of using movies for ministry, mainline Protestant ministers reasoned that if exhibitors refused to close on the Sabbath, why not funnel the crowd into the church to watch a suitable film? Places of worship across the country began installing projection equipment. Sanc-tuaries were sometimes "packed to the limit" for showings of carefully selected "uplifting" movies, followed occasionally "with a dance and a dish of ice cream," *Variety* observed.[4]

Companies were formed to produce films for Sunday school use. *Variety* reported that a "church society" even tried to arrange a deal with film distributors on behalf of 100 churches in greater New York to secure first-run exhibition of films with a promise of 300 days of bookings—Sundays excluded, of course. Churches could put from 1,600 to 2,000 people in the pews. The distributors decided not to take the offer; New York exhibi-tors no doubt breathed a sigh of relief.[5]

Clergy hoped that sold-out sanctuaries would persuade Hollywood that churchgoers were a ready market for inspirational and biblical movies. If producers would make them, ministers were willing to mar-ket and exhibit them, virtually guaranteeing a profitable run. Forging such an alliance became a key, if also contentious, dynamic in relations between the two institutions. Sanctuary showings might have legiti-mized movies for many conservative middle-class Protestants, but ex-hibitors rightly worried about the unfair competition. Clergy complaints about the lack of a reliable supply of educational or religious movies only increased as the movies that attracted the most customers, even in the small towns, exposed middle-class Protestants to commercialized entertainment and modern urban values. Church-oriented films, how-ever, had an unimpressive track record, and producers understandably did not think that much of a market existed for educational films that substituted for sermons. These trends evolved in the late 1910s, and the desire for movies that supplemented church programs likely con-tributed to Protestant support for some kind of government regulation of film production, a business now controlled almost exclusively by vast corporations. The new Protestant head of the Motion Picture Producers and Distributors Association (MPPDA) would invest in a strategy to ride these crosscurrents and build a cooperative relation-ship: a daunting task, given the fundamental divide over the purpose of motion pictures.

Cooperating with the MPPDA

When Will Hays assumed leadership of the MPPDA, he was standing at the crossroads of religious rectitude and political power. A Washington insider connected with a major communication industry and immensely profitable corporations, he also chaired a laymen's committee in the Presbyterian Church, raising $15 million to bolster the denomination's ministerial pension fund. Hays was an icon of the Protestant establishment. With him at the helm, clergy were willing to let Hollywood clean up its act; if the industry could not improve itself under the Presbyterian elder's able and high-minded leadership, then surely it was a "hopelessly corrupted business."[6]

Hays's own views were largely consistent with those expressed by Federal Council leaders. He was in principle opposed to censorship and favored industry self-regulation, not only as a defense against government intrusion, but a means to improve character. Self-regulation, the corporate equivalent of personal self-discipline, he liked to say, "educates and strengthens those who practice it."[7] But industry regulation had to be enforced, if you will, by popular demand for better movies, and so Hays pursued a public relations strategy aimed in part at improving audience taste. If Hays displayed a structural tendency by developing the film industry's mode of self-regulation, deep down he harbored the pietist impulse, seeing ethical problems with film not in its organization or market orientation, but in specific behaviors depicted on screen.

The two expressed purposes of the new MPPDA, which soon became known as the Hays office, were to foster the "common interests" of the film studios and to establish and maintain "the highest possible moral and artistic standards" and develop the educational and entertainment value of movies. Not unlike the National Board, Hays's power depended on simultaneously protecting the industry and improving the movies—mutual aims that were often at cross purposes. Though dubbed the movie "czar," Hays actually had little influence over production. But if he was going to have any legitimacy with the public, the producers had to exhibit some self-discipline. Hays's approach was encapsulated in a frequent assertion: Americans were fundamentally opposed to censorship—but were just as sure to demand it should the industry fail to control itself. Nothing scared the heads of these vertically integrated studios more; any government involvement in the industry's affairs would inevitably lead to regulation of their business practices. Hays sidetracked scrutiny of the industry by managing scandalous news, scuttling censorship legislation, and pacifying critics. To stop the momentum for legal censorship, he tried to win the support of "the forces of morality and idealism" behind it, and to get the producers to make "more human and heart-warming pictures" that did not need to be censored.[8]

The cooperation of Protestant churches and women's organizations—Hays's natural constituencies—was key. There were women's clubs in every town and city, with state federations and a national body representing millions of women across the country. Thirty-two Protestant denominations were part of the Federal Council, representing 19.5 million members and just over 60 percent of the total number of churches in the United States. The Council had federations in more than 50 cities, a biweekly Information Service, and bimonthly *Federal Council Bulletin*; its publicity department was in contact with 150,000 ministers across the country who preached to congregations every Sunday. Hays hoped to leverage their moral authority to keep his employers and their employees in check, using this vast Protestant communication network to promote the best films and to establish a bulwark of public opinion against legal censorship.[9]

Hays's lofty Christian rhetoric created expectations for immediate and pervasive reform; the MPPDA looked like a bona fide opportunity for the Federal Council to get out from under the National Board. The central question put to Hays was how to influence the development of the film industry in a non-censorial way: "If we are not to support a legal censorship (as we have never done), what is to be our alternative as a means of working for a better method of eliminating the evil tendencies from our motion picture films?"[10]

That the Lathrop report sought a resolution in "the social ideals of the whole community" resonated with Hays, who was impressed with the study as "a step in the right direction." He arranged meetings with Federal Council executives right away to discuss possibilities for mutual cooperation. They remained cautious, rightly concerned that any entanglement might damage the organization's credibility. When Hays pushed for "a thoroughgoing liaison arrangement" that would use the Council's extensive network to issue lists of approved films and to promote them in churches, Council officials balked. Passing judgment on movies would open the Council to a constant barrage of criticism over standards and specific rulings—just like the National Board. Everyone agreed, including Hays, that the time to improve the quality of movies was during production.[11]

The Federal Council's Ernest Johnson suggested to Hays that the industry create a direct channel for "mutual interpretation." That way, producers assumed responsibility for their own product; church and civic leaders could help by serving as translators between churches and film companies. Hays, who was struggling with how to implement the MPP-DA's principles, apparently found much to like in the idea; by dealing directly with national organizational leaders, he could effectively control large segments of the influential public.[12] Input from such a committee could perhaps be used to influence the producers. But Hays was more interested in having organizational leaders promote approved films to boost their box office, which in turn would encourage the production of more of them; it was simply a matter of supply and demand.

In June 1922, the MPPDA sponsored a high-profile luncheon at the Waldorf-Astoria Hotel in New York. It was attended by 78 delegates from 62 national organizations with a combined membership of over 60 million. Afterward, a Committee on Public Relations (CPR) was formed as "a channel of inter-communication" between the film industry and national agencies representing public opinion. Protestants assumed top leadership positions. Lee Hanmer (director of the Department of Recreation of the Russell Sage Foundation) was put in charge; Jason Joy (a Methodist and former War Department publicist) became executive secretary. Charles Lathrop represented the Federal Council on the Executive Committee, which was composed of representatives from prestigious Protestant, Catholic, and Jewish organizations. Hanmer thought the committee presented "an unusually favorable opportunity for rendering a real service in this motion picture situation." A number of subcommittees were set up to facilitate the public relations effort, including a Committee on Religious Pictures, whose mandate was "to inform the motion picture industry of the needs of the churches in this respect and to acquaint the churches with the problems involved in meeting this demand."[13]

Content for the time being in cooperating with Hays's public relations effort, the Council tabled its proposal for a federal initiative and eventually disentangled itself entirely from the National Board. Samuel McCrea Cavert resigned from the National Board's General Committee in June 1923; Charles Macfarland followed in December, despite a plea from Executive Secretary Wilton A. Barrett that he not "lose touch with the Board altogether."[14]

Hays's first major challenge was to defeat the Massachusetts referendum on state censorship passed the year before. With church leaders there at loggerheads over the issue, the Federal Council took no official position, but the Hays organization arranged for a special edition of Lathrop's report to be issued, highlighting its emphasis on industry responsibility. That the Council's name appeared on MPPDA anti-censorship tracts drew criticism from constituents who were in favor of the legislation.[15] The referendum was defeated—and with it, film censorship, not only in Massachusetts but likely across the country.

Fresh off the legislative victory, Hays created a firestorm of protest in December for unilaterally lifting the ban on "Fatty" Arbuckle, who had been acquitted of rape and manslaughter charges. Church Federations across the country expressed "shame and outrage" and "emphatic disapproval," and even called for the Federal Council to resign from the Hays committee. Adolph Zukor, not Hays, made the decision not to release Arbuckle's films. Then, over protests by both Hays and the Committee, Zukor went ahead with a film adaptation of the best-selling novel *West of the Water Tower*, which featured illegitimacy and a debauched minister. Realizing that the committee's work was inconsequential, the National Congress of Parents and Teachers and the General Federation of Women's Clubs both withdrew rather than participate in an industry façade. The Committee on Public Relations fell into disrepair.[16]

Hays then began resetting the terms of movie regulation by situating it within the studio system. He replaced the committee and its function with a new MPPDA department and "open door" policy in 1925. A procedure called "the Formula" was instituted in June 1924 to stop producers from outbidding each other for sensational properties. The Hays office was empowered to bar film adaptations of novels and stage plays with salacious or otherwise unacceptable themes. Regular complaints against movies were compiled and codified into a list of "Don'ts and Be Carefuls" in 1927—guidelines to "enlightened public taste" that resembled NAMPI's "Thirteen Points." The studio heads adopted these practices, realizing that there was much less financial risk in negotiating with "censors" during production than releasing a final print that could be cut or even banned from exhibition by an external censor. Depending on the film, foreign ambassadors, government officials, or Protestant or Catholic authorities were used as consultants. "This is not setting up a group of censors, but enlightened self-control," Hays maintained. "By properly interpreting accepted good taste and properties, by helping to shape the pictures properly, and by encouraging the support of the fine pictures resulting, they encourage finer future productions."[17] The standards guided producers in the selection of material; the "open door" policy was a new channel of communication with the public. It all worked to improve movie content and public relations and to better protect studio investments.

Block Booking Must Go

The failure of Hays's public relations effort exposed the industry to a new line of attack. Film production was concentrated in the major Hollywood studios that formed an oligopoly, a small number of companies cooperating together to eliminate competition. The major producer-distributors were vertically integrated firms; they owned the key first-run theaters, monopolized distribution and controlled exhibition, squeezed independents out of business, and ensured a regular outlet for their movies by enforcing compulsory block booking. Given their ironclad control over the industry, the studio heads could ensure the moral and artistic quality of movies. They had repeatedly said so themselves; Hays joined the chorus, citing production as the "one place only where any evils in motion pictures can be eliminated and the good and great advantages retained."[18]

Yet another round of cooperation with the film industry proved a sham. Protestants and others believed that the producers were driven by short-term commercial trends and were cashing in on the most base and lurid tastes, instead of pursuing long-term interests and developing the moral, artistic, and educational value of the cinema. The way to achieve measurable and lasting reform, without resorting to official censorship, was for the federal government to break the stranglehold of the powerful studios by invoking antitrust laws and outlawing the film industry's unfair trade practices.

Briefly, this is how the studio system worked. Movies opened at premium prices and with huge publicity campaigns at first-run metropolitan theaters—nearly all them owned or controlled by MPPDA-member studios—where they earned most of their revenues (between 50 and 80 percent). First-run theaters had exclusive rights to show the best movies first and without competition, a privilege insured by a "protection" clause that prohibited other theaters within a certain distance from exhibiting the same film until after a designated waiting period, a booking policy known as the "run-zone-clearance" system. Most movies were made to appeal to adults and older adolescents who attended these first-run venues. Under the block booking system, these "sophisticated" films were subsequently shown in small cities and towns by exhibitors who were obliged to contract for a whole season (without preview) and play a studio's entire output (regardless of quality). The clientele at these small and medium-sized theaters was mostly families and children.[19]

The studios' position was that block booking was nothing more than a large-scale wholesale practice that kept the exhibitor's rental costs down, even though it also guaranteed the studios a market for their output. Hays and others defended the practice by pointing out that only a small percentage of the total films released annually could be considered objectionable. Independent exhibitors complained that even with a cancellation clause permitting them to reject a percentage of a block, they were forced to show movies that were second-rate either in terms of entertainment value—their top priority—or moral quality. Their main contention, then, was that the blocks available to them contained too many lousy films that were detrimental to their business.

It appears that block booking did function primarily as an efficient way to deliver movies cheaply and in a quantity that matched demand, just as the producers maintained. That most theater owners apparently did not utilize the cancellation clause to its fullest indicates a good deal of satisfaction.[20] Regardless, the slant that Protestant clergy and clubwomen took was that block booking had a moral aspect and was not merely a neutral business practice. By their way of thinking, the cinema also had an educational function, and block booking required exhibitors to show movies that parents, church, and community leaders—and even some exhibitors—objected to. So what if block booking smoothed distribution and enhanced industry profits? Cheap and tasteless pictures, they believed, were detrimental to the social good, and no matter the duration of their run, once such a movie was shown, the damage was done.

Protestant leaders initially invested in voluntary regulation and a consumer-oriented strategy to reform the industry. "Selection Not Censorship" and "Promote the Best and Ignore the Rest" were slogans for a democratic movie reform, with tickets the equivalent of votes. Matters of public morals and social standards had traditionally belonged to the states, and then were left to local communities, where the onus for improving audience tastes and the demand for better pictures fell to schools, churches, and voluntary community groups. The way some Protestant reformers saw it, block booking impeded community cooperation with exhibitors and made consumer-based strategies useless; there was no noticeable difference in the slate of films shown in communities with or without a Better Films Council. Outlawing block booking, they concluded, was necessary to make the film industry responsive to real market demands. And again, they were convinced that if free market conditions were restored, sensationalism would give way to higher quality films reflecting traditional American culture and values.

In sum, Protestant reformers wanted to keep the market for movies fair by preventing huge film corporations from gaming the system. Outlawing block booking and blind selling became the cornerstone of Protestant reform strategies. At work was an optimistic assumption about the high moral tastes of the population that an unrestrained market would feed. This had already been disproved (recall the white slavery films and *The Birth of a Nation*) and would be again. Nevertheless, if their concern with the sensationalism used to boost box office receipts might seem to indicate a pietistic attitude, these reformers were really advocating a structural approach to movie regulation that was at odds with the powers that be in Hollywood.

In May 1922, the Presbyterian Church directed its Board of Temperance and Moral Welfare to unite moral agencies to secure passage of federal legislation that would regulate film production. Three national conferences were held that led to the formation of the Federal Motion Picture Council (FMPC) in 1925. Among its leadership were outspoken industry critics Canon Chase and Mrs. Robbins (Catheryne Cooke) Gilman. A suffragist and settlement house worker devoted to progressive reform, Gilman helped found the Women's Cooperative Alliance of Minneapolis, a local movement that advocated community selection to improve the movies. After campaigning against a Minneapolis censorship bill and working with Hays to defeat the Massachusetts referendum, Gilman discovered that she was being used to control women's organizations. Though opposed to legal censorship, she abandoned industry cooperation as futile and took up the cause of federal regulation. Gilman was elected FMPC president in 1927, and she was also a member of the National Committee for Study of Social Values in Motion Pictures, which later became the Motion Picture Research Council (MPRC). She was a constant thorn in Hays's flesh. The FMPC joined independent exhibitors and rallied behind legislation that would establish and supervise standards of production and regulate the industry's trade practices.[21]

Disaffection with the Hays organization renewed debate over whether to continue cooperating with the industry and supporting Better Films Councils, or to resort to government control. For some, if Hollywood could not regulate itself, then there should be a non-partisan federal commission to do the job; the public welfare was at stake. With the Protestant community starting to split, Hays was looking for ways to carry out the MPPDA's purposes and build goodwill with fellow Protestants. The Committee on Public Relations Executive Committee had recommended that Hays appoint someone to consult with Charles A. McMahon, editor of the *National Catholic Welfare Council Bulletin*, and the Federal Council's Ernest Johnson, and to submit a plan for the non-theatrical distribution of films for use in churches and schools. Nothing came of it. Hays made it clear that he did not want non-theatrical outlets competing with theatrical exhibitors, but he did recognize the reciprocal advantages of involving the industry in the production of religious and instructional films for churches and schools. When *Christian Herald* publisher Graham C. Patterson formed the Herald Non-Theatrical Pictures in April 1923 to supply churches with "wholesome pictures for all the family," Hays offered MPPDA support, in the hope that the venture might bolster churchgoer attendance for worthwhile theatrical releases. Patterson's initiative was short-lived, however, "apparently not appreciated by those on whose behalf it was made."[22] An even more promising opportunity was knocking at Hays's open door.

Will Jesus (Movies) Save?

Congregational minister George Reid Andrews was passionate about making the stage and cinema "an ally of church and home." Andrews went to Union Theological Seminary and started his career in the pastorate, but drama was his real love. More than anything, his "consuming desire" was to produce a film on the life of Christ "so fine and so dramatic" that it would join in permanent cooperation the film industry and "united church forces of America." Andrews's plan was to use a percentage of the profits from the film to establish a foundation that would finance religious films for churches. The arrangement was not entirely unusual. In 1921, George B. Seitz Studios announced plans to shoot a film on the life of Christ in the Holy Land, with any profits going to charitable causes.[23]

In April 1924, Andrews had productive meetings with D. W. Griffith and Adolph Zukor. Both agreed that, given the subject, producing the film under the auspices of a religious organization was a good idea, provided "the terms and conditions could be agreed upon to our mutual satisfaction," as Zukor put it. In August, unexpectedly, Zukor's fierce rival, First

National Pictures, threatened to torpedo the project by announcing plans for a film based on Giovanni Papini's novel, *Storia di Cristo* (The Story of Christ), which the *Christian Century* had praised as "the most vivid portrayal of Christ in our generation." Following Zukor's advice, Andrews asked Hays to intervene so that he and his colleagues might "carry on unhindered our purpose of service to the Churches and the cause of Christianity."[24]

Andrews's proposed project was just the kind of thing Hays needed to bolster relations with disaffected Protestants. Hays had addressed the Presbyterian General Assembly in Grand Rapids, Michigan, that May. Amidst a heated doctrinal clash between modernists and fundamentalists, the Hollywood czar drew laughter from delegates by introducing ministerial pensions as both "modern" and "fundamentally sound." Meanwhile, playing at the local Regent theater was First National Picture's *Son of the Sahara*, with newspaper ads promising "Actual Harem Scenes," "Dusky, Oriental Beauties," and "Kidnapping of White Girls by Sheiks." In Hays's own denomination, moral rectitude was as pressing an issue as the widening theological schism; the assembly denounced evolution as well as unclean, suggestive movies. Even with Hays heading the MPPDA, the Presbyterians reaffirmed the work of its Board of Temperance and Moral Welfare toward "the constructive control of the motion picture industry, local, state and national, in such a way that each shall supplement the other and thus protect public and private morals without injustice to any one." Given such a display of waning confidence in the movie industry, Andrews's idea had not only promise, but tremendous public relations value for Hays and the studios. The *Christian Century* had recently editorialized that after "the smut and filth of the war period with the debasement of public taste," the time was ripe for religious movies.[25]

Hays negotiated a settlement. Both companies would abandon their plans in favor of the MPPDA coordinating an industry-wide production on the life of Jesus with Andrews preparing the story, utilizing parts of Papini's novel. The deal was for Andrews's foundation to secure financing and the MPPDA to cooperate in production and distribution. Andrews set the financial terms: 50 percent of the net profits would go to the film foundation, 25 percent to the MPPDA, and 25 percent to Andrews and associates. It is inconceivable that Zukor or any other studio executive would forgo a direct share in the profits, even if the financing did come from church sources. Hays raised the issue with Andrews and then put the whole matter ("a very serious and pretentious suggestion") before the

MPPDA board. Afterward, preparations just kept unraveling. Griffith and Zukor were unavailable for meetings. The project was postponed in deference to MGM's December release of *Ben Hur* (1925). Hays backpedaled; the MPPDA was not really a production company, and the film would have to be undertaken by one of the studios. Despite the setbacks—a clear sign of diminishing prospects—Andrews remained undeterred. He was sure that his story of Jesus would "supplant conflict with cooperation" between the churches and film industry.[26] As it would turn out, he couldn't have been more wrong.

Andrews took over as head of the Federal Council's Committee on Educational and Religious Drama in 1925. At about the same time, he and L. Roy Curtiss (New York City Federation of Churches) succeeded in persuading William E. Harmon (founder of the Harmon Foundation) to set up a new Religious Motion Picture Foundation (RMPF) with Andrews as executive director. Harmon launched the endeavor with $50,000 in start-up funds; the goal was for the association to become self-supporting through production and distribution to churches of "artistic and reverential pictures of a high order." Andrews envisioned himself at the nexus of cooperation between the RMPF, the Federal Council, and MPPDA. He had two businessmen in the wings, ready to raise $2 million to produce his Christ film, but unanticipated problems—including a dearth of available films for distribution to churches—sidetracked his original plan. Much to Andrews's dismay, Harmon decided that it was better to produce several short, inexpensive films to lay a financial foundation. Andrews's Christ film would have to wait.[27]

The Hays organization took an active interest in all this and struck up a working relationship with Andrews. In cooperation with the Harmon Foundation and the Federal Council's Religious Drama Committee, MPPDA staff collected 800 reels on religious subjects that were edited down to 11 for use in an experiment to test the church market. Andrews's Drama Committee arranged for showings in suburban churches in the New York area, with the MPPDA supplying projection equipment at no cost. The inclusion of the films in Sunday evening services was credited with boosting attendance by 36 percent.[28] By Andrews's account, the MPPDA offered $8,000 to help finance presentations in churches that utilized movies, but after debating whether a church body should receive such money, the Federal Council declined the offer. Andrews was invited to consult on projects like MGM's *The Scarlet Letter* and Famous Players-Lasky's *The Vanishing American*, and Hays offered to pay him $10,000 "for special services, speeches, and advice." And despite the setbacks, Andrews's understanding was that Hays would allow no other movie on the life of Christ to be produced without his "consent and cooperation."[29]

In an address at a Federal Council dinner at the Waldorf-Astoria in March 1926, Hays declared that MPPDA companies would release no film that would "not square with the proprieties as interpreted under all the circumstances by this Committee on Drama of the Federal Council of Churches." Hays appeared to be publicly positioning the Protestant agency as a monitor of movie content. Afterward, Council officials were quick to clarify Hays's remarks and to dispel any notion that it had a censorial function; the drama committee was not assuming "responsibility for the moral qualities of pictures made in America," but only working with producers to attain "the highest possible standards." For its part, the MPPDA stated publicly it had been "actively and closely cooperating" with the Council's drama committee. The Waldorf event "laid down the basic planks," putting Andrews in charge of developing "a constructive program of action leading to closer cooperation and affiliation."[30]

If Hays was hoping that the MPPDA's relation with the Federal Council would increase his influence with Hollywood producers, the Protestant agency simply refused to oblige him. Council officials were against any direct involvement in film production that might even be remotely construed as church censoring. They would do no more than consult on matters related to religion and Protestant constituencies, and they refrained from endorsing specific movies. These dynamics would factor significantly in the MPPDA's alliance with the Catholic Church beginning in the next decade; Catholic bishops had altogether different prerogatives than Protestants, weighing ecclesiastical authority over the individual conscience.

The developing partnership with the MPPDA gave Federal Council executives pause. They decided to make Andrews executive director of a new Church and Drama Association that would be the hub of cooperation between the religious community and the film and theater interests. The association was set up as an independent agency in order to put some distance between its activities and the Council, and also to defuse any negative reaction from constituents still suspicious of the entertainment business. This arrangement also facilitated the inclusion of Catholics, Jews, people with no religious affiliation, and industry professionals not inclined to come under the Council's supervision. Federal Council luminaries, Father William J. Donahue of the Catholic Actors Guild, and Hays were among the speakers at an inaugural dinner at the Plaza Hotel that June.[31]

The MPPDA contributed toward the costs of the dinner at the Waldorf and the launch at the Plaza hotel and pledged $1,000 to the work of the Church and Drama Association. The event was also paid for by the Actor's Equity Association, Church and Drama Association, and Otto H. Kahn, an investment banker, philanthropist, and arts connoisseur. Andrews took this as "keeping with the general understanding earlier arrived at that these cooperating bodies were to finance our enterprise for the sake of the higher interests of the drama." The Federal Council received regular denominational funding, but its commissions also relied on individual donors for financial support. Andrews, who was not on salary with the Federal Council, conceived the Church and Drama Association in the same terms. Hays, MPPDA secretary Carl E. Milliken, and MGM executive J. Robert Rubin joined Council heavyweights Charles Macfarland, Samuel McCrea Cavert, and S. Parkes Cadman on the Drama Association board. Milliken was a central figure. A former president of the Northern Baptist Convention and two-term governor of Maine, he had served in the Federal Council since 1914, including membership on the Executive and Administrative committees. He was also on the board of the Religious Motion Picture Foundation and now the Church and Drama Association's Executive and Ways and Means committees. Milliken was responsible for church relations in the Hays office, and in less than a year would replace Jason Joy as director of the MPPDA's Department of Public Relations. Joy would be put in charge of a Studio Relations Committee in Hollywood to advise producers in the selection of material and applying the "Don'ts and Be Carefuls" to navigate censor boards and avoid public criticism.[32]

In the spring of 1926, the Federal Council and MPPDA appeared to be of one mind, with Andrews and Milliken working together toward their mutual benefit. But events that would prove pivotal for the future of Protestant-Hollywood relations were already in the making.

Getting the *Christ Film*

After a budget riff with Adolf Zukor during *The Ten Commandments* (1923), Cecil B. DeMille formed an independent company under contract with Jeremiah Milbank's Producers Distributing Corporation. DeMille got Milbank, a Wall Street banker, philanthropist, and prominent Baptist, to promise to produce a Christ picture. In June 1926, DeMille, a devout Episcopalian and a consummate Hollywood showman, announced plans to make an epic film on the life of Jesus—or maybe Judas Iscariot. Andrews contacted Hays immediately to confirm their agreement to have "pre-empted the field." He offered to consult with DeMille's writers to ensure "the right sort of a picture of Jesus" in exchange for a "reasonable salary" and paid expenses. Since DeMille was financing the film, Andrews renegotiated the financial terms. He suggested now that 10 percent of the net profits be directed to the Church and Drama Association or the Federal Council's Drama Committee, conditioned upon the ability of these agencies to receive the monies. Otherwise, Andrews would accept the proceeds himself in order to ensure their use for future religious productions.[33]

Hays scheduled a meeting in Hollywood in early July. Andrews, who was disappointed with the Religious Motion Picture Foundation's program, dropped everything and quietly headed for the coast. Dinner at DeMille's home was tense. Twice Hays and the director left the room to confer privately. DeMille finally agreed to sign Andrews on as a consultant, but there was no mention whatsoever of remuneration or the previous arrangement with Hays. Hays made sure to get the Federal Council's stamp of approval so that Andrews, though not employed by the Council, was still serving in some capacity as its agent. In the Council's view, Andrews was an unofficial or semi-official representative. The real benefit of a religious consultant to both DeMille and Hays was not necessarily any applied biblical knowledge, but promotional value and a shield from criticism, which was enhanced by connecting Andrews to the Federal Council.[34]

Andrews found the scenario "most unfortunate in every way," but it was classic DeMille: a religious extravaganza on the life of Christ interlaced with a steamy love affair between Mary Magdalene and Judas Iscariot. This was precisely the sort of commercial pandering that irked Protestant critics. DeMille had also hired Congregationalist minister William E. Barton and his son, Bruce, author of the 1925 best seller *The Man Nobody Knows: A Discovery of the Real Jesus*, as advisers in the project's early stages. The elder Barton initially objected to the love affair, but eventually was persuaded by DeMille and screenwriter Jeanie Macpherson to allow it. "It is not possible to produce a great and successful film dealing with historic characters and not have a love-interest," they explained. DeMille showed him the cost-estimates. "Talk as much as you will about the non-commercial aspects of the business," he said. "They interest me. But there will be no film unless I can see and show the bankers and the managers three millions in quick money." Barton still did not approve, but understood "a little better than I did why it had to be."[35]

Andrews, however, was determined to "get *the* picture of Christ" and reminded Hays that he was on record that no film would be made that did not meet "the proprieties" of the Council's Drama Committee. Using his leverage on behalf of "the united Protestant forces," Andrews managed to get "85% of what I went to secure." Persuaded by both Andrews and the Catholic adviser, Father Daniel Lord, a well-known Jesuit priest, playwright, and drama professor, DeMille nearly eliminated the love affair between Judas and Mary Magdalene. Magdalene, a courtesan who "laughed alike at God and Man," rides off in her zebra-drawn chariot to find Judas in the opening scene and is converted in the next one when she encounters Jesus. Andrews and Lord both extolled the virtues of the final version and, hoping to gain influence with producers, persuaded their respective organizations to publicly endorse the film. Within the Federal Council, Andrews was credited with keeping *The King of Kings* free of "jazzy and sensational elements" that would have "utterly ruined the picture from the standpoint of the churches' interest." With the Protestant and Catholic advisers both "marveling at its scope and power," as Jason Joy put it, everyone involved was supremely confident in the religious epic's potential to bring the life of Christ to "the masses."[36]

Andrews received weekly checks for $125.00 for nearly two months of work on script preparation—no questions asked. Nothing was put on paper. Andrews naïvely assumed that Hays had taken care of the financial details. When shooting began in September, he returned to New York to strategize about promoting the film with Protestant churches. That's when he learned that DeMille knew nothing about the Church and Drama Association getting a share of the net profits. Hays tried to explain that such an arrangement would set an unwanted precedent for other organizations. If that was the case, Andrews proposed that the monies be paid to him personally. As an isolated remark, it might appear that he simply expected a royalty in exchange for his advising and promotional work. Andrews even consulted with an attorney, who advised him that Hays had been unfair and invited him to Hollywood only "to relieve himself of embarrassment in failing to do his plain duty." There was nothing to be done since "moral rights are easily dissipated and quite often disappear over prolonged negotiations." Regardless, despite the changed circumstances, Andrews always thought of *The King of Kings* as his "magnificent dream of the Christ picture" that would create a fund for a religious film program. As another alternative, he suggested to Milliken that some of the film's proceeds be contributed to the Church and Drama Association as a kind of tithe. As it was, the association never accrued any direct proceeds from *The King of Kings*. After hearing about Andrews's original plan, DeMille made a contribution for two years.[37]

The King of Kings had a sensational Broadway premiere on Good Friday, 1927. *Variety* lauded DeMille's "celluloid monument" as simply "tremendous," calling it "the greatest picture ever produced," and predicting that it would become the top-grossing film of all time. After hearing Andrews's account of his consulting work and previewing the film, the Federal Council's Administrative Committee broke precedent and offered an endorsement—unaware that Andrews had been financially compensated for his work. Council officials had earlier made it clear they did not want the Hays organization promoting movies by directly identifying Andrews's unofficial consulting work with the Federal Council. Indicating some confusion over his status with the Council, Andrews promoted *The King of Kings* with mailings to Protestant ministers, sometimes using Federal Council stationery, sometimes at the MPPDA's expense. Andrews's promotional effort was promising enough that Milliken considered establishing a branch of the Church and Drama Association in Los Angeles.[38]

Despite positive notices and Andrews's promotional work with religious leaders, DeMille's masterpiece was not breaking any records at the box office. That fall, controversy brewed as leaders of the Jewish Anti-Defamation League and B'nai B'rith advised that changes be made in the film. To avoid such an eventuality, Andrews had recommended that DeMille include Catholic and Jewish advisers during production, and received letters from rabbis who thought *King of Kings* would foster "better understanding between Jew and non-Jew." He urged DeMille to "stand firm on the picture." Hays stepped in, and DeMille agreed to modify certain scenes and captions.[39]

DeMille was not happy. Despite positive notices, *King of Kings* was not doing enough business to earn a profit against its "generally known" production costs of $2.3 million. *Variety* suggested that the film's shaky box-office performance made the director more amendable to the request by Jewish authorities. DeMille's company was in financial trouble; the expenditures on the film created a crisis that forced Producers Distributing Corporation into a merger with the Keith Albee-Orpheum Corporation and Pathé in 1927. DeMille would later write off his charitable contributions to the Church and Drama Association as a personal "business expense" related to the making of *King of Kings*.[40]

The Church and Drama Association benefited from all the hype over *King of Kings*. After a November membership drive, Andrews called the association "happily launched" and presented Milliken with a plan to preview and recommend movies through a weekly Church and Drama Bulletin.[41] But the controversy and disappointing box office for the religious epic did not bode well for other church-oriented projects—or for Andrews's future as a consultant. There was enough about the *King of Kings* deal left unspoken that divergent interests would soon erupt in a rift that would lead to a tragic and ironic conclusion to Protestant relations with the MPPDA.

4

On the Trail of the Serpent

WILL HAYS AND THE PROTESTANT CRUSADE

I want one good picture a year. That's my policy. Give me a Mr. Deeds or a Jolson Story or an All the King's Men or a Lost Horizon and I won't let an exhibitor have it unless he takes the bread-and-butter product, the Boston Black-ies, the Blondies, the low-budget westerns, and the rest of the junk we make.

HARRY COHN, president, Columbia Pictures

IN THE SPRING of 1928, relations between George Reid Andrews and the Motion Picture Producers and Distributors Association (MPPDA) began to sour. Andrews's Church and Drama Bulletin recommended one exemplary Broadway play and film in each issue (released 40 times a year) and appealed mostly to a constituency in the New York metropolitan area. In the interests of the MPPDA, Carl Milliken urged Andrews to broaden the Bulletin's coverage and distribution to maximize its publicity value; about two-thirds of Protestant churches were located in towns of less than 5,000.[1] Will Hays and Milliken envisioned the Church and Drama Association as the Protestant counterpart to the Motion Picture Bureau of the International Federation of Catholic Alumnae (IFCA). Under the supervision of Rita McGoldrick, IFCA volunteers (all female college graduates) reviewed almost every new release and issued monthly lists of approved films to Catholic schools and newspapers.

Funding was another source of contention. The MPPDA's "invariable policy" was to help with the printing and mailing costs, but not the operating budget (Hays was, however, discreetly covering Rita McGoldrick's travel expenses for movie-related lectures). Hays and Milliken agreed to coordinate screenings for reviewers and provide administrative and clerical help in preparing the Bulletin—all at no cost to the Church and Drama Association. They were also willing to provide some additional financial help until the association could become self-sustaining, but wanted to avoid any public perception that the MPPDA "either controlled or promoted" it. Milliken offered to contribute $6,000 to "underwrite" part of the association's budget, on the condition that Andrews raise the remainder. It was enough to cover the review service, but not Andrews's personal expenses related to speaking and consulting. Andrews recalled no such prior conditions and understood the MPPDA's contribution to be divided evenly between operating costs and his personal expenses.[2]

Federal Council commissions relied on external donors for financial support, and Andrews believed that an "alliance," involving a financial commitment, had been forged between the MPPDA and the Drama Association. The MPPDA paid a quarter of the cost of the Waldorf dinner in March 1926, about $1,000 toward the promotional dinner at the Plaza Hotel in June, and $2,000 to cover the costs of printing and mailing a letter soliciting membership in June 1927. This mailing also advertised *The King of Kings* to clergy by noting the recommendation of the Federal Council's Administrative Committee and mentioning the Hays connection. Andrews went ahead with plans to hire a firm and raise $150,000. He had no intention of functioning merely as a review agency or publicity tool for the film industry, but wanted to be able to weigh in on "the great moral principles involved in the production of pictures."[3]

Circumstances had changed, however, although Andrews was not sure why. His consulting work had dried up, Milliken was dissuading him from lecturing, preferring that he focus on movie reviewing, and MPPDA funding now had strings attached. What he did not know was that in January 1928 the MPPDA started surreptitiously compensating Federal Council officials for consulting with producers and speaking favorably on the movies to church and women's groups—services rendered in connection with their Council duties. Hays and Milliken were circumventing Andrews, who remained unhappy about the treatment he had received on the Christ film and dogged in pursuit of his broader vision to collaborate with the industry on religious productions.

When Milliken kept pressing him for his list of reviewers, Andrews became suspicious and started questioning their working relationship. He put off Milliken's request—supposedly to protect the review process, but also to prevent Milliken from undermining him. The list became a bargaining chip; Andrews made expansion of the review service contingent upon a financial contribution to sustain it. He knew that the membership of Hays and Milliken in the Church and Drama Association linked the MPPDA with prominent church and business leaders. And the MPPDA was having serious public image problems.

Momentum for federal control was building. In July 1927, the Federal Trade Commission released the results of a six-year study that found the studios guilty of conspiracy in restraint of trade and in violation of antitrust laws. The FTC recommended the separation of production, distribution, and exhibition, but, unsure whether it had the authority to force a company to divest itself of property, the commission referred the case to the Justice Department, which took no action. That year, almost 30 states took up censorship bills, and Iowa senator Smith W. Brookhart introduced a bill in the Senate Interstate Commerce Commission to outlaw block booking and blind selling. MPPDA staff urged supporters to accept invitations to the Federal Motion Picture Council's (FMPC) fall conference in 1928, even paying the expenses of some. By prearrangement, they spoke against legislative proposals for federal regulation and left the meeting early so that Hays's publicity staff could report it as a "walkout" in protest of the FMPC's resolutions in favor of the Brookhart bill.[4]

Of much greater significance, a March 1928 Senate investigation of the infamous Teapot Dome affair exposed Hays's complicity in the highly publicized scandals that marred the Harding administration. Hays gave inconsistent testimony, attempting to conceal the fact that he had acted as a fence, covering up and laundering illegal bonds from oil magnate Harry Sinclair in a shady deal to pay off the Republican National Committee's deficit. Through Hays, the signal political scandal of the 1920s was linked to Hollywood and the Protestant establishment. Andrews started receiving queries about whether Hays would remain on the Association's board.[5]

Convoluted charges of bad faith and improprieties went back and forth between Andrews and Milliken, mixed with disagreements over details and personal spin. When Milliken threatened to "organize the church field" apart from the Church and Drama Association, Andrews decided to call his bluff; he stopped the association's film review operation in September 1928.[6]

Familiar enough now with the MPPDA's modus operandi and "utter lack of business ethics," Andrews started to think differently about the offers that Hays and Milliken had made to supplement his salary. Perhaps they were part of a scheme to co-opt individuals and through them control crucial organizations in the interests of the MPPDA. He suggested as much to Milliken; if the MPPDA covered his personal expenses it "would appear to the public to place us on your pay roll." Andrews touched a nerve. Milliken insisted that Andrews's reticence meant that the Church and Drama Association had reached a "final and definite form" and they had reached an impasse, but in his lengthy, detailed reply he omitted any reference to the $6,000 offer to Andrews. Meanwhile, Andrews took notice when a Federal Council employee, Jeannette W. Emrich, was scheduled to lecture on "The Church and Motion Pictures" at an event sponsored by the MPPDA in connection with the Council's Quadrennial Meeting that December.[7] Andrews had not been consulted in the matter, which was against protocol. Were Federal Council officials compromised by some undisclosed financial arrangement with the Hays office?

With Milliken and Andrews at loggerheads, Federal Council general secretary Charles Macfarland arranged a lunch meeting just days after the quadrennial conference. When Andrews alleged that Hays and Milliken had offered him personal compensation, the meeting "broke up in a riot" with sharp denials from Milliken and indignation from MacFarland. Afterward, Macfarland proposed creating an official film commission *within* the Federal Council. This was a complete change in policy, which had long been to establish and maintain organizational relationships through people rather than official action. Though he lacked proof, Andrews sensed a conspiracy. He was convinced that Hays had Council officials on retainer (Jeannette Emrich, maybe others) who were working with Milliken behind the scenes to form a new commission that would displace him and the Drama Association. Andrews started trying to maneuver to make the Federal Council independent of the commercial film and theater interests and confided in Cadman his "profound distrust" of Hays and Milliken.[8]

Macfarland set up a Commission on Motion Pictures and Drama in January 1929. An organizational meeting was held in March, with William C. Redfield chairing a committee of over 30 people, including Jeannette Emrich. The most contentious issue was Andrews's role and the relation of the new committee to the existing Church and Drama Association. In the meantime, Andrews merged the Drama Association with the American Theatre Association and the Drama League of America to form a co-operative enterprise called the Church and Drama League of America. This was another attempt in Andrews's relentless drive to perfect an ecumenical agency that was publicly funded and independent, yet worked cooperatively with commercial film and theater. Andrews became executive director, S. Parkes Cadman president, and Redfield a member of the board, which included Protestants, Catholics, Jews, and others with no religious affiliation. The Church and Drama Association appeared to be on solid financial footing without MPPDA support. Andrews reportedly raised about $30,000 in 1929 from contributors like Otto H. Kahn, John D. Rockefeller Jr., H. D. Walbridge, and others; Rockefeller was reportedly contributing $2,500 a year to the Church and Drama League.[9]

The Federal Council decided to make the Church and Drama League its agent for the stage, separate from the Commission on Motion Pictures to be chaired by Redfield. Andrews was named the Council's Executive Secretary of Drama and a member of the film commission and its executive committee. His purview restricted to theater, Andrews would no longer be the Council's designated gatekeeper in the film industry.[10] Andrews concluded that Hays and Milliken had been hired only to protect the interests and profits of their employers and for that reason they were determined to frustrate church initiatives to improve the quality of movies. That meant preventing others from making worthy films that would compete with Hollywood releases and demonstrate the market viability of religious movies. He set out to quietly warn church officials of the duplicity of Hays and Milliken and to weed out MPPDA influence within the Federal Council.

Hays and the Other Two Movie Musketeers

Guy Emery Shipler was editor of *The Churchman*, a Protestant Episcopal biweekly and the nation's longest-running religious periodical. Shipler had doubts about the Hays organization, so he contacted Andrews, who gave him an earful about his unhappy experiences and suspicions of ethical wrongdoing. In June 1929, at the annual meeting of the Editorial Council of the Religious Press, an association of religious editors set up by the Federal Council, Shipler was appointed head of a committee to investigate the policies of the Hays office. Andrews became his "Deep Throat."[11]

The churches had remained quiet about censorship because of Hays's leadership. But no longer. "THE CHURCHMAN is opposed to censorship on principle," Shipler declared. "In spite of the liberal sentiment in the churches, however, the motion picture industry is going to get censorship— and real censorship—if it doesn't stop hamstringing the public." With that, *The Churchman* launched a blistering campaign against Hays, Milliken, and Jason Joy, asserting that they had sold out their Christian principles. One editorial after another dubbed them a "smoke screen," "moral masks," and "camouflagers" for Hollywood's purveyors of immorality.

Appeals were made to denominational leaders to call the Presbyterian elder Hays and Northern Baptist deacon Milliken to account, the same way "they would any other backslider or hypocrite," and moreover, to investigate their influence with church and women's organizations. Shipler editorialized with the flair of an Old Testament prophet. His scathing rhetoric expressed the deep anger and betrayal that Protestant leaders felt at having been bamboozled by their "brethren."[12] Hays and Milliken were, of course, just as outraged at being subjected to these personal attacks in the religious press.

Shipler's editorial salvo turned up the heat on the Hays organization. His charges were carried by newspapers across the country. Marlen Pew, editor of the trade journal *Editor & Publisher*, praised *The Churchman*'s crusade: "More power to the religious press, say we from the sidelines." The Teapot Dome investigation had damaged Hays's credibility; he was derided now as a "moral perjurer" employing methods of "trickery and deceit," who could no longer hide beneath "his pious mantle of Presbyterianism."[13]

To make matters worse for Hays, newspaper magnate William Randolph Hearst renewed his support for a national censor board. Senator Smith W. Brookhart charged that Hays was not hired to "purify" the industry, but to protect it "against any sort of reform or regulation through public action." An ongoing antitrust suit was making headway in the courts, and the publicity was exposing the absolute control the "Big Eight" studios wielded over the movie business. In November 1929, a federal judge in New York ruled that the trade practices of the producer-distributors violated antitrust laws. Independent exhibitor groups organized the Allied States Association of Motion Picture Exhibitors to better represent their interests. Prominent Protestant groups began calling for an end to block booking; church denominations and agencies passed resolutions urging some kind of federal regulation of the movies. The clamor for federal control brought calls for the Justice Department and Federal Trade Commission to investigate the film industry, including one from Canon William Sheafe Chase.[14] In the midst of it all, Wall Street crashed.

With or Without You

Hays and Milliken had to suspect that Andrews was behind the flogging they were getting in the religious press, and they took steps to make good on Milliken's threat that the MPPDA would manage the Protestant churches with or without the Church and Drama Association.

In August 1929, religious editors received the first in a series of articles on the movies being offered at no cost by freelance writer Charles Stelzle, a familiar and reputable source currently on the Federal Council staff as a publicity specialist. Stelzle had worked for the Presbyterian Board of Home Missions for many years before becoming a freelance public relations agent. Charles Macfarland was instrumental in his appointment as the Council's Field Secretary for Special Service, his salary covered by a benefactor. Andrews recognized the article as Hays's handiwork and passed the piece along to Shipler (who was not included in the offer). *The Churchman* was the only journal to print this first (and last) article, but not without suggesting that "Brother Stelzle" had been surreptitiously hired by the Hays office to write it. Indeed, the MPPDA temporarily hired Stelzle on July 15, 1929, for $125 a week, specifically to offset *The Churchman*'s attacks by writing a series of articles "in acquainting certain editors with the facts which have been misrepresented in a drive against us." Stelzle fired back that *The Churchman* had misconstrued the nature of his business: the MPPDA and Federal Council were just two of more than a dozen clients. But he had not disclosed that upfront. Of greater significance, the exposure directly linked the Hays office and the Federal Council; Stelzle was also a member of its newly formed Motion Picture Commission.[15]

Soon after, correspondence arrived from leaders in women's organizations castigating *The Churchman* for attacking Hays, "an earnest, sincere and honestly religiously minded gentleman." A little detective work showed the letters were all composed by the same person, on precisely the same size, color, and quality of paper, with the same tint of ink and typewriter, and mailed from the same post office within walking distance of the MPPDA offices. *The Churchman*'s charge that they were propaganda from the Hays office was never denied.[16]

That September, some 200 religious, social, and educational leaders attended a Conference on the Use of the Motion Picture in Religious Education. *The Churchman* editorial staff was conspicuously left off the invitation list. A number of key players were on the conference organizing committee, which was headed by Methodist Episcopal minister Howard M. LeSourd (Boston University School of Religious Education and Social Service): Jeannette W. Emrich (National Council of Federated Church Women), Daniel A. Lord (editor, *The Queen's Work*), Rita McGoldrick (Motion Picture Bureau, International Federation of Catholic Alumnae), Harry S. Myers (Board of Missionary Cooperation, Northern Baptist Convention; secretary of the Federal Council's Motion Picture Commission), and Bettie

Monroe Sippel (president of the General Federation of Women's Clubs). The purpose of this "confidential" conference was to recommend a program for industry cooperation on the use of movies in religious education. It was a plain attempt to supersede the Religious Motion Picture Foundation and Church and Drama Association.[17] Hays also used the MPPDA-sponsored event to orchestrate the appointment of Mrs. Thomas G. (Alice Ames) Winter to represent women as a salaried staff member of the MPP-DA's Public Relations Department. It was a move calculated to manage a split among clubwomen over whether to maintain a "support the best, ignore the rest" approach, or to get behind federal regulation to outlaw block booking. A past president of the General Federation of Women's Clubs, Winter was a powerhouse among clubwomen. Hays had out-and-out co-opted one of their top leaders. *The Churchman* cried foul and contended that Winter had really been handpicked by Hays and Milliken: "But how the cunning camouflagers persist!"[18]

While the MPPDA conference was in session, the Federal Council's Motion Picture Commission considered an invitation from the Hays office to preview films—effectively taking over for the Church and Drama Association's Bulletin. William Redfield and Charles MacFarland "locked arms and debate waxed hot" over intimations that Hays and Milliken were making cooperation difficult. To settle the matter, the commission asked the Council's Department of Research and Education to conduct a study of the MPPDA's policies and practices in view of the public welfare. Coincidently, just days earlier, Hays had privately informed Federal Council president Bishop Francis J. McConnell that Shipler's editorial attacks in *The Churchman* jeopardized industry cooperation with the churches. Hays suggested that the Council select an individual with "utter integrity and ability" to investigate the film industry and use the report to refute Shipler's "false charges." Hays not only offered to cooperate, but to fully fund the study. When Redfield later realized the Research Department's inquiry would be conducted under the authority of the Council's Administrative Committee—with Milliken a member—he was convinced that the situation would eventually prove embarrassing and resigned in October 1929.[19]

In December, the New York *Herald-Tribune* ran a story associating Redfield's resignation and Charles Stelzle's release from his Council duties with charges that the Hays organization was trying to control church sentiment through the Motion Picture Commission. Anonymous sources claimed that Hays's staff had disrupted the Administrative Committee and that an ongoing effort to expose the situation would result in other resignations—Milliken rumored to be one. Andrews's fingerprints were all over the report. Macfarland notified him that he was no longer authorized to represent the Federal Council on film-related matters. At an Administrative Committee briefing, Macfarland contended that Redfield resigned rather than relinquish authority over the proposed study and that the press reports of MPPDA influence on the commission were simply "untrue." Charles K. Gilbert, who replaced Redfield as chair of the film commission, issued a statement in January 1930 emphatically denying that anyone associated with the Hays organization had anything whatsoever to do with the formation of the Council's Commission on Motion Pictures or its personnel.[20]

Andrews meanwhile devised a policy change to exclude industry professionals with the intended result that Hays and Milliken were not reelected to the Church and Drama Association board. In a lengthy statement, Milliken accused Andrews of being disgruntled and retaliating against the film industry. He claimed that Andrews expected substantial contributions from the MPPDA to support the Drama Association, "monies which, in ethics and in common sense, we could not supply."[21] Consequently, he and Hays had cut off all official contact and no longer considered Andrews representative of Protestant constituencies. Discrediting Andrews like this was not just underhanded, it was an early warning shot. The Hays organization had launched a crusade against its Protestant opposition.

Courting Catholics

The breach happened at a most inauspicious time. The advent of sound revolutionized the film industry, opening up aesthetic and thematic possibilities while also increasing the costs of production and censorship. By 1929, the cost of state censorship to the film industry was estimated at about $3.5 million a year, more than the annual profits of some of the film companies. To make the changes that boards required and still maintain continuity of sound now required cutting entire scenes and potentially ruining the story, reshooting the scene, or not showing the film in places that demanded changes. Producers wanted fewer restrictions in choosing subject matter and more assurance that their movies would not be hacked up by censor boards. In the summer of 1929, Jason Joy and MGM's Irving Thalberg were working on a revised code to encompass the realities of sound when Martin Quigley, a lay Catholic and publisher of an industrial trade journal (*Motion Picture Herald*) presented Hays with a Catholic proposal written with Father Daniel Lord, the Jesuit priest who consulted on *The King of Kings*. Quigley, who had been badgering Hays about enforcing movie morality, suddenly found him quite receptive. Aware that *The Churchman*'s attacks were eroding Hays's Protestant support, he was suspicious nonetheless of Hays's real purpose in welcoming a Catholic initiative; the distrust was mutual.[22]

With Protestant relations in jeopardy, Hays needed a backup, and he started bolstering his alliance with Catholics. The MPPDA encouraged the studios to buy advertising space in *The Tidings*, a weekly published by the archdiocese of southern California. Hays's public relations staff contributed an article to the Christmas issue and purchased $1,000 worth of copies for distribution. The story featured Alice Ames Winter's appointment, praised Hays for his "open door" policy, and reported that distributors voluntarily renegotiated accounts to refund $1.3 million to independent exhibitors. It was pure MPPDA propaganda. To help persuade Chicago Cardinal Mundelein to support replacing the city's censor board with a previewing agency, Jason Joy suggested that Los Angeles Bishop John J. Cantwell be invited to join a Hollywood previewing group and even offered his personal assurance that movies would contain nothing inimical to the Catholic Church. Aware of how explosive this would be with non-Catholics, Joy advised Hays to destroy his correspondence.[23]

The Skeleton in the Closet

During the press scrap with Milliken, Andrews showed *Churchman* editor Guy Shipler the memo from Macfarland that barred him from speaking about movies on behalf of the Federal Council. Shipler evidently had enough information now to make a dramatic move: "Is the Federal Council of Churches through some of its executive officials, under retainer of the Hays organization?" *The Churchman* called for an investigation. As expected, the editorial created quite a stir within the Federal Council. A top executive paid a visit to *The Churchman* offices to complain about the editor's "reckless crusading." The Council's film commission chair, Charles Gilbert, protested the charge as a "wholly unsupported and unwarranted indictment," and denied again any MPPDA influence on the Motion Picture Commission.[24] At the last moment he tried to withdraw his letter, but it was too late—the issue had already gone to press.

In response to *The Churchman*'s charge of impropriety, Bishop McConnell met with top Council leadership to outline the scope of its Research Department's inquiry. Afterward, Macfarland admitted that he had been on retainer with the Hays organization. From January 1928 through July 1929, Macfarland was compensated $150 a month (the exact amount Milliken had offered to Andrews) as a "counselor" to preview and give advice on films dealing with Protestant religion or clergy. He ended the arrangement in August when *The Churchman*'s attacks became more pointed.[25] The whole matter was kept confidential while the Council's policy committee tried to figure out how to handle it, though it is likely, if only as a matter of courtesy, that Hays had been informed of Macfarland's action.

Hays meanwhile invited Martin Quigley and Daniel Lord to meetings with producers and his staff in January and February 1930. MGM producer Irving Thalberg emphasized the cinema's entertainment value and the importance of the lucrative urban market at the studios' first-run metropolitan theaters. Lord believed that movies should inspire and instruct. The Jesuit priest was concerned about the negative influence films might have, especially on children who attended small-town theaters. He had no problem with movies showing gangsters and prostitutes as long as their activities were depicted as immoral and did not give audiences the wrong impression that sin was "a very profitable undertaking."[26]

The resulting document was a rough mix of high-minded ideals and industry pragmatism. Like the other arts, movies presented "human thoughts, emotions, and experiences" but bore "larger moral responsibilities" as "the art of the multitudes." The cinema was considered primarily entertainment, but socially obligated to uplift the human soul and raise moral and cultural standards. In the new Production Code, the existing "Don'ts and Be Carefuls" were revised a bit and synthesized with Lord's general principles as guidelines for production. The producers adopted the Code as a "play safe" policy. It gave them more latitude in theme while containing narrative treatments—though artificially at times—within a framework of "compensating moral values" requiring that evil not be presented as "attractive."[27]

At the same time that Quigley and Lord were ironing out the details of the new Production Code with studio producers and MPPDA staff, Hays's attorneys were taking legal action against *The Churchman*. Shipler brazenly posted the law firm's libel notice on the cover of the February 15 issue with a rejoinder: the journal's only motive was "to promote the interest of public morality" and it was resolved to continue under the rights of a free press. Hays's lawyers knew there was little hope of succeeding in court, but the suit inadvertently forced McConnell's hand. If he did not conduct a thorough investigation of the Hays organization now, evidence used in Shipler's defense would prove embarrassing to the Council.[28]

Macfarland voluntarily resigned on March 5, 1930. The official announcement came on Friday, March 28, with stories running in the *New York Times* and *Herald Tribune* the following day.[29] At a public lecture on Sunday evening, George Reid Andrews denounced the Hays office for exploiting organizational leaders and revealed, moreover, that Hays and Milliken had personally offered him compensation. The New York papers carried his remarks on Monday, March 31, the same day the MPPDA board ratified the new Production Code. In the meantime, Hays's public relations staff scurried to draft a response to Andrews's charge that Hays was running "a regular paid spy system," as *Variety* put it. *The Churchman's* April 5 headline blared: "The Federal Council of Churches WAS Retained." Shipler demanded that all other organizations involved with the Hays office conduct "a thorough house-cleaning" and called for the Northern Baptist Convention to remove Milliken from the Council's Administrative Committee.[30]

After a ten-month investigation, *The Churchman* uncovered improprieties among high Protestant officials in the MPPDA and Federal Council who were supposed to be responsible for monitoring the moral quality of the movies. During that time, however, the magazine's circulation dropped by 2,000. Churches seemed "languid, if not indifferent" to the Hays organization's improper influence with church and women's groups, "a gesture that threatens Aristophanes and neglects Will H. Hays," Shipler editorialized.[31] Just as bewildering would be the lack of organized church protest to yet another round of broken promises from the producers after instituting the Production Code.

Bamboozled

Between 1927 and 1929, the studios' net profits grew nearly 400 percent. Weekly attendance was nearly three times what it was when Hays took office. "Such an endorsement from the American people could only have come to a form of entertainment that was essentially wholesome," Hays declared. But with movies like *Young Sinners* ("An answer to the youth problem that even youth will love to hear.") and *The Hot Heiress* ("Will knock 'em cold when she flashes her stuff across the screen."), the cinema looked no better to Protestant reformers in the early 1930s than when Hays took office. Especially galling was Fox's *The Cock-Eyed World* (1929), which follows the escapades of two brawling U.S. Marines (Sergeants Flagg and Harry Quirt) as they chase after women of easy virtue, "blondes, brunettes, all shapes and sizes," all over the world. Always trying to get "the lay of the land," a double entendre pointing up the film's ribald humor, the two "pals" even knowingly bed and compete for the same woman, which is played for laughs. Flagg's derisive remark that the Marines fight one war after another just "to protect big business," which conveniently supplies the weaponry, added to the film's cynical outlook. *The Churchman* glibly assumed that Hays had been "absent from his post of duty" when Fox made the movie, or else he could no longer "maintain the polite fiction that he is still a spiritual leader of the Presbyterian Church."[32]

Protestant leaders fully expected Hays to deliver "a body blow" against the commercialization of the movies. They realized now that Hays had little influence over the producers and put most of his energies into placating critics, preventing official censorship, and protecting the major studios from competition. And while clergy and clubwomen were busy promoting the best, people were flocking to see the rest. Having cooperated with the MPPDA, they were now "weary of being bamboozled." The ethically suspect methods that the MPPDA employed with Protestant and woman's organizations did not originate with Hays or Milliken. Nor was this the first time that clubwomen had been exploited by corporate interests. Nevertheless, prominent Protestants rightly or wrongly expected better from Hays, who preached absolutely that "right is right and wrong is wrong, and men know right from wrong." Rather naïvely, it turns out, they assumed common purpose in cooperating with the MPPDA to ensure that movies served the public interest and not just the studios' profits. The Hays organization now looked to be nothing more than a public relations front; Hays provided camouflage, using deceptive methods to secure the endorsement of church agencies and women's clubs, while the "Big Eight" studios monopolized the business. Even more disconcerting, "Hays and the other two movie musketeers" seemed to have sold out to the very forces Protestants wanted to quell: greed, self-interest, materialism, and the commercialization of culture.[33]

Hays took office as an icon of Protestant respectability, and the movie czar was expected to guarantee it. Instead, caught in financial scandals large and small, he became a symbol of corporate business and all the sleaze associated with it. While Presbyterian ministers were making on average $2,584 a year, Hays lived an extravagant lifestyle in the Ritz Tower on Park Avenue. He drew a salary reported to be three times that of the president of the United States (more, even, than Babe Ruth). That he divorced his wife of 27 years amidst rumors he was engaged to an attractive divorcee vexed Protestant clergy and cast him even more in the image of Hollywood decadence. Calls for Hays to be removed increased.

The Federal Council's Research Department was making plans for a thorough inquiry into the MPPDA's official and unofficial relations with religious and civic organizations—including the Federal Council. There was a slim chance that its investigation could rectify the situation, but the way things looked, it was not likely that the report was going to restore Protestant confidence in the Hays office.[34] Hays personified the incongruities of the Roaring Twenties and the correlative fate of the Protestant establishment as well. The stock market crash, the crushing failure of Prohibition, and ineffectual handling of the movie industry—all demonstrated Protestant imprudence and ineptitude in running the country. At least that's how Catholic bishops, eager to assert their moral authority in American life, perceived it. Unable to manipulate the Protestant leadership, Hays would empower the Catholic "interest group" whose influence with the film industry would remain in force for almost 30 years.

5

Protestants and Hollywood at the Crossroads

The motion pictures cannot be made good by the use of scissors.

THE PUBLIC RELATIONS OF THE MOTION PICTURE
INDUSTRY: A REPORT BY THE DEPARTMENT OF
RESEARCH AND EDUCATION, Federal Council of the
Churches of Christ in America, 1931

WHILE THE DRAMA in relations between the Hays office and Federal Council played out in the press and behind closed doors, factional squabbling among Protestant leaders worsened. Around the same time, however, different groups with Protestant leadership began to forge a consensus on their vision for dealing with the film industry. But developments already underway would frustrate Protestant plans to craft a fitting role for the cinema in American life.

On April Fools' Day 1930 the *New York Times* ran concurrent stories that mark a pivotal moment in relations between Hollywood and the religious community. The first, on the front page, announced, "Code of Conduct for Films Revised." The second was Carl Milliken's dismissal of George Reid Andrews's charges that he and Will Hays had offered to compensate Andrews. Milliken tried to make it appear that Andrews had sought to profit personally from *The King of Kings* without the knowledge of Federal Council officials. Andrews countered. Milliken replied that he was weary of the "endless debate" and simply announced that the Hays organization would no longer have anything to do with Andrews.[1]

Hays hoped that the new Production Code would provide a respite from all the bad news the industry was getting—from Andrews's charges of MPPDA corruption to the impending threat of federal regulation. Indeed, at that moment, Hays's nemesis in the women's organizations, Catheryne Cooke Gilman of the Federal Motion Picture Council, was working with eight to ten of "the most powerful of the church reforming bodies" on a bill for a federal commission to license films, supervise production, and eliminate block booking and blind selling.[2]

While Hays singled out the advent of sound as the reason for the new Code, the press interpreted it as a response to relentless Protestant criticism. Hays was mocked as a "Moses of the Movies" with a moral manifesto intended only to impress the public and preempt legal censorship—not to reform the producers. The Code itself was ridiculed as superficial, prone to interpretive ambiguity, and unlikely to be enforced simply because it prohibited too many elements with proven box-office appeal. Didn't its acceptance contradict the industry's contention that "vulgarity and box receipts go hand in hand?" *The Churchman* dismissed Hays's "latest and greatest step" toward industry regulation as just another round of pious pronouncements and promises that would be broken soon enough.[3]

Rumors surfaced immediately that the MPPDA was entertaining "a hands-off policy for the churches" and had acquired a new ally, "another sect as powerful as Protestantism." *Variety* noted that this group was dealing with individual producers and not "the producers as a group," a coded reference to the Hays organization. After the commotion in the Federal Council, Catholic leaders were keeping their distance. Though still secretive, a new alliance with the Catholic Church had begun. As they watched their relations with Hollywood deteriorate, Council officials suspected that Catholics had entered into "some understanding with the industry judging by the attention they are getting."[4]

The disclosure that Federal Council secretary Charles Macfarland was on Hays's payroll was unsettling for leaders of civic and religious organizations. Representatives of 13 organizations released a joint statement affirming they had received no compensation for their cooperation with the film industry.[5]

Then rumors appeared in the press that another Federal Council employee, Jeanette Emrich, had also received payments from the Hays office. Andrews had suspected as much. The Council answered that she had only received expenses for speaking on behalf of the film industry—a "vindication" that left *The Churchman* incredulous. Emrich was on the Council's Commission on International Justice and Goodwill and Committee on

World Friendship Among Children, and also an officer in the National Council of Federated Church Women. These positions gave her access and authority with religious groups that might not have welcomed her as a spokesperson for the film interests. In other words, she was using her Federal Council credentials on behalf of the Hays organization. What happened to the Council's "ethical perception"? Shortly after, the Council's study commission discovered that for almost two years—from January 1928 to December 1929—Emrich had been compensated for delivering speeches to women's and other organizations and for providing the Hays office with contacts and follow-up suggestions.[6] Emrich and Macfarland were both put on retainer at the same time that Hays and Milliken tried to restrict Andrews's activities and turn the Church and Drama Association into an MPPDA promotional tool. The Federal Council accepted her resignation.

With the libel threat against *The Churchman*, calls for further investigations, and all the turmoil swirling around Andrews, Church and Drama League board members worried that they might be dragged into an escalating public controversy. A number of them resigned. *The Churchman's* Shipler inferred that he and Andrews were "marked" men in the Hays organization, and thought that Andrews's supporters were "unconsciously infected" by Hays's operatives "through unsuspected channels." Andrews lost the public relations battle and was forced out of the Church and Drama League in October 1930.[7] His dream of forging a productive alliance between the church and the film industry had come to a disappointing and painful end.

Andrews's charges of impropriety and Milliken's emphatic denial can both be construed as interpretive differences over intent, but there is little doubt Hays and Milliken sought in one way or another to utilize Andrews's services for their own purposes. The MPPDA offers were identical to the arrangements for remuneration to Macfarland and Emrich. Hays also made a similar proposal to Charles McMahon in 1922–1923, when the National Catholic Welfare Conference (NCWC) started issuing monthly lists of approved films. The MPPDA offered to contribute $10,000 to set up a committee to provide the studios with a Catholic viewpoint. When McMahon's superior Father John J. Burke refused to take industry money, Hays proposed that the funds be raised from a wealthy Catholic and donations from Catholic actors and directors.[8]

With Charles Stelzle, Macfarland, and Emrich all retained by the MPPDA while the Federal Council was revising its film policy, the Council's Motion Picture Commission looked like a Hays office party. False rumors that Hays had once been a member of the Federal Council had to be squelched. The film commission, its credibility damaged beyond repair, was quietly dissolved in December 1930. Even though Milliken recused himself from Administrative Committee meetings until the inquiry was completed, the adverse publicity cast a shadow of suspicion on the Research Department's study that was underway.[9]

A Case Study in Corporate Ethics

The Federal Council's report, *The Public Relations of the Motion Picture Industry*, provided a thorough and astute analysis of the studio system. The inquiry focused specifically on the Hays organization as "a case study in corporate ethics." A certified statement by the MPPDA's treasurer showed that 52 people had received some kind of monetary support from the Hays organization, most for attendance at one conference. Some, however, were actively cooperating with Hays to encourage support for the MPPDA's public relations program and opposition to censorship measures. Macfarland was the only top-level administrator on retainer. The methods Hays employed were not uncommon. But paying "honoraria" to officials of a religious agency was a clear ethics violation that invited damaging interpretations and undermined public confidence—however much the services were "conscientiously rendered." On that count, the report chastised the Hays organization.[10]

The committee had a difficult time sorting through "the jumble of facts." Andrews, Hays, and Milliken were each "putting upon every circumstance the one construction that fits in to his own case" in order to discredit the other. According to Andrews, Milliken's daily reports to Hays showed that he was in regular contact with Macfarland, Emrich, and Stelzle while the Motion Picture Commission was being set up; "official records" showed that Macfarland and Milliken met the day after their lunch meeting to draw up the plans for the new film commission. Committee members decided that Andrews had "acted from pure motives, although most indiscreetly," and also that these events were not central to the investigation. The final report included only a short summary with the necessary details—much to Andrews's dismay. On the matter of improper MPPDA influence in the Council, the commission sided with Macfarland, who flatly denied any improprieties, and concluded that there was no plan for the MPPDA to control the Council via its film commission.[11] The judgment left something to be desired.

Privately, Hays thought the Council's report was "reasonably fair." Milliken actually sent a copy to correct a Protestant minister's negative perceptions of film producers. Even so, in an open letter to Federal Council president Bishop McConnell, Hays tried to turn the tables. What about those church officials who were making money by attacking the film industry? Playing loose with the facts, Hays linked Andrews's profit-sharing proposal for *The King of Kings* with the Federal Council.[12] McConnell in turn reminded Hays that he had put "an entirely different construction" on Andrews's letter when it was received in 1926, regarding it as "indiscreetly worded" but without "mercenary intent or improper purpose." At the time Hays made the offer, Andrews thought it was for a desk job, which is what he told Ernest Johnson, who later reminded him that this "was quite inconsistent with an attempt to subsidize you privately." If Andrews perceived Hays's offer as improper, he nonetheless continued to seek financial support for the Church and Drama Association. Andrews subsequently reinterpreted the offers in retrospect and in light of his experiences with the MPPDA. McConnell charged that Hays was clearly misconstruing the purpose of the letter now, since he had involved Andrews in the production of *King of Kings* "in a way that was entirely inconsistent with the interpretation that you now put upon his letter." Andrews's letter was irrelevant; McConnell's suggestion that Hays "face the issues on their merits" was met with silence.[13]

The movies were only one aspect of the Federal Council's wide-ranging work. The release of the report might not have jeopardized the organization, but it certainly did not improve its public standing on the movie matter or its relations with the powers that be in the film industry. Some of the press coverage was mired in misinformation. The *New York Times*, for example, stated in error that 52 Federal Council staffers had received gratuities from the MPPDA. Martin Quigley singled out specific features of the Council's report and ignored others to highlight the importance of the Production Code, a tactic that puzzled Council officials who were still not fully aware of the extent of Catholic cooperation with the MPPDA. Milliken dismissed the "clouded report" for criticizing Macfarland, whose service he thought was completely justified by the Council's educational purposes, while overlooking Andrews's petitions for industry financing. He resigned from the Administrative Committee in a move that *Time* rightly interpreted as "the most painful evidence of the divergence between the Federal Council and the Hays organization." Council secretary Samuel McCrea Cavert stated without reservation that the Council had "no relations of any sort" with the MPPDA now.[14]

Like most news outlets, *Time* found the report not nearly as "sensational" as Milliken's resignation would have indicated. The religious press was looking for the Council to give a bold reproof of the unethical behavior of its officials and clear denunciation of the immoral condition of movies. What they got instead was a timid rebuke and a political compromise. There were "recognized inequities" in the block booking system, but the Council's researchers discovered that there were "relatively few disputes" over the moral quality of films. Exhibitors were far more interested in protecting their box-office revenues by getting rid of the "unpopular pictures" in a block than they were "to escape the necessity of running morally questionable films."

There were no illusions within Federal Council circles about anti-block-booking legislation as a cure-all for what ailed the movies business. Samuel McCrea Cavert, for example, favored measures like the Brookhart and Hudson bills, but with "grave doubt whether, if they were enacted tomorrow, we would really see any noticeable change in the character of the pictures we get." Fred Eastman, professor of religious literature and drama at Chicago Theological Seminary, also did not "expect the movies to be reformed by legislation," but like pure food laws, saw these bills as "simply a weapon in the hands of the people to enforce their will."[15] Attempting to embrace the divergent methods of the National Board of Review and Federal Motion Picture Council (FMPC), the committee argued that whether the industry was competitive or centralized, its leaders needed a greater sense of social responsibility. It was an affirmation of long-standing Protestant themes that lacked, however, a creative vision for the moment. The issue of block booking had become a litmus test for Protestants who were completely disillusioned with industry cooperation. Anyone not opposed to the industry's compulsory trade practices was suspect of being in cahoots with the Hays organization.

The Federal Council's report failed to chart a way forward that would unify Protestant churches and organizations and cast doubt on the Council's capacity to lead on the issue. Council officials admitted being "very much puzzled" over how to solve the movie problem. The one thing they all agreed on was that "under present conditions there is no hope of making progress through the Hays Organization."[16]

Free Speech for Talkies in a "Payneful" Period

Around this time, the Supreme Court ruled, in *Near v. Minnesota*, that, except under rare circumstances, prior restraint in newspaper publishing was unconstitutional. The decision had no immediate effect on the film industry, but established a precedent that might be applied to movies. With synchronized sound and dialogue, movies more than ever evoked clear comparisons with theater and the press. At least one commentator thought this revived "the age-old dilemma of freedom of speech." Why not grant filmmakers now the same legal status as journalists, fiction writers, and playwrights? In the spring of 1927, Hays proposed that a provision be added to the Constitution to extend First Amendment protection to movies. In January 1929, he started speaking against film censorship as an infringement on free speech that was "un-American in its conception." Anticipating that sound would enhance screen realism and amplify censorship difficulties, Hays was preparing the producers, and reportedly waiting for a favorable moment to revisit the question of First Amendment protection for film. Under the circumstances, he wanted them to abide by the association's production standards; this was no time to be testing the boundaries of acceptability.[17]

Hays understood the dynamics of industry profit making and market tastes well enough to want some kind of restraint on film producers who ignored Hays's repeated assertion that the industry's best defense against censorship "was the renewed determination to make pictures of such quality that no reasonable person could claim any need for censorship." Despite Hays's warnings, and with public clamor over movie morals growing, Fox, for example, still purchased the rights to the 1931 novel *Call Her Savage*—mostly for the title—as a vehicle to spark the sagging career of screen sensation Clara Bow. Jason Joy himself found the book "about as far wrong as it is possible," and thought the scenario "took most of the real flavor of the story out" with the result "that only another stupid picture was in prospect."[18]

A self-proclaimed champion of First Amendment rights, Hays was adamant that freedom of the screen "should be maintained not only for the good of the industry itself but in defense of the whole right of free speech."[19] If Hays was going to challenge the legal status quo, the support of eminent Protestant leaders would be crucial. He knew that members of the largest and most important Protestant churches and denominational agencies were on principle opposed to censorship. Federal Council officials refused to put the weight of *the* preeminent Protestant agency behind the movement for a federal film commission. The MPPDA regularly used the backing of the Protestant establishment to sway public opinion and to persuade legislators and judiciaries that government regulation was unnecessary.

Hays's speech at the Waldorf Astoria in March 1926 marked the beginning of MPPDA efforts to empower Protestant leaders as production consultants and film reviewers via the Federal Council's Drama Committee and then the Church and Drama Association—much to the surprise of Council officials who recoiled at even the hint that Protestants might play any kind of censorial role. With the Teapot Dome scandal, Hays's disreputable dealings with the Federal Council damaged his credibility and seriously eroded Protestant support; there was discord among clubwomen and deep suspicion among religious editors. All things considered, could Hays rely on the Protestant press and leadership to support an industry-driven effort to reverse the *Mutual* decision and secure First Amendment protection for movies? The proverbial writing was on the wall; it had to be a bitter realization for Hays.

Near v. Minnesota might have provided the opportunity Hays was looking for, but the MPPDA and the Hollywood studios were not in much of a position to take advantage of the situation. The film industry's problems mounted as the effects of the Depression worsened in the early 1930s. The cost of converting production facilities and theaters to sound was staggering and left the studios heavily in debt. Weekly movie attendance jumped with the advent of "talkies," but then fell from 90 million in 1930 to 60 million by 1932, when nearly one-quarter of the workforce was unemployed. Studio stock plummeted; some MPPDA members were unable to pay their annual dues in 1932. The *Christian Century* taunted producers who long insisted they should be judged at the box office. The verdict was in; cash-strapped Americans were obviously fed up with "stereotypical plots" and "synthetic film-sin."[20]

As many had predicted, the Code seemed to be having little, if any, effect on Hollywood releases. In financial straits, the studios chased their most lucrative audience at the large metropolitan theaters. Producers complained that movies in compliance with the code "will not draw flies at any box-office," while gangster films and sexually charged Mae West vehicles proved box-office gold. But when films like *Little Caesar* and *She Done Him Wrong* reached small-town neighborhood theaters, reformers protested loudly. Rev. Clifford G. Twombly claimed that only 92 out of 228

Hollywood films he reviewed could be considered "morally unobjection-able." A *Parents Magazine* survey found only 17 percent of films surveyed were suitable for children. The MPPDA was flooded with letters criticizing movies for violating "the spirit if not of the letter" of the Production Code. *Film Daily* reported that, with Protestants accounting for nine-tenths of the complaints about movies, Milliken was "lining up" church leaders to establish a preview committee "expected to avert many complaints," with the *Christian Century* injecting, "not to remove their cause." Milliken's was a clear, though short-lived attempt to sidestep the Federal Council and create a Protestant counterpart to the Catholic IFCA. *The Churchman* paro-died the Better Films' slogan now as Hays's way to "Boost the best and put over the worst."[21]

In June 1932, *Harrison's Reports*, a journal for independent exhibitors, published an excerpt from a leaked MPPDA memo that bolstered the case of Protestant critics of the Hays office. Jason Joy spent nearly a month visiting city and state boards coincident with the release of a number of objectionable movies—most notably Howard Hughes's violent gangster saga, *Scarface*, which had initially been rejected by nearly every censor board. Joy personally negotiated with the boards and persuaded them to reverse their decision, though apparently only after securing cuts to the "original, uncut and uncensored version" that was hyped by United Art-ists' publicity people. "This demonstrates," he informed Hays, "in a rather spectacular way that the collective force of the industry can secure the passage of even the most discussed and rejected picture, once the collec-tive industry agrees that the picture conforms to its standards." Editor Pete Harrison pounced on the disclosure as proof that censorship in any form was "impotent to cure the evils of the motion picture industry," and all the more reason to abolish block booking. The *Christian Century* remarked facetiously that Joy's dealings also "demonstrate in a rather spectacular way" the breach in the confidence that church and civic groups had placed in the Hays office, and, moreover, were ample evidence of the "grim deter-mination of the industry" to frustrate public agencies whose purpose was to "defend its children from vicious pictures."[22]

Hays was in a desperate position. Franklin D. Roosevelt's landslide presidential victory in 1932 tossed Hays's political contacts out of office. Iowa senator Brookhart dubbed the Production Code "a failure" and rein-troduced his bill to prohibit block booking and also eliminate blind selling. To avert a public relations disaster, Hays had to dissuade a despondent Alice Ames Winter from resigning in 1932, and then again in July of the following year, when she declared the situation "hopeless." Winter suggested to Hays that Jeannette Emrich could easily replace her.[23]

Adding to the MPPDA's woes was an avalanche of bad publicity that came with the publication of Henry James Forman's *Our Movie Made Children* (1933), a popularized introduction to a massive scientific study on the effects of movies on children and adolescents. The project was headed by William H. Short, a Congregational minister with strong Federal Council connections. Short organized the Motion Picture Research Council (MPRC) to draw public attention to the social value of the cinema and develop a national program of action. A whopping $200,000 grant from the Payne Fund, a private philanthropic foundation, funded research by a group of social scientists and educators under the direction of W. W. Charters, director of the Bureau of Educational Research at Ohio State University. Charters was an active member of the Northern Baptist Convention and was involved with many church education committees. There was some coordinating of effort between the Federal Council's Research Department and the MPRC. Short greeted the Federal Council's 1931 investigation as "assurance of an ally" and decided that the Council's study rendered an analysis of the film industry by the MPRC unnecessary.[24] It was a bit of a relief, as Short did not want these studies to be associated, even tangentially, with the Hays office.

Forman's thesis in *Our Movie Made Children* was that the cinema was "a gigantic educational system with an instruction possibly more successful than the present text-book variety." In a selective presentation of the researchers' findings, he left readers with the impression that movies had a uniform and mostly harmful effect on young people—precisely what Hollywood critics wanted to hear. Chicago Theological Seminary professor Fred Eastman gave the book a ringing endorsement in a seven-part series in the *Christian Century* that was reprinted in other magazines and was published as a pamphlet, with over 100,000 copies sold to churches and schools. Hays's public relations machine went to work trying to discredit what his staff dubbed the "Payneful Studies." Reputable research demonstrating that movies had a harmful effect on youth was far more dangerous than a Federal Council report on the MPPDA's dubious business ethics.[25]

Our Movie Made Children put fuel on the "moral fire," but the Payne Studies themselves actually undermined a central premise of the reform movement. A crucial rationale for regulation was that movies were interpreted uniformly and caused immoral and criminal conduct. The researchers challenged those assumptions. Spectators could have varied interpretations of a film; whatever effect movies had was complex and mitigated by myriad factors, including viewing skills, which were decidedly difficult to isolate. The research demonstrated that movies affected children in unpredictable ways; the net effect was actually small and the tendency was for films to affirm existing attitudes and behaviors. Nevertheless, there was no denying that the cinema was a significant social force and functioned as a "quasi-educational" institution, dispensing "general information, patterns, and not a little in the way of standards and personal ideals."[26]

Instead of mounting a legal battle for movie freedom, Hays would negotiate an unprecedented alliance with Catholics to ensure that studio productions had no "need for censorship." Empowering Catholics who, unlike their Protestant counterparts, had the combined determination and consumer force to exert significant influence over movie content was a risky move for Hays. It was also a sharp rebuff to Protestant leaders. All the same, free speech for talkies would have to wait for another day.

Poetry and the Box Office

Disillusioned with industry cooperation and aware of a growing Catholic influence in Hollywood, the Protestant establishment took up the task of articulating a single approach to the movies. The problems that the cinema presented were complex and could not be pinned simply on salacious public demand, the low ideals of the producers, or the failure of churches, schools, and community groups to improve audience tastes. While there was no complete agreement on strategy, the common goal was to develop a national film policy that would create the right conditions in which movies of high moral and artistic quality could flourish. A concept of movies as the influential products of a popular art industry gave shape to a holistic approach with art, morality, commerce, and social effects all more or less of a piece.

Protestants like Fred Eastman, with a specialty in the dramatic arts, prized movies as a new popular art distinctive in "its vividness, its compactness, its multiple approach to the human mind, and its resemblance to real life." As far back as the Greeks, drama was related to religious and civic purposes, but when it devolved into escape and entertainment it lost this orientation. To achieve its highest purpose, these Protestant drama experts believed, film should be developed along artistic, and not merely commercial, lines. They linked the cinema with traditional social functions of popular art: cultural communication and social criticism.[27]

Serious drama was "a study of life itself." The term *artistic integrity* fused art and life perspective: "Drama deals with the emotions, and out of the emotions come the issues of life." Protestants should judge a movie by asking themselves: Is it good drama? Does it contain crisp dialogue, interesting characters making important choices, a worthwhile theme and well-structured narrative with convincing suspense, conflict, and resolution? How true to life or how "honest" is the movie's treatment? Their main concern was with theme, context, and treatment, and not simply "cutting" objectionable material, which they believed to be censorship. Censorship "waits until a picture is made, and even distributed, and then takes a pair of scissors and tries to cut out the unwholesome parts," Eastman explained. "We cannot cut the devil out of a picture with a pair of scissors; we must go back to the source of production." These critics were not looking for "preachy pictures or sentimental" movies, but great characters, conflict, humor, imagination, and, ideally, "something of the poetry of life." Praise was reserved for films that made an honest attempt to interpret life by presenting "artistically the deeper emotion struggles of the human spirit."[28]

As Eastman and others saw it, however, the bulk of Hollywood's product was "a vicious falsification of human values" stamped with the approval of Hollywood glamour. Movies constantly depicted sexual relationships robbed of "dignity, beauty, and restraint," love as merely "a physical emotion," marriage "an impulsive act," divorce an easy "escape." Gangsters were lionized, foreigners caricatured, and ministers lampooned. Producers blatantly distorted stories adapted from novels and stage plays by emphasizing sensational elements just to boost box office. The film version of Tolstoy's *Anna Karenina* was retitled *Love*; the Broadway comedy *The Constant Wife* became *Charming Sinners*; Joseph Conrad's novel *Victory* became, first, *Flesh of Eve*, and later, *Dangerous Paradise*. Good quality drama need not "depend upon dirt," Eastman maintained. And such sentiments were apparently quite common. Eastman seemed to be drawing on an earlier editorial by New York *World* editor Walter Lippmann, who faulted the Production Code for dealing only with superficial incidents and not Hollywood's "vicious falsification of human values." Lippmann wrote, "If the conventional moralists had a little more moral insight they would realize that this, the materialism of the movies, their constant celebration of the acquisitive and competitive instincts, is far more deeply degrading, even to the sexual life of the adolescent, than ribaldry or coarseness."[29]

Protestants were troubled moreover by the subtle and cumulative impact Hollywood's value system might be having on youth. *Over the Hill* (1931) inspired familial devotion, *Abraham Lincoln* (1930) kindled patriotism, *Les Misérables* (1934) showed that "life is to give and not to take." But far too much of Hollywood's output glorified self-indulgence, sensation, immediate gratification, and material acquisition. This constant parade of movies conflicted with traditional values, confused the young, and tarnished America's reputation abroad. Hollywood seemed to have "lost all sense of spiritual values." If the aim of home, school, and church was to instill character and cultivate concern for the social welfare, Hollywood movies were teaching how "to acquire things, get ahead, be smart, dazzling, a big shot."[30]

If there was a fly in the ointment, it was an exaggerated self-confidence about knowing what constituted an "honest" representation of life, and believing that these standards were widespread. Protestant critics also tended to be rather elitist—preferring film adaptations of literary classics and documentaries over horror, crime, and westerns—and sometimes paternalistic. William Faulkner's *Sanctuary* might have been great literature, the *Christian Century* noted, but for the masses "as material for a picture it is the vilest thing imaginable."[31]

Protestants disparaged producers for treating this inventive medium "as a golden cow to be milked for their own profits" and sparred with them over oppositional readings of the box office. Clergy touted movies like *Cavalcade* (1933), *Silent Enemy* (1930), and *Disraeli* (1929), but the only real moneymaker among the three was *Cavalcade*, a historical drama that won Oscars for Best Picture and Director. *Silent Enemy* was a docudrama about Canadian aboriginals. The Oscar-nominated biopic of the British prime minister *Disraeli* (1929) was the most canceled film of the year. The *Detroit Press* noted that "where a hundred people will go to see George Arliss in *Disraeli*, a thousand will pass it up for a few reels of sensational trash fitted to the moron's taste and designed to separate him from his money." And the MPPDA's Arthur DeBra, a Protestant himself, remarked that film history was "strewn with financial derelicts of a character that the church people want to claim they would support if they had an opportunity to."[32]

Of course, Protestants could wave a list of wholesome box-office hits: Frank Capra's *It Happened One Night* and *Broadway Bill*, the Shirley Temple vehicle *The Little Colonel*, *The Barretts of Wimpole Street*, and *Top Hat*, just to name a few. And an even longer one of salacious flops, mostly unrecognizable titles, but of note, Howard Hawks's *Twentieth Century*, Josef Von Sternberg's

The Devil Is a Woman, and Mae West's *Klondike Annie*. These films did not return nearly as much as *The Thin Man*, *The House of Rothschild*, *Little Women*, or the *Three Little Pigs*—"all fine and wholesome pictures." And when the MPPDA tried to alleviate criticism by pointing out noteworthy Hollywood films—*All Quiet on the Western Front*, *Abraham Lincoln*, *Tom Sawyer*—critics countered easily enough with a slew of sensational titles and taglines: *On Your Back* ("Behind the scenes with dazzling models and playboy millionaires.") and *The Lady Who Dared* ("Where men forget and women remember too late. Where love is the pliant plaything of the devil."). And so the argument went on, with each side claiming its share of commercial successes while pointing out the other sides' failures. It was a constant source of tension and seemingly insurmountable conflict.[33]

Part of the problem was that production and exhibition were conceived in terms of an undifferentiated audience, when in reality the market was segmented by age and geography. Big-budget films with marquee stars were never more than a quarter of studios' annual output. Steady returns came from routine low-budget movies made to excite and amuse Hollywood's bread-and-butter audience—16- to 26-year-olds. This fan base of habitual moviegoers represented the *"best prospects* for picture patronage," and for that reason they were perceived by producers as the real "arbiters of quality in entertainment." Producers targeted these young moviegoers, who frequented downtown first-run venues, but clergy were concerned about children and families who attended small-town neighborhood theaters. Feature films were also shown on a movie program typically put together to appeal to various tastes by coupling a good feature film with "a cheap and tawdry short, or a good short with a mediocre feature," as Eastman observed. "The result is to irritate all tastes, not to please them." MPPDA studio heads flatly rejected a suggestion by Hays to classify films by age, a remedy "urged by churchmen." Studio executives preferred instead an enhanced regulatory machinery to guarantee that every film was suitable for viewing by adults and children.[34]

What it all came down to was that producers and Protestant leaders both adhered to the same basic assumption that "good" movies were somehow those that were commercially successful. With box-office results dictating the terms of quality, film production would always be unsettled and reactive—a slave to momentary fashionable trends. And so it would remain; at the end of the twentieth century, Protestant evangelicals would appeal to the industry's bottom line for PG "family" entertainment, promising to deliver churchgoers for religiously inspiring films.

Toward a National Film Policy

Independent of the Hays office, the Federal Council set up a new Committee on Motion Pictures in February 1933 under the leadership of Worth M. Tippy, executive secretary of the Council's Commission on the Church and Social Service. The committee's twofold purpose was the same as its predecessor's: to facilitate the use of movies in church-education programming and to use the influence of Protestant churches to improve the quality of the commercial cinema.

The Council issued a strong statement stating its opposition to censorship: "The freedom of the screen in its creative process is related to freedom of speech, freedom of assembly and freedom of the press." These rights were not unrestricted, but "always conditioned by public welfare and safety." That continued to be the foundation for the Council's film program: organize local church Better Films Committees, begin a weekly Protestant review service, establish a film bureau to assist pastors in the use of movies, and, of special note, develop a film appreciation curriculum. Also, for the first time, the Council put its weight behind efforts for "remedial legislation" to eliminate block booking and blind selling, at least in their current forms. The objection was not to block booking as a wholesale practice—it reduced the cost of leasing pictures, after all—but only its abuse by the autocratic studios. The public had a right to see the best films; it was in the public interest then for exhibitors to be able to preview and rent individual films in an open market.[35]

The structural motif weighed heavily in the Federal Council's approach, which was much the same as that of William Short's Motion Picture Research Council. The Payne Fund grant covered the groundbreaking academic research; the next phase was to use the results to build "a new attitude and a new outlook toward the motion picture." Payne researcher Edgar Dale (a Lutheran) argued that the major objective of a national film policy was not to curb artistic expression, but, to the contrary, to provide opportunity for genuine artists to bring their interpretations of life to the screen, even if that meant making movies that were "opposed to prevailing notions." This sentiment might have run against demands for harmless and wholesome films, but it affirmed what the MPRC held as "the legitimate function of motion picture drama in national life." Dale's pioneering textbook, How to Appreciate Motion Pictures (1933), exemplified this Protestant-informed approach. His influential model was distinguished by his treatment of the spectator as an engaged viewer and his emphasis on the need to analyze movies in terms of both cinematic art and social and cultural implications.[36]

Guaranteed exhibition gave the studios less incentive to produce high-quality films, and their hold on the market restricted independent production. Legislation curtailing block booking could correct this, and could also remedy Hollywood's perceived lack of artistic integrity by restoring an untrammeled market and free expression to the screen, it was believed. In tandem with improved public taste and demand, this might lead to an increase in the supply of high-quality commercial films. This view was not just fashionable among the Protestant elite. Walter Lippmann also denounced prior censorship and argued that the film industry should operate like theaters, books, newspapers, and magazines, with the studios and independents competing in an open market. Existing obscenity laws would suffice, and audiences would be free to select their movies. The solution was "not to impose standards on the existing monopolistic corporations, but by invoking the anti-trust laws and perhaps new legislation to break their power," Lippmann proposed. "For the evils of the movies come not from too much liberty for the giants but from the destruction of real liberty by the giants." The *Christian Century* and *Harrison's Reports*—constant allies on movie matters—were quick to point out that Lippmann was entirely in accord with the established Protestant position.[37]

By and large, Protestant leaders agreed that Hollywood's mandatory trade practices were the main impediment to improving the cinema. Howard LeSourd was the one exception. LeSourd was on the MPRC's advisory board and was involved with the Federal Council's Committee on Educational and Religious Drama. It had not been established, he felt, that there was a huge market for wholesome movies, and he was not convinced that eliminating block booking would bring about the anticipated results. Perhaps for that reason, he maintained a close relationship with the Hays office. In addition to his Council positions, he chaired the MPPDA's organizing committee for the Conference on the Use of Motion Pictures for Religious Education.[38]

Since surveys showed that there was no difference in the films exhibited in cities with or without a strong Better Films Council, most Protestant leaders believed that local efforts to improve the cinema were futile as long as compulsory block booking was in effect. It seemed that only the national government could wrest control of the market from the powerful studios. For somewhat different reasons, the FMPC's Canon Chase and Catheryne Cooke Gilman thought that a federal film commission was necessary. Chase distrusted the producers; Gilman advocated federal regulation in lieu of an age classification system. Eastman's position seems to have shifted on the issue. He at first expressed reservations about the earnestness of Jewish producers, but would be impressed later with the increase in artistic caliber and number of character-building films under the new Production Code Administration. How could the "low ideals" of the producers be blamed for the "unwholesome tendency" of Hollywood movies, he asked, when these same men were producing "films of real social power and beautiful artistry" that were offering "convincing and satisfying solutions of great human problems?"[39]

The Federal Council never officially endorsed attempts to create a federal film commission. William Short opposed setting up any agency that would restrict community film selection. So did Protestant Episcopalian William Marston Seabury, a former NAMPI general counsel who called for a "commercial renaissance" of the film industry as a public utility. Of course, Hays and Alice Ames Winter also objected to a federal commission as censorship. Bills providing for federal oversight of production actually found little support, in comparison to anti-block-booking legislation that rallied Protestants precisely because it was not censorial. Block booking dealt only with the distribution of films already produced, and not with their production.[40] Though they lacked full accord on the exact mode of regulation, it was a given among Protestant leaders that any church control was beyond the pale.

6

The Worst That Could Happen

A CATHOLIC LEGION OF "DECENCY"

We have been almost a laughing-stock as a moral force or as an interested group for justice to our faith in public affairs. But from now on it must be the Catholic that will be aggressive for the cause of Jesus Christ and therefore for the better welfare of man.

ECCLESIASTICAL REVIEW, September 1934

CATHOLIC CLERGY SHARED Protestant concerns about the harmful influence of the cinema. They knew their parishioners were going to movies that, contrary to Catholic teaching, emphasized carnal pleasures and self-fulfillment, and not devotion to God. To ameliorate the worst elements, local priests protested Sunday movies and specific films depicting Catholics negatively, threatening local boycotts. The Catholic Church began to establish a national voice on social issues with the formation during World War I of what would become the National Catholic Welfare Council (NCWC). But there was no consensus on the movies; a range of strategies, from abstinence to state and even national censorship, were discussed.[1]

Will Hays involved Catholics right from the start. Rita McGoldrick (International Federation of Catholic Alumnae, IFCA) and Charles A. McMahon (NCWC) served on the Committee on Public Relations Executive Board. The MPPDA continued to list the IFCA as one of its supporting organizations and regularly touted its film ratings as proof that the quality of movies was improving. In 1927, the IFCA Film Bureau recommended 40 percent of the movies it reviewed; the number climbed to 51 percent in

1929, 61 percent in 1931, and 71 percent in 1932. Oddly enough, these figures ran contrary to the growing sentiment among bishops, who were fuming at Hollywood's blatant disregard for the Production Code as "just another scrap of paper."[2]

Catholic inaction, prelates believed, had allowed a degeneration of national morals—the failure of Protestantism and paganism—that was mirrored in the deplorable state of the cinema. Their impression was that Protestant leaders were disorganized, lacked unity, power, and even sincere motive, and concerned themselves mostly with trivial matters rather than what Catholics espoused as important moral issues: depictions of nudity, sex, adultery, divorce, and birth control.[3] Where Protestants, and specifically the Federal Council, had failed, Catholic bishops were determined to prevail by stopping the production of indecent movies.

Like Canon William Shaefe Chase, Catholic bishops blamed producers for cultivating, and then catering to, "depraved" tastes for immoral and salacious movies. There were "too many of the wrong kind of people" involved in movie production, Los Angeles Bishop John J. Cantwell maintained—Jews and "pagans" who cared "nothing for decency, good taste or refinement," and had no "respect for religion or for spiritual values." Although Martin Quigley—staunch defender of the Production Code's effectiveness—blasted Our Movie Made Children as "an incorrect and sensational attack upon motion pictures," the book crystallized sentiment among Catholic bishops that movies were having a "decided detrimental effect on morals," and boosted their resolve to take action against the film industry.[4]

In August 1933, Catholic bishops persuaded investment bankers still reeling from the Wall Street crash to put pressure on the studio heads to abide by the Code. Should the church publicly denounce Hollywood, their banks would be tarred with the same brush for financing immoral movies. As Cantwell put it, attorney Joseph Scott and A. H. Giannini, a lay Catholic and president of Bank of America, put "the Jews on the spot." The producers were not worried about Protestant opposition, but a Catholic campaign might be "most hurtful." They were also "naturally anxious to make all the money they can, and do not hesitate to argue that the American people are quite satisfied and rather enjoy the filth that is being produced." Paramount and MGM executives even offered to hire Catholic consultants. In November, Catholic bishops formed the Episcopal Committee on Motion Pictures and began strategizing about ways to target the film industry.[5]

Protestant Overtures

Protestants made attempts to enlist Catholic bishops in their efforts for government intervention. Chase tried unsuccessfully to persuade the Episcopal Committee that federal regulation was necessary. He sought backing for the Patman Bill that was before the House Commerce Committee. The bill outlawed block booking, provided for federal regulation of movies in interstate trade, and also incorporated the Production Code. Chase even indicated that he was amendable to making changes in the legislation to acquire Catholic support. Payne Fund scholar W. W. Charters made headway with NCWC director George Johnson on the issue of block booking. Johnson became convinced that ending the practice would make the industry "amendable to sound public opinion." Quigley also recommended that the bishops petition the federal government to set up the administrative machinery to enforce the Code, and a Catholic sociologist—and member of the Motion Picture Research Council's (MPRC) Advisory Committee—argued in *Ecclesiastical Review*, a journal for priests, that the industry's trade practices were monopolistic and must be eliminated if Catholic opinion were to prevail at the box office. Daniel Lord would also join Protestants in opposing block booking, a move that irritated Quigley, who believed that the only viable solution to the movie problem was producers' adherence to the Production Code.[6]

Cincinnati archbishop John T. McNicholas settled the matter. He clearly displayed the pietist tendency in his approach to Hollywood. Catholic opposition to federal movie regulation was driven in part by a distrust of any government intervention that was likely to be dominated by incompetent Protestants and consequently prone to moral incongruity. They also worried that federal regulation of movies might set a precedent for schooling. Recalling the Prohibition disaster, McNicholas rejected "the mania for legislation as the cure-all of our ills," even though he recognized that the producers were "exercising monopolistic powers." At bottom, McNicholas refused to set up "any civil government as the supreme arbiter of the morality of the cinema."[7] That role belonged exclusively to the Catholic Church. A different rationale, however, would have to be advanced in public. By restricting the Catholic Church's purview to morality—not art or commerce—the bishops avoided taking an official stance on the industry's trade practices. They took care not to discuss block booking, while keeping a close eye on the movement to abolish it.

The National Recovery Administration developed its own code, which contained only a vague assertion that movies should be moral and affirmed

industry self-regulation. It allowed block booking and blind selling to continue, but did give exhibitors the right to cancel up to 10 percent of the
films leased.[8] President Roosevelt signed the NRA's film industry code in
November, over objections from Protestants. The Federal Motion Picture
Council, General Federation of Women's Clubs, and Better Films Councils
all asked that the Production Code be incorporated into the NRA's code,
knowing this would effectively establish federal supervision over movie
content. Quigley also wanted to see at least a summary of the Code included in the NRA code for the film industry, making production of immoral films a violation of federal law. The Federal Council argued that the
licensing of films in groups sacrificed "the public to the merchandizing of
the output of the studios regardless of quality" and recommended amend-
ments to empower local communities in the selection of movies.[9]

Catholic bishops thought that the NRA's cancellation policy put the
onus on exhibitors; to register disapproval, they decided to launch a nationwide boycott of theaters showing immoral movies. With average production costs of about $250,000, just $50,000 in box office—200,000
admissions at twenty-five cents each—could make the difference between
a film's commercial success and failure. Aware of this slim profit margin,
the bishops presumed that by dictating the moviegoing of 20 million
Catholics, they could wield enormous power over film producers. Nevertheless, they had some reservations and remained tentative about the campaign's larger prospects. In an era of open hostility between Protestants,
Catholics, and Jews, they wanted the producers to "feel the result financially" and also to avert an anti-Catholic backlash. Catholic clergy would
rally behind the movement, but would it have sustaining power? All things
considered, they decided that cooperation with non-Catholics would be
"detrimental rather than helpful." The Federal Council's Social Service
Commission was already working cooperatively with the National Catholic
Welfare Council and the Central Conference of American Rabbis when
Worth M. Tippy, on behalf of the Federal Council's Committee on Motion
Pictures, inquired about the purpose of the Episcopal Committee. Bishop
Cantwell replied curtly that it was formed to study the motion pictures.[10]

A Legion of Decency

In April 1934, Catholic prelates announced that they were organizing a
Legion of Decency to generate awareness and take action against "salacious and immoral pictures." In May, Daniel Lord's authorship of the

Code, "kept more or less a secret," *Variety* noted, was made public. A boy-cott of Philadelphia theaters put the Legion in the news, with reports of activities in Chicago and Detroit creating the impression that Catholics were being mobilized en masse—something unprecedented, and unthink-able to Protestants. Studio executives were terrified. There were over 20 million Catholics. They represented only 20 percent of the population, but three-fourths lived in large cities and some of Hollywood's most lucrative markets east of the Mississippi: New York, Boston, Chicago, Philadelphia, and Pittsburgh. The proportions were reversed among Protestants, who lived mostly in rural areas and small towns.[11]

Though they detested the Legion's method, the public groundswell per-suaded Protestant leaders—disenfranchised from the MPPDA—that the time had arrived for "more drastic measures." With no formal agreement, the Federal Council affirmed the Legion's central objective and called for constituents to cooperate by withholding patronage from objectionable films, but only *according to one's conscience*. The Council went out of its way to explain its position as "a thoroughly democratic way" of letting filmmakers know that they were misjudging public desires. And on that count, Protes-tant and Catholic leaders agreed that most Americans were "wholesome and desire clean pictures." Selective patronage of worthy films had always been encouraged; the Council was not about to create "black lists or white lists," or to seek legal censorship. The aim was only to get church members to practice "careful discrimination," a move that garnered support from religious edi-tors who thought Hays and the producers had played the churches for fools long enough. "The Roman Catholic authorities can *command* their members to have nothing to do with bad motion pictures," *Zion Herald* editor L. O. Hartman explained. "Protestant leaders because of their belief in freedom cannot issue orders, but they can appeal to conscience and reason and ask their followers to stay away from demoralizing movies. And this should be the watchword and exhortation of every denomination in the country."[12]

From the Protestant standpoint, even if Catholics were assuming leader-ship now, they were only becoming active in what was an ongoing Protes-tant effort to reform Hollywood. Protestant leaders were willing to align themselves with their religious rivals to create a united front that might fi-nally lead to genuine reform. One reason that Hays was hired was to pre-vent just such an occurrence. *Variety* observed that Hays was in a "most delicate" position with his bosses. *The Churchman* was "shedding no tears."[13]

By the MPPDA's estimate, Protestant support for the Legion was under-whelming. Hays's staff knew that Protestants refrained from completely

endorsing the Catholic drive because its "attempted regimentation of conscience by ecclesiastical authority is not in accordance with Protestant doctrine and practice." The "traditional Protestant methods" were "guidance,
persuasion, leadership and education, rather than expecting unquestioning
obedience to ecclesiastical authority." If the effectiveness of the Legion's
boycott made it seem a "wiser tactic" to some, this was hardly the way that
Protestants wanted to see industry reform take place. Actually, this "burst
of public indignation" worried Federal Council officials. Newspapers across
the country judged public opinion strong enough to bring about federal
supervision; *Variety* reported that the White House and the Justice and
Labor departments were "priming to join the crusade for compulsory
cleanup in Hollywood." Council officials warned that if the interfaith campaign failed, "censorship will almost certainly come"—an unwelcome
prospect. Hays too worried that this massive ecumenical protest "to stave
off national disaster," as one bishop put it, might impress legislators and
inadvertently trigger federal regulation. Nevertheless, Council officials
cooperated with the Catholic campaign and hoped to use public outrage to
advance its own priorities, especially the outlawing of block booking. The
Christian Century contended, "The more the authorities of the Catholic
church consider the issue they are fighting, the surer we are that they will
see the necessity for establishing a free market for the rental of *all* films,
thus making the local exhibitor as responsible for showing bad pictures as
the church now tries to make the producer responsible for filming them."[14]

A Catholic-Hollywood Quid Pro Quo

Hays had gone on record repeatedly promising that salacious pictures
and advertising would end. He expected producers to keep their word and
back him up. They had only themselves to blame for disregarding the
Code and incurring the wrath of the Catholic Church. Increased calls for
federal regulation and heavy financial losses made the studios especially
vulnerable to a large-scale boycott. With film executives alarmed and
bewildered, Hays's hand was strengthened. He negotiated with Quigley
and Joseph Breen, another lay Catholic who was working in the MPPDA's
Studio Relations Committee, to act as an industry liaison. Breen—tough-
minded, religiously devout, and politically conservative—was head of
public relations for the Peabody Coal Company. He handled press relations for the 1926 Eucharistic Congress in Chicago and was working at a
Catholic newspaper there when Hays first hired him to drum up support

for the Code with Catholic editors. Quigley and Breen convinced the Catholic bishops to agree to a proposal that would ensure "strict observance" of the Code.[15]

In July 1934, the Studio Relations Committee was transformed into the Production Code Administration (PCA), with Breen in charge of making sure every film adhered to the Code's provisions. MPPDA members agreed to submit their productions for scrutiny and, moreover, not to exhibit any film without PCA approval. In addition, a new appeals process was put in place. When the Code was adopted, Jason Joy's Studio Relations Committee was responsible for providing a "uniform interpretation of the provisions of the code," but each company remained the final arbiter of whether its films were in compliance.[16] Disputes were settled by a rotating committee of producers who were well aware that one of their movies might come under review. To strengthen the PCA's authority, producer appeals of its rulings went to the MPPDA Board of Directors in New York, and not the "Hollywood Jury."

Movie regulation was fully integrated into the studio system. Enforcement of the Production Code was directly contingent upon theater ownership and compulsory block booking. By controlling the market, MPPDA companies could prevent any film without Code approval from being exhibited in the key metropolitan areas that were critical to a film's commercial success. Catholic bishops understood this and entered into a quid pro quo with the studios: the church would oversee movie content in return for staying out of the industry's business affairs. Movies were produced in Hollywood through a process of negotiation with Breen and his staff. Early prints of a finished film were flown to New York to be classified by Legion of Decency officials, who could require that changes be made in order for the film to receive a certain rating before distribution to theaters nationwide. By avoiding a dreaded "C," for Condemned, a film could reach the Catholic market. In short, the Legion had Breen's back. For all practical purposes, the Legion's demands on the producers, under threat of a nationwide boycott of specific films and even theaters, constituted a church-directed censorship of American movies.

Catholic leaders understood the Production Code as a synthesis of the Ten Commandments and "natural law," which "binds every member of the human race." The purpose of the Code was to keep movies in line with these universally accepted principles. The Catholic hierarchy also perceived themselves as the caretaker of "divine law," and for that reason believed that the church not only had the right and duty to safeguard the faithful from false ideas, opinions, and dogma masquerading as truth, but was also specially positioned as the exclusive and infallible authority in matters moral and religious. Church-directed prior restraint then was consonant with Catholic moral philosophy; the church had a "God given duty to lead in such matters." Rendering judgments on an entertainment that affected the moral standards of the entire nation could not be left to Protestants, Jews, and pagans who confused the issue with a lot of talk about art, business, and free speech, making it out to be "largely a matter of good taste."[17]

Catholic certitude resonated with Hays's own belief there was "no zone of twilight in the matter" of movie morality. What he wanted was a single interpretation and strict application of the Code's provisions, which the no-nonsense Breen, backed by the Legion, was apt to provide. The Legion, however, was not a united movement. Catholic leaders tried to conceal any internal divisions and to maintain the appearance that they were in lock-step on the movies, so as not to diminish their power with the studios. If the producers did not understand this, Hays did. He monitored internal Catholic conflicts closely and gauged public sentiment, which was not mainly in favor of the Legion. It didn't matter. Hays wanted to preserve the specter of a nationwide Catholic boycott, which gave him the leverage he needed to force film producers into complying with the Code—an eventuality impossible with Protestants.[18]

By empowering Catholics, Hays had strategically outflanked his co-religionists. Protecting the industry's profits—for which he was handsomely paid—was Hays's top priority, as critics like George Reid Andrews, Catheryne Cooke Gilman, and others contended. By channeling civic energies into "selection, not censorship," the Hays organization *was* effectively distracting the public from the real threat to the industry—not censorship, but the breakup of the studios' profitable oligopoly. Under the prevailing circumstances, studio executives were willing to follow Hays's lead and submit to a stringent Catholic censorship in order to fend off government scrutiny of their business. Allied with independent exhibitors, Protestant groups worked with legislators, many of them Protestants themselves, in drafting various proposals to break the major studios' stranglehold on the market. They were of accord on two counts: industry cooperation was useless, and block booking and blind selling were "the *sine qua non* of cinema advance."[19] Their persistent efforts to dismantle the studio monopoly made them Hollywood's foes and would bring an end soon enough to any joint Protestant-Catholic endeavors.

Indecency vs. Monopoly

With the International Federation of Catholic Alumnae recommending 75 percent of the studios' output, executives were hopeful that the industry would largely "escape the branding iron" of a Catholic preview. Under Rita McGoldrick's leadership, the IFCA had maintained a close relationship with the Hays organization; the MPPDA covered the agency's printing and mailing costs, along with McGoldrick's MPPDA-related travel expenses. Gilman had suspected as much and queried Catholic leaders about the extent to which the IFCA represented and acted on behalf of the Catholic Church. The Legion, however, was intentionally positioned to avoid any undue industry influence that might taint its efforts. When McGoldrick rebuffed Legion efforts to start a blacklist, she was replaced by her assistant, Mrs. James F. Looram, and IFCA ties to the Hays office were severed. Looram and the film bureau's women volunteers now conducted their reviews in cooperation with, and under the close supervision of, a team of priests.[20]

The bishops refuted charges that the Legion's methods were undemocratic and threatened individual freedoms by claiming that they were only protecting parishioners from the "proximate occasion of sin." Church officials had a duty to inform them ahead of time regarding which movies they should and should not see. They had no qualms about using consumer pressure to coerce filmmakers or with the fact that their decisions were, in effect, binding on Catholics and non-Catholics alike. Catholic control at the source of production, enforced by a persistent threat of financial loss, was the only way to keep those having "no conception of our Christian code of morals" from making indecent movies. And should the Legion succeed in ridding the screen of "morality-mocking films," it would be recognized as "a universal blessing."[21]

By the end of 1934, the IFCA's rate of approved films topped 90 percent, the Production Code Administration (PCA) had reportedly reduced censorship costs by two-thirds, most film companies were profitable, and public opinion took a 180-degree turn "from violent criticism to enthusiastic approval." One Catholic writer compared the advent of the Legion to "the long-awaited tidings of the angels at the Birth of our Redeemer." What was to prevent "this great army of Catholics" now from reviving souls and restoring "the moral happiness of America"? Such triumphal rhetoric struck deep at traditional Protestant worries about the rise of Catholic power. President Roosevelt courted the Catholic vote and appointed more Catholics and

Jews to high-level government and judiciary posts than all presidents before him combined. The two religious groups remained loyal to the Democratic Party. As part of a larger trend of more active Catholic involvement in national affairs, the bishops staked their claim as custodians of American morality and delivered yet another blow to the Protestant establishment.[22]

Moreover, with the effects of the Depression at their worst, Prohibition—*the* symbol of Protestant moral supremacy—ended in December 1933. Prohibition was supposed to eliminate the source of many of the nation's ills—poverty, crime, and violence. When it turned into a fiasco, the Protestant elite were devastated and blamed its failure on the lack of Catholic support, postwar moral confusion and contempt for disciplinary restraint, and, most important, the absence of "scientific and ethical temperance education."[23] While Prohibitionists employed the rhetoric of purity, Catholics countered with an emphasis on individual freedom. An ironic reversal occurred with movie regulation. Catholics now insisted on a central control and "decency," while Protestants amplified the principle of personal liberty, stressed their opposition to censorship, and prioritized educating the public to create demand for high-quality films.

Literary Digest likened the Catholic "spark of indignation" to "a match to a powder-train," but the Legion's interfaith crusade was really an unstable alliance with no lasting potential. Religious leaders formed a short-lived interfaith committee in response to what they called "one of the most spontaneous cooperative movements among those of various faiths in the history of this country." But there was no accord on method. Protestants wanted to "decentralize" moral supervision, Jews wanted a "central committee," and Catholics were "not likely to share the moral guidance of its faithful" with any other agencies.[24]

Federal Council appeals to discuss "next moves and undertakings" with the Episcopal Committee were rebuffed, and sharp differences in perspective emerged. The Council's Worth M. Tippy publicly criticized the Production Code as being too individualistic, too negative, too preoccupied with sex, and its enforcement "too largely an affair between the Catholic Church and the industry." He argued that it should be revised to account for significant differences on moral and social issues that existed among Catholics, Protestants, Jews, and others, and to acknowledge changing tastes and morals. For example, he thought the Code should include the "morality of collective action and responsibility" and permit movies "to portray vested evils and entrenched privileges in their true light, and to embody the struggle for social security and economic plenty."

The Code might have given producers more latitude in themes, but their treatment was constrained within a strict narrative framework of "compensating moral values," which Breen interpreted as "good characters, the voice of morality, a lesson, regeneration of the transgressor, suffering and punishment." But, as the Payne Fund studies showed, young people were preoccupied with the accoutrements of the glamorized world of the film and seldom gave much thought to tacked-on moral endings. The way that many Protestant film critics saw it, the goal was not simply *decency*, "the absence of dirt and impropriety." A film that was made decent by deleting distasteful elements could still be dishonest (in its treatment of life) and dull (as art and entertainment). It was the film's artistic prowess and embodied perspective that mattered most: "The evil in a picture usually is not what is shown but the way it is shown."[25]

Protestant attitudes really soured when Legion officials came out against anti-block-booking legislation. In May 1935, the Supreme Court declared the National Industrial Recovery Act (NIRA) unconstitutional, invalidating the NRA film industry code. The movement to outlaw block booking was revived. Opposed to federal censorship, Congressman Samuel B. Pettengill (Congregationalist) and Senator Matthew M. Neely (Presbyterian) began introducing legislation to prohibit block booking in interstate and foreign commerce and to eliminate blind selling by forcing producers to provide exhibitors with synopses of film content. The Motion Picture Research Council sponsored the Pettengill-Neely bill and claimed that it had the backing of many religious and educational agencies, including the Federal Council, YMCA and YWCA, National Education Association, Women's Christian Temperance Union (WCTU), and individuals like Guy Emery Shipler and Fred Eastman.[26] These bills garnered solid Protestant support and exposed a division among Catholic leaders.

At hearings on the Pettengill-Neely bill (1935–1936), Detroit bishop Michael J. Gallagher broke ranks and came out in favor of its passage. The House Committee received letters from Catholic organizations across the country protesting block booking, including a long telegram from Arthur D. Maguire, president of the Detroit Council of Catholic Organizations, who contended that the Legion's executive secretary, Father Joseph Daly, acted on the advice of Martin Quigley and the Hays organization and did not represent the opinion of the Catholic laity. Legion officials insisted that the church was interested only in the moral aspects of the movies; block booking was "a purely business matter." Insofar as it involved a "moral question," the Legion had urged producers to permit exhibitors to cancel

any films made before July 15, 1934—the date when the PCA began operations under Joe Breen's authority. Given the "marked improvement in the
moral tone of pictures" since then, there was no reason to change the
status quo. In fact, just the opposite. Practically, eliminating block booking
would mean that the Legion would have to deal with over 12,000 theater
owners instead of controlling content at the source. Also, eliminating
block booking was inadequate as a remedy, if only because it did not prevent the production of immoral movies in the first place.[27]

The Legion's unspoken logic was that the church agency's cooperation
with the PCA ensured that every film produced and exhibited conformed
to right moral standards. If exhibitors were free to select their own movies,
sex and crime films were sure to return, with the competition undermining confidence in the efficacy of the Code. And Catholic bishops were not
about to relinquish their newly acquired power. While divisions persisted,
Legion officials squashed any support for anti-block-booking legislation.
House committee hearings also—and more importantly—revealed the
PCA's effectiveness in restricting competition. Only 1 percent of the
movies released from February 1936 to November 1938 had been condemned by the Legion, and not one of those films was produced by a
major Hollywood studio. It was concrete evidence that the studios were
operating under airtight censorship.[28]

The Missiles Are Rarer Today

The Legion was racking up achievements. Box office was up 25 percent,
the family trade revived, and Shirley Temple and Will Rogers were top at-
tractions—all proof that "decency means dollars and dirt deficits." But
films displaying "the so-called Lubitsch touches," referring to the subtle
wit and sexual nuance of director Ernst Lubitsch, still lurked as a harbin-
ger of a possible return to indecency and were enough reason for the
Legion to become the permanent "custodian of morality." Protestants
could only "stand aside and applaud." Yet commentators began questioning the fact that a Catholic agency was acting as the arbiter of taste for the
entire nation and the constitutionality of prior restraint of movies. "Unless we are Catholics do we wish to have our tastes in art set for us by an
authority which we do not otherwise recognize?" one film and drama
critic wrote. "Is Hollywood, already defeated by a financial set-up which
prevents any but the most accidental treatments of reality, to be further
smothered by the repressions of a highly interested group?"[29]

While Catholics cooperated with Hays to control movie morality, Protestants continued working with community groups and legislators. A number of agencies, the National Board of Review and YMCA among them, were previewing movies and rating them based on entertainment value and age-appropriateness. Under the auspices of the MPPDA, the Film Estimate Board of National Organizations (FEBNO) was set up in 1933 so that religious, educational, and women's groups could screen and publish film reviews in organization periodicals. A monthly composite with classifications—popularly known as "The Green Sheet"—was distributed to schools, libraries, and other places to help families in film selection.[30] High schools began offering courses using resources like Edgar Dale's *How to Appreciate Motion Pictures.*

Protestant distrust of the Legion only deepened. Between 1936 and 1943, only 6 of 53 films condemned by the Legion were produced by the major producers, and these were sufficiently revised and reclassified. The others were foreign films, sexploitation "quickies," or films dealing with medical issues and not appropriate for general release. When a Catholic official alleged that block booking actually "crowded out the bad pictures," the *Christian Century* found the assertion utterly incredible. "The Big Eight, apparently, will produce nothing offensive to the Roman Catholic Church provided that the Roman Catholic Church keeps hands off the Big Eight's monopoly and its strangle hold upon the independent exhibitors," the editor contended. "What happens to the whole democratic principle of free enterprise and the right of community choice in the selection of its films seems of no consequence to the legion [sic]. But it matters a lot to some of the rest of us."[31] Regardless, the course had been set, and it was a painful sign of the erosion of Protestant influence.

The Federal Council's loss of credibility had impaired its leadership. Catheryne Cooke Gilman suspected that the "divorcement" from the Hays organization was not complete. When the *Christian Century* learned that Worth Tippy had been elected to the National Board of Review's General Committee, it sharply criticized even this informal connection between the two agencies: public confidence in Council secretaries' "intelligence can hardly stand the strain of further bungling in their motion picture efforts." Didn't they realize that the National Board had tried to discredit the Payne Fund Studies and still operated with industry funding? The *Century* insisted on "absolute independence of the present producers." Tippy resigned from the National Board's General Committee in July 1934 after concluding there was "no hope of accomplishing anything significant through it."[32]

William Short's expectations that the Payne Fund research would be the basis for a united front and national film policy were stymied by the Legion's highly publicized crusade. Ironically, backing the "loose generalization and often unwarranted inferences" in Henry James Forman's popularization of the Payne Fund studies, *Our Movie Made Children*, cast some doubt among supporters about the Motion Picture Research Council's overall direction. The organization lacked sufficient financial resources to carry out additional phases of the project and floundered after William Short's untimely death in 1935. After more than 30 years of crusading against vice and immorality, Canon William Shaefe Chase retired.[33]

A striking instance in the breach between Protestants and Hollywood occurred—not surprisingly—between the Hays office and *The Churchman*. In October 1931, *Harrison's Reports* mistakenly reported that MPPDA general counsel Gabriel Hess, Adolph Zukor, Will Hays, and others had been indicted by the province of Ontario for conspiracy in restraint of trade. Hess was named in the indictment as being connected with the charges, but was not in fact indicted. *The Churchman* carried the story secondhand and then published a retraction in the next issue. Hess sued for libel, asking for $150,000 in damages.[34]

In June 1935, a judge awarded Hess $10,200. Like many church publications, *The Churchman* operated with an annual deficit and did not have the resources to pay the fine. The verdict threatened to destroy the oldest religious journal in the English-speaking world. Outraged, the religious press appealed to readers to contribute to a defense fund. Rabbi Sidney E. Goldstein (Central Conference of American Rabbis) asked Hess to accept the verdict as a moral vindication and not collect the damages. He refused, accusing *The Churchman* of using the threat of increased anti-Semitism to get him to abandon the suit. Goldstein countered that editor Guy Emery Shipler had done "everything possible to keep the religious issue out of the case and to discourage an anti-Semitic reaction." After losing an appeal, Shipler was able to pull together enough to pay the judgment in October 1936 with help from a group of prominent Protestant, Catholic, and Jewish leaders. Hess then announced that the proceeds would be donated to charities. The sentiment in Protestant circles was that Hays could have prevented the libel suit and that it was nothing less than another act of reprisal.[35]

"The missiles are rarer today," *Boxoffice* observed in 1937 of Hays's fifteenth year as head of the MPPDA. The PCA had quieted the industry's harshest critics. By drawing tight parameters around acceptable content,

Breen leveled the playing field considerably and halted the competitive spiral for risqué properties. While it was smart business to attract 16- to 26-year-olds—Hollywood's bread-and-butter audience—he also encouraged a long-term strategy aimed at turning the over-24 age group, roughly 60 percent of the population, into regular moviegoers. Among this group were the social elite in residential areas who were the main source of agitation against the film industry. They seldom went to the movies, under the impression (often from advertising alone) that they were all aimed at youth, which was perhaps one reason that a film like *Disraeli* was a box-office disappointment.[36]

Hollywood's respite was short-lived. Although calls for censorship had subsided, the persistent attention to the studios' trade practices eventually led to a Justice Department investigation and antitrust proceedings in 1938. Thurman Arnold, who headed the Justice Department's Antitrust Division, had a Presbyterian background and was an ardent supporter of Prohibition. The hard-hitting attorney was colorfully described as "cold to feminine charm and deaf to arguments from Hollywood's high-priced legal battery." Arnold's aim was to revamp the entire industry by forcing the MPPDA studios to divest themselves of their theater holdings. Within months, independent producers Samuel Goldwyn, Carl Laemmle, and *Variety* came out against block booking, which the *Christian Century* noted had been its position for 10 years. As a remedial measure, a Consent Decree was signed in November 1940. It called for an end to blind selling and modified block booking by limiting blocks to five films and allowing exhibitors to make substitutions. The studios agreed not to expand their theater holdings. The Production Code Administration was also implicated as a monopolistic tool.[37] Hays and the studio heads realized that the proverbial writing was on the wall; it would only be a matter of time now.

7

One Foot in Hollywood

THE PROTESTANT FILM COMMISSION

*A louder voice in the production of pictures with construc-
tive themes is the goal of the Protestant Film Commission.*
HOLLYWOOD REPORTER, 1948

HOLLYWOOD'S SYSTEM OF self-regulation was entrenched during the 1930s
and 1940s with Joseph Breen's office, the Production Code Administration (PCA), operating in tandem with the Legion of Decency. The Production Code prohibited ridicule of religion, using ministers in comedy or as
villains, and mandated that depiction of religious practices be "supervised
by someone thoroughly conversant with that religion." As a matter of procedure, producers consulted with Father John J. Devlin, the official Catholic film adviser in Los Angeles. The Protestant establishment, however,
had no official representation in Hollywood. Protestant leaders remained
averse to having any influence on productions, beyond helping producers
get the technical details right on church traditions and practices. Filmmakers would find a local minister whenever they needed Protestant
counsel, which was not all that often.

In 1937, Francis Harmon, a top YMCA executive active in the Federal
Council, joined the MPPDA staff as Hays's assistant and head of the New
York office of the PCA, an appointment that *Time* took as a concession to
Protestants. The Federal Council's Samuel McCrea Cavert considered him
a good "friend at court." Tensions remained between the MPPDA and
Federal Council leaders who "squirmed" at the extent of Catholic control
in Hollywood. In response to letters from disgruntled constituents, Coun-
cil officials raised concerns about a perceived discrepancy in Hollywood

films: while Catholic characters were treated with reverence, Protestants were used to generate laughs. Harmon did a statistical analysis showing that only 12 percent of all the movies approved by the PCA in 1939 contained depictions of religious characters. There were exactly 38 Catholic priests, 33 Protestant ministers or missionaries, and one rabbi—mostly in minor roles. Cavert was still not entirely persuaded that Breen's office rejected religiously offensive material and noted that Harmon had failed to address certain depictions of Protestant ministers, like the irreverent Reverend Rosenkrantz in *Drums Along the Mohawk* (1939), which provided "some ground for criticism."[1]

The Protestant leadership perceived that movies were damaging to their public image. The industry also seemed partial to Catholics, whose methods Protestants detested. Something had to be done. Despite Catholic success in securing favorable treatment in movies, Council leaders refused to employ the bishops' strategies and coerce producers under threat of boycott. The challenge was to navigate the industry's apparatus for regulation under Catholic control, which in effect meant finding a way to function within prior censorship, even though it ran against the grain of Protestant principles. This would not be an easy task, particularly because of the diversity of perspectives within Protestantism, and even within the Federal Council. Also, Protestant groups had lobbied for the elimination of the industry's monopolistic trade practices for almost two decades. Events would soon start to undermine the studio system and the existing mode of self-regulation, and with that, the Federal Council would have to reimagine its role with the film industry in order to have an influence appropriate to the new circumstances.

Protestants and Catholics at the Movies

In December 1940, *Reader's Digest* announced that a movie adaptation of Hartzell Spence's best-selling novel *One Foot in Heaven* was in the works. Spence's biography of his father, who gave up a promising career in medicine to become a Methodist minister, was much admired by Protestants. They did not want to see Hollywood make a caricature of William H. Spence. Warner Bros. had a difficult time finding a Methodist adviser, but finally secured help from the Federal Council and Daniel A. Poling, the influential editor of the *Christian Herald*, a conservative nondenominational weekly. Hoping the Spence biopic would compare with Catholic vehicles like *Boys' Town* (1938), *The Fighting 69th* (1940), and *Knute Rockne, All American* (1940), Poling put together an advisory committee and secured Norman Vincent Peale, born a Methodist and pastor of New York's Marble Collegiate Church (Reformed Church in America), to serve as technical adviser during production.

One Foot in Heaven begins with Dr. William Spence (Frederic March) announcing that he plans to abandon medicine and follow a calling to the ministry. Spence's future in-laws are dismayed, but fiancée Hope (Martha Scott) dutifully recites a well-known passage from the Book of Ruth: "Intreat me not to leave thee, or to return from following after thee: for whither thou goest, I will go; and where thou lodgest, I will lodge: thy people shall be my people, and thy God my God." The "new preacher and his blushing bride" start their ministry in a small town in Iowa, making the best out of one run-down parsonage after another. Spence is a man of Christian humility, interminably optimistic and good humored, and deeply devoted to God, his ministry, and his family. At a parish in Denver, rain drips through exactly 20 holes in the parsonage's roof—Spence crawls around the attic counting them—and prosperous parishioners, absent vocal talent, take pride sitting in the choir loft behind the pulpit. Spence's campaign to build a new, redesigned church runs into opposition from these long-standing affluent members. Only after Spence threatens to expose them for spreading a false rumor that gets his son Hartzell expelled from school do they concede to contribute financially to the building project, which includes a new sanctuary with an organ and carillon, recreation facilities, and a parsonage. The film ends with Spence playing a traditional hymn on the new carillon that can be heard all over town. The bells draw the whole community to the Elmwood Methodist Church, singing together "The Church is One Foundation."

Warner Bros. allowed a contractual provision that gave author Hartzell Spence veto power over the final script. Spence was satisfied with the preliminary story treatment, but had a sudden turnabout after conferring with a *Christian Herald* editor who thought the characterization made William Spence "more smart than Christian" and lacking in "those great Christian qualities which characterize most preachers." When Spence registered new objections to what he considered now to be "a second-grade B picture in its present treatment," Harry Warner was "flabbergasted." Just days earlier, Spence had basically approved the story treatment; the "sudden change of opinion" required major rewriting.[2]

In the end, producer Hal Wallis bent over backward to accommodate the church consultants. Wanting to "please the principals involved,"

Spence was brought to Hollywood to work directly with screenwriters, Poling signed off on the script, and Peale advised during production. When a Methodist minister publicly attacked the film during shooting, Poling handled the situation and calmed nervous studio executives by suggesting that such attacks were "of great propaganda value—they would help the picture." The movie's opening credits list Peale as technical consultant and end with an acknowledgment and the names of the committee advisers scrolling up the screen in what looks like a prologue designed to establish the film's credibility with Protestant moviegoers. The studio arranged special screenings for pastors in cities across the country. *Parents' Magazine* gave it the movie-of-the-month award and the *Federal Council Bulletin* called it "glorious entertainment—sparkling with humor and packed full of human interest."[3]

Warner Bros. mounted a full-court press to ensure Protestant support, but even so, some clergy were quite displeased with the movie. One Lutheran pastor faulted it for not emphasizing enough "the most important tenet of all and one which justifies the existence of the Protestant Church: emphasis upon the redemption of the individual through the substitutionary atonement of Jesus Christ." A group of ministers from Florida were more specific, listing their objections to this depiction of a Protestant minister as:

inconsistent, harsh, domineering, turning even the sacrament of baptism into an outrageous triumph over his lovely and longsuffering wife; descending practically to blackmail by threatening with a lawsuit certain evil minded parishioners who have plotted to destroy the reputation of his young son unless they hand over large contributions for his new church edifice and showing a spirit of showy salesmanship with no regard for consistency, or propriety, or a fine sense of honor in securing donations for elaborate features from unworthy hands.[4]

After all the precautions they took, Warner executives had to be stunned by such negative criticism.

"You get a few good Methodists together and they always fight," Dr. Spence tells a parishioner in *One Foot in Heaven*. "They think enough of their church to fight about it." Perhaps the same could be said about clergy reaction to the film; they would not just rally behind a movie, however much the producers consulted with church leaders. The differences of opinion on the merits of *One Foot in Heaven* likely did not boost its commercial prospects. But it was also the case that the congregational squabbling at the heart of the story lacked real dramatic import. Nevertheless, even with extensive Protestant cooperation and a Best Picture nomination, *One Foot in Heaven* did not exactly light up the box office. That it was only mildly successful reenforced doubts about the viability of the Protestant market.

The studios put out a steady stream of films extolling priests and the Catholic Church, including *The Song of Bernadette* (1943), *The Keys of the Kingdom* (1944), *Going My Way* (1944)—which swept the Oscars—and *The Bells of St. Mary's* (1945). It is not that Protestants disliked these movies; the *Christian Herald* ranked *Going My Way* "one of the finest pictures of the year." What bothered them was the disparity between the rosy handling of Catholics, and discourteous depiction of Protestant characters. Letter writers charged that Catholics—sometimes Breen was mentioned by name—monitored movie output and were using the cinema to proselytize. They were tired of paying for "Catholic propaganda" and appealed for a more equitable treatment, especially since "America is predominantly Protestant."[5]

Producers contended that films featuring Catholics were often based on best-selling fiction; other than *One Foot in Heaven*, comparable Protestant source material was simply not available. This was an exaggerated claim: *Boys' Town*, *The Fighting 69th*, *Knute Rockne, All American*, *Going My Way*, and *The Bells of St. Mary's* were all original screenplays. Eric Johnston, who replaced the retired Will Hays as head of the renamed Motion Picture Association of America (MPAA), offered a feeble defense, a list of "outstanding Protestant pictures" that proved uninspiring, especially in comparison to the Catholic vehicles. "The Circuit Rider's Wife" never made it to the screen; the small part of the minister (played by Charles Laughton) in *On Our Merry Way* (a.k.a. *A Miracle Can Happen*) ended up on the proverbial cutting room floor. The others—*Angel and the Badman*, a John Wayne Production for Republic Pictures, *Heaven Only Knows*, and *The Tender Years*—were lackluster fare. The bottom line was that a movie of special interest was highly promoted by Catholic churches and invariably resulted in a box-office success, while movies expected to draw Protestants had disappointing returns. To a Federal Council executive's remark that *One Foot in Heaven* was "an insult to the ethical and moral standards of the Protestant ministry," producers threw up their arms—there was "no way of satisfying the diverse interests of Protestantism."[6]

Council leaders were not entirely convinced, but what they heard producers say was that the studios would make movies giving a good impression of Protestantism provided they had the story material and got hefty box office returns. Afterward, Jason Joy (now at Twentieth Century-Fox) assured Samuel McCrea Cavert that the studio's story department was "earnestly striving to find the best and most significant" material featuring Protestant characters, but the Gilmore-Talmage "Chautauqua" story that Cavert pitched him did not fit the bill. Neither did an idea for a movie on Albert Schweitzer, whose life as a medical missionary in the African jungle Cavert thought was "really a thriller!"[7]

Council and denominational leaders—who apparently were not regular moviegoers—continued stressing educational over entertainment values, believing they could translate church education into an effective strategy to reform Hollywood. "The film story of a soul's redemption is a blessing," the *Christian Herald* maintained. "But let us not be deceived; producers cannot and will not please thoughtful, church-centered Americans unless these religious-minded people *support the product!*" That the film industry seemed impervious to anything but box office results created a dilemma for Protestant leaders. Catholic power was predicated on the notion that church authorities controlled the moviegoing habits of their parishioners, and should the wrath of the bishops be incurred, they could whip up a nationwide boycott. Protestant leaders, by contrast, would do nothing to prevent constituents from attending movies. If they wanted treatment comparable to the Catholics, producers would have to be persuaded that Protestants were good business. The sheer size of the Protestant population—they outnumbered Catholics 43.6 to 24.4 million in 1947—would seem to assure the profitability of Protestant-themed films.[8] But rank-and-file Protestants were at home culturally and enjoyed the same movies as everyone else. They tended to be much less critical viewers than Catholics, who were taught by the church hierarchy to be wary of films, partly because they identified themselves as a subcultural group and were alert to the dangers of acculturation. That church leaders misjudged the movie preferences of large numbers of Protestants would eventually become clear and would undermine efforts to galvanize Federal Council constituencies into a reliable audience for a regular supply of religious and morally uplifting films. This state of affairs shaped the agenda for the Council's next major initiative.

The Protestant Film Commission

Considering the outstanding results of Catholic influence in Hollywood, some kind of comparable Protestant representation seemed inevitable. In 1945, the boards of 19 of the largest denominations and 12 leading interdenominational agencies (including the Federal Council) formed the Protestant Film Commission (PFC) to be the "Voice of Protestantism in Motion Pictures." Paul Heard became the first executive. Heard had supervised production of U.S. Navy films in Hollywood and was aware of the effectiveness of training and propaganda films produced by the governments and armed forces of the United Nations. He believed "similar techniques" could be used to address contemporary problems requiring "spiritual realizations."[9]

The Protestant Film Commission held its first annual meeting in January 1946. The commission had two broad purposes: to centralize and coordinate film production and distribution among denominational agencies and to represent Protestant churches to the film industry. The goal was to eventually produce films for delivery through regular channels and to make the undertaking financially self-supporting; it was an update on the dream George Reid Andrews had for the Religious Motion Picture Foundation in the 1920s. From 1946 to 1952, denominational boards spent $800,000 on independent film productions; the 14 movies made in 1952 represented a high point. The venture was only mildly successful; enthusiasm faded and budgets were reduced, with projects focusing on subjects with limited value beyond church use.[10]

The PFC would also maintain a script review and consulting service offered on a purely voluntary basis—a counterpart to John Devlin's role on behalf of Catholics—checking scripts for accuracy and providing "a reliable index of Protestant opinion" to help producers avoid anything that might alienate Protestant and Orthodox moviegoers. The purpose was to ensure that Protestantism received "dignified recognition" in movies, and also to explore "the dramatic possibilities of religious material and of constructive moral themes."[11] If this was in part a direct response to the rise of Catholic influence, the basic reasoning was familiar enough. By appealing to the producers' commercial instincts, denominational leaders hoped to persuade studio executives of the viability of the Protestant market, believing that such movies would result in a general improvement in the moral, artistic, and entertainment value of films.

While the PFC founders wanted influence comparable to that of Catholics, they had no desire to create an organization anything like the Legion of Decency. From its inception, the commission was not to be "a protest-ing agency," despite contrary public perceptions. A clear separation of its agencies was maintained: one for consulting during production, and an-other offering reviews of finished films for the public. Implied in this strategy was a critique of the Catholic method: Protestant reviews would not be contingent upon producer cooperation. The PFC Hollywood office was prohibited from publicly approving movies; not that such an endorse-ment would be all that effective anyway given "the democratic nature of Protestantism," a reality that would make it impossible to muster the kind of the consumer clout that the Legion had.[12]

The Protestant Film Commission established a cooperative relation-ship with the New York–based *Christian Herald*, whose aim was to draw attention to better films—applaud the good and denounce the bad—as a way to develop more informed and selective viewers. The Christian Her-ald Company formed the Motion Picture Council of Protestant Women in February 1945; a year later, the name was changed to the Protestant Mo-tion Picture Council (PMPC), and a "Picture of the Month" feature was introduced. The review agency functioned under the leadership of Mrs. Daniel Poling, wife of the magazine's editor, and Mrs. Jesse "Golda" Bader, whose husband was a Federal Council secretary; both women were officers in the United Council of Church Women. As the original name indicates, the venture was conceived as gendered, with the council composed ini-tially at least entirely of women, all "with a Church and *Christian Herald* background, wives of leading American churchmen, Christian mothers vitally concerned with the movie diet of their children." With the name change and PFC association, the PMPC maintained about 25 reviewers, including some men, and also representatives of home, school, and mul-tiple denominations to reflect a cross-section of Protestantism.[13]

Unlike its Catholic counterpart, the PMPC was not about to mandate what movies constituents could and could not see. "We aren't censors," Jesse Bader explained. "We evaluate films and let the readers make their own choice." All U.S. and many foreign-produced feature films were reviewed and categorized according to audience: Adults (over 18), Young People (over 12), Mature Young People (mature in experience), Family (en-tertainment for the family to enjoy together). There were also two chil-dren's ratings: CPA (acceptable) and CPR (recommended). On rare occasions, a film was marked "Objectionable" when reviewers found it "so low in moral values as to offend most churchgoers." *Beyond the Forest* (Warner Bros., 1949) fell into this category; the Bette Davis character was drawn as "a selfish, arrogant, immoral and evil-tempered woman with not a single redeeming or relieving feature." The PMPC's monthly *Reviews and Ratings* were syndicated to some 250 Protestant journals and were included in the MPAA-funded digest of organizational reviews, the "Green Sheet."[14]

With an office and reviewing service established in New York, the PFC started implementing plans for its consulting operation in Hollywood. In the meantime, Louis Evans, pastor of the prestigious First Presbyterian Church of Hollywood, was appointed head of a West Coast Committee, a consultative group made up of a cross section of denominational clergy and laypeople ready to advise producers on matters related to Protestant-ism.[15] This laid a fault line down the middle of the Protestants' hopeful new enterprise.

Dueling with David O. Selznick

Famed producer David O. Selznick was sure that his screen adaptation of *Duel in the Sun* would repeat the success of his 1939 classic *Gone with the Wind*. A western, the story centers on a love triangle. Orphaned after her father was hanged for murdering his wife and her lover, Pearl Chavez, a beautiful half–Native American girl, is forced to live with a distant relative in Texas, Laura Belle McCanles, who is married to a cantankerous Senator and rich cattle baron. Pearl finds herself torn between McCanles's two sons, the educated and genteel Jesse, and the spoiled, lecherous Lewt. Re-garding the depiction of a vulgar, itinerant frontier preacher, Breen instructed Selznick to "inject some dialogue" that would "make it quite clear that he is in no sense an ordained minister" and "enable him to play the scenes he does, without the flavor of a travesty on religion." Laura Belle introduces Pearl to the "Sinkiller" saying, "We have no minister in these parts." He interrupts her: "Man doesn't have to wear the cloth to be a Sinkiller, Laura Belle." After exhausting negotiations, a PCA certificate was finally issued in December 1946.[16]

Selznick opened *Duel in the Sun* at the Egyptian Theatre in Hollywood on New Year's Eve in order to qualify for the Academy Awards the following March. While *Variety* labeled it "raw, sex-laden, western pulp fiction" that was "a cinch for resounding ticket sales," a Catholic reviewer attacked the film for making the Code "a sham" and completely disregarding its provi-sion on ministers. Los Angeles Archbishop John J. Cantwell issued a direc-tive warning Catholics not to attend the film, pending classification by the

Legion of Decency. Melvin Harter of the Church Federation of Los Angeles (a Federal Council affiliate) had requested a conference with Selznick in November, but was turned down. Harter informed him that in his judgment the film parodied religion; the Sinkiller provided the only comic relief in the film, was unessential to the plot, and could be eliminated altogether. Likewise, Methodist minister Donald Tippet, who attended the premier with Harter, observed with dismay that every appearance of the Sinkiller on screen was greeted with audience laugher "so that when he came to officiate at the burial of Sam Sears . . . his audience was ready for a laugh and he gave it to them, dragging even death and immortality into the dust to do it. It is clever travesty of religion, expertly done." Martin Quigley's *Motion Picture Daily* reported that Protestant churches, while waiting for Selznick to address their concerns, were considering a boycott. But no official action had been decided upon, and Church Federation members were irked that their communication with Selznick was somehow leaked to Quigley, who wrongly associated their initiative as being in sync with Catholic condemnation of the movie.[17]

Selznick had asked the Church Federation for a week to consider the matter. Aware that his permit to show the film in the important New York market was under review, church officials speculated that he might "seek to protect himself at this point," but were also concerned that the religious furor would only fuel attendance.[18] Contrary to Selznick's impression, Protestant officials did not think that simply eliminating the Sinkiller character would improve the low moral tone of the film. They objected to that as well, but it was not their policy to condemn movies they found objectionable.

Breen and MPAA head Eric Johnston shrugged off Protestant protests; technically, the film was not in violation of the Code. But coming on the heels of Howard Hughes's controversial film *The Outlaw*, and with a movement for local censorship growing, they caved to the Legion's demands for changes by refusing to defend *Duel* even though it had been approved by Breen's office. Under financial pressure, Selznick had little choice but to reedit the film—twice—making cuts and adding a prologue and epilogue before the Legion finally gave it a B rating; the additional editing and delays proved costly. It was a clear victory for the Legion that assured the Catholic agency final cut approval. Afterward, Legion executives let Breen know that he had made "a serious mistake" in approving the film, which was "over-loaded with sex and seduction."[19]

Duel went into general release in May 1947 with a saturation-booking scheme and an intense marketing campaign, but it did not reach the heights that Selznick had hoped. It finished the year tied for second at the box office with the Academy Award–winning *The Best Years of Our Lives*, behind Disney's *Song of the South*. The recent controversies and increased pressure from Catholics and Protestants, however, were enough for Eric Johnston to indicate that the film industry might challenge the legal status of local censorship.[20]

Entering a New Era

When, in January 1947, Paul Heard announced the Protestant Film Commission's plans to open a West Coast Office (WCO) to represent Protestantism in Hollywood, he was asked about the committee's stated purpose "to encourage greater depth and freedom of expression on the screen." Heard said the PFC was "against political and state censorship of films" and planned to work with producers "for higher artistic and moral values in pictures." But he also indicated, in an apparent contradiction, that the committee might have specific recommendations for the Production Code and that the Legion of Decency had made "a contribution to better taste in movies." The *Hollywood Reporter* declared simply enough: "Protestants Plan Own 'Legion.'" PFC officials were aghast at the equation and immediately went to work to correct the "mistaken impression." Heard met with Eric Johnston and studio executives in Hollywood to calm the waters; Louis Evans sent out a statement stressing that the West Coast Office was primarily a consulting agency to provide producers with advice and information on Protestant religion, culture, and church rituals and practices.[21]

After more than a decade of stringent Catholic oversight, industry leaders were leery of the sudden Protestant plan "to rally national support for worthwhile films and suggest and encourage productions of features with high moral values." With *Christian Herald* editor Daniel Poling indicating "something more universal than the Catholic Legion of Decency is definitely in prospect as a result of the lewdness now being unloaded upon the American reading public," the *Hollywood Reporter* speculated that the PFC would "place a church censorship or approval on future product." Protestant officials would often try to get the industry to clean up its act by issuing a warning whenever the threat of political censorship seemed to be gaining momentum. At the time, Hollywood was embroiled in accusations of Communist infiltration that were shaded with anti-Semitic overtones. While Protestants were establishing a physical presence in Hollywood, national Jewish organizations were also setting up a Jewish Film Advisory

Committee there to work with producers. Poling, as the *Hollywood Reporter* noted, was cognizant of the "present outcrop of political spot censorship," and insisted that Protestants possessed "the constructive American answer to the un-American political censorship." Protestants were just as concerned about the threat that anti-Communist hysteria posed to civil liberties as they were with the growing Catholic influence—and not just in the movie industry. In response to a constituent request that the Federal Council intervene with Hollywood producers, Roswell Barnes replied, "The motion picture is only one of the points at which we are giving a great deal of attention to the problems of the influence of the Roman Catholic Church."[22]

As it was, the Protestant Film Commission was trying to make a niche for itself in Hollywood, just as the film industry was undergoing a major transformation. The House Committee on Un-American Activities (HUAC) set out to prove that the Screenwriters Guild was dominated by Communists using movies as propaganda. At sensational hearings in November 1947, HUAC cited a group of writers and directors for contempt. They became known as the Hollywood Ten. The HUAC probe made it look as if Hollywood were defending Communists. Rather than appear unpatriotic, the MPAA and studio heads agreed to blacklist anyone suspected of having Communist affiliations. Fearing more repressive measures on the horizon, industry executives called for the Production Code to be "complied with to the hilt in the future."[23]

The Justice Department, meanwhile, had resumed its antitrust case. In May 1948, the Supreme Court declared that the studios were operating an illegal conspiracy in restraint of trade. The "Paramount Decrees" banned block booking and other restrictive trade practices and resulted in the major studios divesting themselves of their theater holdings. The studio oligopoly was finished at last, the event for which Protestant groups had "long worked." The MPAA studios lost a measure of power over production and, without control of first-run exhibition, they could no longer prevent films without Code approval from being shown in American theaters. In a parenthetical remark in the antitrust ruling, Justice William O. Douglas noted that, although not at issue in the case, the court had "no doubt that moving pictures, like newspapers and radio, are included in the press whose freedom is guaranteed by the First Amendment." It was an indication the court was ready to overturn the *Mutual* decision and extend free speech protection to the movies.[24]

Hollywood's long-standing defense against external censorship—that movies were harmless entertainment—was no longer valid after World

War II. A basic assumption of the HUAC investigations was that movies were a major means of communication affecting American values and beliefs. In an odd twist, during this intense government scrutiny of Hollywood as politically subversive, movies were being recognized as constitutionally protected speech.[25]

A United Front in Hollywood

PFC president Rome Betts met with industry leaders in February 1948 to discuss a Protestant liaison with Hollywood. After the *Duel in the Sun* controversy, Breen was happy to have the Protestant angle covered, as it would relieve his staff from "the avalanche of material" they received. Instead of engaging individual ministers, producers could work with a single official agency that would serve as a kind of Protestant clearinghouse and provide a "backstop in event of any possible criticisms of subjects covered." Breen informed all the major and independent studios that the PFC's West Coast Office (WCO) was available to evaluate scripts and provide production assistance whenever needed.[26]

Operating out of a small space on the KTTV lot on Sunset Boulevard, the West Coast Office began operations that October with Oren W. Evans as its first director. A Script Committee was set up not to censor, but only to give producers "a cross-section of probable Protestant reaction" and advise on the accuracy of depictions of Protestants. A Production Liaison Committee provided immediate technical assistance during production to guard the "authenticity" of the film. It provided technical advice and authorizations for shooting scenes that involved "church exteriors and interiors, correct dress of the clergy, liturgy of the church, proper hymns and scriptural passages." The WCO evaluated around 75 feature film scripts annually in the period 1949–1951 and provided "on-the-set technical advice" for many other projects. By comparison, the PCA staff in a single year (1946) reviewed 397 feature films produced in the United States and 28 produced abroad. A third WCO committee handled fund-raising and public relations. In March 1949, Cecil B. DeMille, Paramount's Y. Frank Freeman, and Paul Heard addressed 100 business leaders in southern California at a fund-raising luncheon in the Sunset Room of the California Club. Evans reported, "Protestants are now united on a strong front in Hollywood."[27]

The West Coast Office also started cooperating with studios in promoting movies to churchgoers. After advising on *Stars in My Crown* (1950), Oren Evans was happy to lend MGM the PFC's nationwide contacts.

Based on a novel by Joe David Brown, the movie tells the story of Josiah Grey, a Civil War veteran who becomes the minister of Walesburg, a small town in the South, and is pitted against the local doctor in a dramatic struggle between faith and science. Special clergy pre-release screenings were arranged through the Council of Churches network in cities across the country; over 800 clergy and guests attended a Los Angeles affair held at the Academy of Motion Picture Arts & Sciences Theater. Evans reported that "with but few exceptions" the Protestant crowd "accepted the film enthusiastically and agreed to publicize it among their various congregations." That was just what MGM executives wanted to hear. The *Christian Herald* named *Stars in My Crown* Picture of the Month ("Please, let's have more of this type of presentation!") and it received the Protestant Motion Picture Council's award for Picture of the Year.[28]

Enforcing the Code was not just about morality; it also had to do with protecting studio investments by making sure that movies would not encounter serious difficulties when released, and guarding the industry's public image. To the extent that the West Coast Office accurately gauged Protestant opinion, it served the interests of Breen and the producers, who could also use its approval of specific screenplays to defuse Protestant criticism in the event that problems arose. Breen had made Protestant sanction of *One Foot in Heaven* a condition for PCA approval. Concerns that Samuel McCrea Cavert and Louis Evans raised with Paramount about the James H. Street novel *The Gauntlet* apparently had some effect on the studio's decision to shelve the film adaptation. WCO members began to assume their status with Breen's office was more or less on par with their Catholic counterpart. At most, however, they were there merely "to protect the characters of the ministers," Geoffrey Shurlock, who would soon replace Breen as head of the PCA, said.[29] Final judgment on whether a film was in violation of the Code remained with Breen—with significant input from Legion officials. The West Coast Office staff would soon test the boundaries of its authority within the Federal Council and with the PCA.

Woman of the Rock

Herman J. Mankiewicz's crowning achievement was the script for the landmark *Citizen Kane* (1941). His health and financial fortunes both in decline, the screenwriter pinned his hopes for a career revival on a script based on a 1949 novel by Hector Chevigny, *Woman of the Rock*. Hollywood columnist Hedda Hopper called it "one of the hottest scripts of the year."

Top stars, studios, and directors wanted it. Though "thinly disguised," the script was recognizably based on the life of the late Aimee Semple McPherson, a colorful evangelist and founder of the Church of the Foursquare Gospel. The theatricality of McPherson's worship services generated controversy and headlines, as did her business and personal ethics. She once disappeared for five weeks and claimed to have been abducted; it was widely reported that she was in Mexico with a married man.

That the Mankiewicz scenario portrayed religion as a "racket" and "cast ridicule" on evangelistic activities was enough reason for Breen's staff to judge it in violation of the Code. A further complication was that the close resemblance to McPherson presented the possibility of public protests and lawsuits. With Mankiewicz's permission, the PCA sent copies of the scenario to the PFC's Hollywood office. Oren Evans returned a scathing evaluation; the story was "damaging to Protestantism in general" and "very offensive to thousands of Protestant people." He found it "unthinkable that with all the content of Protestant religion a script should have to go to the morgue of unestablished rumour of the most insidious kind and portray this as typical of contemporary religion." Mankiewicz "disagreed very violently" with the assessment. Nonetheless, Breen let him know that Evans's "opinion and advice" would be taken into account, since it was the duty of his office to see that the films it passed would not "cause any financial loss to its backers, nor bring ill-will or bad public relations to the motion picture industry in general." Chevigny countered that McPherson's followers should not be considered "a true Protestant denomination," and no one had accused his book of ridiculing religion. "This kind of censorship is against the very spirit of Protestantism," he insisted. In a desperate move, Mankiewciz sent the script to the McPherson family; the initiative backfired when they protested the production and threatened to sue for libel and invasion of privacy.[30]

In July 1950, PCA staff met with Oren Evans and Paul Heard, hoping to find an acceptable solution to their objections. They were aware that Mankiewicz was being hurt financially by the delays and was losing commitments from actors, directors, and other personalities important to the marketability of the project. Heard wanted to find a way forward, but Evans resisted suggestions for ways "the story might be salvaged." At the meeting, it was revealed that Evans's father had been offered the job as preacher at McPherson's church after her death; Breen thought this predisposed him against this story. Bent on protecting the Protestant image, Evans remained unyielding and unwilling to negotiate. Afterward, Breen sought advice from the MPAA's Francis Harmon, who thought the story was acceptable and got assurances from Protestant authorities in New York to that effect. Mankiewicz agreed to Harmon's editorial suggestions "without the batting of an eyelash," and rewrote several pages to address specific objections that Evans and Heard had raised by enforcing the main character's "faith in her mission." Breen hoped this might persuade Evans to change his mind, but regardless, they would go ahead and approve the script. Harmon was confident that even if the PFC tried to "make some trouble for us if this picture is actually produced . . . this is nothing too much to worry about."[31]

Harmon sent the screenplay and correspondence to the Federal Council's Roswell Barnes, who concluded that Heard and Evans in "their judgment and sense of strategy" were in error. He did not think the screenplay ridiculed or depicted the woman preacher "as a hypocrite or a dangerous influence," but showed her to be "naïve and inexperienced," traits that her manager had exploited. More importantly, Barnes asserted that efforts "to prevent the production of such a film comes very close to censorship of legitimate interpretation," a "very unsound strategy for any representative Protestant group." He was making no "official repudiation" of Evans and Heard, but expressed uncertainty over whether the PFC could "claim broad authorization and authority to represent the point of view of Protestantism, at least to the point of censorship."[32] As this exchange indicates, the West Coast Office was operating largely independent of the Federal Council's New York headquarters, and apparently with a different set of assumptions. There were deep differences over the role that the Council's Hollywood operation should play that would be accentuated in years to come.

After six months of negotiations, Breen informed Mankiewicz in August 1950 that his revised script was acceptable under the provisions of the Code. Despite this lengthy ordeal, "Woman of the Rock" never made it into production; Mankiewicz was deeply disappointed. The threat of a lawsuit and the potential backlash from the religious community was enough to scare off studio executives. Three years later, an independent producer inquired about rumors that the PCA had rejected the Mankiewicz script and asked if it was available for purchase. Shurlock replied that it had run "afoul" of the Code and that this producer's project would likely suffer the same fate. "Incidentally, there is quite a file on the Mankiewicz script dating back to 1950," Shurlock wrote. "If you would like to look through it we would be glad to show it to you, should you care to drop by the office."[33]

Wilbur F. Crafts formed the International Reform Bureau in 1895 and campaigned tirelessly against immoral movies, Sunday baseball, and automobile rides that could result in "lifelong shame and woe." Library of Congress, Prints & Photographs Division, LC-DIG-ggbain-03809.

Time dubbed William Sheafe Chase, canon of the Episcopal Church, "the ex officio No. 1 U.S. reformer" because of his lifetime crusade against vice. Chase (center, with attorney Bernard H. Sandler and Immigration Commissioner W. W. Husband, 1924) lobbied for federal oversight of the film producers. Library of Congress, Prints & Photographs Division, LC-DIG-npcc-25997.

Protestant Lee F. Hanmer directed the recreation department of the Russell Sage Foundation and helped found the Boy Scouts of America. He conducted a study on the movies for the Federal Council of Churches and was a top leader in the film industry's Committee on Public Relations in 1922. Courtesy of Stephen Read Hanmer, Jr.

Protestant leaders had high expectations of Will H. Hays, President of the Motion Picture Producers and Distributors of America. A prominent Presbyterian layman, Hays linked Hollywood and the Protestant establishment. Indiana State Library.

A former governor of Maine and past president of the Northern Baptist Convention, Carl E. Milliken served in the Federal Council of Churches while heading the Public Relations Department of the Motion Picture Producers and Distributors of America. Image courtesy Maine State Archives.

Charles S. Macfarland, a chief executive in the Federal Council of Churches (1912-1930), was pivotal in the Council's relations with Will Hays and the movie producers. Library of Congress, Prints & Photographs Division, photograph by Harris & Ewing, LC-DIG-hec-21192.

A longtime executive in the Federal Council of Churches, Samuel McCrea Cavert played a strategic role in Protestant initiatives with the film industry for three decades. Courtesy of the National Council of Churches.

Social activist Catheryne Cooke Gilman helped found the Women's Cooperative Alliance of Minneapolis, a local movement that advocated community selection to improve the movies. Her lobbying for federal regulation of the film industry's trade practices created difficulties for the Hays organization in relating to churches and women's groups. Minnesota Historical Society.

George Reid Andrews was the Protestant consultant on Cecil B. DeMille's *The King of Kings* (1927). Andrews dreamed his Church and Drama Association would form a creative and lasting alliance between the church and film industry. Southern Historical Collection, Wilson Library, The University of North Carolina at Chapel Hill.

The crucifixion scene in Cecil B. DeMille's *The King of Kings* (1927), which was the first in a line of movies on the life of Jesus that would serve as flashpoints among religious groups. Southern Historical Collection, Wilson Library, The University of North Carolina at Chapel Hill.

A Baptist layman and YMCA executive, Francis S. Harmon was active in the Federal Council of Churches before working for the motion picture industry. Kautz Family YMCA Archives. University of Minnesota Libraries.

In an effort to "support the best and ignore the rest," women's organizations reviewed movies and awarded outstanding ones. Director Cecil B. DeMille meets with Mrs. W. Murdoch MacLeod, a Los Angeles representative of the Church-women Council, and United Council of Church Women officers, Mrs. Harper Sibley (Rochester), and Mrs. Jesse Bader (New York) in 1949. Courtesy of the Cecil B. DeMille Archives, L. Tom Perry Special Collections, Brigham Young University.

In 1954, Geoffrey Shurlock (left), an Episcopalian, replaced the retired Joseph Breen, a Catholic, as head of the Production Code Administration. Courtesy of the Academy of Motion Picture Arts and Sciences.

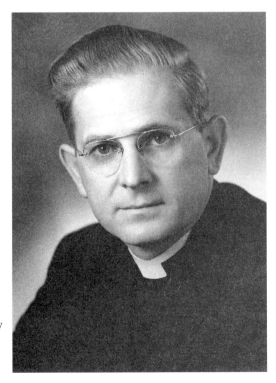

Carl Segerhammar was President of the Lutheran Church in America, Pacific Southwest Synod, and an active member of the National Council of Churches' West Coast Office Committee. Courtesy of the Archives of the Evangelical Lutheran Church of America.

Director Richard Brooks works with actors Burt Lancaster and Shirley Jones on the set of *Elmer Gantry* (1960). The movie's depiction of a Protestant evangelist as an opportunistic charlatan provoked controversy in Protestant circles. Courtesy of the Academy of Motion Picture Arts and Sciences

The depiction of itinerant preacher Harry Powell (Robert Mitchum) as a cold-blooded killer in *The Night of the Hunter* (1955) irked clergy who charged that Hollywood would never show such an offensive portrayal of a priest. Courtesy of the Academy of Motion Picture Arts and Sciences

Some Protestant leaders were outraged when Warner Bros. inserted a love triangle in the film adaptation, *The Sins of Rachel Cade* (1961). Angie Dickinson plays a Protestant missionary nurse who falls for a dashing surgeon and becomes pregnant. Peter Finch plays Henri Derode, the Belgian administrator of the village they serve in the Belgian Congo during World War II. Courtesy of Warner Bros. Pictures/Photofest.

Director George Stevens on the set of *The Greatest Story Ever Told* (1965), which was a critical and commercial disaster that brought an end to the era of biblical spectacles. Conflict erupted when this extravaganza on the life of Jesus was passed over by the Protestant Film Awards. Courtesy of the Academy of Motion Picture Arts and Sciences.

The Pawnbroker (1965), a gritty film about a Jewish Holocaust survivor, was hailed by Protestant critics even though it sparked controversy over the inclusion of nudity in a scene with pawnbroker Sol Nazerman (Rod Steiger) and a prostitute (Thelma Oliver). Courtesy of the Academy of Motion Picture Arts and Sciences.

Members of the National Council of Churches' West Coast Office Committee, Fred Essex, Hubert K. Rasbach, and Clifton Moore consult with Frank Ross, producer of *The Norman Vincent Peale Story*. The movie was based on the life of the inspirational pastor of the Marble Collegiate Church in New York City and author of *The Power of Positive Thinking*. Courtesy of Pastor Mark Rasbach, Hope Lutheran Church, Hollywood.

Executive Directors of the National Council of Churches' Broadcasting and Film Commission, S. Franklin Mack (1954-1963) and William F. Fore (1964-1989), with Harry C. Spencer who was Executive Director of the United Methodist Communications and chair of the Broadcasting and Film Commission (1962-1965). Courtesy of the Presbyterian Historical Society, Presbyterian Church (U.S.A.), Philadelphia, PA.

William Fore, Executive Director of the Broadcasting and Film Commission, and George Heimrich, Director of the BFC's West Coast Office (seated left to right), with others involved in the National Council of Churches' film industry initiatives. Standing (left to right) are Fred Essex (West Coast Office Committee), Robert E. Lee (playwright, *Inherit the Wind*), Arthur Knight (*Saturday Review* film critic), David O. Poindexter (BFC Staff). Courtesy of the Presbyterian Historical Society, Presbyterian Church (U.S.A.), Philadelphia, PA.

F. Thomas Trotter, chair of the National Council of Churches' Film Awards Nomination Panel, presents "Star Crystal Awards" at a luncheon in Hollywood in 1966. Left to right are master of ceremonies Robert E. Lee (BFC member and playwright), Roger Lewis (*The Pawnbroker*), Harry Skolov (*The Sound of Music*), Sydney Glazier (*The Eleanor Roosevelt Story*), Pandro S. Berman (*A Patch of Blue*), actor Ivan Dixon (*Nothing But a Man*), and Trotter. Otto Rothschild Photographic Archive, Department of Special Collections, Charles E. Young Research Library, UCLA and the Presbyterian Historical Society, Presbyterian Church (U.S.A.), Philadelphia, PA.

Recipients of the Protestant Film Awards in 1965 (left to right): Aaron Rosenberg (*Fate Is The Hunter*), John Bachman (National Council of Churches), Max Youngstein (*Fail Safe*), Bishop Kennedy (West Coast Office Committee), George Heimrich (West Coast Office director), Ed Anhalt (*Becket*), and H. K. Rasbach (West Coast Office Committee). Otto Rothschild Photographic Archive, Department of Special Collections, Charles E. Young Research Library, UCLA and the Presbyterian Historical Society, Presbyterian Church (U.S.A.), Philadelphia, PA.

Christian Century editor James M. Wall played a key role in the National Council of Churches' Film Awards Nomination Panel and in Council negotiations with film industry representatives during the launching of the rating system. Courtesy of James M. Wall and the Chicago *Tribune*; copyright Chicago *Tribune*; all rights reserved.

Rev. Patrick J. Sullivan, S.J.
Director
National Catholic Office

Rev. William
Dire
Commis

Christian Century editor James M. Wall, Patrick J. Sullivan (National Catholic Office for Motion Pictures), and William F. Fore (National Council of Churches) addressing the annual meeting of the National Association of Theatre Owners in November 1968 on the theme "Bridge to the Church." Courtesy of James M. Wall.

Jack Valenti, president of the Motion Picture Association of America, recognized the importance of the Protestant and Catholic film agencies in establishing film classification in 1968. "Without their support," he said, "the rating system would never have gotten off the ground." Courtesy of the Academy of Motion Picture Arts and Sciences.

8

Movie Consulting—Protestant Style

We don't want to curb artistry in movies by legislative censorship. Any type of censorship is obnoxious to us. We much prefer the regulation of self-choice. It is this human choice, after all, that is the basis of our religion.

s. FRANKLIN MACK, director, National Council of Churches Broadcasting and Film Commission

THE PARAMOUNT DECREES brought an end to block booking while also allowing exhibitors to lease films without Production Code approval. The result was not exactly what Protestant reformers had hoped for. Movies considered controversial by the Code's standards were finding screen time in American theaters. With the post–World War II emphasis on individual liberties, there was growing public opposition to film censorship and boycotts. Some Protestant and Catholic critics found these trends disconcerting, while others hailed them as expressions of the cinema's new freedom. This gulf widened both within and between the two religious communities along the lines of the pietist and structural impulses as challenges to the Code mounted and the authority of the Production Code Administration (PCA) waned. Facing a confluence of events that were bringing momentous change to the film industry, the Protestant establishment would have to envision new strategies appropriate for the church's role in postwar Hollywood.

In the winter of 1951, Protestant and Catholic groups were on opposing sides, picketing outside New York's Paris Theatre where a short film, *The Miracle*, by renowned Italian director Roberto Rossellini, was playing. In the story, a simpleminded peasant girl is seduced by a bearded stranger, whom she takes to be St. Joseph, and she begins to believe that she is pregnant with the Christ child. After being ridiculed and cast out by the town's religious folks, she gives birth to a son in a deserted church. On top of the film's controversial content, Rossellini's highly publicized affair with actress Ingrid Bergman irked religious leaders and sparked threats of government inquiry into the conduct of the film industry and federal licensing of movies.

The Legion of Decency condemned the film as blasphemous, and New York Cardinal Francis Spellman urged Catholics not to patronize theaters showing it. Protestant clergy countered that no single group had the right to impose its views on the general public and called Catholic efforts to suppress the film an infringement on democratic freedom. Catholic leaders themselves were divided over the film's merit, how to interpret it, and especially the church's official denouncement, which a critic in the liberal Catholic journal *Commonweal* likened to "a semi-ecclesiastical McCarthyism." Another Catholic writer thought the "whoopdedoo" only confirmed the perception of Catholics as not valuing civil and religious liberties.[1]

In May 1952, the Supreme Court struck down a New York State ban on *The Miracle*, declaring that sacrilege was not constitutional grounds for censorship. The decision overturned almost 40 years of precedent, going back to the *Mutual* case in 1915, with the court ruling now that movies were "a significant medium for the communication of ideas" entitled to First Amendment protection.[2] Subsequent decisions clarified the court's position and guaranteed movies the right to advocate ideas, even those considered immoral or unacceptable, eventually leaving only obscenity as grounds for censorship. The breakup of the studio system and the status of movies as protected speech set a new course for the American cinema by undermining prior censorship and with it, church monitoring of movie content. How would Protestant and Catholic leaders respond to this paradigm shift?

The West Coast Office Perspective

In December 1950, the Federal Council became the National Council of the Churches of Christ in the USA. The National Council represented more than half of the Protestant churches in the United States, 29 Protestant and Orthodox denominations, and 12 interdenominational agencies. The Protestant Film and Radio commissions were reorganized and merged into a new Broadcasting and Film Commission (BFC). Facilitating production of films, radio, and now television programs remained its lead objective. They continued to consult (when asked) with producers on religious issues with the same stipulation that the BFC was not "to represent itself or act as a Protestant censor."[3]

When Oren Evans died of a sudden heart attack in 1954, George Heimrich filled in and became director of the BFC's West Coast Office (WCO). Around the same time, S. Franklin Mack took over as the BFC's Executive Director. That same year, Will Hays died and Breen retired, replaced by his longtime chief assistant, Geoffrey Shurlock, a British-born Episcopalian who had an entirely different attitude about industry regulation. After a stint as a screenwriter/editor at Paramount, Shurlock joined the staff of the Studio Relations Committee, the PCA's precursor, in 1932. He took over for Breen amidst swirling charges that the Code was antiquated and a modernized revision long overdue. He was convinced that the industry should join other Western nations and adopt an age classification system, but as long as movies were made for an audience of all ages, producers had a duty to adhere to the Code. Shurlock may have had something to do with Heimrich's appointment, which was an odd one considering Heimrich had earlier threatened the National Council with a lawsuit, claiming that its Department of Evangelism had stolen his ideas for religious advertising.[4]

Heimrich, who came from a background in radio, was a colorful character, always well-dressed and manicured, very friendly, and yet could bluster and be overbearing. He saw himself as a counterpart to Catholic advisers, charged with ensuring that Protestants received the same flattering treatment in movies as priests and nuns.[5] Heimrich was not against free expression, but believed that producers with the right beliefs would make moral movies. Otherwise, a filmmaker's freedom had to be restrained by the Production Code, which he believed was an application of the Ten Commandments. This mind-set, which was compatible with the Catholic view, was the dominant one in the West Coast Office. Its focus was on movies by and for the religiously devout, based on a simple formula for industry reform: a steady slate of uplifting films would prove box-office gold for producers, foster right beliefs and values among Americans, enhance the nation's reputation abroad (aiding the work of foreign missionaries), and even promote the work of the church. This perspective epitomized the pietist approach. However, aside from the biblical spectacles, which were theologically contentious, such films were usually mediocre: neither critically acclaimed nor huge commercial hits. In other words, there might have been an occasional spark, but not enough to make a fire.

Take the screen adaptation of *A Man Called Peter*, Catherine Marshall's biography of her late husband, who served as chaplain of the U.S. Senate. Twentieth Century-Fox's production chief Darryl F. Zanuck, who complained that he was "over-supplied—and *fed up*—with stories about preachers," green-lighted the project anyway, but not because of any sectarian appeal. The best-selling novel was pitched as an American "rags-to-riches" story with romance and "a deep, fundamental *religious* basis without any cant or stuffiness." The film, which contains some 20 minutes of sermons and was voted Picture of the Year by readers of the *Christian Herald*, was produced by Sam Engel. Henry Koster, whose credits included *The Robe* (1953) and an Oscar nomination for *The Bishop's Wife* (1947), directed. Heimrich credited an extensive church marketing campaign with stimulating the turnout for this and similar movies. He reported that a number of studios were planning "at least one big religious production" and were turning to the West Coast Office for more "material in this vein."[6]

With about $4.8 million in earnings, *A Man Called Peter* finished among Fox's top pictures in 1955, behind Marilyn Monroe's *The Seven Year Itch*, and in the company of *The Tall Men* (a western starring Clark Gable and Jane Russell) and *Love Is a Many Splendored Thing* (a romance with William Holden and Jennifer Jones). The box-office champ that year was Disney's *Lady and the Tramp*, which topped $40 million in domestic box office. In short, there was a modest audience for quality church-oriented films, but no more than for westerns, dramas, or other established genres.

Members of the WCO Script Evaluation Committee spent most of their time providing producers with information on technical minutiae: proper dress, procedures, ceremonies, terminology, biblical quotations, church settings, and so forth. For example, several inaccuracies in the biblical drama *Sins of Jezebel* (1953) were pointed out: Jezebel was not thrown to the ground by Jehu, but by eunuchs, and there was no record of a love affair between Jehu and Jezebel. To improve the depiction of a Presbyterian minister in *Gown of Glory* (1954), based on a novel by Agnes Sligh Turnball about a small-town Pennsylvania minister and his family, it was suggested that incidents be included showing "the joy and comradeship of Christian endeavor prevalent between a minister and his congregation." Such advice was helpful, and producers were appreciative, but it hardly mattered to them whether the purpose of marriage as propagation of the family was theologically tenable in *The Remarkable Mr. Pennypacker* (1959), or if a Protestant character conformed "to the prevailing concept of sin as a violation of the social code." Nor could it be shown that addressing these matters had any appreciable influence with Protestant moviegoers. Nevertheless, Heimrich believed that script evaluation was "a vital area of work" and, under his supervision, screenplays were filtered to ensure a correct and positive depiction of Protestantism in the hope that these films might be used by the Holy Spirit to evangelize and foster Christian living.[7]

Protestants had nowhere near as much clout as Catholic advisers. The PCA staff and producers went to great lengths to appease Catholics, radically revising the story in *The Keys of the Kingdom* (1944), for example, a film about a young priest sent to China to set up a Catholic parish, and even assigning a staff person to go on location and monitor directors in their handling of nuns in *Heaven Knows Mr. Allison* (1957) and *The Nun's Story* (1959). By contrast, Oren Evans received one copy of the script for United Artists's *High Noon* (1952), and not until rehearsals were already underway. The film starred Gary Cooper as a marshal left by the townspeople to confront murderous villains. Evans thought the movie was likely to convey "a complete moral failure of a church and church people in a community," which he found entirely unsatisfactory, as the overall impression it gave of Christians was one "of moral lassitude and indifference, in fact, even cowardice." But the failings of the community were central to the film. In retrospect, Shurlock's assistant Albert Van Schmus said pointedly, "I don't think we would've supported them in their feelings on that." In fact, no changes were made. WCO members would complain about receiving scripts at the last moment—just prior to or even after shooting had begun—without sufficient time for careful review. And it was understood that producers were under no obligation to accept their recommendations.[8] That would soon enough be made all too clear to Heimrich and his colleagues.

Stepping Out into the Night of the Hunter

Geoffrey Shurlock and Van Schmus met with independent producers in July 1954 to discuss a screen adaptation of the novel *The Night of the Hunter*. The villain, Harry Powell, is a phony, twisted, itinerant preacher and cold-blooded killer with the words LOVE and HATE tattooed on his fingers. At the story's climax, the religiously devout Rachel Cooper stands guard at night, rocking in a chair with a shotgun across her lap. Outside the house, Powell sings "Leaning on the Everlasting Arms," with Rachel joining in harmony on the familiar hymn. In the end, good triumphs over evil, showing that "God's glory was really in the little old farm woman, and not in the Bible totin' sonofabitch," as producer Paul Gregory put it. The script was revised to address PCA concerns about the depiction of Powell but, wanting to be sure there was nothing to offend Protestants, Breen held off on final approval until it cleared the West Coast Office. "There would be no rules that we *had* to get this Protestant approval for the making of *The Night of the Hunter*. We would *never* do that," Van Schmus explained. "But in order to placate the people, and possibly forestall any organized protests after the picture was made and released, we would try to get some cooperation, if *possible*, to calm the criticism down."[9]

Shooting had already begun. The WCO review committee—quite upset about being brought into the process so late—returned a detailed four-page critique. Heimrich suggested two solutions to the main problem, both requiring significant revisions: either eliminate altogether any scenes and dialogue suggesting that Powell was a minister, or write in a legitimate pastor, "a true man of God," to contrast with the evil and fake preacher. BFC director S. Franklin Mack also could see little value in a film with a "pseudo-evangelist scaring the daylights out of a couple of kids." He let Shurlock know that it would generate "a lot of negative reaction" and put pressure on the National Council to take a harder line on Hollywood. Shurlock thought Mack was overreacting and that the film was "nothing more than a melodrama" that for some people "might be in questionable taste." At a conference in late August with Heimrich and PCA staff, Gregory agreed to make some revisions and include dialogue making it clear that the preacher was not a minister, even having Powell admit it himself. Heimrich was not satisfied; even if Powell was not technically shown to be a minister, the audience was left with the impression that he was. The PCA broke the deadlock. Despite Heimrich's judgment that the film would "do great harm to the Protestant religion," it met the technical requirements of the Code, and that was that.[10]

The Night of the Hunter (1955) opened to lackluster reviews. Many critics were unsure how to categorize it—children's fairy tale, allegory, horror, or religious melodrama—and, unable to decide if it was artful or pretentious, concluded that it failed "honorably." It was a complete flop at the box office.[11]

Heimrich reported that his "firm stand for Protestantism" brought "greater respect and cooperation from the industry," but *The Night of the Hunter* was still produced over his vociferous objections. To strengthen his position, he formed a new West Coast Office Committee, made up of denominational leaders in the Los Angeles area and chaired by Gerald H. Kennedy, a highly influential bishop who presided over the Southern

California–Arizona Conference of the Methodist Church. The heightened prestige was supposed to enhance the committee's authority and the value of its imprimatur. The WCO Committee met officially for the first time in October 1955 and drew up a report outlining its functions. More emphasis was given to script evaluation than in earlier BFC documents and, significantly, the committee intended to compose "an acceptable production code for motion pictures" and to study the need for one in television and radio. A Protestant production code? The Broadcasting and Film Commission's Board of Managers revised the agenda item to read: "To write an acceptable script evaluation procedure for motion pictures."[12] It was a sign of discord within the BFC. The West Coast Office would soon step out on its own.

The number of scripts that the WCO received was declining, and, as Heimrich observed, a higher percentage of them were controversial and were coming from independent producers who tended to take "greater liberties" with their subject matter.[13] Hollywood was actually in transition. The end of the studio system opened the market for independent and foreign films, but the results were not entirely what anti-block-booking advocates had anticipated. With no financial incentive to maintain a steady output for their theaters, the major studios drastically cut production and focused on a few high-budget movies each year. By the end of the 1950s, 65 percent of the movies distributed by Hollywood studios were independently produced. Furthermore, expectations that in a free market the family audience would drive a demand for wholesome movies were frustrated by postwar realities. Suburbanization, the baby boom, and the advent of television revolutionized leisure and entertainment. The general family audience was content to stay at home and watch TV westerns, situation comedies, and detective and variety shows. Movie attendance peaked in the immediate postwar years, but then began to plummet; weekly admissions were cut in half by the mid-1950s and leveled off in the early 1960s. With television the main supplier of family entertainment, Hollywood had to offer something different. Studios tried new technologies, such as color, and widescreen effects like Cinemascope. But the audience of frequent moviegoers was becoming younger and more educated. Faced with stiff competition from television and foreign films—from *The Bicycle Thief* and *La Ronde* to *And God Created Woman* (featuring a sexy Brigitte Bardot) and *La Dolce Vita*—and others not bound by the Code's strictures, some producers began diversifying their product to appeal to young adults harboring more permissive attitudes toward sex and violence.

The Moon Is Blue (1953), a comedy about seduction, *The French Line* (1953), featuring a voluptuous Jane Russell in 3-D, and *The Man with the Golden Arm* (1955), about drug addiction, were all released without Code approval, condemned by the Legion of Decency, and still fared well enough at the box office to rattle the authority of the two monitoring agencies. When the PCA approved *Baby Doll* (1956), which *Time* called "the dirtiest American-made motion picture that has ever been legally exhibited," the Legion condemned it as "an obvious violation" of the Code. New York Cardinal Francis Spellman denounced the film and its advertising as "a contemptuous defiance of the natural law" and warned parishioners not to see it "under pain of sin." In direct response to Spellman and the Legion, Dean James A. Pike, of the Protestant Episcopal Church of St. John the Divine in New York, stated that churches "should not condemn portrayals of real life." Contra Canon William Sheafe Chase, here was a New York Episcopalian speaking out in favor of movie freedom. A *Christian Century* critic understood the moral objections; it was, after all, a finely crafted film in "service of so unpromising a story of what human life is all about." But the film "*registers* not as a pornographic exhibit," as he interpreted it, "but as a comic grotesque—and between the two, I should imagine, there is for any civilized intelligence a world of difference."[14]

At the end of 1956, under strain and criticism, the Code underwent its first major revision since its adoption in 1930. "The first big barrier to the slow reduction of the industry's own self-censorship has been surmounted," *New York Times* critic Bosley Crowther remarked. "That was the reluctance to change."[15]

Heimrich found the direction in which the film industry was heading to be troubling. Protestants were "definitely getting a fair shake" in comparison with Catholic representation in movies—the direct result of the WCO's presence in Hollywood, he maintained, and apparently his top priority. All the same, Heimrich began voicing concerns about a general decline in the moral quality of movies, a growing disregard for the PCA, and the "trash" being imported from Europe under the guise of film "art." His belief that moviemakers would not properly regulate themselves—as the increase in serious movies aimed at adults showed—hardened his resolve to bolster the authority of the West Coast Office and shore up the ailing Code. "We are not censors, nor do we desire to be," he insisted, while also expressing doubts about the viability of BFC policy. The "purely advisory nature" of his consulting work tied his hands; he sometimes had to request scripts for review. And regardless of the outcome, the WCO could not sanction the finished film—or for that matter, even guarantee there would be no criticism. The prohibition on endorsements was a BFC guideline that Heimrich regarded now as "a problem we are going to have to face."[16]

Based on their experience advising producers and facilitating clergy previews, Heimrich and his WCO colleagues understood that the linchpin in script negotiations was increased market access. The only way to reform Hollywood was to work within the existing system by consulting with producers and then promoting favored movies to churchgoers. In practice, however, this could easily become a manner of boycotting those of which they disapproved. But Heimrich thought there were "grey areas involved" with censorship, like classification, and he did not believe that the Catholic Church, even with its "pressure organization," was "for censorship." In February 1959 Heimrich tried to persuade the BFC Board of Managers that the National Council should "get behind" approved films by urging attendance at ministerial previews and cooperating with distributors in premiere showings. Moreover, he recommended placing the Council's review agency, the Protestant Motion Picture Council, under the auspices of his office.[17] The clear intent was to gain leverage with producers by linking pre-release consulting with delivering Protestant-Orthodox moviegoers at the box office, in effect mimicking the Catholic setup. That was precisely what the National Council had taken pains to avoid. Heimrich had operated with a good deal of autonomy, but the BFC board was becoming uneasy now with its West Coast operation. WCO Committee members were just as frustrated by what they took to be a lack of support from the New York office.

A Tale of Three Movies

As soon as word got out that writer and director Richard Brooks was working on a film adaptation of the Sinclair Lewis novel *Elmer Gantry*, about an opportunistic charlatan who becomes an evangelist, controversy erupted. Protestants registered their concerns about yet another movie that they were sure would be a caricature of their religion. Having received inquiries about the film, Heimrich asked Shurlock to send him a copy of the script in May 1959. Though he was aware of a "ground-swell of opposition," Shurlock could only keep him at bay; it was up to the producer to release a script to a third party. The BFC's S. Franklin Mack also requested a copy from Burt Lancaster, who had been cast in the lead role. When producer

Bernard Smith said he would send it, Mack asked that he not wait until it was beyond the point where changes could be made. "There have been occasions," he noted, "when our service to the studios has been of minimal value because a script was so close to production that even changes felt to be desirable could not very well be made." In August, the PCA approved the screenplay, with Smith assuring Shurlock that "in due time" he would send it to Heimrich or Mack.[18]

The West Coast Office, meanwhile, was having a tough time negotiating with Warner Bros. over a screen adaptation of the 1956 novel *Rachel Cade*, written by Charles Mercer, the son of a Baptist minister who had served in Army Intelligence during World War II. Mercer's novel centers thematically on the mysteries of God's creation, pitting Christian belief against superstition. A strong and dedicated American missionary nurse, Rachel Cade's success and travails working in the Belgian Congo during World War II deepen her understanding of self, faith, and love. The film adaptation engages the same theme, but focuses on a love triangle that is not in the book. Rachel (Angie Dickinson) falls for Paul Wilton (Roger Moore), a handsome American surgeon serving as an RAF volunteer. Wilton's plane crashes in the area and Rachel nurses him back to health. After he is called back to duty, a pregnant Rachel seeks help and support from the village administrator, the middle-aged Colonel Henri Derode (Peter Finch), whom she had earlier rejected; she now realizes that she is in love with him. When Wilton learns about his child—via telegram from Derode—he returns. When she discovers that Wilton does not love her after all, Rachel decides to stay and continue her work with the Dibela villagers, and presumably await the return of Derode from active duty.

The screenplay contained some theological errors that were corrected easily enough, but, more important, Heimrich found the script "to a great extent most offensive and degrading," especially "from the standpoint of the over-emphasis on sex." He cited a number of sexual innuendos he considered inappropriate. "Do you think the Colonel will get this Madami to lie with him?" Kulu asks Musinga, who replies, "I don't know. There is a certain stiffness to her walk." Another villager wonders, "What do you suppose a woman with a behind like that is doing in Africa in the first place?" These were, however, minor problems (the lines were dropped) that pointed to a much larger concern.

Had the screenplay adhered more closely to the novel, West Coast Office evaluators actually thought it would make "a very interesting motion picture," but they found that it "twisted and distorted" Mercer's story in two crucial ways. First, the script accentuated the sexual aspect of the story, even introducing the Rachel Cade character as "a spinster missionary in Africa. Her struggle between God's work and her ample sexuality—and its ultimate resolution—is the essential subject of the film." Second, the producers eliminated the character of Caleb Aldrich, a Protestant minister whom Rachel eventually marries—events that occupy the last third of the novel. Heimrich had two meetings that summer with producer Henry Blanke and screenwriter Edward Anhalt, but failed to persuade them that Aldrich, "a strong, forceful person, one with Christian convictions, and a man of integrity, should not be left out of your screenplay."

Heimrich's overriding concern was that the film would discredit the Protestant religion. Along with the offensive depiction of Cade, Heimrich underscored a line of dialogue ("I have seen your people come and go— I've seen you treat the syphilis the men who support your churches brought here two generations ago") as "a vicious attack on the Protestant church, as well as other churches." (As PCA staff suggested, the producers replaced "the men who support your churches" with "the white man.") Missionary work, Heimrich maintained, was "the greatest bulwark against Communism," and he believed, "This screenplay is grist for the Communist mill, as it casts aspersions on those who have dedicated their lives to the service of God in the mission fields." There was another issue as well, and Heimrich put the question directly to Blanke: "What would the Catholic reaction be, Henry, if this screenplay in its present form were to portray a Catholic nun as the medical missionary, and Warner Bros. presented the screenplay to the Catholics for their evaluation?"[19] The pointed reference was undoubtedly to *The Nun's Story*, which Blanke had also produced for Warner Bros. and which was playing successfully in theaters that summer. The two movies are much the same in terms of subject and setting; British actor Peter Finch even plays practically the same role in each.

The Nun's Story follows the spiritual journey of Gabrielle Van Der Mal (Sister Luke) as she becomes a nun and labors as a surgical nurse in a missionary hospital in the Congo and in Belgium after the outbreak of World War II. The film is based on the contentious best-selling novel by Kathryn Hulme, which depicts the utter devotion and self-abnegation of religious life as grim and austere. The spiritual ordeal of the heroine, Sister Luke, proves exhausting, and she eventually renounces her vows. The PCA went to great lengths to ensure that the movie would not offend the Catholic Church, even sending a staffer on location during shooting—an unusual move. Although the film did not escape the novel's controversy, major Catholic critics generally agreed with the Legion of Decency that Warner Bros. had made a movie that was "noble, sensitive, reverent and inspiring."[20] Heimrich expected the same treatment.

Uproar over Sex and Violence

Being snubbed by the producers of *Elmer Gantry* and having their counsel largely disregarded by Warner Bros. put the WCO Committee over the edge. It was time to take action to "ameliorate a rapidly deteriorating relationship" with the PCA. Disregarding BFC policy, Heimrich issued a statement blasting the film industry for an "overemphasis on sex and violence" in blatant disregard of the Code, and hinting at a possible Protestant boycott. *Variety* noted that if "sanctioned" by the National Council, a "moratorium on film attendance" could conceivably influence between 30 and 60 million Protestants and pointed out the disparity: "This marks the first time an official Protestant organization—historically opposed to the banning of films—has gone on record regarding the motion picture industry as a whole."[21] To be clear, Heimrich was not denouncing depictions of sex and violence considered essential to story or character, but only the opportunistic use of these features to boost a film's box-office appeal. Nevertheless, that an agent of the National Council was planning to marshal the forces of Protestantism to boycott movies, save the Catholic-authored Production Code, and shore up prior censorship of motion pictures was unthinkable. But with the full confidence of his committee, Heimrich headed for New York to make his case.

At a New York press conference on August 26, 1959, Heimrich said it was obvious that "either the Code has broken down or it is not being applied. In any event, the Code seems to be running wild." That PCA officials were financially dependent upon the film industry put enormous pressure on them. Heimrich wanted the West Coast Office to be the PCA's strong right arm. Mack "rather soft-pedaled" Heimrich's remarks and, by making it clear that the BFC had no intention of banning offensive films, gave the first public indication of internal division.[22]

The next day, the MPAA released a routine statement with no reference to Heimrich, although it was an obvious rejoinder. The MPAA had good reason to take Heimrich's attack seriously. His criticism was not limited to select films, but was a sweeping condemnation of the industry, including the PCA. And he was consulting with Protestant leaders who opposed banning films as a matter of principle. These were all possible indications that Hollywood had indeed gone too far.[23]

MPAA President Eric Johnston wrote to BFC executive Robert W. Spike, asking him to comment on Heimrich's "blanket charges." Heimrich's condemnation of the film industry "is very far removed from the present thinking of this commission," Spike explained. "Boycott and censorship are most reprehensible to traditional Protestant thinking." Spike wanted to present a counter voice, and with Johnston's permission released their letter exchange to the press. The *New York Times* carried excerpts, noting that Heimrich was irked at being ignored by the producers of the forthcoming films *Elmer Gantry* and *Rachel Cade*. *Time* cited Hollywood insiders who alleged that the real issue was not sex and violence, but movies that criticized Protestants. Producers were reportedly frustrated by the inability of Protestant officials "to spell out a clear opinion" and were having second thoughts about working with the West Coast Office.[24]

The trade press had a heyday with the rift. "Protestants Disavow Pix Rap," a *Hollywood Reporter* headline declared. *Variety* indicated that "this publicly-aired disagreement for all practical purposes nullified whatever influence organized Protestantism may have had in Hollywood." *Film Daily* speculated that Heimrich's charge that the PCA was powerless indicated that federal censorship was the only viable recourse. Indeed, Congressional hearings were held that August on whether to censor American films before they were sent abroad, with H. Allen Smith (R-CA) denouncing movies "which portray immorality or wrongdoing as typical of the United States." *Times* reporter Murray Schumach noted the irony that "one of the strongest reasons given here for strengthening the sex factor in American movies is the fact that foreign films imported here are so heavy on sex."[25]

Damage Control

BFC leaders were shocked by Heimrich's statement and stunned by the subsequent turn of events. To gauge the fallout, they met with Shurlock and MPAA executives on September 18. Three studios indicated that they would not change their policy, but Shurlock suspected that others might. Bernard Smith had already rescinded his offer to submit the "Elmer Gantry" script, and Shurlock, who was also stung by Heimrich's criticism, was quite candid in letting Mack know that he personally "was determined not to let George get his hands on it." As a way forward, Shurlock proposed a top-level conference to establish industry contact with the National Council, and not just the West Coast Office. Afterward, Mrs. Theodore O. Wedel

(National Council vice president and chair of the BFC Board of Managers), Roy G. Ross (National Council general secretary), and Mack met with the MPAA's Johnston, Kenneth Clark, and Ralph Hetzel for an informal, off-the-record luncheon to discuss a way forward.[26]

The same day that he met with BFC executives, Shurlock wrote Jack Warner about the "Rachel Cade" screenplay. In August, just days before Heimrich issued his statement, Henry Blanke and screenwriter Edward Anhalt met with PCA staff and agreed to make numerous deletions and revisions and to handle specific scenes with the "utmost delicacy and good taste." Many changes were clearly in response to Heimrich's objections. Shurlock now informed the Warner Bros. studio head, "There is a fear in some quarters that this story of a missionary woman who sins would seem to reflect on the thousands of other self sacrificing missionaries who have expended their lives for others without sinning." He suggested that if some dialogue were inserted in which Rachel acknowledged that her sinful actions tarnished the reputation of "other self sacrificing missionaries," it would lessen the "danger of a film based on this material irritating people." It was likely an attempt to assuage the thorny situation that Heimrich's indictment had created; Shurlock also presumed the producers would continue to "keep in touch" with a Protestant technical advisor.[27]

Blanke sent Heimrich the final script days later, noting that they had made the corrections Shurlock had requested (though they actually had not made them all). Needless to say, Heimrich was still not satisfied (substituting the French term *derrière* for the English "behind" merely made the screenplay "less offensive than it was"). The PCA and Warner Bros. were willing to make some concessions to Protestant advisors, but reworking the story to include the upright Aldrich character was apparently not one of them; the PCA would issue a certificate of approval in November 1959. In Heimrich's view, this treatment was clear evidence of the weakening of the Code's authority and the harmful result. The exclusion of the Protestant minister, he wrote Blanke, "only serves to further prove our recent contention regarding the over-emphasis on sex for sex's sake, which has become such an evil in too many pictures being produced in Hollywood today, and simply plays into the hands of those who wish to see religion discredited."[28]

That the West Coast Office was exceeding its mandate by meddling in production did not please BFC executives. They assessed the situation at their annual October meeting. "We are not interested in censorship or boycott," Rome Betts insisted, and Heimrich's statement to that effect "should not have been made as this is contrary to our policy." Betts, who presided over the first meeting of the Protestant Film Commission in 1946, had hoped the BFC would serve the film industry "in such a way that there never will arise the danger of our resorting to such devices as a legion of decency."[29] After discussion, it was decided to bring Heimrich in closer consultation with BFC leadership and to appoint a committee to review the role and functions of the West Coast Office.

In the meantime, Heimrich was invited to address several church groups across the country. He attributed the misuse of sex and violence, which he deemed socially detrimental and damaging to the U.S. image abroad, to producers who just wanted to make a "fast buck" and who were exploiting unsound Supreme Court decisions that extended constitutional freedoms of the press to movies. To counter this "low and intolerable situation," it was necessary for Protestants to follow the example of the Legion of Decency. After receiving reports on these lectures, MPAA executives decided, "There is no doubt that Heimrich is out to get us."[30]

That October, Heimrich and WCO member Dean Leonidas Contos made their case to the National Council's Study Commission on the Role of Radio, Television and Film in Religion, which was formed in 1957 to assess the changing media situation and to recommend policy. The 34-member Commission included theologians, university professors (former Payne Fund Studies scholar Edgar Dale), denominational leaders, and media executives Herbert Evans (PBS), Spyros Skouras (20th Century-Fox), and Sig Mickelson (CBS News). Heimrich and Contos argued that movies traditionally addressed a family audience and that producers were evading the industry's code in pursuit of quick profits.[31] This line of reasoning had precedent, but little force, now that movies were protected speech and the industry was adapting to television as the provider of regular family entertainment.

Heimrich kept company with a group in Hollywood whose mind-set was rooted in an old paradigm. He was close with Fox producer and president of the Screen Producers Guild, Sam Engel, who believed that the film industry would be "courting disaster" if it was not "policed by some sort of a code." Heimrich thought 20th Century-Fox was "the only major studio holding the line" against the independent production trend. He empathized with veteran producers who were at a loss over what to do about "the present cycle of horror, sex and violence." Even if they believed that these trends were detrimental to the industry, with their livelihood on the line, they were "caught in the trap of having to do an off-beat type of film" themselves.[32]

Another friend and colleague, James Friedrich of Cathedral Films, a religious production company, had been urging Heimrich for some time to form an organization like the Legion of Decency, going so far as to suggest that church members sign pledge cards promising to avoid forbidden films. And Heimrich did not rule out the possibility that Protestants might have "commitment Sundays on motion pictures," like the Methodists once had on alcoholic beverages. Friedrich owned the film rights to *The Big Fisherman*, Lloyd C. Douglas's novel and sequel to *The Robe*, which had been a huge hit for 20th Century-Fox in 1953. Disney retained him as a consultant for *The Big Fisherman* (1959), but never used his services. When it disappointed at the box office, Friedrich blamed the film's "spiritual mediocrity on a colossal scale," and became convinced that Jewish control of the industry was an impediment to the Christian message.[33]

That the WCO leadership wanted to duplicate the Catholic approach was completely at odds with the Study Commission's outlook, and above all, with the traditional Protestant approach. "We should stop trying to control the content of motion pictures at their source," Union Theological Seminary professor Thomas Driver insisted. "Critical evaluation is demanded by a Protestant emphasis upon freedom, which we must be radical in protecting." Protestant strategies were not bound by the Production Code, which was "a poor thing at best," needing revision, Mack said, but should involve "developing critical faculties all the way up and down the line."[34]

The commission's posture was consistent with important studies of the media sponsored by the National Council. Everett C. Parker, Office of Communication of the United Church of Christ, proposed that by tacitly accepting the industry's commercial standards, the church was effectively commodifying religion and values instead of developing "an aesthetic approach to the media, relating itself to the arts of communication, rather than commercial selling of a product." His main critique of the media was that it encouraged people to think of themselves primarily as consumers and idealized "conspicuous consumption" as a mark of status. Unfortunately, most clergy did not give much serious thought to the impact of the media on their congregations, its potential and limitations for use in religious education and evangelism, or the impact of the media in a religiously pluralistic society. A second study by Wilbur Schramm rejected the parochialism of pressure groups like the Legion of Decency. He proposed instead a theory of "social responsibility" that would call for both producers and consumers to safeguard "the freedom of the person and the vitality of the culture," as the distinguished theologian Reinhold Niebuhr put it.[35]

It was clear that there were conflicting ideas within the BFC. It would be up to the Study Commission to develop policy and set the direction for the Council.

Making Movies for Adults

Heimrich's broadside did much to dramatize widespread sentiment—brewing at least since the Code was liberalized in 1956—that something should be done about the moral condition of the movies. Identifying a number of films "loaded with unnecessary stuff," even *Time* wondered why "the Protestants have waited so long to draw a bead." After more than two decades of morally sanitized movies, the groundbreaking changes taking place in the American cinema elicited contrary reactions; clergy, critics, and producers were disturbed by the same trends that others argued made the cinema "a more mature and honest medium." At the core of the debate was the question of moral acceptability of movies exhibited to people of all ages. Shurlock acknowledged that the cinema's expanded freedom made it increasingly difficult to bring movies with adult appeal in line with the Code, especially when "adult" often meant an emphasis on sex, and not sophistication and complexity in theme or treatment.[36]

The week before the Council's Study Commission heard Heimrich's appeal, Eric Johnston met with studio executives to discuss the possibility of classifying movies for adults as a way to alleviate criticism from Protestant and Catholic clergy. Even if classification gave filmmakers more creative freedom, studio executives did not want their profits reduced by restricting attendance—they wanted neither censorship nor classification. But by the early 1960s, many top producers and directors, as well as major religious and civic organizations, were rallying around an industry-wide movie rating system. Nevertheless, for the time being, classification would remain a "dirty word" in Hollywood.[37]

9

High Noon in the Broadcasting and Film Commission

Dollar for dollar, motion pictures produced on a religious theme make more money than any other picture.
GEORGE HEIMRICH, director, West Coast Office,
Broadcasting and Film Commission

THE TAGLINE FOR *The Nun's Story* was "Her Faith Remained Strong and True in the Face of Africa's Terrors!" In a cover story, *Life* praised the film as "a hauntingly beautiful, tragic account of the battles that raged for 17 years in one nun's soul." The Warner Bros. release featured top talent, with Academy Award winners Audrey Hepburn (in the title role) and Fred Zinneman (directing). The film picked up eight Oscar nominations, including for Best Picture, Best Director, and Best Actress in a Leading Role, and was among the most profitable films of 1959 with around $6 million in domestic box office. Warner Bros. reportedly used leftover footage of the Congo from *The Nun's Story* in the filming of *The Sins of Rachel Cade* (1961). In comparison to Hepburn, Angie Dickinson was a promising newcomer fresh off a sharp performance in Howard Hawks's *Rio Bravo*, and director Gordon Douglas was a lightweight compared to Zinneman. Not surprisingly, the film was faulted by critics for its soap opera quality. "The tolerance of the public for mediocre movies with trashy themes having to do with sex has decreased rather than increased in the last year," Catholic critic Moira Walsh contended, "and I imagine poor Rachel has very little future at the box office." Indeed, the movie did not even make *Variety*'s annual list of box-office earners, indicating a very poor showing. A comparison of the two Warner Bros. films is revealing, and helps to explain Protestant reactions. The luring tagline for *The Sins of Rachel Cade* was "How dare you come preach against sin, Rachel Cade! You . . . and your lover . . . and your baby!"[1]

Catholic leaders took George Heimrich's diatribe against Hollywood as a sign of possible cooperation. In November 1959, a church official said that the Legion of Decency "welcomed recent Protestant criticism of sex and violence in motion pictures as a sign of reactivated interest in a common cause," and Bishop James A. McNulty, head of the Legion's oversight agency, the Episcopal Committee for Motion Pictures, Radio and Television, announced plans for an interfaith campaign for "decency" in movies.[2] The call harkened back to the religious crusade that launched the Legion in 1934, and suggested that Catholics and Protestants might unite behind a pietist approach.

Church membership in the United States reached a high in the postwar years. Although Protestants remained the largest group, their dominance had diminished, and the rise of McCarthyism, as well as the growing power of the Catholic Church, made Protestants fear for American liberty like never before.[3] Protestant-Catholic relations grew "rigid and frigid" during the 1950s, and Protestants mounted new challenges to Catholic control of movie morals. When 20th Century-Fox distributed *Martin Luther* (1953), produced independently by the National Lutheran Council, the *Christian Century* raved about it, *Christian Herald* readers selected it Picture of the Year, *Variety* called it a "box office giant," and *The New Yorker* and *Time* both gave positive reviews. The Legion, however, could neither approve nor condemn the film, and instead assigned it a separate classification for the simple reason that it contained "theological and historical references and interpretations which are unacceptable to Roman Catholics."[4]

A storm of protest erupted when Chicago's WGN-TV capitulated to Catholic pressure and canceled a widely publicized TV premier of the film in December 1957. Various Protestant groups and the ACLU sent a petition with 150,000 signatures to the Federal Communications Commission protesting that the cancellation occurred "under circumstances which are, in effect, sectarian censorship and a violation of freedom of expression." The brief was supported by over 40 Protestant groups, including the Chicago Church Federation, the National Council of Churches, the National Association of Evangelicals, and major Lutheran bodies. It asked the FCC "to correct this injustice and to establish such principles and practices for use of the media of mass communications as will guarantee freedom from such censorship whether direct or otherwise." In March, WISN-TV, an ABC affiliate in Milwaukee, announced that it would premiere *Martin*

Luther. The station manager explained, "We do not find the film morally objectionable or technically inadequate, and those are the principal standards by which we judge." Meanwhile, the station manager at the ABC Chicago affiliate (WBKB), a Catholic, also decided to air the film after he heard from a prominent church official that it was a "false assumption" that the archdiocese was responsible for the WGN-TV cancellation.[5]

Challenges to the Code

Legion reports across the decade documented a drop in family fare, but the agency was under considerable strain and in no position to do much about it. Their main concern was the percentage of films labeled "objectionable in part," which rose from 8 percent in 1937 to 32 percent in 1957. There was also an increase in the number of movies (mostly foreign and independently produced) not submitted for classification. Parishioners were ignoring the Legion and were relying on their own judgment, and there was serious debate over the Legion's authority as its ratings came under increasing criticism.[6] The bishops could no longer keep up the appearance of complete harmony on the movies; Catholics were now divided over the legitimacy of prior censorship.

After the *Miracle* decision, some Catholic leaders tightened their hold on the "essential idea of making the films right at the source," while others began rethinking the church's role. While the Code was being revised in 1956, Jesuit theologian John Courtney Murray broke with traditional Catholic teaching and argued that in a pluralistic society the church could direct its own members, but no minority group had the right to impose its religious beliefs and morals on others. Father Patrick Sullivan, who joined the Legion staff the following year, argued that freedom of expression was inseparable from the expansion of human knowledge, making censorship a "curtailment of a basic human liberty." A 1957 papal encyclical (*Miranda Prorsus*) shifted the official Catholic position by putting an emphasis on praiseworthy films instead of condemning immoral ones, and moved the church closer to the traditional Protestant posture. That year, a landmark Supreme Court ruling established the *Roth-Alberts* test, which treated obscenity as a matter of individual choice, with the government responsible for protecting minors; eventually, the court would embrace different obscenity standards for adults and minors.[7]

In February 1960, MPAA executives were surprised to be asked to testify before a House subcommittee as part of an investigation into the mailing of obscene and pornographic materials. A wary Eric Johnston assured the committee that member studios "do not deal in obscenity or pornography" and touted the association as a model of "how one communications industry successfully practices self-regulation." With fears and tensions mounting over obscenity, freedom, and idea control in mass communication, Johnston dismissed calls for government classification of movies as censorship and emphasized "breadth and diversity, not blind conformity" in movies. Contra the Production Code's originators, he argued that the Code's main purpose was not to make movies suitable for everyone, but rather to keep "the screen open to subjects that are an inherent part of life, of literature, of drama." PCA head Geoffrey Shurlock advanced the theme by stressing that the PCA's basic concern was not with subject, but treatment, which was characteristic of the long-standing Protestant position. Shurlock stated emphatically that "the Code is as strong and effective today as it ever was."[8]

To demonstrate the PCA's success in assuring "basic moral standards in American motion pictures," Shurlock highlighted the fact that the Legion of Decency had condemned only four films and, along with the Protestant Motion Picture Council, regularly reviewed and rated movies. Catholic and Protestant support for the PCA remained important to the MPAA studios, especially with support for film classification starting to gather momentum. But within both religious camps there were widening divisions over the legitimacy and effectiveness of the Production Code, and the idea of an interfaith campaign to support it was never more than an idea.

Later in February, just months after McNulty's proposal for cooperation of Catholics and non-Catholics in the cause of "decency and morality," Legion officials backed off their support for the "uprising" against sex and violence in films. The reason given was that the attack was too broad, "a nice-sounding slogan which lacks sufficient definition and clarification," and there was concern it "might be carried to excess." But the Broadcasting and Film Commission's (BFC) S. Franklin Mack had recently made the National Council's position clear. "We have no desire to hit the headlines with accusations or threats or denunciations," he said, drawing a sharp distinction between Catholics who sought to "proscribe, prescribe and to limit by edict from above" and the Protestant emphasis on enabling churchgoers to make their own, informed decisions.[9] Catholic leaders probably realized that Heimrich's stand on enhanced code enforcement was getting no traction with Protestant officials and, under the circumstances, trying to mount a united front against the film industry was futile—at least for the moment.

Committed to its role as the church's liaison with the film industry, National Council officials took Shurlock's advice and arranged a series of conferences with high-level studio executives, film producers, and MPAA administrators. Given the ruckus over *Rachel Cade* and *Elmer Gantry*, Shurlock tried to arrange screenings of the two films for Eric Johnston and MPAA vice president Kenneth Clark so that they might be prepared to defend themselves. After seeing the finished film, PCA staff had thought it possible that Heimrich might find *Rachel Cade* "a pleasant surprise," and it appears that Shurlock also wanted Johnston and Clark to consider whether screening the film for National Council officials might relieve their concerns. It seems, based on a published review in July 1960, that some Protestant leaders did preview *Rachel Cade*. Aware that "many Christians will deplore this portrayal of a missionary," the *Christian Herald* gave *Rachel Cade* qualified praise as a "colorful, shocking, and at times inspiring drama" that nevertheless "shows understanding of the motivation of missionary service. Forgiveness takes precedence over all other considerations which are relative." In other words, *Herald* readers were probably not going to vote it "Movie of the Month." It is reasonable to assume that a lackluster response from Protestant clergy factored in the studio's decision to shelve the picture. Warner Bros. finally released it in April 1961 with the more lurid title *The Sins of Rachel Cade*, obviously intended to draw more than Protestant churchgoers.[10]

The Church and the Mass Media

The National Council's Study Commission issued its report, "The Church and the Mass Media," in June 1960. At the core of the analysis was a critique of the media's assumption that the purpose of life was to achieve "material advantage, power and pleasure" through competition, manipulation, and exploitation of others. This ultimate concern affected both content—"the pathological preoccupation with sex and violence"—and industry policies. At a fundamental level, the media propagated a vision that was "often poles apart" from the Christian view that humans were created in the image of God and charged with love of neighbor. The church could play a constructive role in two ways: first, by developing "consultative relationships" with like-minded people in the industries and by exploring creative possibilities for addressing "the moral and spiritual condition" of the time; and second, by pursuing a corresponding program in media education to make churchgoers more knowledgeable, selective viewers who would then encourage production of better movies. Because the Council valued self-discipline over "restraint or coercion by any outside group—including the church itself," the commission opted to support industry self-regulation and criticized "the attempts of irresponsible individuals to circumvent both the spirit and the letter of the code," even as it found the Production Code "to have become increasingly ineffective."[11]

The long-awaited report was hardly groundbreaking, especially since there was already a movement afoot among religious organizations pressing the film industry to adopt an age-classification system. Nevertheless, the commission signaled an important change in perspective. The BFC would no longer be content to cooperate with the industry just to get religiously themed entertainment, but was ready to "be critical of it where it was not meeting human need, where it was not ethically sound," future BFC director William F. Fore explained.[12] A committee was appointed to implement the findings.

In conjunction with the report's release, and in an effort to continue smoothing things over after the George Heimrich imbroglio, the National Council sponsored another luncheon with high-level industry personnel at the Beverly Hills Club. The MPAA's Kenneth Clark worked with BFC head Mack on a guest list that included Eric Johnston, Geoffrey Shurlock, top leaders in the Association of Motion Picture Producers (AMPP), and nearly 20 studio representatives, independent producers, and BFC and West Coast Office members; Heimrich was noticeably absent. Remarks by Johnston and Eugene Carson Blake, a past National Council president and a towering figure in Protestantism, were followed by an informal discussion that centered on the perpetual debate over industry standards and public desires. *Variety* reported that Johnston blamed non-MPAA members—"fly-by-night" companies—for most objectionable films. George Stevens, John Ford, and other directors "stood solidly" behind the Production Code Administration (PCA). Council members urged producers not to "merely give the public what it wants," but to maintain high standards that would "improve taste." Filmmakers countered that they were not leading "the parade in offensiveness," but mostly following trends with adaptations of novels and plays, and at times "hitting bulls' eyes" with outstanding and worthwhile movies. All agreed that mutual understanding was crucial. Church officials had to get a handle on the industry's changing conditions; producers needed to know who represented Protestantism and what role the churches might play with regard to the commercial cinema.[13]

After the industry luncheon, BFC officials realized that their film strategy was too narrow, largely ineffective, and out-of-date. Religious programming was of poor quality and ineffective, and the churches were having little effect on the commercial cinema. The loosening of the Production Code's restrictions had more to do with competition from television, the influence of foreign films, and the spirit of the times than with the rise of independent production, and American producers were more dependent now on revenues from crowded overseas markets. Individual creativity and, conversely, a lowest common denominator appeal to sex and violence were the immediate results. The onus was on the church to envision a fitting role for the cinema in a pluralistic society and to develop an approach in line with the industry's new freedoms, challenges, and responsibilities. It was a classic expression of the structural motif. The central question was: How could a national Protestant agency remain principally in support of free speech on the one hand, and advocate some kind of system of regulation or restraint on the other?[14]

A *Christian Herald* writer, for example, declared that "when literature deals with a sex theme, no censor should abridge its freedom to treat of anything—from adultery to nymphomania, from homosexuality to fetishism or sado-masochism—*so long as these are points of departure in a journey toward the truth.*" But when it came to movies falling into this category, he simply branded them all excessive, sensational, and a "sick-sex trend," even though they were homogenized adaptations of successful literary works. Apparently, artistic integrity and a measure of complexity in exploring moral issues were fine for the cultural elite, but not for the untutored masses. Shurlock pointed this out to Mack and suggested that Protestants could play a more constructive role if they had "some really trained fair-minded and literate Protestant critics and assessors of both morals and aesthetics in films."[15] In other words, Protestant critics needed to catch up with their own rhetoric and consider movies on a par with art and literature, treating them as cultural discourse and not merely as vehicles for propagating Christian values.

Not for Sinners under 16

The PCA-approved *Elmer Gantry* reached theaters in July 1960 without any Protestant "technical" advice. National Council executives previewed the film on June 24, but only after Richard Brooks had held several screenings for Legion of Decency officials that resulted in the deletion of two lines and the addition of a prologue:

We believe that certain aspects of Revivalism can bear examination, that the conduct of some Revivalists makes a mockery of the traditional beliefs and practices of organized Christianity. We believe that everyone has a right to worship according to his conscience. But freedom of religion is not a license to abuse the faith of the people. However, due to its highly controversial nature, we strongly urge you to prevent impressionable children from seeing this film.[16]

The statement demonstrated that Brooks was really concerned with protecting the film's box-office potential from the Legion of Decency. Setting new precedent, United Artists labeled *Elmer Gantry* suitable for "adults only," a tactic that worked to avoid a "C" rating from the Legion as well as promote the film's controversial aspects. *Variety* quipped that UA was recommending the movie for "adult sinners" and not those under 16, but the MPAA took a dim view of the action as cracking the door to classification. The Legion gave it a "B" rating (objectionable in part for all); the *Christian Herald* wrote if off as missing the mark on "spiritual discernment."[17]

Even though Brooks "softened the story," *Variety* doubted that the film would "escape agitating the Bible Belt." But there was no public outrage. Bishop Gerald Kennedy, chair of the West Coast Office Committee, thought the film packed "dramatic punch," but lamented its depiction of religion as "cheap and unethical." The real issue was whether Hollywood ought to produce adult fare and become "the legitimate theatre on a larger scale," or "mass entertainment for the family and the interpreter of American life around the world." Kennedy might have preferred the latter, but his own denomination's periodical, the *Christian Advocate*, disagreed. "Hollywood may come of age artistically and responsibly when it can cast its light on all institutions and examine them with candor and sincerity," Claremont Seminary professor F. Thomas Trotter wrote. "Those who have looked to Hollywood to break out of the slumbers of the mythical 12-year-old mentality see some hope in the realism of *Elmer Gantry*." Most reviewers judged it an impressive adaptation that was "almost wholesome" in comparison to the book, if also ambivalent in its attitude about religious revivalism.[18] *Elmer Gantry*'s $5.2 million box-office performance was respectable, but disappointing, and not enough to start the trend that some Protestant leaders feared. More important, that movies like *Elmer Gantry* and *The Sins of Rachel Cade* were distributed in the United States and abroad over Protestant objections showed that the West Coast Office was not having a discernible impact on the making of Hollywood films. Distraught, Heimrich and his WCO colleagues traced the growing disregard that producers had for their input on matters related to Protestantism directly to the declining authority of the Code. The BFC leadership, however, was beginning to see it instead as a sign that the West Coast Office was not just ineffective, but outmoded.

Richard Brooks picked up an Oscar for his screenplay, and actors Burt Lancaster and Shirley Jones also won for their roles in *Elmer Gantry*, which was nominated for Best Picture. The Best Picture award went to *The Apartment* (1960), a Code-approved movie about corporate executives using an employee's apartment to rendezvous with their mistresses. These movies signified the changes taking place in Hollywood. Most releases in 1960 were unobjectionable; it was just that producers were making more films that were adult-oriented in theme and treatment and therefore inappropriate for those under 16. At the same time, "art" and "realism," as *New York Times* writer Murray Schumach observed, also provided "wonderful camouflage" for producers looking to enhance box-office prospects by emphasizing sex and violence. With Russ Meyer's "happy-go-lucky nudie," *The Immoral Mr. Teas* (1959), playing in regular theaters, an industry contingent defended the Code as a necessary restraint. The persistent fear remained that screen sensationalism would push too far, ignite a public backlash, "and thereby kill the goose that hatched the golden age," as a writer in *Life* cleverly put it.[19]

In the early 1930s, Code enforcement was considered vital to the industry's economic well-being. Along with its expanded freedom, the industry's financial woes and competition from television contributed to a loosening of the Code's strictures during the 1950s. In Hollywood there was growing disinterest—even contempt—for church agencies meddling in movie production. At the same time, the power of church authorities to dictate opinion was giving way to greater individual freedom; censorship and boycotts to safeguard the public were increasingly rejected as curtailments of individual liberty—more characteristic of totalitarian societies than of the United States. By the early 1960s, PCA approval no longer counted for much.

Protestant and Catholic Concerns

With the Legion of Decency experiencing a drop in the number of films submitted for classification, Bishop McNulty cited an "alarming" increase in morally objectionable movies during 1960. He rebuked the film industry for its "sensational presentation of religion as well as for its new-found predilection for pornographic and perverted subject matter." Noting widespread criticism of Hollywood, he recommended that the American Roman Catholic bishops get behind "an unmistakable national protest." Under the circumstances, he suggested that they consider supporting an industry classification system and insist that adult-oriented movies "conform to the spirit of the Production Code." *Christian Herald* editor Daniel Poling agreed with the Legion's findings and thought the time had come for Protestants, Catholics, Jews, and all people of good will to rally "against Hollywood's steadily growing output of objectionable pictures."[20]

West Coast Office personnel were fully aware of these trends. They, too, were increasingly dissatisfied with the scripts they saw, and they faced more resistance from producers who routinely disregarded Protestant advice—except, of course, when churchgoers might flock to the theaters. Then they might be willing to cooperate, securing screenings for clergy; sermons and church bulletins were free advertising. Heimrich's industry criticism notwithstanding, it was also the case that WCO personnel had acquired a reputation for being disorganized, not very capable, and at times too demanding and uncompromising. Producers started circumventing the BFC's West Coast operation.

The Remarkable Mr. Pennypacker (1959) is an apt illustration. In the film, based on a Broadway play, Horace Pennypacker is a free thinker, president of the Darwin League, and above all, a bigamist. He's "remarkable" for having fathered 17 children, 8 in Harrisburg and 9 in Philadelphia. Harrisburg wife Emily asks of his "plural marriage," which came first, the "philosophy or the glands?" In a debate over moral standards with the local minister, Dr. Fielding, Pennypacker argues, based on natural selection, that "morality is really a matter of geography" and the true purpose of marriage is "propagation of the family, naturally," with Fielding adding: only in "a union blessed by God." With little emotional turmoil—it is a farce after all—the whole dilemma is resolved when it is revealed that Mrs. Pennypacker in Philadelphia had passed away eight years ago. Horace's sister takes over care of her children; the movie ends with Emily and Horace renewing their marriage vows and Horace emphasizing "forsaking all others."

The WCO Script Committee found the film's concept itself "objectionable from a moral and ethical point of view" and thought the clergyman was made to "look inept, uneducated and tongue-tied in the face of the serious moral delinquencies with which he is confronted." After two rounds of negotiations, first over general Protestant concerns and then specific Episcopalian ones, a Fox producer simply made the minister amorphous and eliminated any reference to the Episcopal Church rather than revise

Dr. Fielding's "theologically untenable" position. Heimrich would nevertheless cite *Pennypacker* as an example of successful industry cooperation. Afterward, when producer and director Stanley Kramer sought approval for *Inherit the Wind* (1960), his critically acclaimed film on the Scopes Trial, Shurlock referred him to Heimrich. But Kramer went ahead and secured approval from an Episcopalian prelate instead. That was enough to satisfy the PCA. Heimrich managed to frustrate production of "The Moneychanger," a screenplay whose main character was based on the popular evangelist Billy Graham, and another titled "Adam and Eve," but these were small victories that contributed to Heimrich's sense that he was "fighting a losing battle."[21]

The West Coast Office was not having much success in other areas either. Heimrich's nonprofit production company (Imperator Corporation) was unable to secure a studio deal for two Protestant-themed properties to which he held the screen rights: German pastor Hans Lilje's *Valley of the Shadow* and Courtney Anderson's *Toward the Golden Shore*, a story of Adoniram Judson, the first Baptist missionary to Burma. The objective of Heimrich's company was identical to that of George Reid Andrews's Religious Motion Picture Foundation, namely "to inject this type of film into the mainstream of theatre film distribution" in anticipation that "acceptance at the box office would provide additional funds for future production development and an additional source of income for BFC."[22]

Script review and production consulting were given such priority in the West Coast Office that other functions received inadequate attention, including developing relations with local church councils, women's groups, and denominational executives that were essential to fund-raising. Los Angeles was becoming the center for television production, but the WCO was unable able to cash in on the opportunities—"failures" Heimrich attributed mostly to "a matter of inadequate budget and time necessary to fulfill our objectives."[23]

WCO Committee members tried to pressure Mack and the BFC board to support Heimrich and they mustered some church support. But Bishop Kennedy's claim that dissatisfaction with Hollywood was widespread and that the BFC was "in a position to demand some reforms and a new spirit of responsibility" from the producers was vastly overstated. Nevertheless, Mack thought it urgent that the BFC adopt a coherent policy since there was some possibility that individual denominations might rush ahead and "act unilaterally." "Least of all can we content ourselves with safe-guarding the image of the church and of the clergy."[24] There was more than a hint of sarcasm in the remark. Instead of igniting a campaign to clean up the movies, Heim-rich's broadside marginalized him in Hollywood, damaged his credibility as the Protestants' representative, and made it clear how much the BFC's West Coast operation was out of sync with the organization's purposes.

Though beleaguered, Heimrich remained undeterred, believing that his office was not just representing Protestantism, but was mounting a defense against a great evil: "Pictures which portray religion in a derogatory and disrespectful manner can serve only one purpose—the communist line."[25] Heimrich still had a powerful ally in Bishop Kennedy and the full support of the WCO Committee. His work continued with those producers who voluntarily submitted scripts, and special clergy previews were arranged for movies like *King of Kings* (1961), *The Norman Vincent Peale Story*, and *To Kill a Mockingbird* (both 1962). Most significant, Heimrich and his committee were working closely with a two-time Academy Award winner, director George Stevens, on an epic film on the life of Jesus, *The Greatest Story Ever Told*. Once again, a Hollywood heavyweight with a major distributor was bringing the central story of the Bible to film. It was the stuff that pietists' dreams were made of, but would it be *The King of Kings* all over again?

An Audacious Proposal

The West Coast Office dodged a bullet in February 1961 when the BFC board rejected a proposal to remove the WCO from its jurisdiction and put it under direct control of the Department of Public Interpretation, where it was presumed it would "starve for lack of funds." The practical advantage of a Hollywood location weighed heavily in the board's decision, and Heimrich "had a pretty good set of chess moves left because he held the strong bishop," William Fore said, referring to Kennedy. Though not out of jeopardy, the WCO Committee seized the moment to make an audacious recommendation. It proposed to establish a permanent three-member board in Hollywood to evaluate every script submitted to the PCA and issue a tentative classification on age suitability, from Family to Totally Objectionable. The board would advise producers on revisions to merit a "more favorable classification and gain broader audience scope," with a final rating issued upon completion of the film.[26]

The West Coast Office was barely raising enough money to support its existing activities, let alone a full-time reviewing staff. The parallel to the Legion of Decency setup was simply unmistakable—if also incredible—and garnered extensive press coverage. The proposal had no chance of adoption. The Council's own Study Commission had rejected any censorial measures and, as an anonymous official put it, such a system "goes against the traditional Protestant stand against pre-production censorship, and it is exceedingly unlikely that the council would alter that tradition." Seminary professor Thomas Driver judged the move "a betrayal of the spirit of Protestantism."[27]

The WCO proposal was on the agenda for discussion with top-level film executives on March 22, 1961. Industry personnel were quick to highlight a number of practical problems. The script is only one stage in production and could undergo significant changes while the material is adapted for the screen; further revisions might occur during shooting. There were also matters of confidentiality that prohibited such a review and, as Arthur Krim of United Artists pointed out, classification based on the screenplay would create a bad precedent and "oblige the industry to do it for others." In short, film producers unanimously nixed the idea; better to keep preproduction advice separate, with the BFC classifying finished films for its own constituents.

When National Council secretary Roy G. Ross raised the question about "the efficacy of the BFC's West Coast Office," the producers declined comment. The MPAA's Ken Clark made it clear that Heimrich's blanket denunciation of movies created a situation that was not conducive to studios "working happily" with him. Ross wanted them to know that although the West Coast Office was not authorized to make public statements on behalf the National Council, Heimrich's remarks "represented a very considerable body of Church opinion." WCO Committee member Dean Leonidas Contos admitted that Heimrich could be "intemperate on occasion," and considering how much his remarks had "done a lot to produce this new climate," thought he should be "enjoined from making further speeches." Even so, Heimrich still had good relations with a number of studio executives. Contos was confident that the West Coast Office could be "made much more helpful and much less of a thorn in the flesh." The producers of *Inherit the Wind* and *Rachel Cade*, for example, could have benefited from the WCO's counseling. But Clark pointed out that Heimrich had consulted on *Rachel Cade* "but without much effect."[28]

BFC leaders came away from the meeting with agreed-upon guidelines for mutual cooperation, but how to deal with the West Coast Office remained up in the air. Heimrich and his colleagues were clearly at odds with the recommendations of the Council's Study Commission. As expected, the WCO Committee's plan for a Protestant rating board was derailed. The BFC's aim was to be engaged in a high-level, industry-wide dialogue; the question was how to make this happen with the current West Coast Office personnel. The board took steps to overcome "groupthink" in its Hollywood operation, to bring it in line with the organization's policies, and to make it more accountable. Mack started attending West Coast meetings. The board changed the status of the WCO from an advisory group to an officially recognized committee and increased its size from 8 to 26 members. Tight parameters for a "limited liaison" with the film industry were drawn up to overcome the negative image of "censor." The Board also required that time be spent selecting films for special promotion and developing categories for an annual awards program. Mack set the terms of the "ideal church-film industry liaison" as "one that fosters a meaningful dialogue between the churches and the industry at all levels and that is as much concerned to develop viewer discrimination as to communicate the Protestant-Orthodox view to the film industry." The emphasis was clearly away from church mediation in production and toward cooperation and film education. That the BFC board kept its West Coast operation during a "severe retrenchment" in 1962 shows that maintaining a Hollywood presence was still a high priority.[29]

When the reformulated WCO Committee met in October 1962, Mack, who was one of the founders of the Protestant Film Commission, treated it as a new beginning for Protestant engagement with Hollywood.[30] But conflict between the competing factions in the BFC would only intensify with new leadership implementing board-approved policies that would lead to a restructuring of the organization. At the same time, dynamics in Protestant-Catholic relations were shifting and would soon undergo a radical makeover.

Considering Classification

The Catholic bishops' Episcopal Committee for Motion Pictures, Radio and Television released a statement in December 1962 urging the film industry to adopt a voluntary age-classification system. With the Legion's own monitoring in decline, Catholic bishops argued for this new approach by affirming what had been a perennial Protestant concern, namely, that the cinema presented "an unhealthful and false outlook on life." In January, Mack told members of the WCO Committee that the film industry was "quite shaken" by the Catholic action, suspecting it was a "first step toward censorship." Frustrated that the Catholic agency got the jump on them,

Bishop Kennedy asked, "Are we by the very nature of the National Council set-up forever doomed to have to react to what the Catholics do, instead of once in awhile saying something first?" He pointed out that "this statement by the Catholics is the kind of thing we have been trying to say for several years, but officially could not. The public gets the idea that the Catholic Church always takes the lead on these things."[31]

The Council's Study Commission report in June 1960 would have been a timely occasion for the Protestant agency to put itself at the vanguard. The commission rejected Catholic coercion of filmmakers, but only recommended support for PCA efforts to improve the Code and the existing mode of self-regulation. There were probably two reasons that the report gave no official credence to movie classification. Political expediency was one. The National Council is a deliberative body; its commissions represent the position of its members. Critics charged that the Council's "cumbersome bureaucracy can do little more than issue position papers on current problems." If this was a downside to its organizational structure, the Council's democratic process also helped prevent knee-jerk reactions, and Council-sponsored studies often resulted in substantive analyses.[32]

The Study Commission's report on the mass media was prepared while some church groups were rallying behind the West Coast Office. Heimrich's own denomination, the Augustana Lutheran Church, supported his action by issuing a protest against "the production of motion pictures which over-emphasize sex and violence," and calling on other churches to do the same. The resolution was addressed to the National Council, the World Council of Churches, the National Lutheran Council, and the Lutheran World Federation, organizations representing over 250 million Protestants worldwide. In February 1960, the National Lutheran Council in turn urged the National Council to "strengthen" the work of the BFC, and especially that of the West Coast Office. Similar resolutions came from the American Baptist Convention, the Television, Radio and Film Commission of the Methodist Church (TRAFCO), and Southern California and Washington chapters of the National Religious Publicity Council. A local Hollywood Ministerial Association issued a statement commending Heimrich's "forthright stand in opposition to objectionable films." *Worship and Arts*, an official publication of the Los Angeles Church Federation and the Southern California Council of Churches, championed him and charged that "Hollywood has gone far enough and that the time has come for churchmen to protest." This position had some support in Protestant circles and was likely taken into account in the commission's final reporting.[33]

The deeper issue behind Protestant reluctance on classification, however, was probably the likelihood of further Catholic influence over movies.
If the profit-motivated industry could not be trusted to police itself, the
crucial question, which Kennedy raised, was "Who's going to do the classifying?" Heimrich offered to do the job on behalf of Protestants, but
BFC leaders wanted the church to have no part in curbing productions
to achieve a certain classification. The Legion was already set up to
classify movies in cooperation with the PCA. Should Hollywood adopt
a classification system, it was not unthinkable that the Legion's staff
would be put in charge of it. This would also explain Mack's remark that
classification was unworkable, given that it was made in conjunction with
comments that called the Catholic approach restraint "imposed from
without." He preferred instead a "really discriminating" film review service that would help people make their own decisions.[34]

Nevertheless, if the Catholic agency was out in front on classification,
Protestants would soon get a head start in altering industry perceptions of
the relation between church and cinema with a high-profile film awards
program that would become the public face of the changes taking place
within the BFC.

IO

And the Winner Is

THE PROTESTANT FILM AWARDS

> *As helpful as they may be, a few sporadic personal contacts*
> *simply are not going to get the job done for the Protestant*
> *Church in relationship to the entertainment arts.*
> WILLIAM F. FORE, executive director, Broadcasting and
> Film Commission

THE WEST COAST Office submitted a plan for a film awards program in the fall of 1962. Their recommendation was to create a committee "with full authority" to honor movies that emphasized "the faith and ideals that made America great," with other categories for films that presented an individual, the family, and a contemporary situation in keeping with Christian principles. The BFC board found the proposal lacking. It was significantly modified, starting with a broadening of the categories to include a wider range of films. The awards committee became a nominating panel and was expanded to include members of church media staff, critics and professors with theological and film expertise, and board members. The Board of Managers reserved the last word on nominations.[1]

When S. Franklin Mack resigned at the end of 1963, William F. Fore took over as BFC executive director. Fore had a course in religious television production at Yale Divinity School and afterward produced the nation's first children's religious television program, which was picked up by CBS. He served as director of Visual Education of the Methodist Board of Missions and worked with the National Council as a representative of the Methodist Church, in which he was ordained. Throughout his career, he worked tirelessly on behalf of the public interest in film and broadcasting.[2]

The board expected Fore to bring about significant change, especially with regard to its maverick West Coast operation. Over a year after its reorganization, the WCO Committee still floundered for lack of leadership. Bishop Gerald Kennedy was too busy to be more than a "passive chairman," and George Heimrich was "not only ineffectual but actually a drag on our work," according to Thomas Trotter, a professor at Claremont School of Theology who taught courses on art, religion, and contemporary literature. Another new member, playwright Robert E. Lee, thought the Protestant agency suffered from "delusions of accomplishment."[3]

Fore argued that, "So long as we are viewed by the industries as a place which censors scripts, approves ministerial images, and occasionally boosts a show which carries our 'message,' we are utterly lost." He wanted the West Coast Office to work to overcome this negative image "as one more private interest group in Hollywood" by emphasizing concern with "the total philosophical assumptions and values conveyed by a film and their total effect upon audiences." With the board's support, Fore pursued an ambitious agenda and became the architect of the reforms already underway in the BFC. His plan was to fully integrate the West Coast operation into the BFC's overall strategy. He wanted to see the entire agency function as a single entity, serving as a "catalyst" for genuine dialogue between the church and entertainment industries.[4] Fore strived for a consolidated Protestantism that would speak collectively to the culture-forming film industry in a structural way. This approach, which was aimed at challenging fundamental industry assumptions about profit making over artistic responsibility, was far from the thinking of Heimrich and his WCO colleagues. Differences in perspective between the BFC's East and West Coast factions became much more pronounced during Fore's administration, eventually leading to a showdown.

Firm supporters of liberty and artistic freedom, the BFC's East Coast faction fashioned a theology of the arts from theologian Paul Tillich's understanding of religion as an "ultimate concern" that is the source of all human activity. Religion and culture were inseparable: "religion is the substance of culture, culture is the form of religion."[5] The very organization of the film industry, then, revealed underlying presuppositions (ultimate concerns) about human purpose and values. Movies were analyzed both as cultural texts, using traditional art and literary criticism to uncover the artist's religious vision, and as a social medium in terms of their impact on culture.

It followed that the BFC's first priority was to make executives and creative people in film and broadcasting, who controlled "culture's most powerful forms," realize that they were "expressing the religion of our time, and then challenge them to the responsibility which is theirs." There was an assumption that religious leaders could still call studio heads to mind their social responsibilities and not just the bottom line, an indication perhaps of the lingering notion that Protestants, in concert with Catholics and Jews now, remained custodians of the culture. The aim of this dialogue between church and industry was not to protect the Protestant image and serve as a source of free publicity for certain kinds of films, but rather to ensure a pluralistic media that allowed room in the discourse for a Christian understanding of the human condition and the hope of redemption. The second task was to pursue media education to help church leaders and laypeople understand the relation between culture, as expressed in mass-produced entertainment, and a Christian understanding of life and the world. The goal was to make churchgoers more knowledgeable, selective viewers who would be able to interpret what they were seeing. A third priority was to find ways of cooperating with Catholics and Jews.

There were four basic issues to be addressed at both national and local levels: securing greater diversity of programming in the public interest; addressing the relationship between freedom of speech, free access to information, and separation of church and state; developing definitions of obscenity that balance parental rights to nurture children's development with every citizen's right of free speech and free access to information; and fostering community action to confront the power centers of the mass media with the implications of their messages.[6]

If the East and West Coast groups both recognized the cinema's potential to communicate the Gospel, they advanced radically different visions for Christian involvement. This was not a creative tension; each side was intransigent and saw the other as detrimental to carrying out their mission. That Heimrich's idea of industry reform was to hold a "prayer meeting on the back lot of Paramount" was much more than East Coast humor. Emphasizing the structural motif, they found it incredibly naïve to think that personal ministry to a grip, an actor, or director could have a serious effect on the direction of the film industry. Instead, the East Coast group pursued a two-pronged strategy. One was to change public and industry perceptions by using the annual film awards to highlight a Protestant approach to film and to encourage production of movies that honestly explored the human condition. The other was to change the industry's fundamental structure by replacing the Production Code with an age classification system.[7]

Hold the Dancing Girls and Orgies

Relations between the East and West Coast offices had not improved by the time Fore took over. George Heimrich ran afoul of National Council executives in July 1963 when he used National Council stationery to petition the State Department and the Senate Foreign Relations Committee on behalf of a group of evangelical Christians who were refused asylum at the U.S. Embassy in Moscow. Mack reported, "This is only one of many points at which I have had problems in knowing how to deal with George without telling him flatly what he could and could not do, and where his operations as a private citizen conflicted with his operations as a member of the NCC staff and BFC's west coast executive." The BFC board had been telegraphing its dissatisfaction over what was—or, rather, was not—being accomplished, but the WCO Committee stood firm and still equated protecting the image of Protestantism with successful "dialogue between the church and the industry," a statement made in reference to *The Norman Vincent Peale Story* (1962). The WCO consulted on the script and arranged previews so that denominational leaders could meet with the producer to provide "a clearer cross-section of opinions" and generate ideas on how to promote the film among clergy.[8] Needless to say, functioning merely as a publicity tool for the studios was not at all how the BFC board conceived Protestant "dialogue" with the industry.

Regardless, there was much enthusiasm in the West Coast Office over its collaboration with George Stevens, a devout Christian, on the production of *The Greatest Story Ever Told*. Stevens's staff conducted over four years of research—including a trip to the Holy Land—and gathered information on the religious audience for what the acclaimed director hoped would be another biblical blockbuster like *The Robe* (1953) and *The Ten Commandments* (1956). Stevens's idea for yet another definitive Christ film was "to capture the spirit and power of the Biblical account" by focusing on the simple, basic story, and "not clutter it up with dancing girls and orgies," as was typical of the genre. The austere approach still turned into a mammoth production, with the budget ballooning from $10 to $20 million.[9]

The West Coast Office was among the first to receive the script. Reviewers submitted a list of minutiae that Stevens's staff slighted as "various little suggestions and corrections, none of which, however, are of great importance." Heimrich arranged for church leaders to visit shooting locations and worked vigorously to promote the film to church groups and to get coverage in religious publications. The American Baptist Convention Magazine, *The Crusader*, featured a two-page article that included a photo of Stevens on the set with WCO Committee member Fred Essex and his Radio and Television Committee. Committee member H. K. Rasbach and his wife spent time on location, hosted by Ann del Valle, whom he had met six years earlier on the set of Cecil B. DeMille's *The Ten Commandments* (1956). WCO personnel had been very much involved with DeMille's production. Bishop Gerald Kennedy had—to del Valle's delight—publicly defended *The Ten Commandments* from Protestant attacks. Rasbach even arranged for the tablets from the film to be displayed at his church during a Thanksgiving Day Service. He and Heimrich both received specially bound copies of the screenplay, signed by DeMille. The WCO staff had high expectations for Stevens's film. Echoing George Reid Andrews's feelings about *The King of Kings* in 1927, Heimrich predicted *The Greatest Story Ever Told* would be "one of the truly great pictures, and certainly the greatest ever filmed on the life of Christ."[10]

The day after the release of the Legion of Decency's 1964 annual report, which criticized Hollywood for a "substantial decrease" in family-friendly films, the BFC announced its film awards program. It had been a long time since Protestants led the way with a constructive film initiative. But the first BFC film awards were inconsequential. The winners—*Becket*, *Fate Is the Hunter*, and *Fail Safe*—would soon be forgotten, while the disregarded *Dr. Strangelove* went on to become a classic. At the awards luncheon, *Becket* screenwriter Edward Anhalt, whose recent credits included *The Young Savages* (a *Blackboard Jungle*–type story of juvenile gang crime), the Elvis Presley vehicle *Girls! Girls! Girls!*, a sex comedy, *Wives and Lovers*, and incredibly, *The Sins of Rachel Cade*, remarked that his next project was a "sex farce." If some Protestant clergy found the comment disconcerting, they also got a glimpse of how much the industry was driven by business imperatives.[11]

Afterward, the panel took a hit from Malcolm Boyd for awarding movies that failed artistically or lacked moral or existential significance. Boyd, a civil rights activist and one of the Freedom Riders in 1961, had worked in the entertainment industry before becoming an Episcopalian priest. He blamed the southern California school of "pseudo-criticism" for being "theologically and aesthetically unsound." If his intent was to spark debate, he succeeded. BFC chair John W. Bachman and Bishop Kennedy both issued sharp rejoinders, the former defending the awards process, the latter Protestant diversity of opinion on movies. Boyd charged that

Kennedy and others found "inspiration in soap-opera-type religious themes and 'profound' meaning in the banalities of pop religion."[12] A friend of both DeMille and Stevens, Kennedy had lavished praise on *The Ten Commandments* (1956) and called *The Greatest Story Ever Told* the ultimate film on the life of Christ. But the air had recently been let out of his unqualified endorsement for the Stevens picture.

On February 8, 1965, United Artists hosted special invitation-only premieres for *Greatest Story* in both New York and Los Angeles. The film ran very long—3 hours and 41 minutes (Kennedy's wife left at intermission)—and elicited lukewarm applause from an audience filled with clergy who were supposed to recommend it to their congregations. Critics panned it for its "Hallmark-like" treatment. *Time* was typical, labeling the film "impeccable boredom. As for vigorous ideas, there are none that would seem new to a beginners' class in Bible study." Neither could the religious press find much of value. Catholic critic Moira Walsh admitted that whatever she wrote would "sound like damning with faint praise," and a *Christian Century* reviewer, who found the script "inane," faulted the church advisers "who ought to have known better."[13]

A critical and commercial disaster, *Greatest Story* dashed any hope of persuading producers that it was advantageous to work with the West Coast Office; the Protestant gatekeepers could not even deliver an audience for an epic film on the life of Jesus. Moreover, since DeMille inaugurated the trend with *Samson and Deliah* (1949), the studios had been trying to beat each other to market with Bible-based dramas. There were several big hits like *The Ten Commandments*, *Ben-Hur*, and *The Robe*, but *The Greatest Story Ever Told* brought an end to the era of biblical extravaganzas. Ambitious plans for a series based on the books of the Bible ended abruptly when the first installment, *The Bible*, an $18 million production, failed to recoup its costs.[14]

Movies That Explore the Human Condition

The Production Code Administration (PCA), meanwhile, was faced with a new challenge when an independent production, *The Pawnbroker*, based on the novel by Edward Lewis Wallant and directed by Sidney Lumet, was submitted for approval in December 1964. Producer Ely Landau did not present the screenplay or the finished film to the PCA for evaluation, but had signed a distribution deal with Allied Artists. As a member of the MPAA, the distributor was required to submit the film for approval or release it through a subsidiary. Allied could have distributed it without a seal, but was struggling financially, and, hoping for more than an art house hit, decided that a Production Code controversy "could only help sell an otherwise difficult picture."[15]

The story centers on Sol Nazerman, a Jewish pawnbroker in Harlem who was a philosophy professor in Leipzig before his family was killed at Auschwitz. He manages to cope with his guilt at having survived by squelching any human connectedness. As the anniversary of their deaths approaches, the most mundane things spark agonizing recollections, until in one scene a prostitute offers herself to him, baring her breasts and inviting him to "look." It triggers a horrid memory (seen in flashback) of a German soldier smashing Nazerman's head through a window and ordering him to "look." What he sees is his wife sitting bare-breasted on a bed about to be raped by a German officer. The moment links his past and present and emotionally connects stunned viewers to his personal devastation. The producer argued that the scene was "integral to the story" and was not meant to "titillate." Geoffrey Shurlock agreed, but the Code prohibited nudity, and PCA approval was denied.[16]

Shurlock had an introductory lunch meeting in March 1965 with James M. Wall, editor of the *Christian Advocate*, a Methodist church periodical. A Southern liberal and ordained minister, Wall was tough-minded, energetic, inquisitive, and a cinephile. As soon as he took over the editorial reins, he put out an unprecedented special issue on "Church and Cinema" that prodded readers to abandon their moralistic denunciation of movies, and urged the film industry to adopt its own voluntary classification system. Wall had sent Shurlock his review of *Becket*, which he found to be a soul-searching dramatization of the Archbishop of Canterbury's violent conflict with Henry II, and another one critical of Billy Wilder's *Kiss Me, Stupid*, which staged the unintentional results of imposture and double adultery as hilarity. In the film, Orville Spooner, a would-be songwriter, sleeps with a prostitute whom he hires to pose as his wife, while Dino, the famous entertainer he's trying to get in a melody-buying mood, ends up spending the night elsewhere with Spooner's wife, one of Dino's adoring fans whom the drunken singer mistakes for the prostitute. It all ends happily for everyone. Though impressed with Wilder's earlier comedies, *The Apartment* and *Some Like It Hot*, Wall blasted *Kiss Me, Stupid* as nothing more than a "dirty joke"—cynical and morally vacuous. "An artist can present an immoral situation realistically," Wall maintained, "but if he begins with immorality on the real level, he must conclude with a response of disgust, anger, remorse and a possible redemption." Shurlock was impressed; Wall fit the bill as an evenhanded Protestant critic, and the two hit it off. Shurlock confided in him about the PCA's dilemma with *The Pawnbroker*. If the scene was dramatically necessary, it should be included, Wall said, and suggested that a cautionary note be added to let audiences know what to expect.[17]

Two weeks later, the MPAA Code Review Board overturned the PCA ruling, but not without some consternation about the precedent that was being set. The board was under some pressure; Landau planned to bring an antitrust suit against the MPAA if the board did not overturn the PCA's ruling. MPAA executives also realized that the decision would likely lead to abuses by some producers, would have an incalculable impact on the viability of the Code, and might elicit a public outcry, perhaps leading to stricter regulations. Wall interpreted the appeals ruling as "a trial balloon to determine whether the public will accept nudity in American-produced films as it has accepted nudity in imports from abroad." And although he agreed with the decision, he was also wary that it would pave the way for exploitation.[18]

As expected, the Legion of Decency condemned *The Pawnbroker*, but drew criticism from Catholic writers who found the scene dramatically motivated and not prurient. James A. Pike, now Episcopal bishop of California, also took exception to the Legion's condemned rating and issued a statement praising *The Pawnbroker* as "one of the truly significant religious (because it deals with ultimate matters) films of our time." The actions of the PCA and Legion highlighted the superficiality of judging elements in isolation and ignoring contextual and situational meaning, which had long been a Protestant critique of the Code and the Catholic "decency" approach. *The Pawnbroker* and *Kiss Me, Stupid* were the only two major Hollywood movies condemned by the Legion since *The Moon is Blue* and *Baby Doll* in the mid-1950s. Playing only in key cities during its initial run, *The Pawnbroker* earned nearly $3 million. Reviews were mixed, ranging from "remarkable" and "shockingly good" to "seldom deeply moving" and a "pretentious parable that manages to shrivel into drivel." Critics noted matter-of-factly the scene involving nudity, but few commented on it, and then only to affirm dramatically or morally its inclusion in the narrative. Only *Newsweek* mentioned a religious theme, but it was precisely the film's treatment of the horrors of the Holocaust and their theological implications that fascinated film enthusiasts in the BFC.[19]

The two main objectives of the awards program were to educate moviegoers by publicizing the selected films and generating discussion about them, and to alert the industry that at least a portion of the churchgoing public was interested in high-quality movies. At the same time, BFC director William Fore hoped that the Awards Nomination Panel Committee would become a crucible for discourse within the BFC and would lead to reform in the West Coast Office. Thomas Trotter became chair of the nominating panel when H. K. Rasbach resigned after suffering a heart attack in the spring of 1965. James Wall and Malcolm Boyd both joined the panel that year, and with others like Trotter and the distinguished *Saturday Review* film critic Arthur Knight, tipped the panel in favor of the east coast perspective. Knight was a Hollywood insider, a film scholar who taught courses at USC. He represented no church denomination, but was there to give the Awards Committee "a real anchor in the Hollywood ethos, not just a bunch of clergy who were outsiders," as Trotter put it, adding that Knight was "very worldly—made the rest of us look like monks." An ardent advocate of free speech, Knight agreed to serve on the BFC's awards panel because he believed that it facilitated a larger purpose, one that corresponded with his own interest in "raising the level of film discrimination in the nation," Trotter explained.[20]

Finding movies that qualified and determining their acceptability in the categories proved difficult in the first year. The panel now decided to focus its award criteria on the phrase "within the perspective of the Christian faith." What made for a distinctively Christian judgment on films? The new categories for 1965 citations emphasized honest and compassionate portrayals of the human situation that enhanced understanding of culture and society. The merit of movies on religious subjects was gauged by the "perceptiveness, accuracy, and pertinence" in treatment; exceptional entertainment for children and family were also to be recognized. Designating films of outstanding artistic merit within the Christian perspective put the awards "under a point-of-view umbrella," Wall explained. "This was an acknowledgment of the award's source, not an establishment of overt standards." But it also created a bias against movies with explicitly religious content, or a big-budget release that "almost by definition waters down any sharp personal directorial vision or incisive comment on public mores."[21]

Controversy at the Christian Oscars

During the panel's deliberations in January 1966, the awards came down to six nominations. *The Pawnbroker, Patch of Blue, The Eleanor Roosevelt Story, Nothing But a Man*, and *Sound of Music* all received a clear majority vote; the decision went 6 to 5 against *The Greatest Story Ever Told*. For the minority, the effect that denying an award to the biblical drama might have with constituents and producers was reason enough to overlook the film's artistic and theological failings. But the majority was firm that the panel's judgments should be made in reference to the categories and its mandate to award films of outstanding artistic merit. Panelist Frederick Essex (American Baptist Convention) resigned in protest of the exclusion of Stevens's film.[22]

At the February meeting of the BFC board in New York, discussion of the film nominations was "desultory and short," as William Fore put it. Despite forceful opposition from Bishop Kennedy, who argued that the BFC ought to support Stevens's film regardless of its lack of merit, the board voted nearly unanimously in favor of accepting the nominations. That day, the American Baptist News Service reported that Fred Essex "could not in good conscience be a party to the final recommendations." The next day, it was revealed that he had been employed by United Artists to solicit support for the film from Protestant leaders. Essex had taken a leave and had used vacation time to arrange promotional events, with the film studio picking up the tab, circumstances that would indicate he was aware of a potential conflict of interest. In his response, he noted that his denominational board had approved the arrangement and that other panel members were aware of it. It was the George Reid Andrews affair redux. Questions followed about who knew what and when, with Fore finally stating that the committee was not about to "run a security check" on each panel member. He put the onus on Essex. Among BFC leaders, there was agreement that Essex should have recused himself from the vote. Had Trotter known of Essex's "conflict of interest," he said, he would not have allowed him to vote. Coverage in the trades drew attention to the Protestant awards; the controversy showed how crucial it was for the BFC to keep any consulting and promotional work by its staff separate from its review agency and awards program.[23]

Variety ran a piece on the BFC awards that quoted Wall. "A sensitive filmmaker like Stevens," he maintained, "must have known that his characters were all lifeless, stereotyped, cardboard figures out of ancient Sunday-school literature." Afterward, WCO Committee member Carl Segerhammar wrote apologetically to Stevens. He was embarrassed by his colleagues' disregard for *Greatest Story*, which he thought was "a magnificent epic, well-told, and so far as I am concerned creates an atmosphere of worship." The BFC's action represented "the attitude of a few sophisticated and somewhat angry young men," but not "what the Church at large thinks."[24] Believing that, supporters of the film tried to mend the situation and communicate a different message to the film industry.

The Los Angeles Council of Churches, which included West Coast Office members, announced that it was giving one of its ecumenical awards to George Stevens for *Greatest Story*. The event was scheduled for the same day as the BFC awards luncheon—a perfect symbol of the unequivocal breach in the BFC. Disgruntled Protestant leaders also issued a statement calling the BFC's rejection of the movie a "grievous act of omission" and warning that endorsing movies that violated "basic Christian principles" only gave license to exploit nudity and obscenity in the name of "plot development."[25]

Bishop Kennedy played a part in the local council giving Stevens an award, which is what he wanted the BFC to do, but not in the statement of protest. His views on movie regulation were changing. The bishop, surprisingly, had never read the entire Production Code. When Shurlock sent him a copy, Kennedy likened its rules to "a maiden aunt's fuzzy regulations." He was not yet willing to grant movies the same freedom as the stage, but he believed that the code should be rewritten to give producers "the freedom to deal with life realistically." Kennedy was also persuaded by Trotter's argument that the BFC's task was "to encourage films of serious artistic purpose that are neither innocuous, simplistic moral tales nor debilitating immorality under the guise of 'harmless' entertainment."[26] Kennedy would remain personally supportive of Heimrich and the West Coast Office even as he came to see the value of the approach that his East Coast BFC colleagues were advocating.

The awards controversy proved a decisive moment that brought the protracted conflict between the East and West Coast factions—and with it the pietist-structural confrontation—to a showdown. Each group heralded one film as a quintessential illustration of its approach, and the other film as the antithesis. *The Pawnbroker*, an edgy art-house picture with religious overtones that illumined the plight of humanity, was the perfect movie to illustrate film criticism "within the perspective of the Christian faith." Moralists were upset over a contextual scene with brief nudity, though the thematic thrust of the entire film was grounded in the Holocaust. The film awards were supposed to encourage churchgoers to support movies that aspired to art. *Greatest Story* failed on that count; its absence of theological perspective or contemporary relevance rendered it a superficial, literal representation of the Gospel narratives. And for these reasons, the BFC judged the story of a Jewish Holocaust survivor to be a profoundly moral and religious film, and a biblical epic on the life of Christ to be theologically vacuous.

The 1965 awards did much to advance the BFC's first two purposes. New avenues for dialogue with the film industry were opened, and in terms of media education, public attention was drawn to a Christian model for film criticism that was not moralistic, but was distinguished by its emphasis on the vision embedded in the world of the film. Progress was being made on the goal of interfaith cooperation as well.

Ending an Era

Long-standing religious rivalries continued in the decades after World War II, even as the three great religious traditions were finding common ground and Americans were becoming more accepting of pluralism. As the cultural force of the liberal Protestant tradition diminished, an unprecedented ecumenism emerged among Protestants, Catholics, and Jews. The civil rights movement that started in black churches in the 1950s gave expression to the postwar emphasis on individual rights, and also united religious leaders in a moral cause to end racial segregation. It was a tumultuous time, however, and Protestant churches were not immune to the deep divisions that beset the country. Moderate and liberal clergy who advocated racial justice could be branded Communists, or might come under fire from religious conservatives who either opposed civil rights legislation or believed that the church should refrain from political involvement. With its liberal agenda, the National Council was alleged to have Communist sympathies; BFC awards to movies containing nudity and profanity were fodder for the Council's critics.[27]

In December 1965, the Legion of Decency changed its name to the National Catholic Office for Motion Pictures (NCOMP) to represent the "far-reaching transformation of its objectives and services" that had begun with the publication of the encyclical on the mass media (*Miranda Prorsus*) in 1957 and continued in the wake of the Second Vatican Council (1962–1965). The emphasis on boycotts to bolster Code enforcement and keep producers in line gave way to a positive approach: endorsing outstanding movies and promoting film education. In many respects, the Catholic agency was moving in the same direction as its Protestant counterpart. Actually, Fore and Father Patrick Sullivan, now NCOMP's executive secretary, were well acquainted and knowingly used each other to prod their organizations to change. Both wanted to eliminate the overly simplistic and moralistic approach that had long defined the Legion and had come to be identified with the BFC's West Coast Office.[28]

In April 1965, Heimrich suffered a mild heart attack and was only able to return to work on a part-time basis in September. That fall, the BFC underwent a major reorganization. During the 1960s, mainline Protestant denominations began to experience significant membership losses. National church attendance declined 5 percent between 1958 and 1966, with the sharpest drop among young people in their twenties—a trend that would only continue. It was a clear signal of the decline of mainline Protestantism in terms of resources, clout, and culture-shaping pretensions. A decrease in denominational support, over-budgeting, and a loss of income from its film distribution left the BFC in severe financial straits. Cuts were made in budget and personnel, and there was some consolidation of activities. A part-time director of utilization was added in New York to develop a program of film criticism and information and assume duties previously under the purview of the West Coast Office, including administering the Film Awards program and arranging pastoral film previews. Between 1964 and 1967, the BFC curtailed its film operation, moving away from production to facilitating network and denominational programs. Fore had hoped that BFC productions would be of a caliber to reach general audiences and get them "to take religion itself seriously," but despite an investment of resources, most church productions remained "from fair to awful, and some of the BFC material is at the bottom of the list." *Time* dubbed church productions "almost as cliché-ridden as a Hollywood comedy series." No productions were scheduled for release in 1966.[29]

In January of that year, Fore held a "brainstorming" session with Trotter, Wall, Knight, Kennedy, Robert Lee, and others. Afterward, Fore outlined the functions of a reformed West Coast Office and decided that small ad hoc committees assigned specific tasks could sufficiently carry out the work. He was convinced that the WCO was no longer absolutely essential to the BFC's relationship with the film industry. Despite efforts to get the WCO Committee to modify its role, it was clear that Heimrich and his colleagues were determined in their course, regardless of what the board in New York wanted to see happen. Meanwhile, the BFC's budget woes continued; a major drop in income for the year was projected. In September 1966, the BFC board was forced to reduce staff and operations for the next fiscal year. The decision was made to close the West Coast Office, effective January 1, 1967.[30]

At the final meeting of the WCO Committee, tempers flared. Members were not persuaded that the closure was due to a budget crisis. "The West Coast Office was set up to review screenplays," Heimrich said. "This has nothing to do with William Fore. He took a position the West Coast Office had to be closed. He took projects away from the West Coast Office—Film Awards is one example. Besides money, this office is being closed because of my objection to the garbage coming out of Hollywood. I had only the guidelines of the Motion Picture Producers Code to go by—'no minister shall be portrayed in a bad light.'" His comment was not off the mark, even as it revealed how outdated his outlook was. That Heimrich thought his job was to make sure Hollywood gave the same positive treatment to Protestant ministers as priests revealed "the depth of his understanding of the role of Christian relation to the industry," Fore said. Though he saw himself in a rivalry with Catholics, Heimrich adopted an approach to the cinema that was compatible with theirs. Arthur Knight wrote that Heimrich "sincerely believed that prior controls were the only way to influence the film-makers." But the courts had put an end to prior censorship, and the new head of the MPAA, Jack Valenti, had recently made the Production Code a relic of the past. Protecting the image of Protestantism belonged to a paternalistic mind-set that was no longer compelling in a pluralistic society. But Heimrich was tenacious and kept the West Coast Office on course as he envisioned it. The fiscal crisis was real, but the West Coast Office had been working at cross-purposes with the BFC's goals and policies. As it was, Heimrich's approach was out of sync with his own organization, the law, the movie business, the church, and the times: "theologically unsound and culturally outmoded," as Fore put it.[31] At the same time, the institutional power behind Fore and the East Coast faction was starting to leak badly.

As it was, two Protestant-Catholic alliances actually formed: the one a display of the pietist tendency, if only in principle, between the West Coast Office and Legion conservatives, and the other a structural one, with the two film agencies embarking on cooperative ventures. One year after the BFC started its awards program, NCOMP launched its own to honor "films whose artistic vision and expression best embody authentic human values." The rhetoric was nearly identical to that of the Protestant agency. The church awards garnered significant press coverage because they signaled a "change in the church's thinking about filmmaking," *Variety* observed. "What this means is that the Church no longer expects the film industry to provide nothing but easily digested pablum, designed just 'for entertainment or for profit,' but it has accepted the motion picture as an art form capable of dealing seriously and thoughtfully with human problems and with the world as it exists, not as it might be in a picture-book primer." The East Coast contingent could not have been more pleased. Fore was thrilled with the discourse in the nominations panel and the fact that the national press treated the awards as significant news. As hoped, the BFC was gaining respect from people in the film and broadcasting industries.[32]

In the fall of 1966, BFC and NCOMP officials began discussing ways in which they could work together. These initiatives validated and, insofar as they received press attention as examples of church unity, drew attention to and encouraged the larger ecumenical movement. The first joint Protestant-Catholic citation was given in 1967 to *A Man for All Seasons*, on the martyrdom of Sir Thomas More. The next year, *In the Heat of the Night* and *The Battle of Algiers* were awarded. A priest at the reception said, "It's as if in this one evening they've negated the entire work of the Legion of Decency all those years."[33] Indeed, these events—the transformation of the Legion, the closing of the West Coast Office, and the joint Protestant-Catholic film awards—were signposts of a new church posture, setting the stage for extensive cooperation with the film industry in finally bringing the Production Code Era to an end. The two national church agencies now set their sights on an industry rating system that would guard a filmmaker's freedom and an adult's right to view, while also protecting young people and children from exposure to material above their emotional level.

I I

No Longer a Dirty Word

THIS FILM WILL NOW BE RATED

My basic approach remains the same: classification is the
best available method both to protect the young and guar-
antee a maximum freedom for the creative artists.
JAMES M. WALL, editor, the Christian Century

IN THE SPRING of 1966, Jack Valenti, special assistant to President Lyndon
Johnson, left the White House to become the third president of the Motion
Picture Association of America (MPAA). That summer, the Production
Code Administration (PCA) denied approval to several films, most notably the profanity-laden *Who's Afraid of Virginia Woolf?*, which even the National Catholic Office for Motion Pictures (NCOMP) had not condemned.
According to one report, no more than 60 or 70 percent of the films shown
in American theaters were being monitored by the PCA. The Code's provisions were clearly out of step with contemporary mores. This precipitated
a major MPAA policy change. "I junked immediately in 1966 the foolish
constructions of the Hays Code," Valenti explained, for the reason that "it
was just palpably censorship and I wanted to be no part of it." The question was how to deal with the "expanding urgency of directors" to push the
boundaries of accepted limits, mindful that a public outcry might impede
progress toward artistic freedom and invite government censorship. A
top-notch lobbyist and public relations guru, Valenti's warning to industry
leaders that "unless we make an honest effort at self-restraint there will be
such a race toward excess that we are bound to injure progress toward adult
artistic statements as well as cripple the industry itself," echoed the sentiment of his predecessor, Will Hays.[1] Valenti was the Catholic equivalent of

the Presbyterian Hays, and just as Catholics helped Hays set up the Production Code Administration, Protestants would play a key role in helping Valenti transform it into a Classification and Rating Administration.

While consulting with the church agencies, MPAA staff were surprised to learn that Broadcasting and Film Commission (BFC) executives were not much interested in a Code revision. They preferred to talk about misrepresentation in advertising, and urged Valenti to adopt a voluntary classification system administered by the industry with assistance from civic groups. A rating system would allow a serious filmmaker to treat any subject for adult audiences and also protect children from "banal and salacious films," as BFC head William Fore put it. The BFC was doing its part, advancing a program in film education by assembling a stable of Protestant critics, encouraging discussion of movies in churches, conducting film seminars, and presenting its annual film awards.[2]

The powerful studio heads—Valenti's bosses—were not ready to adopt a system that they were sure would only restrict attendance and diminish profit margins. The MPAA implemented a halfway measure; the PCA would label certain films "suitable for mature audiences," and revise the Code by condensing it and turning its prohibitions into a set of guidelines that would encourage artistic freedom and responsibility by keeping producers in harmony with the tenor of the times. "This is still self-restraint, self-regulation and self-discipline," Valenti assured. "We want to make clear that expansion of the artist's freedom doesn't mean tolerance of license." The newly formed National Association of Theater Owners (NATO), representing 90 percent of the nation's exhibitors, got on board with a unanimous endorsement.[3]

The Protestant response, predictably, varied. Former WCO Committee member Clifton Moore was convinced that the revised Code would only lead to greater permissiveness. The industry was "so degenerated morally that we're going to have some form of censorship, " he said, and called for a government-appointed national film review board of 50 to 75 members representing a cross section of the American public: Protestant ministers, rabbis, priests, psychologists, doctors, teachers, parents, and "even the far out guys with the long hair." Bishop Kennedy considered the revision an improvement, while warning that "obscenity under the cloak of freedom of expression" would eventually "bring the censor down on all of us." The BFC and NCOMP gave circumspect approval. Fore welcomed the new approach, insofar as it promised to expand "possibilities for the honesty of production and the artistic merit," but, he insisted, the standards had to be "wisely administered" to be of any real value.[4]

In April 1968, the Supreme Court completely changed the terms of engagement. Obscenity remained a matter for the courts to decide, but two concurrent rulings implied that it was possible to draw a legal demarcation between movies suitable for adults but not minors, and that a system of film classification with clearly defined guidelines might be constitutionally valid. The court dispatched the MPAA's philosophical opposition to classification—that classifying movies was censorship—and also opened the prospect of a sudden proliferation of state and local regulatory boards across the country. The situation recalled the years before the Production Code, when state and city boards demanded expensive cuts in prints before they would allow exhibition.[5]

Valenti and NATO president Julian Rifkin knew they needed to act quickly. Besides the possibility of local censorship, there was good reason to think that federal legislators might step in and create a national rating system. The President's Commission on Obscenity and Pornography was authorized by Congress in October 1967, and the Senate was considering a resolution by Senator Margaret Chase Smith for a feasibility study of film classification. Fore, denominational officials, and NCOMP's Patrick Sullivan, all aware that industry plans were in progress, filed statements in favor of Smith's proposal with the Senate Commerce Committee in June 1968, in an obvious attempt to put pressure on the studios to act. Though opposed to government regulation, they indicated support for some kind of statutory classification of films if the industry did not adopt its own rating system.[6]

Exhibitors had been clamoring for a classification system. Top-level studio executives remained opposed, but, with the backing of Lew Wasserman (Universal) and Arthur Krim (United Artists),Valenti was able to sell them on the idea. Long-standing adversaries, the producer and exhibitor organizations moved swiftly to launch a voluntary rating system, an idea that industry leaders had long been attacking as contrary to the American tradition.[7] Almost overnight, the industry underwent a dramatic shift that would require a major public relations effort and strong support from opinion makers.

Building Bridges Between Church and Cinema

That April, a Methodist minister in Detroit issued a veiled boycott threat in an attempt to get a theater manager to cancel showings of The Graduate. Milton H. London, a NATO executive and president of the Michigan chapter, tried to alleviate his concerns by citing positive reviews of the film in religious publications, including the Methodist *Christian Advocate*. The minister appealed to editor James Wall, who responded that the film was a genuine artistic effort to deal with "the problem of alienation in modern life." The Methodist clergyman was at once "surprised," "disappointed," and "disturbed" by Wall's response: "Calling a film an art form or giving it an academy award doesn't change the fact that it is 'dirty.'" The conflict was resolved with Detroit area exhibitors announcing that they would not admit children or young teenagers.[8]

London forwarded the correspondence to Julian Rifkin, who invited Wall to speak at the NATO meeting in July. It was at this meeting that NATO's executive committee approved a tentative plan for a rating system. That the Protestant film buff commended adult and sophisticated movies like *The Graduate, Bonnie and Clyde*, and *The Pawnbroker* as having "moral and religious significance, as well as artistic merit" was an unexpected surprise. According to the trades, Wall's speech had "a profound effect" on NATO executives, and the meeting raised "prospects of vastly improved lines of communication between organized exhibition and religious organizations." Wall facilitated a meeting of NATO, BFC, and NCOMP leaders during the New York Film Festival that would lay the groundwork for future cooperation.[9]

Rifkin was convinced that "the imprimatur of the church people" was crucial to winning respect from legislators and the public. The church endorsement gave the industry "a respectability we did not have ourselves" and was "a very important factor in talking to legislators of each community," Rifkin said. "Don't forget the basic reason for having this was to avoid legal classification and to eliminate being arrested for pornography." Valenti was less sanguine about the prospect of involving church agencies in classifying films. Given the history of antagonistic relations, there were still many movie people "who nurse old wounds," as one executive put it. Conversely, church officials were leery of the industry's propensity for putting profits ahead of the public welfare. The BFC and NCOMP were visible points of contact with the religious community, however, together representing about 43 percent of the U.S. population. Already on record in favor of classification, they could give the new rating system cachet, help educate the public, bolster the industry's case with legislators, and defuse any major organized religious opposition. The Protestant and Catholic film agencies proved to be valuable industry allies at this critical juncture. It was agreed that the church agencies would have no part in rating films, but would serve in an "advisory capacity." This partnership assumed a measure of cooperation between church, family, and the MPAA ratings board to maintain artistic freedom and inform parents about the suitability of certain movies for young people. With this cooperation came a measure of scrutiny on the part of the church agencies. They would collaborate with the MPAA and NATO in publicizing the new program and would issue a periodic performance review based on the administration of ratings, exhibitor compliance, and the adequacy of advertising in displaying a film's rating.[10]

On September 27, 1968, industry heavyweights held a closed-door meeting at Geoffrey Shurlock's office for final approval of the new rating system; Fore, Sullivan, and Wall were there, with endorsements from their organizations.[11] The MPAA established four ratings and copyrighted the three less restrictive ones: General, Mature, and Restricted. A non-trademarked X rating (signifying material not suitable for those under 16) could be self-applied by non-MPAA members who chose not to submit a film to the new Code (later Classification) and Rating Administration (CARA).

The plan was announced at a press conference on October 7, with the MPAA acknowledging that the film industry served a differentiated audience. The following day, the BFC and NCOMP issued a joint statement endorsing "in principle this MPAA rating system as being consistent with the rights and obligations of free speech and artistic expression, as well as with the duty of parents and society to safeguard the young in their growth to responsible adulthood." The statement was carefully crafted to make it clear that church endorsement would remain contingent upon the industry's performance. "We were under no illusion the industry was trying to help parents make decisions about their children or anything like that," Fore said. "That was not their motivation." Still, it was better to support self-regulation than risk the emergence of nationwide censorship. "So, we supported it for First Amendment reasons, but we went into it knowing it was going to be a very flawed system."[12]

In his opening address at the NATO convention in November, Rifkin highlighted support for the rating system by clergy "opposed to statutory censorship" and "not as appalled as many might think about the addition of four-letter words to film dialog." Wall, Fore, and Sullivan presented a panel at the convention as part of a "Bridge to the Church" program. So began a cooperative public relations effort on the part of the church and industry organizations to win support for movie classification.[13]

Wall especially relished his liaison role and became a sharp apologist for the program. He published a number of articles on the rating system, and took every opportunity to address industry and church groups. Wall explained to his Methodist readers that deciding "what is suitable or appropriate for viewing in a pluralistic society is an almost impossible task." Milton London called the article "a giant step on the educational road that faces us." Margaret Twyman, MPAA vice president and director of Community Services, arranged distribution of some 2,000 copies of another article that Wall wrote, explaining how parents might utilize the ratings. "Building Bridges Between the Church and the Theatres" became Wall's stump speech, delivered at NATO's Celebrity Luncheon at the 50th Annual Motion Picture Industry Convention in Detroit that March. Copies of a brochure with suggestions for ways that theater owners could cooperate with local churches were provided and also made available to exhibitors at a "Show-a-rama" in Kansas City. Wall's book, *Church and Cinema: A Way of Viewing Film* (1971), was promoted in a *NATO Flash News Bulletin* as "'Must' reading for the exhibitor."[14]

As Wall envisioned church-industry cooperation, the MPAA would designate movies like *The Pawnbroker* and *Kiss Me Stupid* as adult, with a Christian review labeling the one as "an excellent portrayal for adults and older teen-agers," as he put it, and "*Stupid* as limited to those adults desirous of sitting through a two-hour dirty joke." Like his colleagues, he believed that for the rating program to work, those responsible for implementing it had to be "motivated by something other than purely commercial ends." The MPAA represented companies liable to "take advantage of the freedoms provided them under the First Amendment," he wrote. "For this they must be criticized and constantly watched. But their freedom must be protected." That was a role the church agencies were equipped to play, and in their view, this made church involvement with the industry rating program imperative.[15] It was a classic articulation of the structural motif.

The Mark of Cain: X-Rated

Classification gave filmmakers new freedom. Content prohibited under prior censorship was now permissible. But for some moviegoers, the new Hollywood came as something of a shock, and there was concern about detrimental social effects. Not surprisingly, the MPAA encountered a number of problems implementing the new system and getting the public to understand it. The biggest issue concerned the X rating. Public perception was that an X was tantamount to sexploitation. By August 1969, a number of newspapers announced that they would not carry advertisements for X-rated films, and many theater managers refused to book them in a move that threatened to undermine the effectiveness of the system. NATO's Rifkin called it "catastrophic and in the epidemic stages," and asked the church agencies to issue "a joint statement condemning this most insidious form of censorship."[16]

Wall instead came out with what *Daily Variety* called "one of the sharpest criticisms of X-rating films." He suggested amending the rating system with a special category for what he called "clean X films—pictures clearly aimed at an adult audience because of their over-all erotic or violent content, but still possessing authentic artistic merit." Wall actually started pitching the idea to the MPAA shortly after the rating program was approved in September 1968. Since the X category would include both "skin flicks" and artistically mature films, he could foresee a situation developing with the latter being rated R in order to distinguish them from sex-exploitation. As a remedy, he suggested that an "Adult" category be included to designate mature artistic movies, in effect "establishing two different kinds of 'X' films." The idea was noted, but came too late; the MPAA was confident that it had covered the legal bases and was ready to run with the new system. As problems developed, Wall again urged Valenti to make the change, but Valenti perceived it as venturing too far in asking CARA, the rating administration, to make "qualitative" judgments on artistic merit and whether a movie was obscene—a decision for the courts. The MPAA also wanted to protect itself from antitrust and discrimination charges of arbitrarily restricting trade. Wall understood the MPAA's position, but argued that value judgments were inherent in the process; categorizing a film "X" because of a nude scene was in effect a value judgment that "frontal nudity is not appropriate."[17] Drawing a distinction between adult-oriented movies and exploitation fare would remain as contentious as it was crucial to the viability of the rating program.

The rating system came under attack from groups as diverse as the General Federation of Women's Clubs, the American Civil Liberties Union (ACLU), and the Hollywood AFL Film Council, an industry group composed of unions in Hollywood. It was reported that film executives found the system in need of "serious revisions," and with speculation that an X-rated film might get only 10 to 15 percent of the bookings it would with an R rating, at least one executive suggested that a U (Unsubmitted) category be added to make the X rating viable. In January 1970, the MPAA announced two revisions to clarify and strengthen the program: the M category was changed to "GP: All ages admitted. Parental Guidance Suggested," and the age limit for the R and X categories was raised from 16 to 17.[18]

A *Stinging Rebuke*

The BFC and NCOMP issued a performance review in May 1970, warning that the rating system was "in proximate danger of failure." It was not just that there was public dissatisfaction with the program; officials of the two agencies sensed "a new public sympathy for censorship" emerging with the rise of President Richard Nixon's conservative "Silent Majority." The church groups reported evidence of theater noncompliance, inconsistency in advertising displaying the rating symbols, unreliability of film ratings (especially GP), and noted that trailers for R- and X-rated films were being shown before G and GP movies. They recommended that the criteria distinguishing the R and X categories be sharpened and that a new symbol be added to distinguish mature adult movies from exploitation films. These were practical concerns that could be dealt with easily enough; their critique of how the ratings were being administered echoed a traditional Protestant theme.

Ratings were based on isolated "language and visuals" instead of "overall treatment and theme," the BFC/NCOMP report pointed out, and therefore without regard for "the basic values a film proposes and their effect upon the viewer." It was naïve to think that a few editorial cuts could transform an adult-themed movie into one suitable to the emotional capabilities of children or adolescents. Gauging a young viewer's "ability to judge its content and to properly integrate it into his own experience and developing sense of values" should factor significantly in determining the suitability of a film. The current method was too moralistic and gave more weight to box-office aspirations than to the public welfare.

The report also noted that rating officials were employees of the MPAA studios, which compromised the system. Suggestions for alternative review panels, including a "blue ribbon" committee and, if all else failed, an independent one established by the government, were really idle warnings of what might happen if the industry failed to make the rating system credible. Wall, for example, had already rejected a government panel as "a prospect frightening in the extreme" and a blue ribbon board as elitist.[19]

The *Hollywood Reporter* headline read, "Church Groups Blast Code," and the *Los Angeles Times* called the evaluation "a stinging rebuke." The Catholic journal *America* hailed the BFC-NCOMP statement as "the key to a solution that respects the freedom and rights of both viewers and film-makers." Clifton Moore, former WCO member, again seized on aspects of the report to step up his campaign for a blue ribbon citizens committee and called for Valenti's resignation.[20] After a lengthy meeting with Fore and Sullivan, Valenti acknowledged that the ratings had to become more accurate and informative, and exhibitors had to tighten box-office enforcement and be more effective in monitoring trailers. Per their request, the MPAA commissioned a nationwide survey to gauge the effectiveness of the system, and a new policy was adopted that all trailers had to be approved for a general audience. But that was about it.

Afterward, Valenti became too busy to with meet with church officials; Margaret Twyman became their primary liaison. Fore and Sullivan felt the MPAA had become unresponsive to their interests and became even more vexed when a number of movies that should, in their judgment, have been rated R were designated GP. MGM's *Ryan's Daughter* (1970) was a case in point. The film was rated R for its adultery theme and a love scene involving nudity. But with the studio in financial trouble and in need of a large number of bookings to turn a profit, MGM went ahead and released it in New York and Los Angeles without a rating. The appeals board subsequently revised it to GP. Wall thought the whole affair made the rating system look like "an industry patsy." The basic problem with self-regulation, he maintained, was that "it remains in constant danger of self-interest," and if the MGM film was any indication, the New York appeals board could undermine the credibility of the system "with its overconcern for economics." He suggested broadening the appeals board to include non-industry personnel with expertise in film criticism or education so "there will at least be voices on the committee that will bring something other than a purely commercial concern to bear." Twyman dismissed his concerns and cautioned him not to editorialize so as to "blow it up out of proportion, resulting in some loss of faith in the system."[21] Wall disregarded her warning and editorialized against MGM's defiance and the appeals board's capitulation.

With the MPAA making minimal effort to address their concerns, the BFC and NCOMP review committee decided to revoke their endorsement of the rating system. Box office "was always the only issue as far as the MPA was concerned," Fore said. Any changes to the program were weighed against their potential effect on a member company's ability to make money. By Wall's account, Sullivan, under pressure from conservative Catholics, was the stronger advocate of this course, though his ecumenical stance kept NCOMP from "reverting to a less tolerant position." Wall anticipated that the action would not count for much "in the total scheme of things" and had argued against it.[22] But Fore and Sullivan believed they owed it to their constituencies to say that they did not endorse the rating system as currently administered. It was a dramatic and risky move that laid their influence with the industry on the line, but it was entirely consistent with the prophetic role the BFC had adopted in the early 1960s. The unsettled issue was whether the action would make any difference with the MPAA.

The announcement was made at a press conference in May 1971. The two church agencies withdrew their official endorsement of the program "as presently administered," but would continue to evaluate it in hope that the industry would develop "a workable, dependable and credible system of self-regulation as an alternative to governmental censorship." Valenti blasted the statement as "inaccurate and unfair" as well as based entirely on conjecture. He called their contention that the rating board was influenced by industry pressure "a lie—a cruel and unjust statement based solely on hearsay." The MPAA tried to pin the attack on Fore and Sullivan personally, claiming that their agencies did not represent "high official church sanction," and went so far as to cast them as unwitting opponents of free speech. The counterattack recalled the dispute between Will Hays, Carl Milliken, and George Reid Andrews. Valenti twisted remarks made about the need to improve the system in order to fend off legal censorship as a "subtle attempt" or "a possibly unconscious attempt" to tear down public support for the rating system in order to make way for government regulation. Fore and Sullivan emphatically denied the charge. Although they could not vouch for the sufficiency of the rating program, they had made it clear that they remained opposed to censorship and reiterated the fact that they had long been on record favoring industry self-regulation.[23]

The timing of the church groups' action was most disadvantageous for the MPAA. Its legal experts could cite the success of the rating system in arguments against the need for legislation aimed at creating classification boards. The MPAA's Legislative Department monitored 329 bills introduced in 50 states and 89 proposals before the U.S. Congress that affected the film industry in some way. Some of these statutes proposed censorship or classification boards or changes in, or enactment of, obscenity proposals. Some incorporated the rating program, while others had to do with sales and admission taxes. Those in favor of more restrictive measures, however, seized on the BFC-NCOMP statement to advance their cause.

That was unfortunate, but Fore and Sullivan replied that industry executives were fully aware of their concerns and had done little to address them. The MPAA's survey of parental satisfaction was not adequate; its verdict of "useful to very useful" was simply too vague to honestly assess the effectiveness of the system. And theater owners were likely to exaggerate their level of compliance for a NATO survey. A visit to a local theater was all that was needed to see that exhibitors were admitting underage people to R-rated films.[24]

The BFC-NCOMP announcement sparked a wave of press reports that brought the MPAA a lot of bad publicity. Stories were recounted of underage viewers being allowed into R-rated movies. *Time* found the ratings of a number of films unreliable and likened the categories to "just so much alphabet soup." *Life* pointed out enough flaws and inadequacies to put the program on "the long list of human endeavors which failed— things like the Crusades, Prohibition and Edsels." MGM threatened to withdraw because the system was "confusing and impractical," and a student intern with CARA said publicly, "Pubic hair and breasts, that's what they're worried about."[25] These reports mostly substantiated the church agencies' central claims.

Under pressure, Valenti admitted that there was confusion over the GP category and considered splitting it into two separate categories, but settled for publishing clearer explanations of the existing ones. He also weighed the possibility of changing the composition of the appeals board to include parents and professionals in psychology and education "who would not be subject to the film industry's politics and economic pressures," but the proposal met "with resistance within the industry." In June, Aaron Stern took over the rating administration with a view that producers of X-rated movies should stand by their "artistic convictions, instead of entering negotiations for less restrictive ratings." Stern's approach initially seemed compatible with the BFC's position. Although *The Summer of '42* (1971) contained no nudity and some profanity, he judged the movie's theme—a young boy having an affair with an older woman— enough to warrant an R rating. But the psychiatrist exhibited a Puritanical streak that irked producers, and "his shift to dealing with visuals only rather than total theme and context of a film," struck church officials as an ineffectual call back to the practices of the Breen office. The MPAA was making some effort to "bring critical church groups back into the fold," *Variety* observed, but it was not nearly enough to satisfy Protestant and Catholic officials.[26]

As it was, 16- to 24-year-olds accounted for 43 percent of annual admissions. It was estimated that an X rating meant losing up to 50 percent of a film's potential gross; an R-rated film lost about 20 percent. The tendency was for movies to gravitate toward the middle ratings to increase their commercial prospects (a trend that has not abated). The majority of films fell into the important GP and R categories, with some straddling the two and sending "parents dragging their children out of theatres, with dirty looks to the house managers enroute," a *Variety* reporter remarked. By the end of 1971, about 30 newspapers in major U.S. cities refused to review or accept advertising for X-rated films, with some even rejecting ads for R-rated movies.[27] The church film agencies had identified problems that would vex the rating program for years, and although the MPAA resisted their suggestions, additional pressures would eventually lead to the implementation of most of them, one by one, over the course of the next two decades.

Letting the Dust Settle

James Wall tried to alleviate the tensions and patch things up with the MPAA and NATO. Though he did not agree with the BFC-NCOMP action, the fight might have been avoided had the MPAA made a better effort to deal with their discontent. The onus was on the MPAA now. Julian Rifkin set up a symposium at the NATO Convention in October 1971 to facilitate discussion between church and industry leaders. *Boxoffice* editor Ben Shlyen welcomed the initiative; waning public confidence in the rating program made regaining "the support of these important clerical elements" all the more important to stem the tide of legislation for local, state, or federal classification or censorship. Rifkin presided over a panel of industry and religious heavyweights: Valenti; NATO president Eugene Picker; Myron Saland, executive director of the International Film Importers and Distributors of America (IFIDA); *Los Angeles Times* film editor Charles Champlin; Fore; Wall; Sullivan; and Rabbi Balfour Brickner of the Joint Commission of the Union of American Hebrew Associations.[28]

Afterward, the MPAA gradually instituted a number of changes that followed church groups' recommendations. First, the standards for a GP rating were toughened, and a "cautionary tag" was added to certain GP films, which effectively created a new category, a "qualified GP," *Variety* called it. Then, in February 1972, the GP rating was replaced with PG (Parental Guidance Suggested: Some material may not be suitable for pre-teenagers). Valenti decided to keep the appeals board "strictly an industry operation." Instead of adding outside experts, he invited Catholic, Protestant, and Jewish representatives to attend appeals hearings, but without voting rights. They would serve as public observers, monitoring the appeals procedure to ensure its legitimacy or "to bear witness to how the system works," as Valenti put it. BFC and NCOMP officers met several times a year with MPAA, NATO, and IFIDA staff. The meetings were largely perfunctory; for the most part, church officials would listen to "PR reports and kibitz and complain," Fore said.[29] The politically shrewd Valenti was playing it out to see what, if any, real effect the BFC-NCOMP action might have.

Change was in the air, however. Like the film industry, television producers were increasingly reflecting the sensibilities of the youth culture, looking at the under-30 market that appealed to advertisers. Looming on the horizon were advancing technologies—cable, pay-TV, and satellite broadcasting—that promised a proliferation of channels. This would present a challenge to the church, Fore predicted, in "helping preserve an informational structure in our nation which will serve the vital needs and interests of the public welfare."[30]

In 1972, the Southern Baptist Convention (SBC), now the largest Protestant denomination with nearly 12 million members, declared that many contemporary films were "utterly degrading, lacking in redeeming social value" and called for legislation to prohibit "exhibition of obscenity" in movies and television programs. The SBC resolution was in response to the 1970 Report of the President's Commission on Obscenity and Pornography, which found no reliable evidence to establish a link between sexually explicit materials and juvenile crime. Nixon dismissed the report of his own commission as "morally bankrupt," and the Senate voted overwhelmingly to reject the findings.[31] The Supreme Court would decide to revisit the issue of obscenity and movie standards. The outcome would have a direct impact on relations between the MPAA and the Protestant film agency.

12

A Changing of the Guard

The youth of America cannot follow the gods and goddesses
of the silver screen and the true God of Heaven at the same
time!

ROBERT L. SUMNER, Hollywood Cesspool (1955)

THE RATING SYSTEM contributed to the making of a "Hollywood Renaissance," with American movies displaying a new diversity and a high level of creativity. The commercial and critical success of youth-oriented movies, starting with *Bonnie and Clyde* and *The Graduate* in 1967, inaugurated a shift in the studios' production strategy toward the under-30 age group. Domestic box office began to surge, more than doubling: from $1 billion in 1971 to $2.8 billion in 1979. The R-rated and award-winning gangster saga, *The Godfather* (1972), replaced a family musical, *The Sound of Music* (1965), as the highest-grossing film ever. At the same time, however, a spate of movies featuring explicit sex and graphic violence pressed the boundaries between artistic liberty and license. Exploiting the X rating, three independently produced hard-core sex films—*Deep Throat, The Devil in Miss Jones*, and *Behind the Green Door*—achieved a new scale of commercial success, outpacing most major studio releases. Fears that "porno chic" would become a trend created widespread alarm.[1]

Nixon appointees gave the Supreme Court a conservative majority, and the court issued new guidelines for determining obscenity. *Miller v. California* (1973) dismissed the supposed national standard that had evolved since the *Roth* and *Alberts* decisions in 1957, with the court allowing a "community" to apply local standards. Further, disregarding the Nixon commission's findings, the court allowed legislators to assume a causal connection between pornography and antisocial behavior, even in the absence of "conclusive evidence or empirical data." The ruling sent a shock wave through the film industry. It encouraged the creation of state or local censorship boards and put distributors and exhibitors at risk of prosecution in one locality, even if a film was found unobjectionable elsewhere. Fearing lengthy and expensive lawsuits, studios began canceling projects and put others under close scrutiny; it was reported that they now refused to release any X-rated pictures.[2]

Though directed at hard-core pornography, it was not clear how the *Miller* guidelines would be applied by communities across the country. In March 1972, a local jury in Albany, Georgia, had declared *Carnal Knowledge*, a critically acclaimed R-rated film, to be obscene; the theater owner was convicted and fined. On appeal, the Georgia Supreme Court upheld the conviction and cited the *Miller* ruling. Jack Valenti wanted the Supreme Court to review the case "so that it is plain and clear that artistic films with a serious intent are not liable to indictment."[3]

With more than half of the state legislatures debating censorship laws, Valenti and Julian Rifkin thought the odds were good that the Broadcasting and Film Commission (BFC) would relent and reendorse the rating system—even if it meant living with its flaws. They made an appearance before the BFC board in February 1974, with Rifkin contending that the church groups had dealt a "serious blow" to freedom by withdrawing their backing. "Every time we tell a state legislature that our rating system is preferable to censorship, they want to know, 'Why don't the churches support you?'" he said. That was a concern, but the BFC would not be used as a public relations front for the film industry, and without significant improvement, the rating program remained "inadequate and unsupportable." The "three sticking points" remained: improve exhibitor compliance, provide better information to the public on the meaning of the ratings, and rate films more "on a total contextual basis."[4] This was the old Protestant agenda, guarding the public welfare, for the new times.

Troubled by the specter of censorship, the BFC decided to "soften its blow" by issuing a carefully worded statement affirming its "opposition to local film censorship" and confidence that "a voluntary effective, educationally oriented industry system is preferable to no system at all." They authorized a six-month study of the rating program that would begin with Aaron Stern's successor—who they hoped would adopt a more contextual approach to rating movies. Pending the outcome of that evaluation, an endorsement could be voted on at the October board meeting. Valenti and Rifkin came away with "at least half a loaf they can take for legislative nibbling," as James Wall put it. Wall was now the editor of the *Christian Century*, sixth in a line of succession stretching back to Charles Clayton Morrison in 1908, the year that the Federal Council was formed. Wall informed NATO's Paul Roth that the evaluation period would tell "whether the ratings serve merely to keep censor boards at bay" or to keep parents adequately informed of a movie's content. "As long as we fear that commerce rather than public interest motivates ratings, we would be obliged to withhold our endorsement," Wall maintained.[5]

"Protestants Needed by MPAA," *Variety* declared, but it was too early to gauge the political import of the church's imprimatur. The board was hoping to use whatever leverage it might have to make the rating program as effective an alternative to government regulation as possible. That two "motion picture bigwigs" made a personal appeal indicated that BFC support could be "a potent weapon." If that were true, perhaps Valenti would be able to persuade the studio heads to "heed church criticisms." If not, then the Protestant agency would "have to weigh the danger of withholding endorsement and the influence this may have on censorship forces."[6]

Shortly after the meeting with Valenti and Rifkin, the BFC held a conference of representatives from 30 religious, educational, and public service organizations to discuss ways to inform their constituencies about "this erosion of their intellectual and religious freedoms." Among them were the ACLU, American Library Association, Anti-Defamation League, Association of American Publishers, MPAA, National Association of Broadcasters, NATO, National Education Association, National Urban League, and the United States Catholic Conference. In the wake of the *Miller* ruling, 250 obscenity bills had been introduced in 37 state legislatures. BFC director William Fore said, "Our big concern is to make freedom respectable—so it will not be confused with smut." Speakers highlighted the problem of defining "community" and the confusion resulting from the Court's new guidelines. "In recent years, Protestants, Catholics and Jews have taken the position that since film has the possibility—as all art has—of opening us up to humanity, we have a right to be morally indignant about censorship," Wall said. In an editorial, he faulted the court's definition of a community as a geographic entity. "In a pluralistic and highly mobile society, culture is not geographic," he wrote. "Only the assumption that 'local' is a sacred word would permit such an interpretation."[7]

In June, the Supreme Court settled the matter with a unanimous decision that reversed the lower court ruling and declared that *Carnal*

Knowledge was not obscene under *Miller* standards. With this precedent established, studio executives could be reasonably sure that an R-rated film would not be ruled legally obscene. And the MPAA no longer had a pressing need for the Protestant agency's support for the rating system.

Movie Ratings and Deregulation

The BFC was reorganized in 1975 as the National Council's Communication Commission and issued a report that *Variety* considered "the strongest endorsement of the MPAA's rating system by a major religious body in at least four years." Even so, the Protestant agency still pressed for improvements in two main areas. The first was to modify the ratings by making them more age-group specific; insert a category between PG and R, basically splitting the Restricted category in two—one for children 13 to 17, and another for those under 12. Second, append extra symbols to the ratings (V for violence, L for language, and so forth) and/or taglines like "strong language," "brief frontal nudity," "mild comic violence," to help parents understand why a film was rated PG or R. Valenti entertained the ideas, but nothing changed until public outrage over PG ratings for *Poltergeist* and *Gremlins* forced the MPAA to institute a new PG-13 category for Steven Spielberg's *Indiana Jones and the Temple of Doom* in 1984.[8]

Amidst the uproar, the National Council commissioned a two-year study of violence and sexual violence in the media, with public hearings held in New York, Los Angeles, and Washington. That movies produced for theatrical exhibition had become much more accessible to young people was part of the problem. By 1986, video was a distinct market, accounting for about half of the studios' total revenues. The number of households with VCRs jumped from 1.85 million in 1980 to 32.5 million in 1986, and would reach 65 million (70 percent of the population) by the end of the decade; those with basic cable grew from 17.6 to almost 55 million. During that time, the number of adult theaters fell from 700 to about 250, while the adult video business was estimated at $1 billion in 1987. Cable television presented a whole new set of issues; because they did not transmit via the public airwaves, cable providers were exempt from Federal Communications Commission (FCC) regulations governing content. If the National Council preferred a course of media education and encouraging studios to develop a "corporate conscience," the new delivery systems made it necessary to make "some adjustment to the conflict between artistic freedom and commercial exploitation."[9]

The commission arrived at two important conclusions. Based on expert testimony from scholars like George Gerbner, dean of the Annenberg School for Communication at the University of Pennsylvania, who conducted extensive studies on media effects, the commission contended that media violence, and especially sexual violence, contributed to aggressive behavior in real life. Second, the prevalence of sexual violence in entertainment was attributed to the monopoly on production of a small number of powerful companies, a drive for excessive profits, and a weakening of federal oversight. Deregulation policies begun under Nixon continued during the Reagan administration. Entertainment companies reestablished their monopoly over production, distribution, and exhibition—the very structure that earlier Protestant reformers had labored for so long to abolish. *The Sound of Music* had fueled a trend of overproducing big-budget musicals, many of them flops that generated over $60 million in losses between 1967 and 1970 and contributed to the major studios' financial instability. Their stock undervalued, most of the studios were absorbed by large, diversified corporations. The oligopoly dismantled by the Supreme Court in the 1940s was being put back together through openings in the cable, satellite, and videocassette markets. The studios would eventually get back into theatrical exhibition, making the Paramount Decrees moot by 1987. Today, almost all of the film studios are subdivisions of vast entertainment conglomerates like Time Warner, News Corporation, Viacom, and Sony.[10]

In the past, fear of government regulation motivated producers to act voluntarily in adopting measures aimed at protecting the public welfare. But media companies were now part of a huge and complex corporate system that tended to diffuse personal responsibility. Moreover, the entertainment industry had little to fear from Protestants who were devoted to the First Amendment. Wall, who chaired the National Council's commission on media violence, noted the irony that "our greatest threat to the industry—government control—is undercut by our commitment to freedom."[11]

National Council leaders remained steadfast in their opposition to government censorship, while also believing that government had a role to play in preventing monopolistic control and ensuring media access. As the Council leadership saw it, deregulation brought about a fundamental shift: entertainment companies were perceived as profit-based businesses operating in a commercial environment and requiring minimal government oversight. Corporate strategies had less to do with the public welfare than with maximizing the interests—whether economic or ideological—of company owners.[12]

Among the study commission's recommendations were reversing deregulation of the television industry and restoring oversight power to the FCC, improving the Classification and Rating Administration (CARA) system and applying it to broadcast and cable television, making a "lockout" feature available to cable subscribers, requiring regular public hearings on entertainment programming, and including a media education curriculum in public and private schools. The commission also called for the industry to take seriously its social responsibility and not eliminate, but voluntarily curb, *exploitative* sex and *gratuitous* violence.

The commission warned that failure to demonstrate "a sensitivity to the impact of violence and sexual violence, especially upon children" would likely lead to censorial measures. CBS called the report "frightening," but National Council officials feared that, with the confluence of conservative politics and religion, explosive growth of the adult home video market, and an impending report on pornography by Reagan's attorney general Edwin Meese, calls for government control might prevail. The Council wanted to redirect the discourse, Wall said, by taking "this battle away from the new conservative right."[13]

The New Evangelicalism

While mainline Protestant denominations continued to suffer losses, membership in evangelical churches surged. By 1976, dubbed the "Year of the Evangelical," 34 percent—almost 50 million Americans over 18—claimed to have had a "born again" experience, the hallmark of the evangelical faith. A subculture of Protestantism, this "new evangelicalism" took shape in the post–World War II era as a transdenominational movement centered on biblical orthodoxy and the imperative to proclaim the Gospel and preserve the Christian character of the nation.[14] Evangelicals established their own periodicals, institutions, and even national organizations as alternatives to the National Council of Churches and mainline Protestantism. They believed they were a remnant of orthodoxy and a bulwark against liberal theology and modernism, perceiving themselves as a persecuted religious minority whose values were under assault by the secular mainstream culture.

Evangelicalism gathered momentum in the wake of the social and political upheaval of the 1960s. The national conflict over Vietnam and civil rights, the hippie counterculture and sexual revolution, Supreme Court rulings prohibiting prayer in public schools and legalizing abortion, the Commission on Pornography's report—these events convinced evangelicals that America had lost its way and was in decline. Aligning themselves with a rising political conservatism, many evangelicals claimed to be part of a "Moral Majority" (the name of Jerry Falwell's organization); their mission was to reverse the effects of the 1960s social revolutions and to establish a moral consensus based on biblical principles and evangelical values.

Evangelicals approached the media with different strategies from their mainline Protestant counterparts. When reports surfaced that *Soap*, a new sitcom in ABC's 1977 fall lineup, would be saturated with sexual situations, Protestant, Catholic, and evangelical leaders were all alarmed; it looked as if the network was pushing the prime-time envelope with a racy program. The National Council, United Church of Christ, United Methodist Church, and the National Conference of Catholic Bishops urged constituents to watch the first two episodes and communicate with local ABC stations on its suitability for viewing by children during prime time. The issue was not the show's content per se, but the appropriateness of the time slot; the strategy was to hold local affiliates accountable to the public interest.

Considering the moral dimension of how to exert economic pressure without becoming repressive, Fore proposed that church groups adopt a generic approach rather than target individual programs. The idea was to direct criticism, based on the findings of responsible experts, at the overall quality of programming, the inclusion of gratuitous sex and violence, or the commercial exploitation of children, for example, instead of objecting to an idea presented in a specific film or television show.

United Methodist minister Donald Wildmon, a fundamentalist and head of the newly formed National Federation for Decency (a name echoing the old Catholic organization), utilized a different tactic. He orchestrated a letter-writing campaign to protest the airing of *Soap* and, along with the Southern Baptist Convention and United States Catholic Conference, to put pressure on the show's commercial sponsors. The aim was to prevent programs containing excessive sexual, violent, or anti-Christian content from being shown, or to have them removed.[15]

With the election of Ronald Reagan to the presidency, evangelicals saw the tide changing, and under the banner of "family values," large parts of the movement identified a conservative political agenda with true Christian religion. Stressing personal piety as a means of social reform, a coalition of evangelical groups emerged as a potent force in American religion, politics, and the media by emphasizing moral issues, while also promoting an anti-government platform and the values of free enterprise.

Wildmon's anti-obscenity campaign got a boost from a partnership with Moral Majority leader Jerry Falwell. Wildmon formed the Coalition for Better Television, which represented over 3 million viewers, to monitor television programming and pressure advertisers. There was apparently more bark than bite to Wildmon's boycott threats, but advertisers were nervous about being entangled in controversy. With increasing competition from cable and videocassettes, the major television networks were willing to spice up their programming, and also to take seriously boycott threats that might diminish their already reduced audience share.[16]

Protestant leaders thought that evangelical maneuvers were undermining the effectiveness of church efforts with the media industries. Wildmon launched a boycott of Holiday Inn for showing "pornographic movies," but the hotel chain already had a firm policy that prohibited the showing of X-rated films. Playing loose with the term *pornographic*, Wildmon used it to describe movies like *Tootsie* and *Platoon*. By dubbing whatever they disliked as "pornography," Wall noted, these moral crusaders "erode public confidence in the church," and "by misrepresenting the situation they make it less likely that corporate officials will respond to criticism."[17]

Alarmed by increasing levels of media sex and violence, a number of evangelical organizations popped up to counter the ambiguity of CARA movie ratings. They advised Christian parents on the suitability of movies and television programs by providing tallies of incidents of sex, violence, and the use of expletives. Such "moralistic-content analysis" was having no effect, Wall maintained, highlighting the differences between pietist and structural tendencies. "This image-counting fails to deal with the deeper problem of the 'message' a given image conveys in context, and it allows the entertainment industry to brush aside the religious community's criticisms as naïve."[18] Evangelical critics however, had little patience for theories about interpretive context or audience receptivity; the direct communication of the surface message, and not the medium, was what mattered to them. They emphasized communication as Christian outreach; the religious conversion of individuals, they believed, was the way to redeem the culture. If movies can be used to evangelize, it stood to reason, they could also lead to spiritual corruption. And so evangelicals protested movies they found offensive and championed those they believed advanced their agenda by propagating the faith or espousing conservative ideals. But evangelicals were also beginning to assume the mainline Protestants' old role as cultural custodians, and they saw movies and television now as critical tools in their effort to revitalize the Christian character of the nation.

Movies with a Message

As a rule, conservative Protestant groups did not go to the movies even during the Production Code Era, considered by some to be a golden age in family movies. During the 1950s, the Billy Graham Evangelistic Organization formed World Wide Pictures to produce and distribute independent movies to evangelize youth—and not reform Hollywood. Hoping to reach "the black-jacket and beatnik crowds," *The Restless Ones* was booked in commercial theaters instead of churches in 1965. That year, 20th Century-Fox's *The Sound of Music* lured out even some of the most conservative Protestants; their numbers swelled the box office for the charming musical, which temporarily replaced *Gone with the Wind* as the top-grossing movie of all time. By the end of the decade, *Christianity Today*, the flagship evangelical magazine, reported that evangelicals felt free from "fundamentalist taboos" and could be counted among regular moviegoers—an occurrence that coincided with the advent of the MPAA rating system.[19]

Evangelicals made their explicit presence felt sporadically at the box office with support for movies like World Wide Pictures' *The Hiding Place* (1975), based on the true story of Corrie ten Boom, a Christian who hid Jews in Amsterdam during World War II and then survived a Nazi concentration camp. Warner Bros. hired an evangelical marketing firm to promote a British movie about two gifted runners that centered on class, faith, and the human spirit. *Chariots of Fire* (1981) topped $30 million at the box office and raised evangelical expectations; here was a "non-Christian" film distributed by a major studio that contained "a powerful Christian message" and won the Oscar for Best Picture. Surely this would alert Hollywood producers to "the vast, uncharted, unwritten, unfilmed, unacted territory of the Christian life and experience," a writer in *Christianity Today* remarked, echoing an argument long used by Protestants with film producers. But despite support from evangelical leaders, *Tender Mercies*, a beautiful film about a down-and-out country singer who becomes a Christian, failed at the box office in 1983.[20]

When Universal announced that it was distributing a Martin Scorsese film based on the controversial Nikos Kazantzakis novel, *The Last Temptation of Christ*, the studio started receiving angry letters, calls, and boycott threats. Like the novel, the film emphasizes Christ's humanity and shows Jesus struggling with his messianic fate and, tempted by Satan, fantasizing about living as a married man with children. Universal executives braced for a confrontation, but underestimated the deep hostility the film would elicit from Protestant conservatives, who perceived themselves as the nation's religious authority, under attack by a mainstream secular culture that was hostile to Christianity.

To deal with the religious community, the film company hired marketing consultant Tim Penland, an evangelical who was involved in the promotion of *The Mission* and *Chariots of Fire*. Scorsese, a Catholic, said he was intent on making "a deeply religious film which is an affirmation of faith," but evangelical leaders remained skeptical. Wildmon, head now of the renamed American Family Association (AFA), obtained a bootleg copy of a draft of the screenplay that included scenes deemed offensive. In one, while hanging on the cross, Jesus fantasizes about making love to Mary Magdalene and tells her, "God sleeps between your legs." When Universal postponed a scheduled prerelease screening for evangelical leaders (ostensibly because of postproduction delays), they were furious. Penland resigned. "I knew the chances were high that I was being used," he said, "but I was hoping to develop genuine dialogue between Christians and Hollywood." Universal did set up a special screening in July for Protestant and Catholic clergy, but miffed evangelical ministers refused to attend. Their indignant response was comparable to that of Catholics over *The Miracle*; they decried the film as an assault on Christianity, and called on Universal not to exhibit it out of respect for the Christian community. The MPAA issued a strong statement in support of Universal and attacked the evangelical effort to ban the film as censorship: "The key issue, the only issue, is whether or not self-appointed groups can prevent a film from being exhibited to the public, or a book from being published, or a piece of art from being shown."[21]

On August 11, 1988, the day before *Last Temptation*'s scheduled release in select cities across the country, fundamentalist and evangelical leaders organized a protest at Universal Studios that drew an estimated 25,000 people. "We're unleashing a movement," Donald Wildmon told the crowd. "Christian-bashing is over. . . . We demand that anti-Christian stereotypes come to an end." Protests against the film, however, were stained with an ugly anti-Semitism. Demonstrators waved placards denouncing Universal as "anti-Christian," and the crowd reportedly shouted "Jewish money, Jewish money." A group protested outside the home of MCA/Universal chair

Lew Wasserman by having a man dressed as Jesus kneel as a movie producer hovered nearby, carrying a lash. Jerry Falwell predicted the release of the film would ignite "a wave of anti-Semitism."[22]

Last Temptation had a solid opening weekend, but did meager business at the box office. It was a low-budget production, part of a three-film deal Universal had with Scorsese, and it was not expected to be a huge commercial hit. Nevertheless, evangelical leaders took credit for the film's poor outing. Furthermore, they called for a boycott of all Universal releases, and specifically urged constituents not to buy the videocassette of *E. T.: The Extraterrestrial* as a show of protest against Universal's "callous indifference to the Christian faith." Regardless, Universal set a sales record selling 14 million videocassette copies of its theatrical blockbuster hit.[23]

After previewing *Last Temptation*, the National Association of Evangelicals (NAE) issued a statement calling it "insensitive, offensive" and full of "flawed theology," while also acknowledging Universal's right to produce and distribute it. *Christianity Today* weighed the merits of the protest and rejected accusations that it amounted to censorship. But evangelical leaders went beyond the exercise of free speech. They tried to intimidate Universal into withdrawing the movie by threatening MCA/Universal with financial ruin. Bill Bright, the head of Campus Crusade for Christ, publicly offered to raise $10 million to buy the negative and prints from Universal so that they could promptly be destroyed. Exhibitors were pressured not to book the movie. These actions turned dissent and theological debate into a First Amendment issue and constituted an attempt to censor a movie on grounds of sacrilege.[24]

Having failed to prevent exhibition of the film, Falwell called for "an all-out effort to cripple Hollywood and make it regret ever releasing this piece of garbage." Conservative political commentator Pat Buchanan called the battle over the *Last Temptation* "one more skirmish in the century's struggle over whose values, whose beliefs, shall be exalted in American culture, and whose faith may be derided and disparaged." The protest over the movie took on enormous symbolic significance. A coalition of evangelicals opened a new Hollywood front in the "culture wars."[25]

In Retrospect

Having developed an approach to film as art, cultural discourse, and a theologically revealing medium, the National Council's East Coast group was at odds with the pietist perspective of evangelicals and fundamentalists. In his *Christian Century* review, James Wall called *Last Temptation* "a flawed film that doesn't deserve the publicity that fundamentalist Christian preachers have given it." William Fore, who attended the prerelease screening for clergy, found the movie "a bit pompous," but "consistent with an important stream of Christian theology," and criticized those Christians who sought to prevent its exhibition. Even if they found the rating system deficient in some ways, Council officials had helped establish a mode of industry self-regulation that affirmed the traditional Protestant emphasis on guarding both freedom of expression and the public welfare. The National Council would continue to monitor the appeals process and press for improvements in the rating program, but, as Fore put it, "When the church has made a point it is time to move on to a new task."[26]

The film awards program advanced the BFC's goals by setting the stage for church involvement with the rating system and increasing interfaith cooperation. In March 1971, NBC aired a one-hour special, *The Protestant-Catholic Movie Awards, A Public Affairs Presentation of NBC News*, with Hugh Downs moderating a panel with *Life* movie critic Richard Schickel, Father Sullivan, and the BFC's Robert Lee. The next year, the Synagogue Council of America participated in the first Inter-Religious Film Awards televised on NBC, *Cinema '71 Films That Matter*. But the awards program lost its luster and Protestant criticism its distinctiveness. The kinds of issues that Protestant criticism addressed—debate over the morality of *Bonnie and Clyde* and *The Graduate*, for example—were taken up by national reviewers who were highlighting quality films for large audiences. In the fall of 1973, the BFC board decided to discontinue the awards and emphasize film education. When the MPAA stopped distributing the Green Sheet in 1969, the BFC launched *Film Information*, a monthly periodical to provide churchgoers with a religious perspective on newly released films. Circulation never reached expectations, and the publication was terminated in 1978. In 1980, the Catholic Church closed its film office and, after more than 40 years, stopped publishing film recommendations.[27]

Media education proved frustrating. Like most moviegoers, rank-and-file Protestants just wanted to be entertained. If the West Coast mentality proved anachronistic, the East Coast approach tended toward elitism. Two of the winners at the 1971 Inter-Religious Film Awards, for example, were obscure movies: *One Day in the Life of Ivan Denisovich*, based on Alexander Solzhenitsyn's novel about a prisoner at a Siberian labor camp, and foreign film Oscar winner *The Garden of the Finzi-Continis*. The next year, the interfaith committee awarded two Oscar-nominated films, *The Emigrants* and *Sounder*, but overlooked the box office record-setting and critically acclaimed gangster classic, *The Godfather*. The awards had become too esoteric and were having no recognizable impact on the habits of Protestant moviegoers.

The Protestant establishment negotiated the historic transition from Protestant America to an increasingly pluralistic democracy, maintaining its responsibility for the nation's well-being, while recognizing the loss of its inherited religious and cultural authority. The key question in the National Council's Communication Commission remained how to relate to media personnel and institutions in terms of "the *human* uses" to which the media is being put.[28] The Commission continued to address problems related to the film and broadcasting industries and to educate constituents. But these efforts were largely out of public view, as evangelicals moved to center stage.

Evangelicals were aware of America's pluralistic complexion, but, believing that the nation could only survive with their religion and core values as its foundation, they followed the earlier examples of Protestants, and later Catholics, by assuming the role of the nation's moral custodian. Evangelicals took their turn now at protecting Christianity and asserting their hegemony over American culture. Their proposals and tactics represented a significant departure from those of their recent Protestant predecessors, who thought evangelical conservatives were undermining church efforts to guard freedom of expression and influence the film industry. Evangelical leaders would soon reinvigorate talk of prior censorship in what looked like a throwback to the heyday of the Legion of Decency.

13

The Curious Case of Evangelicals

*When I started this in 1977, I thought I was dealing with
sex and violence on TV. I've discovered we are dealing with
a war between the Christian view of man, and a secular, or
humanistic or materialistic, view of man.*

DONALD WILDMON, founder, American Family Association

IN 1990, THE Motion Picture Association of America (MPAA) adopted a
new NC-17 rating for adult-themed movies that were not pornographic,
but also not appropriate for viewers under 17. At the same time, brief
explanations were included with a film's rating, beginning with R-rated
films in September, and then for those rated PG and PG-13 in 1992. These
were both adjustments for which the Protestant film agency had lobbied years earlier. Now, however, James Wall interpreted the move as the
MPAA relenting to pressure from producers who wanted to put more
sex and violence in movies for general release. He editorialized that, by
replacing "the pejorative X rating" with NC-17, "the industry has decided
that responsibility is less important than freedom." Under the existing
circumstances, any designation for artistic adult movies "would quickly
evolve into a public stigma."[1]

Wall's longtime friend and associate, William Fore, now teaching at
Yale Divinity School, disagreed. When pornographers started exploiting the X rating as an advertising device, many theaters refused to show
X-rated films and studios stopped producing them. The effect of this de
facto censorship was to undermine two of the rating system's objectives:
averting censorship and encouraging artistic freedom. The NC-17 designation promised to correct this. Jack Valenti also weighed in. "I am proud
of our movie rating system, for it is a nourishing element in our grand

experiment in a free, democratic society," he wrote. "I cannot but believe that my old friend James Wall agrees with that." He did, in principle, but his confidence in the system was shaken. "Quite simply, freedom is being abused by the industry," he had remarked a few years earlier.[2] Even though Wall represented the National Council on the Classification and Rating Administration's (CARA) appeals board, he was disappointed with how the rating program was working. Box office enforcement was still lax, and producers were pushing the envelope and skirting the system by releasing movies unrated.

Throughout the religious community, there was widespread concern over the effect the new rating might have. Evangelicals were quite skeptical, with some interpreting it as a smoke screen for the film industry to mainstream pornography. Donald Wildmon's American Family Association threatened to boycott Blockbuster Video if the nation's largest video rental chain stocked NC-17 titles. Under his leadership, a coalition of church leaders called CLeaR-TV (Christian Leaders for Responsible Television) issued a "Statement of Concern" to top studio and network executives. Echoing a familiar theme, they called for a reduction in the levels of sex, profanity, and violence in movies and on television under threat of boycott, and also demanded an end to what they construed as "anti-Christian bigotry." Movies like *Ghost* and *Nuns on the Run* and specific episodes of TV shows *MacGyver*, *Matlock*, *Cheers*, and *Knots Landing* were among the programs cited as anti-Christian.[3]

Revisiting the Past

At a public forum in February 1992 sponsored by the Knights of Columbus, Los Angeles Cardinal Roger M. Mahony lamented a "breakdown of our social fabric," and suggested that "perhaps the time is ripe" for the industry to voluntarily adopt a moral code. Mahony had been persuaded by Dennis Jarrard of the Archdiocese's Commission on Obscenity and Pornography to get behind a revised Motion Picture and Television Code prepared by Ted Baehr, an evangelical Protestant. According to Baehr, "Between 1933 and 1966, representatives of the Roman Catholic Church and the Protestant Film Office read every script from every major studio to make sure it conformed to the high moral character of the Motion Picture Code." It was an exaggerated claim that invested the BFC's West Coast Office with far more power than it ever had. Nevertheless, Baehr maintained that shutting down the West Coast Office at the end of 1966 (and supposedly the Catholic agency around the same time) opened the "floodgates to violence, sex, Satanism, homosexuality, and anti-Christian bigotry," alienated the family audience, and led to the advent of the MPAA rating system in 1968. "The liberals had won. Fort Hollywood was closed," he wrote. "It was the end of an era." The solution was to return to the conditions that existed during the glory days of the Production Code Administration (PCA) and the Legion of Decency.[4]

Inspired by George Heimrich, Baehr formed the Christian Film and Television Commission (CFTVC) to reestablish a church presence in Hollywood and, specifically, "to resurrect the work of the Protestant Film Office and the Legion of Decency." The CFTVC's goal was to get the film and television industries to adopt and adhere to Baehr's revised production code, which was "only a reflection of eternal principles" that would "help filmmakers understand the concerns of moral Americans." And Baehr claimed nothing less than that the CFTVC had its "finger on the pulse of the entertainment preferences of moral individuals and families around the world." He conceived of censorship narrowly, "prior restraint by the government," as distinguished from "a united effort to make obscenity and immorality unprofitable," and based on such reasoning, he concluded that his plan for prior censorship was not censorial. Like Heimrich before him, he wanted his organization to play a role akin to that of the Breen Office, scrutinizing film scripts, which he believed would "inaugurate a second Golden Age of Hollywood movies and television programs," and would be profitable as well.[5] In a long line of Protestant and Catholic reformers, Baehr now offered his expertise and services to ensure that movies met with Christian proprieties.

Cardinal Mahony's support for a new production code created a furor in Hollywood. Valenti dubbed the code "an anachronism," and the *Los Angeles Times* estimated that, if implemented, the code's provisions "would probably prevent the production of most films now showing in theaters." The cardinal backpedaled. Dennis Jarrard was fired, and after consulting with Valenti and MCA/Universal's Lew Wasserman, Mahony issued a pastoral letter in September highlighting "human values" to serve as a guide for entertainment producers and consumers. Mahony was close with Wasserman, who had helped plan the visit of Pope John Paul II to Los Angeles in 1987 and had donated $1 million to the archdiocese's Education Foundation in 1990. During the uproar over *The Last Temptation of Christ*, Mahony criticized the "anti-Semitic implications" in evangelical attacks on the film and Universal, and expressed confidence that Wasserman would not release a movie that would be offensive to a large group of American moviegoers. "Because I reject censorship," Mahony said in regard to his pastoral letter, "I do not propose a code to govern what filmmakers may create, nor do I wish to dictate what intelligent viewers may see." Mahony's missive defended artistic freedom, and as *U.S. News & World Report* put it, asked "Hollywood, ever so politely, to clean up its act."[6]

Veiled support for Mahony's code came from film critic and conservative commentator Michael Medved. In an op-ed piece in the *Los Angeles Times*, he declared that "Hollywood no longer reflects, or even respects, the values of most American families." The producers of entertainment, Medved alleged, suffered from "a sickness of the soul." That was the theme of his soon-to-be released book, *Hollywood vs. America*. In the early twentieth century, some Protestants had faulted Jewish producers (ostensibly ignorant of "Christian" mores) for reaping huge profits from immoral movies believed to be detrimental to the social good and out of sync with the majority of the public. In the late twentieth century, the accent shifted from religion to ideology, the "Other" being Hollywood liberals charged by conservatives with forsaking profits to undermine the "traditional values" of most American families. Medved popularized the notion and his book was particularly influential in evangelical circles. He pilloried the entertainment industry as "an all-powerful enemy, an alien force that assaults our most cherished values and corrupts our children," contending, moreover, that Hollywood only became hostile to family and religion when the industry was taken over by countercultural liberals in the late 1960s. Prior to that time, under the leadership of Jewish immigrants, Hollywood "presented America and its institutions in a very uplifting, hopeful, optimistic way," Medved told *Christianity Today*.[7] This remark completely misconstrues the religious dynamics and industry conditions that existed prior to the 1960s.

Nevertheless, those in the Religious Right perceived Medved, who is not evangelical but Jewish, as a Hollywood insider, and he told them precisely what they wanted to hear: the secular ideology of Hollywood producers was preventing the entertainment industry from responding naturally to market forces. As proof, studies were presented showing that the studios released a higher percentage of R-rated films even though G and PG-rated movies on average performed much better at the box office. A survey by the Michigan-based Dove Foundation, an evangelical non-profit and pro-family organization, for example, showed that G-rated movies on average earned over 8 times the gross profit of R-rated ones, had a 78 percent greater rate of return on investment, and also that the studios produced 17 times more R-rated than G-rated films. Copies of the Dove Profitability Study were delivered to studio executives with CEO Dick Rolfe's exhortation to "give the public more of what it wants—for profits sake."[8]

An Evangelical Approach

The explanations that religious conservatives put forth owed more to their own predilections than to historical realities. First, however much they claimed to be against prior censorship, critics like Ted Baehr and Michael Medved romanticized the Production Code Era as "once upon a time" when Hollywood, working in harmony with the church, made movies that respected religion and family. They lamented the end of the Code, and were vulnerable to charges that they favored a censorial prior restraint of movies, and also that their proposals for reform were unrealistic. "I never for one moment countenanced using any of these things Ted Baehr was talking about," Valenti said, "but I certainly listened." Medved acknowledged that reinstituting a production code was unworkable, but his main remedy for what ailed the entertainment industry was for producers to sign on to the basic principle of the 1930 Code: "No picture shall be produced which will lower the moral standards of those who see it."[9] As we have seen, the film industry might lend its rhetorical assent, but would not voluntarily monitor itself according to such a nebulous ideal, and without an enforcement mechanism the Code had proved largely ineffectual.

If they were not expecting to reverse the evolution of movies as protected speech, religious conservatives wanted their moral vision to reign supreme over Hollywood. Appeals for family-oriented programming were not just meant to curb sex, profanity, and violence; they were also aimed at restricting ideological content. The majority that evangelicals claimed to represent were identified variously as churchgoing, moral, and conservative; evangelical reviewers were just as likely to denounce a movie on ideological as moral or theological grounds.

Second, a significant demographic shift in the moviegoing audience was underway by 1990 that indicates the studios *were* responding to box-office trends. Hollywood was preoccupied with the youth market during the 1980s, which a *Los Angeles Times* critic referred to as "a decade of demographic tunnel vision during which people out of the twelve to thirty-four range were statistically irrelevant to Hollywood." With the exception of *E.T.*, the ten top-grossing movies of the 1980s were all driven by the repeat business of teenagers—especially adolescent males. But by the end of the decade, the percentage of the population under 18 dropped significantly. Between 1990 and 1994, as increasing numbers of baby boomers entered their thirties and forties, the under-30 share of the box office dropped from 56 to 45 percent, while the 30-and-over share rose from 44 to 54 percent. While network television was getting racier to compete with cable, film producers charted demographic trends that showed a bifurcated market emerging; it made commercial sense to produce PG movies aimed at the general or "family" audience, and others with "provocative themes" for the over-40 group who did not care about a film's rating.[10]

After a lackluster period in the 1970s and 1980s, Disney struck gold with *The Little Mermaid* in 1989, selling not just movie tickets, but the soundtrack, videocassettes, and children's merchandise. The movie merchandizing market skyrocketed from $7 billion annually in 1977 to more than $70 billion by the end of the 1990s, with children's products accounting for 65 to 76 percent of the market. Hollywood was no longer primarily in the business of making movies for theatrical exhibition. Box-office constituted only 25 percent of studio revenues in the 1990s as media corporations sought to synergize a movie into an event that could reap financial rewards in multiple markets. Disney followed up *The Little Mermaid* with a series of animated films that, along with the *Home Alone* hits, solidified the viability of the family audience. G- and PG-rated movies grew from just over 16 to almost 21 percent of all releases between 1991 and 1994. With some exceptions, the top-grossing films of the decade were aimed at the general family audience or adults, while still appealing to the 16- to 24-year-old group of regular moviegoers.[11] "Family values" critics tapped into widespread concerns about the pervasiveness and potentially harmful effect of the entertainment media that materialized with the availability of movies on videocassette, and the explosive growth of cable channels like MTV that gave youth exposure to movies and music—including controversial rap. These fears animated the evangelical-led movement for family entertainment, which was as much about market demographics and the changing media landscape as it was about cultural conflict.

Finally, evangelicals embraced profit making as their modus operandi for movie reform with much more intensity than any of their predecessors; their appeal ultimately was to the corporate bottom line, not social responsibility. In the main, those Protestants who took the structural approach believed themselves to be a countervailing force to the film industry's incessant drive to maximize profits. Any aspirations to deliver an audience large enough to redirect Hollywood's production schedule were dispelled by *The Greatest Story Ever Told*. Evangelical leaders, however, recycled—and amped up—the premise that movie producers would reap a financial bonanza by catering to a vast majority of God-fearing Americans. They put their full confidence in the consumer ethos and approached the entertainment industry single-mindedly as lobbyists on behalf of a potentially lucrative market. Surveys showing that the vast majority of Americans believed in God and that high numbers attended church regularly were used both to demonstrate the prowess of the religious market, and to mark Hollywood personnel as secularists out of touch with mainstream America. It was common for evangelical groups to petition Hollywood for more "wholesome family entertainment" based on the existence of "the huge untapped market of consumers who want exciting movies, but without explicit portrayals of sex, violence and profanity."[12]

This market-based strategy harbors an inherent contradiction—one that always seems to escape its adherents. The obvious assumption, grounded in consumer choice and maximized profits, is that a free market will produce movie morality. On what basis then can religious conservatives limit screen exploitation other than profitability? The gauge of commercial success can be used to justify family movies as much as crude teen comedies or misogynistic slasher films; the Christian-themed *The Blind Side* and raunchy *The Hangover* each earned over $200 million domestically in 2009. Furthermore, if the strategy of delivering an audience of churchgoers was not new, the scope was; the by-product of increased family fare was not just more movies and programs, but an avalanche of merchandise marketed to children.

The evangelical approach can also be understood as part of a larger pattern of postmodern culture. Various pressure groups—whether from the Left or the Right—have assumed the role of media watchdog, protesting specific programming and trying to influence producers on representations of gender, race, religion, sexuality, and more. The working assumption is that the raison d'être of entertainment corporations is to maximize profits, and these groups expect to exert some control over media depictions by demonstrating the existence of a lucrative market for movies representing their particular ideals and values. To some extent, this consumer-based censorship has come to be understood as a feature of the regulation of free expression.[13]

Boycotting Disney

In 1995, evangelicals joined conservative Catholic groups in their outrage over the movie *Priest* and spearheaded a boycott of the Walt Disney Company. The film's depiction of a homosexual priest, plus another engaged in an ongoing affair, was a far cry from Bing Crosby's Father O'Malley in *Going My Way*. William Donohue, president of the Catholic League for Religious and Civil Rights, claimed that *Priest* was "designed intentionally to insult the Catholic Church and Catholics nationwide." The Assemblies of God, American Family Association, and many other evangelical organizations joined the effort. The campaign got a boost in 1997 when the Southern Baptist Convention and evangelical James Dobson's Focus on the Family announced that they too would boycott the world's largest provider of family entertainment, not just for objectionable movies and television programs, but also for its "anti-Christian" policies, such as providing health and other benefits to same-sex domestic partners. Religious conservatives were meddling in the corporation's internal policies, and they were making homosexuality a top issue.[14]

Like the other major studios, Disney owned production and distribution companies, cable and broadcast channels, radio stations, theme parks and resorts, retail outlets, and more. Even some Southern Baptists thought the boycott was unrealistic. "If you approve this, you will have the moral obligation to go home and cancel ESPN, get rid of the A&E channel, stop watching Lifetime, and never watch ABC's *Good Morning America*," one delegate observed. At the end of the year, Disney's chief executive, Michael Eisner, said the company was "not pushing any agenda" and the boycott was having no "financial effect."[15] Even so, the campaign paradoxically contributed to the industry's growing awareness of the existence of a "Christian" market for religiously themed products.

There were a number of films that pleased the evangelical palette, including the C. S. Lewis biopic, *Shadowlands* (1994), *Dead Man Walking* (1996), Mel Gibson's *Braveheart* (1996), and *A Walk to Remember* (2002). Not all met commercial expectations. *The Prince of Egypt* (1998), an animated version of the story of Moses that was heavily marketed to evangelicals, received good reviews, but had a mediocre box office run. *The Passion of the Christ* became a significant event in 2004; conservative evangelical and Catholic groups that had protested *The Last Temptation of Christ* to no avail became a potent box-office force behind the film's astounding commercial success. Mel Gibson's ultraviolent depiction of the torture and crucifixion of Jesus of Nazareth was embroiled in controversy—its detractors charging Gibson with anti-Semitism, its defenders treating it as a major battleground in the ongoing culture wars. Evangelicals heralded *The Passion* as an extraordinary evangelistic opportunity, with some churches buying blocks of tickets. The movie finished third among 2004 moneymakers—behind *Shrek 2* and *Spider-Man 2*—earning $370 million in the domestic market and over $600 million worldwide.[16]

Meanwhile, the incredible success of *The Lord of the Rings* trilogy (2001–2003), based on the fantasy novels by J. R. R. Tolkien, a British Catholic, drew serious attention to the "Christian" market. Disney partnered with Walden Media, owned by evangelical billionaire Philip Anschutz, in the production of *The Chronicles of Narnia: The Lion, the Witch and the Wardrobe* (2005), an adaptation of Christian writer C. S. Lewis's children's book. Walden Media aimed its output at Disney's demographic—children and families—with the intent of making "some small improvement in the culture," as Anschutz put it. The marketing budget for *Narnia* was around $80 million, with over $5 million spent pitching the movie directly to churchgoers as an occasion for evangelism. With $291 million in domestic grosses and $745 million worldwide, the Christian allegory was a resounding box-office success.[17]

In 2005, the Southern Baptist Convention, American Family Association, and Focus on the Family called off their boycott of Disney—in part an effect of the Disney/Walden Narnia venture. The eight-year campaign apparently had no real effect on Disney's bottom line. Much more than an indication of whether evangelicals "love Jesus more than we love entertainment," the failure of the boycott highlighted the fact that the real driving force in Hollywood was the formation of huge global entertainment conglomerates that were cultivating international markets for American movies, television programming, and ancillary products. The irony is not hard to miss. In their alliance with political conservatives to advance a moral agenda, evangelicals signed on to a program of deregulation that reversed the gains made by earlier Protestant reformers to dispel the concentration of power in the industry. Consumer protests might have an effect on a select product, but would hardly make a dent in these powerful media corporations.[18]

In 2006, conservative Catholics were up in arms over *The Da Vinci Code*. Despite a huge controversy and horrible reviews, the film adaptation of Dan Brown's runaway best seller still finished in the top ten and earned $217 million in domestic box-office grosses and $758 million worldwide.

That year, 20th Century-Fox created FoxFaith, a new home entertainment division focusing on movies with appeal to the "Christian" audience. Movie marketers set their sights on those Christians who generated hundreds of millions of dollars in sales of religious books, Christian-themed music, and merchandise.

Making the Most of the Christian Market

Evangelicals started to create their own consumer subculture in the 1970s by merging religion with commercial values and practices: celebrity, sales and profits, consumer tastes and audience demographics, marketing and merchandising were means to propagate the Gospel. By the time *Entertainment Weekly* dubbed Christian popular culture "entertainment's newest boom industry" in 1999, "Christian" was widely understood as a marketing label identified with content that was variously faith-affirming and evangelistic, or at least family-friendly, and perhaps ideologically specific.[19]

With Christian outreach paramount, movies made by evangelicals were notable for exhibiting a distinct lack of cinematic merit and still scoring in the CBA (former Christian Booksellers Association) market. Based on the best-selling novel by Tim LaHaye and Jerry Jenkins, the low-budgeted *Left Behind* (2000) was distributed direct-to-video and sold over 3 million copies. One reviewer began with a caveat. "Immediate disclaimer: This is not to denigrate the religious beliefs that inform *Left Behind*. . . . This is simply to address the hilariously bad manner in which those beliefs are expressed." Whatever it lacked in artistic quality, *Facing the Giants* (2006), a small-budgeted Baptist-funded film about a football coach whose spiritual renewal turns his life around, grossed $10 million against a mere $10,000 in production costs. Some evangelicals were irked when CARA slapped a PG rating on *Facing the Giants* and charged it was only because of the movie's explicitly evangelistic message. *Fireproof* (2008) was a step up, featuring *Left Behind* star Kirk Cameron as a fireman whose life and marriage are restored by a religious conversion. When this low-budget ($500,000) film was niche marketed to Christian consumers, it earned $38 million in a theatrical run and sold 2 million DVDs. *Fireproof*'s surprising success drew comparisons among evangelicals to the mainstream hit *My Big Fat Greek Wedding*.[20]

The "Christian" market had its distinct peculiarities, but to tap its largest potential, marketers sought a lowest common denominator to exploit. A 2005 MarketCast study cosponsored by *Variety* revealed that the viewing tastes of religious and nonreligious people were nearly indistinguishable. Evangelicals might turn out in droves for an explicitly religious film like *The Passion* and exhibit disdain for Michael Moore's politically charged *Fahrenheit 9/11*, but for the most part, their penchant for sentimental, melodramatic fare put them pretty much in the mainstream of American tastes in entertainment. Moreover, this Hollywood marketing firm discovered that at least some Christians were much less bothered by violence than by sex, nudity, and profanity. "What you find is that people with conservative religious doctrine are the most likely to see movies rated R for violence," a MarketCast executive said. "If you compared it to liberals, it's a third more." These marketing gurus were finding a formula for box-office appeal by connecting with an evangelical theological ethic that stresses sexual purity and an eschatology that embraces violence, imagining Christians as apocalyptic warriors bent on eliminating infidelity and immorality in order to hasten Christ's return and usher in the millennial kingdom of God. Also, what researchers discovered was that movies directly targeting the "Christian" audience were tricky to market; a safer bet was "sanding the edges off dialogue that might offend churchgoers" in a general release. Film studios hired religious marketing consultants, the *New York Times* reported, "to scan their family-friendly scripts for objectionable content and to devise marketing plans to reach the Christian audience."[21]

The results were mixed. *Constantine* (2005), a *Matrix*-like Warner Bros. release starring Kenau Reeves as a noir-styled detective who battles spiritual beings in the earthly realm, managed only mediocre reviews and mild box office, about $75 million, roughly the same as Sony's low-budget *The Exorcism of Emily Rose* (2005), which actually exceeded expectations by drawing churchgoers and fans of horror films. In 2006, *Amazing Grace*, a William Wilberforce biopic, and *The Nativity Story* were given special screenings for Christian leaders and were accompanied with study materials for church use. Both were commercial disappointments. *Bruce's* 2007 sequel, *Evan Almighty*, was a box-office disaster. The second installment in the Narnia series, *Prince Caspian* (2008), made only about half as much as *The Lion, the Witch and the Wardrobe*, while one Harry Potter film after another finished in the top-ten grossing movies of the year.[22] Christian theme alone was no guarantee with evangelical moviegoers, and evangelical critics were apparently no better at predicting—or influencing—their fickle constituents than their mainline counterparts were.

In 2009 Warner Bros. scored a huge hit and a Best Picture nomination with *The Blind Side*, a touching movie based on the true story of a wealthy, white, Christian, politically conservative family that takes in a homeless African American teen who goes on to play in the NFL. Sandra Bullock picked up the Oscar for Best Actress. The studio tapped Grace Hill Media to promote the film in Christian circles. This Hollywood-based marketing firm specializes in the church community and was originally set up "to bridge the chasm that existed between Hollywood and the relatively untapped market of Religious America." The same slogan could have been used by George Reid Andrews or the BFC's West Coast Office. Grace Hill Media was hired to promote a wide range of movies from *Constantine*, *The Lion, the Witch and the Wardrobe*, and *The Exorcism of Emily Rose*, to *Ratatouille*, *The Notebook*, and *Elf*.[23] What this suggests is that film distributors conceived the "faith-based" audience in much the same way as other minority markets. Distributors preferred movies with broad appeal that would still draw in specialized groups, and appeared to have the impression that faith convictions did not count for too much with Christian moviegoers. Otherwise, it was mostly a matter of keeping sex and profanity tantalizing, but within reasonable limits.

Paradoxical Rapport

Depending on how one looks at it, the entertainment industry's strategizing to make the most of the Christian market proved a mixed blessing. There was more quality family-oriented entertainment. At the same time, this religious community existed as little more than a market for specific kinds of products. Moreover, the label "Christian" carried only the most superficial meaning as a way of thinking about film. "Kid-friendly" became the defining feature of a "Christian" aesthetic that ultimately prized those movies that entertained the whole "family," meaning movies rated PG and tuned to the level of children. Recall that one purpose of the BFC Film Awards in the 1960s was to develop and promote a distinctive Christian approach to movies in the hope that it would take root with Protestant moviegoers and have some effect on production. The awards panel treated film as art and free expression, a means of cultural reflection and discourse. The emphasis was on the extent to which a movie honestly explored the human condition using a distinctly Christian interpretative strategy. This approach still exists in academic circles and among some Protestant, Catholic, and evangelical reviewers, but this "Christian" model faded from public perception as the evangelical consumer culture blossomed during the 1980s and 1990s and acquired a distinctiveness of its own that was indebted to the pietist tradition. Reversing the aims of the BFC Film Awards program, evangelicals set themselves up as an identifiable consumer group for Hollywood's "easily digested pabulum, designed just 'for entertainment or for profit'," as *Variety* put it in 1966.[24] Ironically, in some sense the aspirations of the BFC's West Coast Office staff found their fullest realization in this Christian consumerism.

The emphasis that evangelicals put on market-based strategies ran against the grain of the central Protestant route to substantial and lasting industry reform. While understanding the need for the studios to make money, mainline Protestants had long argued that the bottom line had to be about artistic integrity and social responsibility, not just profits. The history of Protestants and the movies reveals that a dramatic shift in American cultural values occurred over the course of the twentieth century. Indeed, while writing this book, I was struck by the extent of the subjugation of traditional Protestant values—like service and love of neighbor, sustaining community, and concern for the public welfare—to the primacy of self-interest and the acquisition of wealth and power in American society. In confronting the excessive individualism and apparent lack of social responsibility that has come to characterize the American ethos in the twenty-first century, it might be worthwhile to recover the communal resources of the Protestant tradition.

Regarding the cinema, the values-discourse tends to be limited to the content of specific movies, when in reality, cultural values have just as much to do with the function of entertainment and the corporate systems that provide it—a central concern of the structural approach. At the same time, the strategy for reform that I have identified with the pietist motif has come under sharp criticism for neglecting the complexity of culture, misjudging the power and role of institutions in cultural change, and, consequently, for having failed to bring about the kind of transformation that its adherents await.[25] Understanding the interrelation of culture and institutions and promoting a value system that stresses the relationship between public and private life and the importance of both individual *and* corporate responsibility for the common good seems especially important today, given the rapid developments in technologies and the vast transformations taking place in the media industries.

Conclusion

Unconstrained, free communication is the basis for a
pluralistic society.
WILLIAM F. FORE, executive director, National Council of
Churches Communication Commission

WHEN SOME PROTESTANTS objected to MPAA president Jack Valenti's
revision of the Production Code in 1966, William Fore wrote, "The genius
of Protestantism is that it holds in tension a diversity of opinion within a
common unity of faith, and there is plenty of diversity when it comes to
the question of how we should relate to motion pictures!"[1] In the main,
Protestant movie reform was characterized and circumscribed by basic
beliefs derived from a religious heritage that sought both individual freedom and community welfare. Protestant leaders recognized the cinema as
a multifaceted phenomenon—a popular art, a means of communication,
an arena for cultural discourse, and a commercial product—and always
weighed free expression against the common good. The tension between
the industry's pursuit of profits and the church's long-standing concern
with civil liberties and the public welfare was at the forefront of the struggle that Protestants waged over the movies. This was a distinct part of the
Protestant discourse on movie regulation.

Despite the diversity of Protestantism, within the mainstream of this
broad religious community there was a remarkable persistence of vision
that weathered and adjusted to social, legal, and industrial changes. Persistence, of course, does not necessarily mean coherence or consistency, nor
does it preclude violation of principle. Theological differences, religious
and racial antagonisms, ideological conflicts, the legal status quo, and immediate exigencies informed Protestant motivations and interpretations

of their role, shaped their attitudes and strategies, and at times tarnished their ideals. Even so, their basic beliefs about the relationship between the individual and society served the Protestant community as a guide, if also at times a restraint, in the quest to secure a fitting role for the cinema in an American society that was growing increasingly pluralistic, socially fragmented, and institutionally complex.

What are we to make of the historical interaction of Protestants and the film industry? One way to understand the course of these events is as evidence of *secularization*, not in the sense of a decline of religion, but rather the diminishing scope of religious authority. This interpretation would be consistent with the increasing "privatization" of religion in American life, a development that has been compatible with religious pluralism but has also tended to compartmentalize faith in a way that prohibits religious communities from challenging the dominant ideals, values, and assumptions in society.[2]

To look at it another way, this narrative traces the struggle to establish an autonomous institutional status for a new twentieth-century popular art form, a progression that, like theater and the other arts, involved church, government, legal, and other institutions. In 1995, the year the Disney boycott began, Valenti told a group of Christian communicators that the central question that the rating system addressed was, "Where to mark the boundary of speech and conduct beyond which society is affronted, and what's the penalty for crossing that line?" To address that question, the MPAA devised an age-classification system, and Valenti credited the Protestant and Catholic film agencies. "Without their support," he said, "the rating system would never have gotten off the ground." Indeed, the Protestant thread and its vicissitudes are an essential part of the Hollywood story. Protestants helped to secure a freedom for movies that necessitated a diminished church influence. With constitutional protection and an age classification system, the cinema was freed from church control and was integrated into our complex and differentiated society as a legitimate "art world" with its own province, authority, rationales, and responsibilities.[3]

Since the advent of the rating system, however, the media landscape has changed considerably. New delivery systems have outpaced the MPAA's monitoring apparatus. When Congress mandated a television rating system in 1997, the networks adapted the MPAA's ratings, rather than have the Federal Communications Commission (FCC) set categories. Today, movies are readily available for viewing by children via multiple outlets, and the movie and television rating programs do not cover the expanse of available programming. Close to 90 percent of television viewers subscribe to cable or satellite services that are not regulated by the FCC. Neither is the Internet. Digital technologies have created new horizons for the production, distribution, and marketing of moving images, and have also energized the convergence of media by linking computers, cell phones, televisions, DVDs, video games, and the Internet—all means of accessing entertainment programming.[4]

The explosion in communication technologies and services has led to a sweeping overhaul of government policy. Deregulation to foster competition spawned a media oligopoly with corporations consolidating through mergers and alliances of phone companies, cable and broadcast networks, and computer firms. The Telecommunications Reform Act (1996) raised the limit on the number of TV and radio stations that a single corporation could own and increased the percentage of households reached. It also mandated that TV sets include "V-chips" to allow parents to block out select programming designated not suitable for young viewers; other provisions aimed at protecting children from obscenity communicated over the Internet were ruled unconstitutional by the Supreme Court.

In the wake of the Columbine High School shootings, a Federal Trade Commission report found that companies routinely violated their own rating systems and targeted children in promotional campaigns for movies, music, and video games containing violent content. To head off the prospect of legislation with enforced restrictions and penalties, the MPAA and NATO voluntarily adopted a 12-point initiative that limits the advertising of R-rated films containing violence to people over the age of 17. The new guidelines made it harder for R-rated movies to make money and precipitated a drop in the number of R-rated releases, from 212 in 1999 to 147 in 2004. That year, PG films reportedly grossed more than R-rated ones for the first time since the introduction of the PG-13 rating in 1984.[5]

Valenti denied that there was any connection between a film's rating and its box office, but a less restricted rating was likely to improve potential earnings, especially for big commercial films. "You're leaving tens of millions of dollars on the table with an R rating," a studio marketing executive said. "Why? For artistic integrity? Let's be real." Producers now wanted more PG-13 films so that they could use a blanket marketing campaign. Not surprisingly, PG-13 movies starting looking more like R-rated ones. A 2004 study of releases between 1992 and 2003 showed "ratings creep," with significant increases in sex, violence, and profanity in movies with the same rating. In terms of sexual and violent content, PG-13 films in 2003 looked like R-rated ones in 1992; the same was true for the PG and PG-13 categories. This study also showed higher gross revenues for films rated PG-13 and R for violence, and that R-rated movies including sex and profanity had higher profitability margins. And so the tension between commercial interests, audience tastes, and the public welfare continues. The researchers called for a single "universal media rating system" to keep parents informed in the "new integrated media environment," with cross-marketing and convergence of media products.[6]

As all this suggests, we are still finding our way in an age of high-tech communication that is intensely individualistic and pervasive, its commercial prospects vast but undetermined. Hopefully, the account I have offered will not just deepen our understanding of Hollywood-Protestant relations, but will shed new light on perennial issues that are especially perplexing as emerging technologies and delivery systems present new challenges to existing regulation of the cinema and new media: the entanglement of free speech, censorship and media access; tensions between the industry's drive to maximize profits and concerns about artistic quality and social responsibility; the status of film as an uncensored art and fears that the influence of the cinema has exceeded reasonable limits. These dynamics continue to unfold today, erupting in periodic, yet seemingly arbitrary and unprecedented crises that are sensationalized by the industry and churches alike. Perhaps recovering this important missing piece in film history will help everyone gain a broader perspective.

The Cast

Individuals

George Reid Andrews was executive director of the Church and Drama Association (1926–1930) and a consultant on *The King of Kings* (1927).

Rome Betts was president of the Protestant Film Commission (1946).

William A. Brady was president of the National Association of the Motion Picture Industry (1916–1922).

Joseph I. Breen was head of the Production Code Administration (1934–1954).

S. Parkes Cadman was president of the Federal Council of Churches (1924–1926) and the Church and Drama Association (1926).

Samuel McCrea Cavert was an executive in the Federal Council of Churches and general secretary of the National Council of Churches (1950–1954).

William Sheafe Chase was rector of Christ Episcopal Church in Brooklyn and cofounder of the Interdenominational Committee for the Suppression of Sunday Vaudeville (1906).

Rev. Wilbur F. Crafts was founder and superintendent of the International Reform Bureau (1895).

Fred Eastman was a contributing editor to the *Christian Century* and professor of drama and literature at Chicago Theological Seminary during the 1930s and 1940s.

Frederick Essex was associate director, Division of Communication, American Baptist Convention, and served on the BFC Film Awards Panel (1965–1966).

Oren W. Evans was the director of the BFC's West Coast Office (1948–1954).

William F. Fore was executive director of the Broadcasting and Film Commission (1964–1989).

Charles K. Gilbert was chair of the Executive Committee of the Federal Council of Churches' Commission on Motion Pictures (1929–1930).

Mrs. Robbins (Catheryne Cooke) Gilman was a founder of the Women's Cooperative Alliance of Minneapolis and was elected president of the Federal Motion Picture Council in 1927.

Lee F. Hanmer was director, Department of Recreation, Russell Sage Foundation (1907–1937).

Francis Harmon was vice president of the MPPDA, then MPAA (1936–1952) and was active in the Federal Council of Churches.

Will H. Hays was president of the Motion Picture Producers and Distributors of America (1922–1954).

Paul Heard was director of the Protestant Film Commission (1946–1951).

George Heimrich was director of the BFC's West Coast Office (1954–1966).

F. Ernest Johnson was head of the Federal Council of Churches' Department of Research and Education during the 1920s.

Eric Johnston was president of the Motion Picture Association of America (1945–1963).

Jason Joy was head of the MPPDA's Department of Public Relations (1925) before heading a new Studio Relations Department in Hollywood (1927).

Gerald H. Kennedy was bishop of the Southern California–Arizona Conference of the Methodist Church and chair of the BFC's West Coast Office Committee (1955–1966).

Charles N. Lathrop authored the Federal Council of Churches' study, *The Motion Picture Problem* (1922).

Howard M. LeSourd chaired the MPPDA's organizing committee for the Conference on the Use of Motion Pictures for Religious Education (1929) and was on the Motion Picture Research Council's Advisory Council and the Federal Council's Committee on Educational and Religious Drama.

Daniel Lord was a Jesuit priest who consulted on *The King of Kings* and was a writer of the 1930 Production Code.

Charles S. Macfarland was general secretary of the Federal Council of Churches (1912–1930).

S. Franklin Mack was executive director of the Broadcasting the Film Commission (1954–1963).

Rita McGoldrick was head of the Motion Picture Bureau of the International Federation of Catholic Alumnae (1922–1930).

Carl E. Milliken replaced Jason Joy as head of the MPPDA Public Relations Department in 1927, and as early as 1914 began serving on various committees of the Federal Council of Churches, including the Executive and Administrative committees.

Clifton E. Moore was director, Radio and Television, United Presbyterian Church, and member of the West Coast Office Committee (1955–1966).

Harry S. Myers served on the Federal Council of Churches' Commission on Motion Pictures (1929–1930).

Martin Quigley was publisher of *Motion Picture Herald* and a writer of the 1930 Production Code.

H. K. Rasbach was a member of the West Coast Office Committee (1955–1966) and BFC Film Awards Panel (1965–1973).

William C. Redfield was chair of the Federal Council of Churches' Commission on Motion Pictures (1929).

Julian Rifkin was president of the National Association of Theater Owners (1968–1970).

Roy G. Ross was general secretary of the National Council of Churches (1954–1963).

Carl Segerhammar was president of the Pacific Southwest Synod in Los Angeles, Lutheran Church in America (1963–1975), and member of the BFC's West Coast Office Committee (1955–1966).

Guy Emery Shipler became editor of the Protestant Episcopal *The Churchman* in 1922.

William H. Short organized the Motion Picture Research Council in 1927 (under the name National Committee for Study of the Social Values in

Motion Pictures), and secured funding for the Payne Fund Studies (1929–1932).

Geoffrey Shurlock replaced Joseph Breen as head of the Production Code Administration (1954–1968).

Charles Stelzle was the Federal Council of Churches' field secretary for special service (1929) and a member of the Commission on Motion Pictures (1929–1930).

Patrick Sullivan joined the Legion of Decency staff in 1957 and became executive secretary of the newly named National Catholic Office for Motion Pictures (1965).

Worth M. Tippy was executive secretary of the Federal Council of Churches' Commission on the Church and Social Service (1917–1937) and head of the Council's Committee on Motion Pictures (1933).

F. Thomas Trotter was dean and professor of Theology at the Claremont School of Theology, a member of the West Coast Office Committee (1962–1966), and chaired the BFC Film Awards Panel beginning in 1966.

Jack Valenti was president of the Motion Picture Association of America (1966–2004).

James M. Wall was editor of the *Christian Advocate* (1964–1972) and the *Christian Century* (1972–1999), served on the BFC Film Awards Panel (1966–1973), and represents the National Council of Churches on the CARA appeals board.

Mrs. Thomas G. (Alice Ames) Winter was a president of the General Federation of Women's Clubs and joined the MPPDA's Public Relations Department in 1929.

Organizations

Broadcasting and Film Commission of the National Council of Churches (BFC)

Classification and Rating Administration (CARA)

Federal Council of the Churches of Christ in America (Federal Council of Churches)

Federal Motion Picture Council (FMPC)

General Federation of Women's Clubs (GFWC)

Motion Picture Association of America (MPAA)

Motion Pictures Patent Company (MPPC)

Motion Picture Producers and Distributors of America (MPPDA)

Motion Picture Research Council (MPRC)

National Association of Evangelicals (NAE)

National Association of the Motion Picture Industry (NAMPI)

National Association of Theater Owners (NATO)

National Board of Censorship/Review of Motion Pictures (NBR)

National Catholic Office of Motion Pictures (NCOMP)

National Catholic Welfare (Council) Conference

National Council of the Churches of Christ in the USA (National Council of Churches)

Production Code Administration (PCA)

Protestant Film Commission (PFC)

Protestant Motion Picture Council (PMPC)

Religious Motion Picture Foundation (RMPF)

West Coast Office of the Broadcasting and Film Commission (WCO)

Women's Christian Temperance Union (WCTU)

Abbreviations Used in Notes

AALA	Archives of the Archdiocese of Los Angeles, Mission Hills, CA
AANY	Archives of the Archdiocese of New York, St. Joseph's Seminary, Yonkers, NY
AP	George Reid Andrews Papers #4184, Manuscripts Department, Library of the University of North Carolina, Chapel Hill, NC
BFC	Broadcasting and Film Commission
CFTVC	Christian Film and Television Commission
DMA	Cecil B. DeMille Archives, L. Tom Perry Special Collections, Harold B. Lee Library, Brigham Young University, Prov, UT
EDP	Edgar Dale Papers, The Ohio State University Archives, Columbus, OH
FCC	Federal Communications Commission
FCCCA	Federal Council of the Churches of Christ in America
FMPC	Federal Motion Picture Council
FTT-PP	F. Thomas Trotter Personal Papers
GSC	George Stevens Collection, Margaret Herrick Library of the Academy of Motion Picture Arts and Sciences, Beverly Hills, CA
IFIDA	International Film Importers and Distributors of America
JMW-PP	James M. Wall Personal Papers
KF-YMCA	Kautz Family YMCA Archives, Elmer L. Anderson Library, University of Minnesota, Minneapolis, MN
LOD	Legion of Decency
MGM	MGM Collection, USC Cinema-Television Library, Los Angeles, CA

MJA	Daniel A. Lord Collection, Midwest Jesuit Archives, St. Louis, MO
MPAA	Motion Picture Association of America
MPPDA	Motion Picture Producers and Distributors of America
MPPDA-MA	Motion Picture Producers and Distributors of America, Inc., Microfilm Archive (A copy is available at the Margaret Herrick Library of the Academy of Motion Picture Arts and Sciences)
MPRC-HIA	Motion Picture Research Council Records, Hoover Institute Archives, Stanford University, Stanford, CA
NBR	National Board of Review of Motion Pictures Records, New York Public Library, New York, NY
NCC	National Council of the Churches of Christ in the USA
NCOMP	National Catholic Office of Motion Pictures
NCWC-ACUA	National Catholic Welfare Conference Records, OGS, American Catholic History Research Center and University Archives, Catholic University of America, Washington, DC
NP	John Francis Noll Papers, Notre Dame Archives, South Bend, IN
QP	Martin J. Quigley Papers, Special Collections Division, Georgetown University Library, Washington, DC
PCA	Production Code Administration Archives, Margaret Herrick Library of the Academy of Motion Picture Arts and Sciences, Beverly Hills, CA
PFC	Protestant Film Commission
PHS	Presbyterian Historical Society, Philadelphia, PA
RBC	Richard Brooks Collection, Margaret Herrick Library of the Academy of Motion Picture Arts and Sciences, Beverly Hills, CA
RMPF	Religious Motion Picture Foundation
RNS	Religious News Service
TCF-USC	Twentieth Century-Fox Collection, USC Cinema-Television Library, Los Angeles, CA

WBA	Warner Bros. Archives, USC Warner Bros. Archives, Los Angeles, CA
WCO	West Coast Office
WFF-PP	William F. Fore Personal Papers
WHP	Will H. Hays Papers, Indiana State Library, Indianapolis, IN
WWCP	Werrett Wallace Charters Papers, The Ohio State University Archives, Columbus, OH

Notes

INTRODUCTION

1. James M. Wall, E-mail, January 18, 2011.
2. A. O. Scott, "Some Material May Be Inappropriate or Mystifying, and the Rating May Be as Well," *New York Times*, September 1, 2006, E8; Jack Valenti, *Address at the North American Branch of the World Association of Christians in Communications (NABSWAAC)* (1995), Videocassette.
3. "The Christian Century," *Christian Century*, January 4, 1900, 4.
4. Bishop Francis J. McConnell, "The New Heathenism," *Association Men*, January 1930, 228; Charles S. Macfarland, *The Progress of Church Federation* (New York: Fleming H. Revell, 1917), 14.
5. John R. Rice, *What Is Wrong with the Movies?* (Grand Rapids, MI: Zondervan, 1938), 10; H. J. Kuiper, "Moving Pictures," *The Banner*, December 1931, 1076.
6. Warren I. Susman, *Culture as History: The Transformation of American Society in the Twentieth Century* (New York: Pantheon Books, 1984), 284; Untitled Manuscript, n.d., NBR box 170, folder: Papers Relating to the Formation and History of the NBRMP, 1908–1915. See William D. Romanowski, "John Calvin Meets the Creature from the Black Lagoon: The Christian Reformed Church and the Movies 1928–1966," *Christian Scholars Review* 25, no. 1 (September 1995): 47–62.
7. Benjamin B. Hampton, *A History of the Movies* (New York: Covici Friede Publishers, 1931; reprinted Arno Press, 1970), 283; Raymond Moley, *The Hays Office* (New York, Bobbs-Merrill, 1945), 133–134. See also Lewis Jacobs, *The Rise of the American Film: A Critical History* (New York: Harcourt, Brace and Company, 1939); Terry Ramsaye, *A Million and One Nights: A History of the Motion Picture Industry Through 1925* (New York: Simon & Schuster, Touchstone, 1926).

8. William R. Hutchison, *Religious Pluralism in America: The Contentious History of a Founding Ideal* (New Haven: Yale University Press, 2003), 61; Frederic C. Howe, *The Confessions of a Reformer* (Chicago: Quadrangle, 1967), 17. Howe coined the phrase "moral coercion" to describe the National Board of Censorship's method of voluntary film review. Howe, "What to Do with the Motion-Picture Show: Shall It Be Censored?," *The Outlook*, June 20, 1914. Richard Blake applies the term *afterimage* to Catholic filmmakers whose work exhibits something of their religious backgrounds. Richard A. Blake, *Afterimage: The Indelible Catholic Imagination of Six American Filmmakers* (Chicago: Loyola Press, 2000).

9. Wilbur F. Crafts, *National Perils and Hopes: A Study Based on Current Statistic and the Observations of a Cheerful Reformer* (Cleveland: F. M. Barton, 1910), 39; on perspectives, Calvin Seerveld, "What Makes a College Christian?," in *In the Fields of the Lord: A Seerveld Reader*, ed. Craig Bartholomew (Toronto and Carlisle, UK: Toronto Tuppence Press and Piquant, 2000), 122.

10. Worth Tippy, "Social Work of the Federal Council of Churches," *Journal of Social Forces* 1, no. 1 (1922), 37. On defining Protestant see "Preface" in William R. Hutchison, ed., *Between the Times: The Travail of the Protestant Establishment in America, 1900–1960* (Cambridge: Cambridge University Press, 1989), vii–xv; "Introduction," in *Women and Twentieth-Century Protestantism*, eds. Margaret Lamberts and Virginia Lieson Brereton Bendroth (Urbana: University of Illinois Press, 2002), xi–xv.

11. There are of course exceptions to this scheme. Certain Reformed groups in the neo-Calvinist tradition embrace a conservative theology, emphasizing total depravity, and also institutional reform. On different religious perspectives on the media, see Daniel A. Stout and Judith M. Buddenbaum, *Religion and Mass Media: Audiences and Adaptations* (Thousand Oaks, CA: SAGE, 1996).

12. American obscenity standards (the Hicklin Rule) were inherited from an English case, *Regina v. Hicklin* (1868). Though juridically suspect, the basic tenets of *Hicklin* were not challenged in American courts until 1933—the book in question, James Joyce's *Ulysses*. By definition, prior restraint restricts or prevents a communication from occurring; an *ex post facto* punishment is applied as a judgment rendered after the communication has occurred. See Thomas L. and Dale A. Herbeck Tedford, *Freedom of Speech in the United States*, 4th ed. (State College: Strata Publishing, 2001), 214.

13. Fred Eastman and Edward Ouellette, *Learning for Life: Better Motion Pictures*, Pamphlet (Boston: Pilgrim Press, 1936), 48–49 (italics in original), MPRC-HIA box 76.

14. P. C. Kemeny, "Banned in Boston: Commercial Culture and the Politics of Moral Reform in Boston During the 1920s," in *Faith in the Market: Religion and the Rise of Urban Commercial Culture*, eds. John M. and Diane Winston Giggie (New Brunswick: Rutgers, 2002), 138. A Protestant involved in movie reform, William Marston Seabury cited an influential book by Gustave Le Bon, *The Crowd: A Study of the Popular Mind* (1896) in "The Wicked Consumers," *The Churchman*, May 24, 1930, 10–12.

CHAPTER 1

1. See Warren I. Susman, *Culture as History: The Transformation of American Society in the Twentieth Century* (New York: Pantheon Books, 1984), 271–285; Richard Wightman Fox, "The Culture of Liberal Protestant Progressivism, 1875–1925," *Journal of Interdisciplinary History* 23, no. 3 (1993), 639–660.

2. F. Ernest Johnson, "The Teaching of the Protestant Church," *Annals of the American Academy of Political and Social Science* 103 (1922): 85.

3. William Henry Roberts, quoted in Elias B. Sanford, *Origin and History of the Federal Council of the Churches of Christ in America* (Hartford: S. S. Scranton, 1916), 245; Charles S. Macfarland, *The Progress of Church Federation* (New York: Fleming H. Revell, 1917), 23–24.

4. Lewis Jacobs, *The Rise of the American Film: A Critical History* (New York: Harcourt, Brace and Company, 1939), 271. Erwin Panofsky, "Style and Medium in the Motion Pictures" in *Film Theory and Criticism: Introductory Readings*, 5th ed., eds. Leo Braudy and Marshall Cohen (New York: Oxford University Press, 1999), 279–292; Lawrence Levine, *Highbrow/Lowbrow: The Emergence of Cultural Hierarchy in America* (Cambridge, MA: Harvard University Press, 1988).

5. Kathy Peiss, *Cheap Amusements: Working Women and Leisure in Turn-of-the-Century New York* (Philadephia: Temple University Press, 1986), 6–8.

6. Jane Addams, *The Spirit of Youth and the City Streets* (Urbana: University of Illinois, 1972), 159, 76; Episcopal Bishop H. Greer quoted in "Christianity and Amusements," *Everybody's Magazine* 10, no. 5 (1904): 701.

7. Quoted in Terry Ramsaye, *A Million and One Nights: A History of the Motion Picture Industry Through 1925* (New York: Simon & Schuster, Touchstone, 1926), 473.

8. John Collier, "Cheap Amusements," *Charities and the Commons: A Weekly Journal of Philanthropy and Social Advance* 20 (1908): 74, 76. See "Picture Shows," *New York Times*, January 12, 1909, 8.

9. "Hear Two Sides on Sunday Closing," *Variety*, December 26, 1908, 8; Chase quoted in "Sabbath Champions Rap New Sunday Law," *New York Times*, January 9, 1908, 8. Chase was also active on the boards of the Lord's Day Alliance and Society for the Prevention of Crime.

10. "Open Sunday Law Is in Force Now," *New York Times*, December 20, 1907, 7; "Picture Men Organize," *Variety*, December 28, 1907, 6.

11. Quotes taken from "Say Picture Shows Corrupt Children," *New York Times*, December 24, 1908, 4.

12. "Committee to Censor Cheap Amusements," *New York Times*, February 24, 1909, 6; Daniel Czitrom, "The Politics of Performance: Theater Licensing and the Origins of Movie Censorship in New York," in *Movie Censorship and American Culture*, Francis G. Couvares, ed. (Washington, DC: Smithsonian Institution Press, 1996), 17; "Picture Shows All Put out of Business," *New York Times*, December 25, 1908, 1; "Pastors Open War on Sunday Shows," *New York Times*, January 19, 1909, 8.

13. Terry Ramsaye, "The Motion Picture," *Annals of the American Academy of Political and Social Science* 128 (1926): 16.

14. Untitled Manuscript, n.d. NBR box 170, folder: Papers Relating to the Formation and History of the NBRMP, 1908–1915; Orrin G. Cocks, "Public Amusements Safe-Guarded for Moral Health," Unpublished Manuscript, May 1915, NBR box 170, folder: Papers Relating to the Formation and History of the NBRMP, 1908–1915.

15. Cocks, "Public Amusements Safe-Guarded for Moral Health." George William Knox of Union Theological Seminary chaired the governing board and at least 80 percent of the National Board's members were church people from various Protestant denominations. W. D. McGuire to P. O. Warren, March 16, 1921; Charles Stelzle to Dr. Herbert W. Gates, March 17, 1921, NBR box 43, folder: Stelzle, Charles; NBR box 164, folder: Analysis of Personnel of the National Board of Review of Motion Pictures. See Lary May, *Screening out the Past: The Birth of Mass Culture and the Motion Picture Industry* (New York: Oxford University Press, 1980), 54–55. On Board policies see "The National Board of Review and Its Field of Work," Unpublished Paper, n.d. [circa 1920], PHS RG 18, box 15, folder 2.

16. National Board Secretary and Presbyterian minister Orrin G. Cocks wrote in tribute that Charles Sprague Smith believed in the "fundamental wholesomeness of the people and also in their power to preserve freedom of speech and thought at the same time they assisted in the elimination of those elements which were evil." Cocks, "Public Amusements Safe-Guarded for Moral Health." Collier quoted in Charles Matthew Feldman, *The National Board of Censorship (Review) of Motion Pictures, 1909–1922* (New York: Arno Press, 1977), 28.

17. Untitled Manuscript, n.d.

18. Russell Merritt, "Nickelodeoon Theaters 1905–1914: Building an Audience for the Movies," in *The American Film Industry*, ed. Tino Balio (Madison: University of Wisconsin, 1976), 67. Robert C. Allen, *Vaudeville and Film, 1895–1915: A Study in Media Interaction* (New York: Arno Press, 1980); Kathryn H. Fuller, *At the Picture Show: Small-Town Audiences and the Creation of Movie Fan Culture* (Charlottesville: University Press of Virginia, 1996).

19. Untitled Manuscript, n.d., NBR box 170, folder: Papers Relating to the Formation and History of the NBRMP, 1908–1915. Edison's Trust was inoperative by 1914; it was officially dissolved by action of an antitrust suit in 1918.

20. *The Vitagraph Bulletin* quoted in William and Roberta E. Pearson Uricchio, "'You Can Make *the Life of Moses* Your Life Saver': Vitagraph's Biblical Blockbuster," in *An Invention of the Devil?: Religion and Early Cinema*, eds. André Gaudreault Cosandey, Tom Gunning (Sanite-Foy: Les Presses de L'Université Laval, 1992), 202; "'Saviour' Film Falls Down," *Variety*, April 17, 1914, 19.

21. Exhibitor association quotes in "Petitioning Against Censoring," *Variety*, May 22, 1914, 19; "Censoring Date Postponed," *Variety*, June 5, 1914, 18; "Anti-Censor Fight On," *Variety*, November 7, 1914, 21. On the white slavery films, see Shelley

Stamp, "Moral Coercion, or the National Board of Censorship Ponders the Vice Films," in *Controlling Hollywood: Censorship and Regulation in the Studio Era*, ed. Matthew Bernstein (New Brunswick: Rutgers, 1999), 41–59; Janet Staiger, *Bad Women: Regulating Sexuality in Early American Cinema* (Minneapolis: University of Minneapolis Press, 1995).

22. Quoted in "Dr. Wilbur F. Crafts Crusader, Dies At 73," *New York Times*, December 28, 1922, 15; Wilbur F. Crafts, *National Perils and Hopes: A Study Based on Current Statistics and the Observations of a Cheerful Reformer* (Cleveland: F. M. Barton, 1910), 33 (italics in original).

23. "Pretty Pictures Subjects!," *Variety*, January 8, 1910, 12; survey cited in Crafts, *National Perils and Hopes*, 37.

24. Wilbur F. Crafts, "Fit Motion Pictures," *New York Times*, May 19, 1914, 8. See Feldman, *The National Board*, 68–69, 83–84.

25. The unanimous ruling was delivered by Justice Joseph McKenna, one of two Roman Catholics on an otherwise Protestant court. See Garth Jowett, "'A Capacity for Evil': The 1915 Supreme Court *Mutual* Decision," in *Controlling Hollywood: Censorship and Regulation in the Studio Era*, ed. Matthew Bernstein (New Brunswick: Rutgers, 1999), 16–40.

26. "National Censorship Now Warmly Discussed," *Variety*, October 31, 1913, 15; "National Board Censorship Answers Some Charges," *Variety*, November 14, 1913, 15; Edward M. McConoughy, *Motion Pictures in Religious and Educational Work*, Pamphlet, n.d. (internal references indicate a 1915 publication date), PHS RG 18, box 52, folder 17.

27. John Collier, "Censorship and the National Board (1915)," in *The Movies in Our Midst: Documents in the Cultural History of Film in America*, ed. Gerald Mast (Chicago: University of Chicago Press, 1982), 149. The Board passed the film initially and it opened in Los Angeles on February 15, 1915.

28. "Reformer Jane Addams Critiques *The Birth of a Nation*," History Matters: The U.S. Survey Course on the Web, http://historymatters.gmu.edu/d/4994/.

29. Frederic C. Howe, "What to Do with the Motion-Picture Show: Shall It Be Censored?," *The Outlook*, June 20, 1914, 412.

30. "National Censorship Board Has Prolapsus of Bankroll," *Variety*, December 31, 1915, 26.

CHAPTER 2

1. "Bans 'Scarlet Letter'," *Variety*, May 31, 1913, 8; "Censored All but Scenery," *Variety*, April 2, 1910, 16; "Obscene Picture Costs $1,000," *Variety*, August 1, 1908, 13.

2. Alva W. Taylor, "Shall We Censor the Movies?," *Christian Century*, February 10, 1921, 18.

3. Jacob Binder quoted in Charles Matthew Feldman, *The National Board of Censorship (Review) of Motion Pictures, 1909–1922* (New York: Arno Press, 1977), 97;

Benjamin B. Hampton, *A History of the Movies* (New York: Covici Friede Publishers, 1931; reprinted, New York: Arno Press, 1970), 290. See Lee Grieveson, *Policing Cinema: Movies and Censorship in Early-Twentieth-Century America* (Berkeley: University of California Press, 2004), 204–205.

4. Quoted in William Sheafe Chase, *Catechism on Motion Pictures in Inter-State Commerce*, Pamphlet, 1921, 16–17, PHS RG 18, box 72, folder 20.

5. George D. Baker quoted in "Censorship at Last," *America*, April 9, 1921, 600. The "public mind" and following quotes are from "For Better Motion Pictures," FCCCA Press Release, June 22, 1934, PHS RG 18, box 15, folder 1.

6. Memorandum of Points for Discussion with New York Members of the Advisory Committee, 1916, NBR box 170, folder: Papers Relating to the Formation and History of the NBRMP, 1916–1951; Chase, *Catechism*, 17–18; "President Leaves on Trip to Omaha," *New York Times*, October 4, 1916, 1.

7. Edward M. McConoughy, *Motion Pictures in Religious and Educational Work*, Pamphlet, n.d., PHS RG 18, box 52, folder 17.

8. Johnson to W. D. McGuire, June 28, 1920, NBR box 25, folder: FCCCA.

9. "National Board of Censorship Changes Its Name," Press Release, March 19, 1916, NBR box 170, folder: Papers Relating to the Formation and History of the NBRMP, 1916–1951; *The Public Relations of the Motion Picture Industry* (New York: Department of Research and Education, FCCCA, 1931), 54–55, 59.

10. Untitled Manuscript, n.d.; Memorandum of Points for Discussion with New York Members of the Advisory Committee, 1916, NBR box 170, folder: Papers Relating to the Formation and History of the NBRMP, 1916–1951; W. D. McGuire, Form Letter, March 16, 1921, NBR box 43, folder: Stelzle, Charles; Ruth A. Inglis, *Freedom of the Movies: A Report on Self-Regulation from the Commission on Freedom of the Press* (Chicago: University of Chicago Press, 1947), 63–65.

11. Orrin G. Cocks to Lee F. Hanmer, April 8, 1919, NBR box 28, folder: Hanmer, Lee F., 1916–1922. See correspondence between Johnson, McGuire, and Cocks, May 1919–June 1920, NBR box 25, folder: FCCCA. For context on the sex hygiene films, see Eric Schaefer, *"Bold! Daring! Shocking! True": A History of Exploitation Films, 1919–1959* (Durham: Duke University Press, 1999), 21–37.

12. "Rochester Convention Hears All Censorship Attacked," *Variety*, August 18, 1919, 54.

13. "Pictures Blamed by Angry Baptists," *Variety*, May 21, 1920, 35; "Protestant Churches Giving Own Motion Picture Shows," *Variety*, November 14, 1919, 63; "Catholic Review of Films Serves 17,000,000 Readers," *Variety*, September 3, 1919, 66.

14. Johnson to McGuire, May 20, 1920, NBR box 25, folder: FCCCA.

15. Cavert to Cocks, December 21, 1920, PHS RG 18, box 14, folder 24. See related correspondence in NBR box 25, folder: FCCCA.

16. HFS [Herbert F. Sherwood], Assistant Secretary, NBR, to Rev. Christian F. Reismar, March 30, 1918, NBR box 34, folder: Methodist Episcopal Church; "Moving Pictures in a Typical City," *Christian Century*, July 29, 1920, 3.

17. Crafts quoted in Terry Ramsaye, *A Million and One Nights: A History of the Motion Picture Industry Through 1925* (New York: Simon & Schuster, Touchstone, 1926), 483. "Dr. Crafts Renews Attack on Movies," *New York Times*, December 27, 1920, 24; Inglis, *Freedom of the Movies*, 70–71.

18. Morris L. Ernst and Pare Lorentz, *Censored: The Private Life of the Movie* (New York: Jonathan Cape and Harrison Smith, 1930), 122. Democrats were less inclined to regulate personal morality and amusement than Republicans, and counted Jewish and Catholic immigrants and anti-prohibitionists among their ranks. See Thomas R. Pegram, *Battling Demon Rum: The Struggle for a Dry America, 1800–1933* (Chicago: Ivan R. Dee, 1998); Joseph R. Gusfield, *Symbolic Crusade: Status Politics and the American Temperance Movement* (Urbana: University of Illinois, 1963).

19. Cavert to Cocks, January 10, 1921, NBR, box 25, folder: FCCCA; Memorandum of Questions on Motion Picture Regulation That Have Developed in Connection with a Study of the Motion Picture Situation Throughout the United States Made by the Department of Recreation of the Russell Sage Foundation, n.d. PHS RG 18, box 72, folder 19.

20. Hampton quoted in "Should Moving Pictures Be Censored?," in *Current Opinion for May* (New York: Current Literature Publishing Company, 1921), 652; "Overdoing the Sex Motive in Moving Pictures," in *Current Opinion for March* (New York: Current Literature Publishing Company, 1921), 362–363; Taylor, "Shall We Censor the Movies?," 18. On the *Brooklyn Daily Eagle*'s reporting, see Feldman, *The National Board*, 172–180.

21. "Producers Agree to Reform Films," *New York Times*, March 15, 1921, 11; Feldman, *The National Board*, 194–197; Inglis, *Freedom of the Movies*, 85–86.

22. "A Danger to the Arts," *New York Times*, March 20, 1921, 2; "Proposes Federal Film Censorship," *New York Times*, March 18, 1921, 26; "Brady Wants Trade to Reform Movies," *New York Times*, March 21, 1921, 11.

23. "Nat'l Association Frames Informal Censorship Truce," *Variety*, March 18, 1921, 36; "Movie Producers Take a Hand at Self-Reformation," *Christian Century*, October 6, 1921, 4. This was Crafts's last stand for movie regulation; the tireless reformer died of pneumonia in December 1922 at the age of 73. Of note, Hampton recounts that Wilbur Crafts "earnestly advocated" for a system of industry self-censorship such as Will Hays would eventually establish. This suggests that industry self-regulation might have been a principled ideal for Crafts, but under the existing circumstances he continued to pursue a federal commission. Hampton, *A History of the Movies*, 293–294, 302–303.

24. FCCCA Press Release, "The Crisis in the Motion Picture Industry," March 15, 1921, KF-YMCA, Program Records: Religious Work, folder: YMCA Church Relations, Federal Council of Churches Commission on Church/Social Service, 1921; "Board of Censors Is Condemned," *Christian Century*, March 31, 1921, 4–5. Cavert to National Association of Motion Picture Industries, March 24, 1921, PHS RG 18, box 14, folder 24.

25. Cavert to Everett Dean Martin, March 16, 1921; McGuire to Martin, March 31, 1921; McGuire to Cavert, March 31, 1921, NBR box 25, folder: FCCCA.

26. Harris D. H. Connick quoted in Chase, *Catechism*; "Censorship at Last," 600; "New York Governor Backs Drastic Picture Censorship," *Variety*, March 11, 1921, 33.

27. The Massachusetts measure was subject to referendum. "Censorship out in 31 States; Would Have Ended Ohio Shows," *Variety*, May 6, 1921, 47. "Legal Censorship Is Being Defeated," *Christian Century*, March 31, 1921, 3–4; "School Children Like Pictures of 'Blood and Thunder' Type," *Variety*, February 17, 1922, 1; Robert S. and Helen Merrell Lynd, *Middletown: A Study in Contemporary American Culture* (New York: Harcourt Brace, 1920), 265–269. According to the Lynd's study, historical and educational films were a "flat failure" that bored young and old alike.

28. J. Ray Johnson, "The Church and the Movies," *Christian Century*, January 6, 1921, 18–19; "Presbyterians Ask Action on Divorce," *New York Times*, May 25, 1921, 17; Richard Koszarski, *An Evening's Entertainment: The Age of the Silent Feature Picture 1915–1928*, ed. Charles Harpole, vol. 3, *History of the American Cinema* (New York: Charles Scribner's Sons, 1990), 13.

29. William Sheafe Chase, *Catechism on Motion Pictures*, 9, 10, 35, 6.

30. Charles N. Lathrop, *The Motion Picture Problem*, Commission on the Church and Social Service, FCCCA, Pamphlet, 1922, 28, PHS RG 18, box 52, folder 17, 12, 13, 8, 25. Lathrop was with the Department of Christian Social Service of the Protestant Episcopal Church. See also "The Church and the Motion Picture Problem," *Federal Council Bulletin*, August–September, 1922, 18, PHS RG 18, box 80, folder 16.

31. Hanmer to Lathrop, May 27, 1921. The government oversight scheme came from Hanmer, who considered it a practical means of regulation consistent with other kinds of public service that rightly put "the responsibility upon those asking for the privilege of carrying on such public service." Hanmer to Chase, June 3, 1921, PHS RG 18, box 72, folder 19; "Congress' Censorial Measure Includes Indecent Pictures," *Variety*, July 8, 1921, 31.

32. "Screen: Facts for Reformers," *New York Times*, June 18, 1922, 75; "Screen: Danger Ahead," *New York Times*, June 25, 1922, 3. FCCCA, Press Releases, June 10, 17, 24 and July 1, 1922, WHP box 17, folder July 1–12, 1922. See "The Pros and Cons of Censorship," *Christian Century*, July 13, 1922, 869.

33. This alliance remark is attributed to C. C. Pettijohn (Selznick Corporation) in "Report of a Conference Between the Committee on Motion Pictures of the Federal Council of Churches and a Committee of the National Association of the Motion Picture Industry," October 17, 1921, 1, PHS RG 18, box 77, folder 21. The "indirect influence" comment is in Memorandum for Meeting of the Administrative Committee Concerning Possible Cooperation with Motion Picture Industry in Securing films Depicting Religious and Humanitarian Efforts, May 11, 1921, PHS RG 18, box 14, folder 24. On these events, see correspondence in

PHS RG 18, box 14, folder 24; Minutes of a Meeting of the Committee on Motion Pictures of the Federal Council of Churches, November 3, 1921, PHS RG 18, box 77, folder 21.

34. Hanmer to Lathrop, June 1, 1921, PHS RG 18, box 72, folder 19; "Movies Arraigned by Senator Myers," *New York Times*, June 30, 1922, 9; "Motion Picture Producers Are in Politics," *Christian Century*, July 6, 1922, 832.

35. "The Movies and Profits," *Christian Century*, February 10, 1921, 4. See "Exhibitors Not for Hays," *Variety*, January 13, 1922, 43. Ellis W. Hawley, *The New Deal and the Problem of Monopoly: A Study in Economic Ambivalence* (Princeton, NJ: Princeton University Press, 1966).

36. "Would Scrap Nat'l Ass'n for Organization of Producers and Distributors; Mention Hays," *Variety*, December 9, 1921, 39; "Probing the Hays Mystery," *Variety*, January 20, 1922, 1, 38, 99; "N. A. M. P. I. Passing in a Fortnight; Association Quits in Favor of Hays," *Variety*, April 28, 1922, 46.

CHAPTER 3

1. "Oswego Votes for Sunday Film," *Variety*, May 9, 1919, 57. See "New Sunday Opening Bill Before State Legislature," *Variety*, February 28, 1919, 63; "New York Grants Sundays," *Variety*, April 11, 1919, 61.

2. "Presbyterians Ask for 'Clean Movies,'" *New York Times*, May 24, 1922, 21. "Griffith Forced to Retake Scenes in "Mother and Law"," *Variety*, April 7, 1916, 1; "Catholics Make Objection," *Variety*, April 21, 1916, 23; "Ban Against Feature Film by the Catholic Church," *Variety*, July 28, 1916, 18.

3. Elizabeth Ewen, "City Lights: Immigrant Women and the Rise of the Movies," *Signs: Journal of Women in Culture and Society* 5, no. 3, Supplement (1980): S61.

4. "Presbyterians Ask for 'Clean Movies,'" 21; "Churches Find Success in Moving Pictures," *Christian Century*, November 25, 1920, 24; "Protestant Churches Giving Own Motion Picture Shows," *Variety*, November 14, 1919, 63. For the fundamentalist separatist rationale, see "Moving Pictures in the Church," *Moody Bible Institute Monthly*, February 1921, 272.

5. "100 N. Y. Churches Offer 300 Days' Film Bookings," *Variety*, November 5, 1920, 46. On films produced for church use during the Silent Era, see Terry Lindvall, *Sanctuary Cinema: Origins of the Christian Film Industry* (New York: New York University Press, 2007).

6. "Movie Men Still Defy Public Sentiment," *Christian Century*, May 18, 1922, 613.

7. Will H. Hays, *The Memoirs of Will H. Hays* (Garden City, NY: Doubleday & Company, 1955), 327 (italics in original).

8. "Speech Delivered by Will H. Hays, Publishers of the United States," April 26, 1922, PHS RG 18, box 14, folder 24; Hays, *Memoirs*, 346.

9. "The Federal Council of Churches of Christ in America," *Industry: A Semi-Monthly Interpretation of Industrial Progress*, 2, no. 14 (June 15, 1920), 3–12, PHS

RG 18, box 8, folder 23. Hays began receiving daily reports immediately on censorship efforts and the activities of church and women's groups. Report to the Honorable Will H. Hays, May 1, 1922, WHP box 17, folder May 1–9, 1922.

10. Unsigned letter [Cavert?] to Hays, April 3, 1922, PHS RG 18, box 14, folder 24.

11. Charles N. Lathrop, *The Motion Picture Problem*, Pamphlet, 1922, 28, PHS RG 18, box 52, folder 17; Hays to Cavert, June 12, 1922, PHS RG 18, box 14, folder 24.

12. Johnson to Hays, April 24, 1922. See related correspondence in PHS RG 18, box 14, folder 24; John M. Glenn, Lilian Brandt, and F. Emerson Andrews, *Russell Sage Foundation, 1907–1946*, Vol. 1 (New York: Russell Sage Foundation, 1947), 323.

13. Ralph Hayes to Macfarland, July 15, 1922, Attachment; Hanmer to Macfarland, September 25, 1922; Minutes, Executive Committee of the Committee on Public Relations, MPPDA, March 10, 1923, Civil Committee File, MPPDA-MA, Reel 01, Frame 0156–0161.

14. Barrett to Macfarland, December 29, 1923, NBR box 25, folder: FCCCA.

15. Hays, *Memoirs*, 332. See correspondence between Fred Winslow Adams, James Elvin Wagner, and Cavert, October–November 1922, PHS RG 18, box 14, folder 24.

16. M. P. Hunt, Western Union Telegram, December 26, 1922; C. McLeod Smith to Macfarland, December 29, 1922, PHS RG 18, box 14, folder 24. "Federal Council Opposes Arbuckle Films," *Federal Council Bulletin*, December 1922–January 1923, 16, PHS RG 18, box 80, folder 16.

17. Hays to Rev. S. Parkes Cadman, December 20, 1929, 12, AP box 2, folder 42. See Richard Maltby, "'To Prevent the Prevalent Type of Book': Censorship and Adaptation in Hollywood, 1924–1934," in *Movie Censorship and American Culture*, ed. Francis G. Couvares (Washington, DC: Smithsonian Institution Press, 1996), 97–128.

18. Address of Will H. Hays Before the Men's Bible Class Annual Dinner-Baptist Church (John D. Rockefeller, Jr.), "What Is Being Done for Motion Pictures," January 25, 1923, 9, WHP box 19, folder: January 21–27, 1923.

19. Mae D. Huettig, *Economic Control of the Motion Picture Industry* (Philadelphia: University of Pennsylvania Press, 1944), 79; Suzanne Mary Donahue, *American Film Distribution: The Changing Marketplace* (Ann Arbor: UMI Research Press, 1987, 1985), 21.

20. See F. Andrew Hanssen, "The Block Booking of Films Re-examined," in *An Economic History of Film*, eds. John Sedgwick and Michael Pokorny (London and New York: Routledge, 2005), 121–150.

21. "Presbyterians Ask for 'Clean Movies,'" 21; "Reformers All Set to Jam Federal Censorship Bill through Congress," *Variety*, December 27, 1923, 20; "Church Meeting," *Variety*, January 10, 1924, 23; "Woman Reformer Says Censorship Is Failure," *Variety*, July 20, 1927, 10.

22. Arthur Edwin Krows, "Motion Pictures—Not for Theatres," *The Educational Screen* (1943): 96. Minutes of the September 15, 1922, Meeting of the Executive Committee; Hanmer to Macfarland, September 25, 1922, PHS RG 18, box 14,

folder 24; Address of Will H. Hays Before the Men's Bible Class Annual Dinner-Baptist Church, 12–13, WHP box 19, folder: January 21–27, 1923.

23. Quoted in "Andrews Says Hays Offered Him $10,000," *Brooklyn Eagle*, March 31, 1930, PHS RG 18, box 15, folder 3; [Andrews] to Will H. Hays, June 14, 1926, AP box 1, folder 6; "To Film the Life of Christ," *Christian Century*, March 10 1921, 4.

24. Zukor to Curtiss, April 14, 1924; Andrews to Hays, August 13, 1924, AP box 1, folder 2; "Papini's Vivid 'Life of Christ'," *Christian Century*, March 1, 1923, 260.

25. Hays quoted in "Hays Champions New Movement to Help Pastors," *Grand Rapids Press*, May 24, 1924, 1, 2 (movie advertisement on page 10); "Pass Resolutions upon Morals and Church Education," *Grand Rapids Press*, May 27, 1924, 3; "What Kind of Pictures Do People Want," *Christian Century*, September 28, 1922, 1181. See James D. Bratt and Christopher H. Meehan, *Gathered at the River: Grand Rapids, Michigan and Its People of Faith* (Grand Rapids, MI: Eerdmans, 1993), 127–131.

26. Hays to Andrews, December 23, 1924; [Andrews] to Hays, December 19, 1924, AP box 1, folder 3. See additional correspondence in AP box 1, folders 3, 4, and 5. Andrews unsuccessfully pitched the concept to Harry Warner. Andrews to Warner, January 14, 1926; Warner to Andrews, April 26, 1926, AP box 1, folder 6.

27. William E. Harmon to National Committee of Advisers, Religious Motion Picture Foundation, March 23, 1926, NBR box 28, folder: Harmon Foundation. Andrews to J. E. Ingram, October 28, 1925, AP box 1, folder 5; Joseph Lewis Bridges, "A Historical Study of Cooperative Protestant Religious Film in America from 1914 to 1972" (Dissertation, University of Southern California, 1975), 48–52. Among the church leaders involved were L. Roy Curtiss, Rev. William B. Millar (secretary of the New York City Federation of Churches), William H. Short (executive secretary of the Non-partisan Association for the League of Nations, and later with the Payne Foundation), and Charles P. Fagnani (Union Theological Seminary). Lee Hanmer (Russell Sage Foundation) provided assistance in setting up the RMPF. John M. Glenn, Lilian Brandt, and F. Emerson Andrews, *Russell Sage Foundation, 1907–1946,* Vol. 2 (New York: Russell Sage Foundation, 1947), 508.

28. Lamar Trotti, "The Attitude of the Church Toward Motion Pictures," Typescript of Article, No. Publication Reference, 6. 1925, Trotti, L. Special Articles File, MPPDA-MA, Reel 02, Frame 1110–1117; "Can the Movies Save the Churches?," *Christian Century*, December 31, 1925, 1629–1630.

29. "Andrews Says Hays Offered Him $10,000," *Brooklyn Eagle*, March 31, 1930, PHS RG 18, box 15, folder 3; Executive Director of the Church and Drama League of America [Andrews], Unpublished Paper, n.d., PHS RG 18, box 15, folder 2; Chapter 15, 170–171, AP box 3, folder 56; Andrews to Hays, July 12, 1926, AP box 1, folder 7; MPPDA Press Release, July 27, 1926, WHP box 31, folder: July 18–31, 1926.

30. Speech Delivered by Will H. Hays at Dinner Given by the Federal Council of Churches, Waldorf-Astoria Hotel, March 3, 1926, WHP box 29, folder: March 1–5, 1926; Unsigned Letter to Christian Herter, April 24, 1926, AP box 1, folder 6. MPPDA Press Release, "Church and Theater Plan Work Together," March 6, 1926; MPPDA Press Release, March 8, 1926, WHP box 29, folder: March 6–11, 1926; Macfarland to Christian Herter, April 9, 1926, AP box 1, folder 6; "Churches to Help the Stage Reform," *New York Times*, March 4, 1926, 1, 3.

31. Chapter 5, AP box 3, folder 53; Chapter 10, 109–110, AP box 3, folder 55; MPPDA Press Release, June 10, 1926, WHP box 30, folder: June 6–17, 1926; "Church Joins Stage to Elevate Plays," *New York Times*, June 11, 1926, 23. See The Church and Drama Association, Pamphlet, n.d., DMA King of Kings Subseries, box 285, folder 8.

32. Chapter 5, AP box 3, folder 53. Andrews to Milliken, June 22, 1926, AP box 1, folder 6; Milliken to Church & Drama Association, August 11, 1926, AP box 1, folder 7.

33. [Andrews] to Hays, June 14, 1926, AP box 1, folder 6. Charles Higham, *Cecil B. Demille* (New York: Charles Scribner's Sons, 1973), 83, 143.

34. Chapter 6, 49–53, AP box 3, folder 54. Johnson to Andrews, June 24, 1931, PHS RG 18, box 14, folder 26. See Richard Maltby, "*The King of Kings* and the Czar of All the Rushes: The Propriety of the Christ Story," in *Controlling Hollywood: Censorship and Regulation in the Studio Era*, ed. Matthew Bernstein (New Brunswick: Rutgers, 1999), 60–86.

35. Andrews to Charles P. Fagnani, May 2, 1927, AP box 1, folder 12; William E. Barton, "Chaplain-in-Ordinary to a Film," *The Dearborn Independent*, April 9, 1927, 22, PCA King of Kings File. Of note, the Jesus that "nobody knows" in Bruce Barton's book is really a prototype of a successful 20th-century business and marketing executive.

36. Andrews to Hays, July 12, 1926, AP box 1, folder 7; Cavert to Wallace Hayes, March 30, 1927, PHS RG 18, box 14, folder 26; Jason Joy to Alfred D. Moore, March 8, 1927, PCA King of Kings File. See Chapter 6, 54, AP box 3, folder 54; Daniel Lord to John J. Burke, n.d., MJA folder DeMille, King of Kings; Frank Walsh, *Sin and Censorship: The Catholic Church and the Motion Picture Industry* (New Haven: Yale University Press, 1996), 52–54.

37. Chapter 6, 59, AP box 3, folder 54; Pliny W. Williamson to Andrews, July 19, 1926, AP box 1, folder 7. DeMille gave $2,000 for 1927–1928 and $1,000 with a matching pledge from Pathé for 1928–1929. See correspondence between DeMille, Andrews, and Gladys Rosson in AP box 1, folder 17; DMA box 50, folder 15; DMA box 791, folder 8.

38. "The King of Kings," *Variety*, April 20, 1927, 15. S. Parkes Cadman to Hays, June 10, 1927, PCA King of Kings File; FCCCA Press Release, 1927, AP, box 1, folder 14; Milliken to Joy, June 15, 1927, PCA, King of Kings File; Cavert to Joy, August 3, 1926, PHS RG 18, box 14, folder 26; Andrews to DeMille, November 1, 1926, DMA box 285, folder 8.

39. Rabbi Simon Greensburg to Andrews, October 23, 1927; Andrews to DeMille, November 25, 1927, DMA box 285, folder 8. "By Requests of Jews, DeMille Is Modifying 'King of Kings'," *Variety*, January 11, 1928, 4.

40. "'Godless Girl' Film Full of Atheism," *Variety*, January 11, 1928, 15; Gladys Rosson to Andrews, November 9, 1929, DMA, box 791, folder 8. The MPPDA's Arthur DeBra would include the religious drama on a list of money losers. Inter-Office Memo, DeBra to Wilkinson, January 23, 1930, WHP box 41, folder: January 15–31, 1930. See also "The King of Kings," 15; FCCCA Press Release, 1927, AP box 1, folder 14; "'King of Kings' on the Screen," *Federal Council Bulletin*, March 1927, 27, PHS RG 18, box 80, folder 19.

41. George Reid Andrews, "How the Churches Are Working for Better Drama," *Federal Council Bulletin*, November 1927, 16, PHS RG 18, box 80, folder 19; Andrews to Barrett, November 23, 1927, NBR box 21, folder: Church and Drama Association.

CHAPTER 4

1. See Andrews and Milliken correspondence in AP box 1, folder 16, and AP box 1, folder 18. Data Book Prepared for the Quadrennial Meeting of the Federal Council of the Churches of Christ in America, Rochester, NY, December 5–12, 1928, 31, KF-YMCA Program Records: Religious Work, folder: Federal Council of Churches 6th Quadrennial Meeting Reports, December 5–11, 1928.

2. Milliken to Andrews, October 1, 1928, AP box 1, folder 18. See Andrews and Milliken correspondence between January and May 1928 in AP box 1, folders 15 and 16. On McGoldrick see Leigh Ann Wheeler, *Against Obscenity: Reform and the Politics of Womanhood in America, 1873–1935* (Baltimore: Johns Hopkins, 2004), 168. The MPPDA's $6,000 offer was for $150 a week toward the $400 minimum weekly budget for ten months. That the Association did not operate during July and August was another source of irritation with Milliken. The Church and Drama Bulletin had somewhere between 11,000 and 12,000 subscribers.

3. Andrews to Milliken, October 4, 1928; Milliken to Andrews, October 1, 1928, AP box 1, folder 18, October 1–15, 1928.

4. "Unexpected Decision," *Variety*, July 13 1927, 5, 14. The Brookhart Bill was introduced in December 1927 and hearings before the Senate Interstate Commerce Commission took place February 27 to March 2, 1928. William Marston Seabury, "The Futile Exhibitor," *The Churchman*, February 1, 1930, 13–15; David A. Horowitz, "An Alliance of Convenience: Independent Exhibitors and Purity Crusders Battle Hollywood, 1920–1960," *The Historian* 59, no. 3 (1997): 563–564; "The Facts on Block-booking and Blind-selling of Motion Pictures," Unpublished Paper, n.d., PHS RG 18, box 15, folder 1; *The Public Relations of the Motion Picture Industry* (New York: Department of Research and Education, FCCCA, 1931), 92–93; "Canon Chase, Champ Reformer, Slams Pictures and Will Hays," *Variety*, February 2, 1927, 5, 13.

5. Chapter 9, 86, AP box 3, folder 54; Andrews to Otto H. Kahn, September 26, 1928, AP box 1, folder 17. On the Senate investigation, see M. R. Werner, *Privileged Characters* (New York: Arno Press, 1974).

6. Andrews to Milliken, September 25, 1928, AP box 1, folder 17.

7. Chapter 9, 84, AP box 3, folder 54; Andrews to Milliken, October 4, 1928; Milliken to Andrews, October 11, 1928, AP box 1, folder 18.

8. Chapter 10, 107–108, AP box 3, folder 55; Andrews to Cadman, March 20, 1929, AP box 2, folder 26. The luncheon took place on Friday, December 14, 1928, at the Harvard Club. Macfarland to Andrews, November 24, 1928, AP box 1, folder 20.

9. Andrews to Cadman, June 5, 1929, AP box 2, folder 31; Chapter 11, 116, AP box 3, folder 55. Fosdick to Andrews, November 20, 1930, AP box 3, folder 48. The Drama League of America raised $35,000 and the American Theatre Association another $10,000. On the Church and Drama League, see Press Release, September 16, 1929, NBR box 21, folder: Church and Drama Association.

10. Redfield was secretary of commerce in the Wilson Cabinet and president of the National Institute of Social Sciences. On the film commission, see Minutes of the Meeting of the Executive Committee of the Commission on Motion Pictures, September 26, 1929; Organization Meeting of the Commission on the Motion Picture and Drama, March 25, [1929?]; Minutes of the Meeting of the Commission on Motion Pictures, May 27, 1929, PHS RG 18, box 77, folder 21; Andrews to Macfarland, May 14, 1929, AP box 2, folder 29.

11. Chapter 11, 123–124, AP box 3, folder 55; Shipler to Harry Emerson Fosdick, June 22, 1930, AP box 3, folder 48. The Editorial Council of the Religious Press was organized under the auspices of the Federal Council. Shipler worked closely with Don C. Seitz, author and veteran journalist with the New York *World*, who recently joined *The Churchman*'s editorial staff.

12. "Mr. Hays and the Movies," *The Churchman*, June 29, 1929, 8; "Men, Movies and Money," *The Churchman*, July 20, 1929, 8; "Selling Synthetic Sin," *The Churchman*, August 3, 1929, 8–9; "The Camouflagers," *The Churchman*, July 13, 1929, 8; "Tear Off the Masks," *The Churchman*, July 6, 1929, 8.

13. "As Seen by Marlen Pew," *The Churchman*, October 26, 1929, 16–17 (Reprinted from *Editor & Publisher*, October 12, 1929); Welford Beaton, "Will H. Hays Is Done," *The Churchman*, October 5, 1929, 12–13.

14. "Brookhart Proposes Film Regulations," *The Lewiston Daily Sun*, May 8, 1929, 1; Horowitz, "An Alliance of Convenience," 565–566; William Randolph Hearst, Editorial, "Purer Films Vital to Industry and Public Morals; Federal Censorship Alone Will Guarantee Them," *Los Angeles Examiner*, October 13, 1927, PCA, Censorship (1924–1936).

15. "Consummate Movie Camouflaging," *The Churchman*, September 14, 1929, 8–9; Memo From Mr. Borthwick to Will H. Hays, January 4, 1930; also Inter-Office Memo, Budget 1930, WHP box 41, folder: January 1–14, 1930. Charles

Stelzle, *A Son of the Bowery: The Life Story of an East Side American* (New York: George H. Doran, 1926), 175; Stelzle to the Editor of The Churchman, [September 12, 1929], WHP box 40, folder: September 11–30, 1929.

16. "The Movie Masqueraders," *The Churchman*, September 21, 1929, 15–16.

17. *The Churchman*, October 20, 7–8; "Consummate Movie Camouflaging," 9; Beaton, "Will H. Hays Is Done," 12. Committee on Use of Motion Pictures for Religious Education, Press Release, April 20, 1930, WHP box 41, folder: April 16–30, 1930. Minutes of the Meeting of the Commission on Motion Pictures of the FCCCA, October 25, 1929, PHS RG 18, box 77, folder 21. See press materials in PCA, Biography-Alice Ames Winter (Mrs. Thomas G. Winter). Afterward, Sidney Weston (Congregational Publishing Society) resigned from the committee, believing it had been compromised by the MPPDA. "The Movie Camouflagers," *The Churchman*, February 22, 1930, 13–14.

18. "Continuing Camouflage," *The Churchman*, October 26, 1929, 16; "Let the Senate Investigate," *The Churchman*, October 19, 1929, 9; MPPDA Press Release, [November 12, 1929], WHP box 41, folder: November 1–13, 1929. See Wheeler, *Against Obscenity*, 79–85; Anna Steese Richardson, "Lobbying in Women's Clubs," *New Republic*, June 11, 1930, 91–93. If observers at the time had little doubt—and Wheeler has confirmed—that Hays and Milliken had arranged Winter's appointment, Raymond Moley contends just the opposite. Commenting on these events, he includes an aside: "Hays himself, *who had certainly not consciously inspired these proposals*, was delighted with the friendly interest they bespoke and the concrete results they promised" (italics mine). Moley, *The Hays Office* (New York, Bobbs-Merrill, 1945), 144. Moley and Hays, who provide the first accounts of the MPPDA, both carefully sidestep Protestants, even when considering events that centrally involve them. Moreover, they plainly leave out any consideration of the Federal Council of Churches or charge its leaders with having censorial intentions. See Moley, 81; Will H. Hays, *The Memoirs of Will H. Hays* (Garden City, NY: Doubleday & Company, 1955), 449.

19. Chapter 12, 131–134, AP box 3, folder 55; Hays to McConnell, September 20, 1929, WHP box 40, folder: September 11–30, 1929. Minutes of Committee on Nominations of the Commission on Motion Pictures, October 23, 1929, PHS RG 18, box 77, folder 21; Redfield to Andrews, December 14, 1929, AP box 2, folder 41; Chapter 12, 135–136, AP box 3, folder 55.

20. "Stelzle Forced out by Federal Council," 23. Andrews was a source for Wayne Parrish, the *Herald Tribune*'s religion editor. Chapter 13, 144, AP box 3, folder 55. Macfarland to Andrews, December 16, 1929, cited in Chapter 13, 141, AP box 3, folder 55; Minutes of the Administrative Committee of the Federal Council of Churches, December 27, 1929, NBR box 25, folder: FCCCA; "Motion Picture Commission Defines Policy," *Federal Council Bulletin*, January 1930, 23, PHS RG 18, box 18, folder 1.

21. MPPDA Press Release, December 16, 1929, PHS RG 18, box 14, folder 26. The letter cited was Andrews to Milliken, October 4, 1928. "Hays Offered Him Film Pay, Says Andrews," *New York Herald Tribune*, March 31, 1930, PHS RG 18, box 15, folder 3.

22. Edwin W. Hullinger, "Free Speech for Talkies?," *North American Review* (June 1929): 737–743. See Richard Maltby, "The Genesis of the Production Code," *Quarterly Review of Film & Video* 15, no. 4 (1995): 13–14. Hays continued his dubious business dealings. Father Daniel Lord accepted an "honorarium" and expense money for his work on the Production Code, and the MPPDA covered all of Quigley's expenses related to his activities with the Legion. See correspondence between Lord and Quigley, February 1930 to May, 1931, MJA folder, Movie Production Code, Quigley, Martin, 1927–1932.

23. Joy to Hays, November 12, 1929, WHP box 41, folder: November 1–13, 1929. Frank Walsh, *Sin and Censorship: The Catholic Church and the Motion Picture Industry* (New Haven: Yale University Press, 1996), 57–58; J. P. S., "Motion Picture Problems, How Producers Meet Them," *The Tidings*, December 13, 1929, 19, 21, 31.

24. "Is the Federal Council Retained?," *The Churchman*, January 4, 1930, 8–9; Chapter 13, 142–143, AP box 3, folder 55; "The Federal Council of Churches WAS Retained," *The Churchman*, April 5, 1930, 9. Ernest Johnson paid "interpretive visits" and Macfarland specifically tried to persuade Shipler to refrain from attacking the Council's connection to the Hays organization. Andrews to Johnson, June 26, 1931; Cavert to Johnson, July 15, 1931, PHS RG 18, box 14, folder 26; Charles K. Gilbert, "The Open Forum: The Federal Council and Motion Pictures," *The Churchman*, January 18, 1930, 2.

25. "Dr. Macfarland Quits Federal Church Council," *New York Herald Tribune*, March 29, 1930, PHS RG 18, box 15, folder 3.

26. Quoted in Richard Maltby, "The Genesis of the Production Code," 19. See also Maltby, "The Production Code and the Hays Office," in *Grand Design: Hollywood as a Modern Business Enterprise 1930–1939*, ed. Tino Balio (New York: Charles Scribner's Sons, 1993), 47.

27. Joy to Hays, May 23, 1932, cited in "Ten Years of Will H. Hays—Article No. 6," *Harrison's Reports*, June 18, 1932, 97, 100, NBR box 159, folder: Harrison's Report, 1932; Maltby, "The Genesis of the Production Code," 18.

28. "A Letter and an Answer," *The Churchman*, February 15, 1930, 1. The proceedings were initiated on behalf of Hays, Milliken, and Joy, with a request for damages in the sum of $250,000. Edgar Souza to Hays, April 5, 1930, WHP box 41, folder: April 1–15, 1930; Alfred A. Cook to Hess, April 21, 1930, WHP box 41, folder: April 16–30, 1930. Journalists were up in arms over Hays's action. See "Hays Should Go," *The Churchman*, March 1, 1930, 13; "Some Comments on the Movies," *The Churchman*, March 8, 1930, 12–13.

29. "Dr. Macfarland Quits Federal Church Council," *New York Herald Tribune*, March 29, 1930, PHS RG 18, box 15, folder 3; "Macfarland Quits in Church Dispute," *New York Times*, March 29, 1930, 21.

30. "Hays Plagued by Religionists but Issues 'Don'ts' on Schedule," *Variety*, April 2, 1930, 2; "The Federal Council of Churches WAS Retained," 9. "Charges Hays Funds Balk Film Reforms," *New York Times*, March 31, 1930, 23.

31. "Church and Drama," *The Churchman*, August 23, 1930, 9; "Documents Concerning a Libel Case," *The Churchman*, August 1936, Section 2, I–VIII.

32. Hays quoted in MPPDA Press Release, April 2, 1930, WHP box 41, 1930, folder: April 1–15, 1930; "The Hays 'Moral Codes'," *The Churchman*, July 5, 1930, 9; "As a Newspaper Sees It," *The Churchman*, October 26, 1929, 17 (reprinted from Houston's *Southern Advance* as "Brother Hays and 'The Cock-eyed World'"). Marlen Pew, editor of the newspaper trade journal, *Editor & Publisher*, complained at having "suffered the humiliation of sitting through a performance of *The Cock-Eyed World*, in the presence of a crowd of boys and girls of my family circle." "As Seen by Marlen Pew," *The Churchman*, October 26, 1929, 16–17 (reprinted from *Editor & Publisher*, October 12, 1929). Robert Sklar, *Movie-Made America: A Cultural History of American Movies* (New York: Random House, Vintage Books, 1994), 153. Weekly attendance exceeded expectations in 1929, increasing 15 percent.

33. "Will Haysing Presbyterianism," *The Churchman*, March 22, 1930, 14; "Federal Council Report Called Inhibited," *The Churchman*, August 8, 1931, 17; Address of Will H. Hays Before the Men's Bible Class Annual Dinner-Baptist Church (John D. Rockefeller, Jr.), "What is Being Done for Motion Pictures," January 25, 1923, 5, 9, WHP box 19, folder: January 21–27, 1923; "As a Newspaper Sees It," *The Churchman*, October 26, 1929, 17. A Congressional investigation exposed the questionable practices of public utility companies making use of university professors and civic organizations, including the General Federation of Women's Clubs, for propaganda purposes while they expanded their power and increased their profits. See "Anti-Movie Revolt in Women's Clubs," *The Churchman*, May 3, 1930, 12–14; Anna Steese Richardson, "Lobbying in Women's Clubs," *New Republic*, June 11, 1930, 91–93; "Mr. Hays and the Women's Clubs," *The Churchman*, June 28, 1930, 9.

34. "Hays Champions New Movement to Help Pastors," *Grand Rapids Press*, May 24, 1924, 1, 2; "The Way of the Hays-Milliken Uplift," *The Churchman*, November 9, 1929, 13; "Hollywood Promises," *Commonweal*, April 16, 1930, 667; Stephen Vaughn, "The Devil's Advocate: Will H. Hays and the Campaign to Make Movies Respectable," *Indiana Magazine of History* 101, no. 2 (2005): paragraph 33; "Plans Made for Research Study of Motion Picture Situation," *Federal Council Bulletin*, February 1930, 24, PHS RG 18, box 81, folder 1.

CHAPTER 5

1. "Code of Conduct for Films Revised," *New York Times*, April 1, 1930, 1, 18; "Andrews Got Pay, Hays Aide Replies," *New York Times*, April 1, 1930, 18. "Andrews Explains Asking 10% on Film," *New York Times*, April 2, 1930, 3; MPPDA Press Release,

April 2, 1930, WHP box 41, folder: April 1–15, 1930. Hays shrewdly did not reply to Andrews's June 14, 1926, letter.

2. "Hudson Introduces His Censor Bill; No Mention Church Bodies Behind Act," *Variety*, February 19, 1930, 9, 66; "Revising Hudson Bill for Fed'l Censorship," *Variety*, February 12, 1930, 8. This was a revision of the Hudson Bill introduced by Congressman Grant M. Hudson, a lay Baptist leader, former Anti-Saloon League official, and member of the FMPC's board of directors. The bill drew on earlier proposals by William Sheafe Chase to regulate the industry as a public utility and enforce NAMPI's Thirteen Points.

3. "Virtue in Cans," *The Nation*, April 16, 1930, in "Some Movie Comments," *The Churchman*, April 19, 1930, 17; "Hollywood Promises," *Commonweal*, April 16, 1930, 667–668; "The New Motion Picture Code," *The Churchman*, April 12, 1930, 9.

4. "Hays Plagued by Religionists but Issues 'Don'ts' on Schedule," *Variety*, April 2, 1930, 2; Tippy to Eastman, March 2, 1931, PHS RG 18, box 14, folder 26. Lord to Father Provincial, February 17, 1930, MJA folder, Movie Production Code, Quigley, Martin, 1927–1932.

5. Lee Hanmer, Russell Sage Foundation, Press Release, April 7, 1930, WHP box 41, folder: April 1–15, 1930; "13 Welfare Bodies Deny Hays Paid Fees," *New York Times*, April 7, 1930, 25; "Both Sides Deny Movie Retainers," *New York Times*, April 3, 1930, 31.

6. "The Trail of the Serpent," *The Churchman*, May 31, 1930, 9. Emrich received $3,258.72 from the MPPDA during 1928 and 1929 and logged 215 appearances; she was paid $15.00 and expenses for each one. Memorandum, Johnson to Cavert, "Mrs. Jeannette W. Emrich's Relationship with the Motion Picture Producers and Distributors of America, Inc.," August 18, 1930, PHS RG 18, box 14, folder 26. Disbursements from an MPPDA "Special Reserve Fund" used to pay "Speakers" stopped that August (1930). Summary of Receipts and Expenses, January 1st to August 31st, 1930 (inclusive), MPPDA, WHP box 42: June 1, 1930—May 31, 1931, folder: September 1–30, 1930.

7. Shipler to Fosdick, June 22, 1930; Andrews to Cadman, October 27, 1930, AP box 3, folder 48. Andrews became a pastor at the Park Street Congregational Church in Bridgeport, Connecticut.

8. Frank Walsh, *Sin and Censorship: The Catholic Church and the Motion Picture Industry* (New Haven: Yale University Press, 1996), 31–32.

9. Cavert to Gilman, January 8, 1931; Gilman to Cavert, January 28, 1931; Milliken to Weigle, April 23, 1931, PHS RG 18, box 14, folder 26; "Federal Council of Churches Accepts Resignation," *The Churchman*, May 3, 1930, 21. On the Motion Picture Commission, see Cavert to the Members of the Commission on Motion Pictures, February 6, 1931; Cavert to Fred Eastman, February 14, 1931; Cavert to Jerome Davis, February 27, 1931, PHS RG 18, box 14, folder 26.

10. *The Public Relations of the Motion Picture Industry* (New York: Department of Research and Education, FCCCA, 1931), 144, 48. Herbert Shenton, professor of

Sociology at Syracuse University and vice-chair of the Council's Research and Education Department, headed the study commission. Hays fulfilled his offer of cooperation to McConnell and provided access to pertinent files.

11. Johnson to Andrews, February 9, 1931, AP box 3, folder 49; Johnson to Andrews, June 24, 1931, PHS RG 18, box 14, folder 26; Chapter 10, 108, AP box 3, folder 55. See Henry "Hawk" Smith Leiper to Andrews, April 21, 1930, AP box 3, folder 49, 1931; Andrews to Johnson, June 26, 1931; Memorandum, CSM [Macfarland] to Johnson, November 5, 1930, PHS RG 18, box 14, folder 26.

12. Hays to Roy W. Howard, June 26, 1931; MPPDA Press Release, Will H. Hays to Bishop Francis J. McConnell, June 26, 1931, WHP box 43, folder: June 26–30, 1931; "More Milliken Manipulating," *The Churchman*, August 15, 1931, 9; Johnson to Cavert, June 30, 1931, PHS RG 18, box 14, folder 26.

13. McConnell to Hays, July 3, 1931; Johnson to Andrews, June 24, 1931; also Andrews to Johnson, June 26, 1931, PHS RG 18, box 14, folder 26. See "Bishop McConnell Refutes Hays," *The Churchman*, July 11, 1931, 9; George Reid Andrews, "An Open Letter to Bishop McConnell," *The Churchman*, July 25, 1931, 15–16.

14. "Milliken Statement Re Report Issued by the Federal Council on Movies," MPPDA Press Release, June 29, 1931, WHP box 43, folder: June 26–30, 1931; "Federal Council *v.* Hays," *Time*, July 6, 1931, 21; Cavert to John J. Rothermel, July 9, 1931, PHS RG 18, box 14, folder 26. "Bishop Says Hays Evades Film Issue," *New York Times*, July 6, 1931, 19; Martin Quigley, "Federal Council Report One of Most Heartening Development Insists on Continued Cooperation," *Motion Picture Herald*, July 18, 1931, 12–13; Cavert to Johnson, July 16, 1931, PHS RG 18, box 14, folder 26. The Federal Council's 1931 report noted Catholic authorship of the Code and cooperation with Hays in getting the industry to adopt it, but underplayed Catholic influence by pointing out that the concept "was also in the minds of Hollywood studio heads." *The Public Relations of the Motion Picture Industry*, 129–130.

15. *The Public Relations of the Motion Picture Industry*, 44; Cavert to Fred Eastman, February 26, 1931; Eastman to Cavert, March 3, 1931, PHS RG 18, box 14, folder 26.

16. Cavert to Andrews, November 5, 1931; Cavert to William D. McRae, September 28, 1931; also Chase to McConnell, July 8, 1931, PHS RG 18, box 14, folder 26. See "Federal Council Report Called Inhibited," *The Churchman*, August 8, 1931, 17.

17. Edwin W. Hullinger, "Free Speech for Talkies?," *North American Review* (June 1929): 737; "Hays Decries Censoring," *New York Times*, January 14, 1929, 10. See Hays to Eugene Chrystal, Eastman Kodak, August 28, 1928, Censor, Sound File, MPPDA-MA Reel 05, Frame 0054–0067; "Hays for Amendment to Bar Movie Censors," *New York Times*, March 26, 1927, 20; Will H. Hays, "Motion Pictures and Their Censors," *The American Review of Reviews*, April 1927, 393–398; "Hays Says Censors Bar Film Progress," *New York Times*, March 26, 1929, 15; Richard Maltby, "The Genesis of the Production Code," *Quarterly Review of Film & Video* 15, no. 4 (1995): 14; Laura Wittern-Keller, *Freedom of the Screen: Legal Challenges*

to *State Film Censorship, 1915–1981* (Lexington: University of Kentucky Press, 2008), 79–80; Murray Schumach, *The Face on the Cutting Room Floor: The Story of Movie and Television Censorship* (New York: William Morrow, 1964), 188–189.

18. Will H. Hays, *The Memoirs of Will H. Hays* (Garden City, NY: Doubleday & Company, 1955), 394; Joy to Hays, June 24, 1932; Inter-Office Memo, McKenzie to Kelly and Trotti, April 19, 1932, PCA Call Her Savage File.

19. Hays, *Memoirs*, 394.

20. "The Movies Are Brought to Judgment," *Christian Century*, December 30, 1931, 1648; David A. Cook, *A History of Narrative Film*, 4th ed. (New York: W. W. Norton & Company, 2004), 250; Joseph I. Breen to Quigley, May 1, 1932, QP box 1, folder 3.

21. "Producers' War Brews," *Hollywood Reporter*, June 25, 1931, 1–2. Twombly cited in "Biography of Bishop Noll: He Warns Against Effects of Immoral Movies," *Our Sunday Visitor*, May 27, 1951, 3, NP CNOL 5/03 Group: LOD: Clippings 1934–1935. See "Annual Report, "[MPPDA] Community Service Department," February 5, 1935, 7, NBR box 8, folder: Company Papers, Motion Picture Producers & Distributors of America, Inc., folder 1; "Milliken Lining up Protestants to Aid Films," *Christian Century*, October 26, 1932, 1292 (in reference to *Film Daily*, October 12, 1932, 1, 13). The phrase actually appeared in *The Churchman* as "Boost the best (Mr. Hay's [sic] phrase) and put over the worst." "The Better Movies," *The Churchman*, November 12, 1932, 8.

22. Joy's memo is cited in "Ten Years of Will H. Hays—Article No. 6," *Harrison's Reports*, June 18, 1932, 97, 100; "Movie Censors Hear Their Master's Voice," *Christian Century*, July 13, 1932, 877.

23. "Brookhart Attacks Movie Industry," *Spokane Daily Chronicle*, February 23, 1932, 3. Winter quoted in Leonard J. Leff and Jerold L. Simmons, *The Dame in the Kimono: Hollywood, Censorship, and the Production Code*, 2nd ed. (Lexington: University of Kentucky, 2001), 25, 42. Winter to Hays, November 4, 1931, WHP box 43, folder: November 16–30, 1931. Brookhart's bill tried to deal with blind selling by requiring producers to supply exhibitors with a 1,000-word synopsis before leasing a film.

24. Short to Charters, March 25, 1930; also Short to Dr. Wesley C. Mitchell, March 25, 1930, WWCP RG 40/117, box 32, folder 52; Cavert to Paul Leinbach, May 20, 1931, PHS RG 18, box 14, folder 26.

25. Henry James Forman, *Our Movie Made Children* (New York: Macmillan, 1933), 64–65; Leff and Simmons, *The Dame in the Kimono*, 38. Eastman's *Christian Century* series ran from May 3 to June 14, 1933.

26. Short to Charters, January 23, 1933, WWCP RG 40/117, box 32, folder 20; Paul G. Cressey, "The Motion Picture as Informal Education," *Journal of Educational Sociology* 7 (1934): 505–506, 13. The Payne Studies researchers privately faulted Forman's summary for its "anti-movie tone" and biased arguments against the movies. Charters to Forman, January 21, 1933, WCCP RG 40/117, box 32, folder 20; Charters to Short, January 21, 1933, WCCP RG 40/117, box 33, folder 9. This

summary is also drawn from Cressey to Charters, May 5, 1933, WCCP RG 40/117, box 33, folder 19; Ruth C. and L. L. Thurstone Peterson, *Motion Pictures and the Social Attitudes of Children* (New York: Macmillan, 1933), 92–93.

27. Fred Eastman and Edward Ouellette, *Learning for Life: Better Motion Pictures*, Pamphlet (Boston: Pilgrim Press, 1936), 23, MPRC-HIA box 76; Fred Eastman, "The Dramatist and the Minister," in *The Arts and Religion: The Ayers Lectures of the Colgate-Rochest Divinity School, 1943*, ed. Albert Edward Bailey (New York: MacMillan, 1944), 137; Eastman, "Introduction," in *Modern Religious Dramas*, ed. Fred Eastman (New York: Henry Holt, Red Label Reprints, 1928), vi.

28. George Reid Andrews, "Educational Use of Drama and Pageantry," *Religious Education* 22, no. 10 (1927): 1030; Eastman and Ouellette, *Learning for Life*, 54–55. Fred Eastman, "The Movie Outlook: What Is Wanted by the Public," *The Churchman*, January 1, 1935, 13; Eastman, "What Can We Do About the Movies?," *Christian Century*, June 14, 1933, 781; "The Legion of Decency's First Year," *Christian Century*, March 27, 1935, 393; Fred Eastman, "The Battle in the Theatre," *Association Men*, May 1930, 429; "Decency Plus!," *Christian Century*, June 13, 1934, 790–791; Fred Eastman, "The Motion Picture and Its Public Responsibilities," *The Public Opinion Quarterly* 2, no. 1 (1938): 44–46.

29. Eastman, "What Can We Do About the Movies?," 779; Eastman and Ouellette, *Learning for Life*, 4–5; Eastman, "The Movie Outlook: What Is Wanted by the Public," 13; Walter Lippmann, "Morals for Profit," *The World*, April 2, 1930, 10; "Morals for Movies," *Outlook and Independent*, April 16, 1930, 612.

30. Eastman and Ouellette, *Learning for Life*, 54–55; Eastman, "What Can We Do About the Movies?," 779; Eastman, "The Movies and Your Child's Conduct," *Christian Century*, May 24, 1933, 690; Eastman, "The Movies and Your Child's Emotions," Christian Century, May 17, 1933, 653.

31. "The Better Movies," 8.

32. Eastman, "The Movies and Your Child's Conduct," 688; "Cleansing the Movies," *Detroit Free Press*, April 2, 1930, in "Comments on the Movies," *The Churchman*, April 12, 1930, 13. Inter-Office Memo, Mr. DeBra to Mr. Wilkinson, January 23, 1930, WHP box 41, folder: January 15–31, 1930.

33. Eastman and Ouellette, *Learning for Life*, 34; "The Hays 'Moral Codes," *The Churchman*, July 5, 1930, 9; MPPDA Press Release, March 22, 1931, WHP box 42, folder: March 13–31, 1931.

34. Joseph I. Breen to Maurice McKenzie, March 5, 1931, WHP box 42, folder: March 1–12, 1931; "Annual Report, "[MPPDA] Community Service Department," February 5, 1935, 2–3, NBR box 8, folder: Company Papers, MPPDA, folder 1; Fred Eastman, "The Movie Outlook: The Dark Side," *The Churchman*, December 1, 1934, 16, 35; "Nix Classifying of Pix," *Variety*, August 28, 1934, 7, 51.

35. "Federal Council Plans Motion Picture Program," Press Release, n.d. [1933?]; Better Films Councils: Suggestions to Churches on Work for Better Films, Federal Council's Committee on Motion Pictures, Department of the Church and

Social Services, November 1933; Cavert to William H. Parsons, March 9, 1934, PHS RG 18, box 15, folder 1.

36. "The Payne Fund Studies: An Evaluation," October 15, 1937, 2, EDP RG 40/105, box 6, folder 22; First Symposium on Elements Out of Which a Program Looking Towards National Film Policies in Motion Pictures Can Be Selected, September 15, 1933, 1, 19, MPRC-HIA box 57, folder: Symposium—MPRC Researchers. See correspondence in PHS RG 18, box 14, folder 26; MPRC-HIA box 12, folder: National Foundations, and folder: Payne Study and Experiment Fund; WWCP RG 40/117, box 33, folder 4.

37. Walter Lippmann, "The Morals of the Movies," *Milwaukee Sentinel*, January 14, 1935, 8; "Source Material on Motion Pictures for Pastors," Federal Council Committee on Motion Pictures, October 21, 1934, PHS RG 18, box 15, folder 1; "The Legion of Decency's First Year," 393; "The Further Duty of the Legion of Decency," *Harrison's Reports*, April 13, 1935, 57, NP CNOL: 4/99 folder: LOD: Reports and Newsletters 1934–1935.

38. Howard M. LeSourd, "Block-Booking—Cause or Camouflage?," *Literary Digest*, June 9, 1934, 28; Short to May, April 12, 1933, MPRC-HIA box 12, folder: May, Mark A.—Shuttleworth (1931–1932). A side note: LeSourd, Payne Studies researcher Mark A. May, and Arthur DeBra on the MPPDA Public Relations staff, were classmates at Union Theological Seminary.

39. Eastman and Ouellette, *Learning for Life*, 35. Federal Motion Picture Commission, Hearing Before the Committee on Interstate and Foreign Commerce House of Representatives, Seventy-Third Congress, Second Session on H. R. 6097, March 19, 1934, NP CNOL: 4/99 folder: LOD: Reports and Newsletters 1934–1935; David A. Horowitz, "An Alliance of Convenience: Independent Exhibitors and Purity Crusders Battle Hollywood, 1920–1960," *The Historian* 59, no. 3 (1997): 570; Fred Eastman, "The Movie Outlook: A Practical Program," *The Christian Leader*, November 17, 1934, 1452.

40. William Marston Seabury, *The Public and the Motion Picture Industry* (New York: Macmillan, 1926), 193, 89; Cavert to Mrs. Mary C. Smith, n.d. [circa February–March, 1931]; Tippy to Axling, May 21, 1931, PHS RG 18, box 14, folder 26; First Symposium on Elements Out of Which a Program Looking Towards National Film Policies in Motion Pictures Can Be Selected, September 15, 1933, 2–3, MPRC-HIA box 57, folder: Symposium—MPRC Researchers; Alice Ames Winter, "And So to Hollywood," *The Women's Journal*, March 1930, 9.

CHAPTER 6

1. On early Catholic strategies, see Frank Walsh, *Sin and Censorship: The Catholic Church and the Motion Picture Industry* (New Haven: Yale University Press, 1996), 18–22, 27. The name was changed to the National Catholic Welfare Conference in 1922.

2. Archbishop Cardinal Mundelein quoted in "Production Code Scrap of Paper Says Mundelein," *Motion Picture Herald*, June 9, 1934, 40. IFCA statistics in Alice Ames Winter, "Better Pictures in Your Home Town: Suggestions to Local Better Films Committees," Brochure (Hollywood: Public Relations, Motion Picture Producers and Distributors of America, Inc., 1932), 7; Annual Report, [MPPDA] Community Service Department, February 5, 1935, 9, NBR box 8, folder: Company Papers, MPPDA, folder 1.

3. Cantwell to McNicholas, September 1, 1936, with Enclosure, NCWC-ACUA box 198, folder 7; Unpublished and undated paper concerning the Encyclical, 1936, AALA LOD #55, Motion Picture Industry, Breen File; LOD #57, Material for AER Article; LOD #57, John J. Devlin Correspondence Files, box 58.

4. John T. McNicholas, "The Episcopal Committee and the Problem of Evil Motion Pictures," *Ecclesiastical Review* 91, no. 2 (1934): 115; John J. Cantwell, "Priests and the Motion Picture Industry," *Ecclesiastical Review* 90, no. 2 (1934): 143; John F. Noll, "A Real National Welfare Drive: Movie Campaign Must Be Continued," *Our Sunday Visitor*, October 21, 1934, 14; Quigley to McNicholas, July 11, 1935, NCWC-ACUA box 198, folder 39. Payne scholar Edgar Dale discovered that Catholic bishops were interested "merely with the moral and social values side of the program [Payne Studies]" and not reforming the industry's trade practices. Memorandum, June 1, 1934, WWCP RG 40/117, box 33, folder 26.

5. Cantwell to John J. Burke, September 20, 1933, AALA LOD #55, LOD File—1934–1942; Cantwell to McNicholas, December 28, 1933, NCWC-ACUA box 198, folder 6; Breen to Lord, August 3, 1933, MJA folder, Movie Production Code, Breen, Joseph, 1933–1942.

6. George Johnson to McNicholas, July 9, 1934, and related correspondence with William H. Short in NCWC-ACUA box 198, folder 21. See also in box 198, Chase to McNicholas, February 21, 1934 (folder 17); Michael J. Ready to McNicholas, March 8, 1934 (folder 33); Quigley to McNicholas, March 27, 1934 (folder 37); McNicholas to Cantwell, April 17, 1934 (folder 6); Breen to McNicholas, May 22, 1934 (folder 5); Dinneen to McNicholas, June 2, 1934 (folder 10); Paul H. Furfey, "The Priest and the Motion-Picture Problem," *Ecclesiastical Review* 90, no. 5 (1934): 480–491; Furfey, "Children and the Cinema," *Ecclesiastical Review* 90, no. 3 (1934): 262; Daniel A. Lord, "The Motion Pictures Betray America," (St. Louis, MO: The Queen's Work, 1934), 47.

7. McNicholas to Chase, March 22, 1934, NCWC-ACUA box 198, folder 17.

8. Fred Eastman, "Social Issues in the Movie Code," *Christian Century*, September 20, 1933, 1170–71; "The President and the Movie Code," *Christian Century*, October 25, 1933, 1326–28.

9. "Appeal to President on Motion Picture Code," *Federal Council Bulletin*, November–December 1933, 14, PHS RG 18, box 81, folder 2.

10. Cantwell to McNicholas, December 28, 1933, NCWC-ACUA box 198, folder 6; The Pledge: Its Nature and Purpose, Unpublished Manuscript, LOD, [n.d.], 5, AANY S/C—37, folder #6 (Microfilm); Meetings of the Episcopal Committee,

NCWC-ACUA box 198, folder 8. See Tippy to Burke, November 22, 1933; Burke to Cantwell, November 28, 1933, QP box 1, folder 3; Cantwell to Tippy, December 13, 1933; Cantwell to Burke, December 13, 1933, LOD #57, John J. Devlin Correspondence Files, box 58; Cantwell to Burke, September 20, 1933, AALA LOD #55, LOD File—1934–1942. Production and box-office estimates in Fred Eastman and Edward Ouellette, *Learning for Life: Better Motion Pictures*, Pamphlet (Boston: Pilgrim Press, 1936), 41; MPRC-HIA box 76.

11. McNicholas, "The Episcopal Committee and the Problem of Evil Motion Pictures," 113; James M. Wall, *Oral History with Geoffrey Shurlock* (Los Angeles: Louis B. Mayer Library, American Film Institute, 1970), 110; "Church Drive Progresses," *Variety*, May 29, 1934, 5, 23.

12. "For Better Motion Pictures," FCCCA Press Release, June 22, 1934, PHS RG 18, box 15, folder 1; "Plans Perfected for Movie Clean-up," FCCCA Release, 1934; FCCCA Press Release, July 14, [1934?]; L. O. Hartman, Editorial, "Keep Away from Bad Movies," *Zion Herald*, July 11, 1934, 651–652, PHS RG 18, box 15, folder 1. The Central Conference of American Rabbis also denounced the "harmful influence" of movies on youth. "Jewish Conference Joins War on Dirt," *Hollywood Reporter*, June 19, 1934.

13. *Variety* cited in "The Movie Worm Has Turned," *The Churchman*, July 1, 1934, 9.

14. Annual Report, [MPPDA] Community Service Department, 9; Magaret Farrand Thorp, *America at the Movies* (New Haven: Yale, 1939), 203; "12,000,000 Expected to Aid Movie Drive," *New York Times*, July 8, 1934, 1, 8; "Uncle Sam on Warpath in Crusade for Compulsory Cleanup of H'wood," *Variety*, June 12, 1934, 1, 57; FCCCA Press Release, July 14, [1934?], PHS RG 18, box 15, folder 1; Cantwell, "Priests and the Motion Picture Industry," 146; "Decency Plus!," *Christian Century*, June 13, 1934, 790–791. It was estimated that only 4 million Protestants pledged cooperation with the Legion's campaign compared to between 6 to 11 million Catholic pledge signers.

15. Report by John J. Devlin to John J. Cantwell, n.d., AALA LOD #57, Material for AER Article. Breen to Quigley, October 7, 1930, WHP box 42, folder: October 1–31, 1930.

16. MPPDA Press Release, April 2, 1930, WHP box 41, folder: April 1–15, 1930.

17. McNicholas to Goldstein, December 27, 1934, NP CNOL 4/98 folder: LOD: Correspondence 1934–1952; Maguire to McNicholas, March 12, 1934, NCWC-ACUA box 198, folder 30: Maguire, Arthur D., 1934–1936. See Michael Cromartie, *A Preserving Grace: Protestants, Catholics, and Natural Law* (Grand Rapids: Eerdmans 1997). In the Catholic worldview, natural law is accessed by reason alone and without the aid of faith or divine revelation. In traditional Protestant thinking, human reason is both informed by faith and corrupted by sin. God's grace does not make people morally superior, but liberates them from sin to work in the redemption or restoration of God's creation.

18. Address of Will H. Hays Before the Men's Bible Class Annual Dinner-Baptist Church (John D. Rockefeller, Jr.), "What Is Being Done for Motion Pictures,"

January 25, 1923, 9, WHP box 19, folder: January 21–27, 1923. Breen had little respect for Hays and even less for Jewish producers, "a dirty, filthy lot" concerned only with "the standard of the box-office," in his estimate. "To attempt to talk ethical values to them is time worse than wasted." Breen to Quigley, May 1, 1932, QP, box 1, folder 3. See Thomas Doherty's perceptive consideration of Breen's attitudes toward Jews in *Hollywood's Censor: Joseph I. Breen and the Production Code Administration* (New York: Columbia, 2007), 203–212.

19. "A Fateful Hour for the Movies," *Christian Century*, May 27, 1936, 757. As Richard Maltby shows, "For all industry parties, issues of oligopoly control and industry trade practices were much more important than censorship." Maltby, "The Production Code and the Hays Office," in *Grand Design: Hollywood as a Modern Business Enterprise 1930–1939*, ed. Tino Balio (New York: Charles Scribner's Sons, 1993), 42. Maltby observes that Protestants criticized the immorality of both movie content and the industry's trade practices in "More Sinned Against Than Sinning: The Fabrications of 'Pre-Code Cinema'," *Senses of the Cinema*, November 2003, http://www.sensesofcinema.com/contents/03/29/pre_code_cinema.html. For reasons that the studio magnates were willing "to institutionalize what was clearly a system of de facto censorship and prior restraint," see David A. Cook, *A History of Narrative Film*, 4th ed. (New York: W. W. Norton & Company, 2004), 238.

20. "Clean Pix's Fan Kickback," *Variety*, May 1, 1934, 51. Gilman to James E. Cummings, April 18, 1934, NCWC-ACUA box 198, folder 33. After receiving her cloned letter praising Hays, *The Churchman* always suspected that McGoldrick was being compensated by the MPPDA. "The Movie Masqueraders," *The Churchman*, September 21, 1929, 14–16. The change in the Legion's review policy also marked a gender paradigm shift that affected the role and authority of women in the anti-obscenity movement. Leigh Ann Wheeler, *Against Obscenity: Reform and the Politics of Womanhood in America, 1873–1935* (Baltimore: Johns Hopkins, 2004), 178–179.

21. McNicholas, "The Episcopal Committee and the Problem of Evil Motion Pictures," 118; Cantwell to McNicholas, December 28, 1933, NCWC-ACUA box 198, folder 6; John F. Noll, "A Real National Welfare Drive: Movie Campaign Must Be Continued," *Our Sunday Visitor*, October 21, 1934, 3, 14, NP CNOL 5/01 Group: LOD: Clippings 1934–1935.

22. Annual Report, [MPPDA] Community Service Department, 6; Owen A. McGrath, "Catholic Action's Big Opportunity," *Ecclesiastical Review* 91, no. 3 (1934): 287, 81. See Meetings of the Episcopal Committee, NCWC-ACUA box 198, folder 8; James J. Hennesey, *American Catholics: A History of the Roman Catholic Community in the United States* (New York: Oxford University Press, 1981), 260; William B. Prendergast, *The Catholic Voter in American Politics: The Passing of the Democratic Monolith* (Washington, DC: Georgetown University Press, 1999), 112, 15.

23. "The Defeat of Prohibition," *Christian Century*, August 2, 1933, 976.

24. "Legion of Decency Campaign Intensified," *Literary Digest*, December 22, 1934, 20; "Interfaith Amity Seen in Film Fight," *New York Times*, July 6, 1934, 13; "Clergy Act Today on Film Control," *New York Times*, July 17, 1934, 21. According to Andrea Friedman, rabbis feared campaigns against Hollywood would morph into active anti-Semitism and in self defense denounced objectionable films to fend off harmful stereotypes and demonstrate Jewish solidarity with Protestant and Catholic morality. The Legion's campaign coincided with the growing Nazi threat. See *Prurient Interests: Gender, Democracy, and Obscenity in New York City, 1909–1945* (New York: Columbia University Press, 2000), 140–146.

25. Tippy to Quigley, March 20, 1935, QP box 2, folder 6. Breen quoted in Ruth A. Inglis, *Freedom of the Movies: A Report on Self-Regulation from the Commission on Freedom of the Press* (Chicago: University of Chicago Press, 1947), 162; Fred Eastman, "The Movie Outlook: What Is Wanted by the Public," *The Churchman*, January 1, 1935, 13; Better Films Councils: Suggestions to Churches on Work for Better Films by the Federal Council's Committee on Motion Pictures, FCCCA, Department of the Church and Social Services, November 1933, 9, PHS RG 18, box 15, folder 1.

26. Pettengill to Noll, May 15, 1936, NCWC-ACUA box 198, folder 34; "Important Motion Picture Bill," *The Churchman*, April 1, 1935, 2–3; Motion Picture Research Council, Press Release, March 19, 1935, NBR box 164, folder: Block-Booking Controversy. For a brief summary of differences in Protestant and Catholic approaches to movie reform, see "The Catholic Drive for Decency," *Christian Century*, August 15, 1934, 1038–1039. On the FMPC, MPPDA, and block-booking legislation, see materials in MPRC-HIA box 60, folder: Analysis of Neely Bill, and box 60, folder: Why You Should Support the Neely Bill; box 66, folder: Motion Pictures: Block Booking and Blind Selling. For a list of block-booking legislation from 1927 to 1940, see Benjamin Werne, "The Neely Anti-Block Booking and Blind Selling Bill—an Analysis," in *Contemporary Law Pamphlets*, ed. New York University of Law (New York: New York University of Law, 1940).

27. "Statement Issued by the Episcopal Committee on Motion Pictures," February 25, 1936, NCWC-ACUA box 198, folder 3; Quigley to McNicholas, March 24, 1936, Enclosure, Excerpts from Testimony in the Hearing on Pettengill Bill—Tuesday, March 17, 1936, NCWC-ACUA box 198, folder 40.

28. See "Catholic Women Protest Movie Code," *Christian Century*, October 11, 1933, 1259–1260; Chase to McNicholas, February 21, 1934, NCWC-ACUA box 198, folder 17; Quigley to McNicholas, July 11, 1935, NCWC-ACUA box 198, folder 39; Father McClafferty phoned from New York about the Neely Bill abolishing block booking, n.d., NCWC-ACUA box 198, folder 27; International Federation of Catholic Alumnae Motion Picture Bureau, Mrs. James Looram, Chairman, Report of the Chairman, 1934–1936, 20, QP box 2, folder 10.

29. Legion executive secretary Joseph A. Daly quoted in "Legion's Work to Be Pressed, States Priest," *Motion Picture Daily*, February 14, 1936, 1, 8, NP CNOL 5/03 Group: Legion of Decency: Clippings 1934–1935; "Profit in Decency Is Seen for Films," *New York Times*, February 14, 1936, 23; "Decency and Censorship," *Christian Century*, July 29, 1936, 132; Robert Forsythe, "Who Speaks for Us?," *New Theatre*, August 1936, 9. For commentary on Catholics and the Legion, see the three-part series by Leo H. Lehmann, "The Catholic Church in Politics" in *New Republic*, November 16, 1938, 34–36; November 23, 1938, 64–66; November 30, 1938, 94–96; Ben Ray Redman, "Pictures and Censorship," *Saturday Review of Literature*, December 31, 1938, 3–4, 13–14; "Censorship of Motion Pictures," *Yale Law Journal* 49, no. 1 (1939): 87–113.

30. "Pictures Worth Watching For," *Association Men*, January 1930, 220; "The Free Screen Censored: Statement of the Motion Picture Association of America Before a Committee of the United States Congress," February 2, 1960, 15–16, PHS RG 16, box 3, folder 5.

31. "The Legion of Decency and the Big Eight," *Christian Century*, March 20, 1940, 373; Richard Corliss, "The Legion of Decency," *Film Comment* (Summer 1968): 32.

32. Gilman to William T. Bannerman, July 31, 1934, NCWC-ACUA box 198, folder 21; "A Friendly Warning to the Federal Council," *Christian Century*, February 28, 1934, 276–277; Cavert to McConnell, July 5, 1934 (also Cavert to Parsons, March 9, 1934; Robinson to Cavert, April 17, 1934), PHS RG 18, box 15, folder 1. Tippy to Barrett, January 5, 1934; Tippy to Barrett, April 3, 1934, NBR box 25, folder: FCCCA.

33. George W. Kirchwey to Hanmer, October 2, 1933, NBR box 28, folder: Hanmer, Lee F., 1923–1935; Related Papers. "'Little Giant'," *Time*, January 11, 1937, 45–46. The MPRC was unable to coordinate the forces of movie reform. "Maps Broad Aid for Movies Drive," *New York Times*, June 30, 1934, 18; "Undertone of Pique over Publicity as Research Council Formulate Drive on Pictures," *Variety*, July 3, 1934, 5.

34. "Untitled," *The Churchman*, November 14, 1931, 7; *The Churchman*, November 21, 1931, 7; "Troubled Waters," *Harrison's Reports*, October 31, 1931, 176; "A Correction in the Interest of Truth," *Harrison's Reports*, November 14, 1931, 184, NBR box 159: Harrison's Reports, folder: Harrison's Report, 1931; "What Editors Are Saying," *The Churchman*, October 15, 1935, 13; Schwegler to Quigley, August 27, 1935, QP box 2, folder 1.

35. Goldstein quoted in "Documents Concerning a Libel Case," *The Churchman*, August 1936, Section 2, I–VIII. Hess also recovered $5,200 from *Harrison's Report* editor, P. S. "Pete" Harrison. See "$10,200 Judgment Against the Churchman," *The Churchman*, July 1, 1935, 1; "The Religious Press Stands By," *The Churchman*, August 1, 1935, 9; "As Seen by the Religious Press," *The*

Churchman, August 15, 1935, 12–15; "What Editors Are Saying," *The Churchman*, October 15, 1935, 13; "Rabbi Goldstein to Assist Churchman," *The Churchman*, October 15, 1935, 21; "Churchman: Creed Fences Fall to Save Christian Fortnightly," *Newsweek*, October 5, 1935, 27; "$10,200 Libel Judgment Sustained," *The Churchman*, July 1 & 15, 1936, 1; "The Churchman Associates," *The Churchman*, October 1, 1936, 9.

36. A. L. Finestone, "Will H. Hays' Fifteen Years in the Motion Picture Industry," *Boxoffice*, March 6 1937, 12–13. Annual Report, [MPPDA] Community Service Department, 3–4; Breen to Maurice McKenzie, March 5, 1931, WHP box 42, folder: March 1–12, 1931; "X: Moving Pictures," *Fortune*, April 13, 1936, 222.

37. "Movie Moguls Worried," *Independent Exhibitor*, January 1939, 9, MPRC-HIA box 76. "Another Jolt for Block Booking," *Christian Century*, January 11, 1939, 43–44; "Justice Department Statement on Suit Against Leading Movie Interests," *New York Times*, July 21, 1938, 6; "Consent Decree," *Time*, November 11, 1940, 70–71. Thurman Arnold, *Fair Fights and Foul: A Dissenting Lawyer's Life* (New York: Harcourt, Brace & World, 1951, 1960, 1965), 6; Alan Brinkley, *The End of Reform: New Deal Liberalism in Recession and War* (New York: Alfred A. Knopf, 1995), 107; Gene M. Gressley, ed., *Voltaire and the Cowboy: The Letters of Thurman Arnold* (Boulder: Colorado Associated University Press, 1977), 46.

CHAPTER 7

1. Cavert to Rev. C. Lawson Willard, June 14, 1946; Cavert to Edwin T. Dahlberg, April 9, 1946, PHS RG 18, box 15, folder 2; "Harmon to Hollywood," *Time*, November 2, 1936, 36; "Clergymen in Motion Pictures: A Statistical Analysis of Clerical Characterizations in 1939," n.d., attachment, Cavert to Francis S. Harmon, August 9, 1940, PHS RG 18, box 15, folder 1. Harmon received acclaim as the head of the film industry's War Activities Committee and afterward became vice president of Motion Picture Export Association. He remained an MPAA vice president until 1952, chaired the Budget Committee during the formation of the National Council of Churches in 1950, and served as vice president of the National Council of Churches (1958–1960). Statement in Connection with Visit to Latin America Being Made by Francis S. Harmon, January 4, 1961, KF-YMCA box 83, folder: Francis S. Harmon, Biographical Data.

2. Paul Maynard to Hartzell Spence, December 30, 1940; Spence to Jacob Wilk, n.d., attached with previous; Harry Warner to Wilk, January 8, 1941, WBA One Foot in Heaven, Production File, 2143, folder 1. Further details on the production can be found in PCA One Foot in Heaven File; WBA One Foot in Heaven, Production File, 2143, folders 1–5.

3. Warner to Wilk, January 8, 1941; Poling to Bishop Charles W. Flint, May 1, 1941, WBA One Foot in Heaven, Production File, 2143, folder 1; "One Foot in Heaven,"

Federal Council Bulletin, November 1941, 5, PHS RG 18, box 81, folder 8. "Minister Attacks WB Selection of Advisor for 'Foot in Heaven,'" *Daily Variety*, April 24, 1941, 4.

4. W. Harry Krieger to Warner Bros. Studios, October 31, 1941, WBA One Foot in Heaven, Production File, 2143, folder 1; Charles S. Miller, et al., Open Letter to the Editors of the Federal Council Bulletin, January 4, 1942, PHS RG 18, box 15, folder 1.

5. A. O. Dillenbeck, "New Movies to See," *Christian Herald*, August 1944, 47; Catherine Brown to Eric Johnston, January 25, 1947; Marjorie J. Slowen to Johnston, March 12, 1946, in PCA PCA-Religion. For a Catholic reply to charges that Hollywood played favorites, see William H. Mooring, "Hollywood in Focus," *The Tidings*, January 4, 1946, 10; "Legion of Decency in New Steps to Force 'Cleanup' of H'wood Pix," *Variety*, April 3, 1946, 1, 26.

6. Roswell P. Barnes to Rev. A. Melendez, July 25, 1946, PHS RG 18, box 15, folder 2. Eric Johnston to Don Chase, May 13, 1947, PCA PCA-Religion.

7. Joy to Cavert, May 27, 1946; Cavert to Harmon, October 15, 1947, PHS RG 18, box 15, folder 2.

8. Roscoe Gilmore Stott, "What's Right with Movies?," *Christian Herald*, October 1944, 74. In 1947, the Federal Council represented 25 denominations comprised of 142,354 local congregations with a total communicant membership of approximately 28,000,000 cooperating through the accredited agency. There were 600 local councils of churches across the country. John M. Alexander, "The Voice of Protestantism," *Presbyterian Outlook*, September 29, 1947, 4.

9. "A Statement and Request to Foundations by the Protestant Film Commission, Inc.," n.d., 1; Minutes, Protestant Film Commission, Incorporated, First Annual Meeting, January 30, 1946, PHS RG 18, box 17, folder 13. Together these agencies represented about 34 million Protestants. "Protestant Film Commission," n.d., PHS RG 16, box 3, folder 31; William F. Fore, "A Short History of Religious Broadcasting," Unpublished Paper, National Council of Churches, 1968, 2. Rome A. Betts (American Heart Association), was president; S. Franklin Mack, vice president; Mrs. Norman Vincent Peale, secretary; Fred G. Kraft, treasurer; Paul F. Heard, executive secretary. *The Protestant Film Commission: The Voice of Protestantism in Motion Pictures*, Pamphlet, Fall 1949, PHS RG 16, box 3, folder 31.

10. Fore, "A Short History of Religious Broadcasting," 2. On religious film production, see Terry Lindvall and Andrew Quicke, *Celluloid Sermons: The Emergence of the Christian Film Industry, 1930–1986* (New York: New York University Press, 2011).

11. Heard to Robert D. Jordan, August 23, 1946, PHS RG 18, box 15, folder 2; A Statement and Request to Foundations by the Protestant Film Commission, Inc., n.d.; Minutes, Protestant Film Commission, Incorporated, First Annual Meeting, January 30, 1946, PHS RG 18, box 17, folder 13; "Protestants Advise," *New York Times*, August 13, 1947, 3.

12. E. C. Farnham to Barnes, January 17, 1947; Heard to J. Quinter Miller, August 15, 1947, PHS RG 18, box 15, folder 2.

13. Daniel Poling, "A Militant Protestant Voice," *Christian Herald*, February 1945, 36. See Greg Linnell, "'Applauding the Good and Condemning the Bad': *The Christian Herald* and Varieties of Protestant Response to Hollywood in the 1950s," *Journal of Religion and Popular Culture* XII, no. Spring (2006), http://www.usask.ca/relst/jrpc/art12-goodandbad.html.

14. Bader quoted in "Better Than Censorship," *National Council Outlook*, May 1953, 6; Poling, "Other Current Films," *Christian Herald*, January 1950, 74. Golda Bader, "What the Protestant Motion Picture Council Does," *Christian Herald*, July 1956, 59; "Picture of the Month: Spellbound," *Christian Herald*, February 1946, 88–89.

15. Heard to J. Quinter Miller, August 15, 1947, PHS RG 18, box 15, folder 2; Johnston to Chase, May 13, 1947, PCA PCA-Religion.

16. Breen to Margaret McDonnell, January 24, 1945; Breen to Selznick, February 27, 1945, PCA Duel in the Sun File. See Ruth Waterbury, "The Case of 'Duel in the Sun'," *Photoplay* (1947): 38, 127–129.

17. "Duel in the Sun," *Variety*, January 1, 1947, 14; William Mooring, "Hog-Wash Served in Golden Canteen," *The Tidings*, Friday, January 3, 1947, 15–16; Harter to Selznick, January 6, 1947, PCA Duel in the Sun File. Harter copied Breen and Heard. Tippet quoted in E. C. Farnham (Church Federation of Los Angeles) to Barnes, January 17, 1947, PHS RG 18, box 15, folder 2; "Churchmen Object to 'Duel in Sun'," *Motion Picture Daily*, January 16, 1947, PCA Duel in the Sun File.

18. Farnham to Barnes, January 17, 1947, PHS RG 18, box 15, folder 2. Heard requested a special preview of the film in New York and used the occasion to introduce the services of the Protestant Film Commission, but I could find no record of Selznick's response. Heard to Selznick, January 20, 1947, PCA Duel in the Sun File.

19. Masterson to Breen, February 18, 1947; Breen to Masterson, February 21, 1947, PCA Duel in the Sun File. "'Duel' Disfavor with Catholics Brings H'wood Fear of Widening Censorship," *Variety*, January 22, 1947, 5.

20. "Protestants Warn Pix Not to Play 'Sugar Daddy' to Indecent Novelists," *Variety*, March 6, 1946, 1, 62; "Legion of Decency in New Steps to Force 'Cleanup' of H'wood Pix," 1, 26, "Censors Face MPAA Court Test," *Variety*, April 3, 1946, 9, 26.

21. "Protestants Plan Own 'Legion," *Hollywood Reporter*, January 31, 1947, 1, 4. "Protestant Leaders Due for Huddles," *Hollywood Reporter*, March 4 1947, 3. According to Geoffrey Shurlock, PCA staff interpreted the move as "a little bit of interloping on the part of the Protestants." James M. Wall, *Oral History with Geoffrey Shurlock* (Los Angeles: Louis B. Mayer Library, American Film Institute, 1970), 328, 110.

22. "Protestant Legion to Sift Pix," *Hollywood Reporter*, March 5, 1946, 1, 10; Barnes to Rev. A. Melendez, July 25, 1946, PHS RG 18, box 15, folder 2. "Legion's 'C' Rating

on 'Amber' Makes It Tough to Recoup That $6,000,000," *Variety*, October 29,
1947, 5, 18; Judith E. Doneson, *The Holocaust in American Film* (Philadelphia:
Jewish Publication Soceity, 1987), 62.

23. "Pix' Public Relations Problem," *Variety*, November 12, 1947, 3, 18; "Film Industry's Policy Defined," *Variety* November 26, 1947, 3, 18; "Film Industry Rules
'No Jobs' for Reds; Will Fire or Suspend the Cited 10," *Variety*, November 26,
1947, 3, 18.

24. "U.S. Court Decision Ends Block-Booking," *Christian Century*, August 28, 1946,
1028; "U.S. Verdict Shocks Film Biz," *Variety*, May 5, 1948, 1, 18. See "Test Suit
May K.O. Pix Censors," *Variety*, May 26, 1948, 5, 20; Michael Conant, "The
Paramount Decrees Reconsidered," *Law and Contemporary Problems* 44, no. 4
(1981): 79–107.

25. See "Are Movies the Opium of the People?," *Christian Century*, January 8, 1947,
36; Margaret Frakes, "You Can't Film That!," *Christian Century*, March 5, 1947,
305. In a book written under the auspices of the Commission on Freedom of the
Press, or the Hutchins Commission, Ruth Inglis recommended that movies be
granted constitutional protection under freedom of the press and offered qualified support for the industry's self-regulation. Ruth A. Inglis, *Freedom of the
Movies: A Report on Self-Regulation from the Commission on Freedom of the Press*
(Chicago: University of Chicago Press, 1947).

26. "Protestant Body Set Up Here to Assist on Pix," *Daily Variety*, February 6, 1948,
PCA NCC—BFC; Report of the West Coast Office of the Protestant Film Com-
mission, Protestant Film Commission, Inc., Meeting of the Administrative
Committee, New York, June 29, 1949, PHS RG 16, box 3, folder 31. Harter to
Breen, January 23, 1947; Breen to Harter, January 24, 1947, PCA Duel in the
Sun File. In 1948, the Protestant Film Commission represented 19 denominations
with some 200,000 churches and 34,000,000 members. "Protestant Organi-
zation Set Up for Studio Liaison," *Hollywood Reporter*, October 12, 1948, 3.

27. Protestant Film Commission, Inc., Meeting of the Sub-Committee on the
Hollywood Office and Outline of Set-Up of Hollywood Office, October 20,
1948; Annual Report of the Hollywood Office, September 1949–September
1950; Hollywood Office Annual Report, September 1949, PHS RG 16, box 3,
folder 31; Fore, "A Short History of Religious Broadcasting," 2. Some Facts
Regarding Liaison with the Motion Picture Industry, Attachment, BFC An-
nual Report, 1951 (reports 264 scripts submitted to WCO to date; a PFC
script evaluation form is attached to this report), PHS RG 16, box 1, folder 3.
Geoffrey Shurlock, "The Motion Picture Production Code," *Annals of the
American Academy of Political and Social Science* 254 (1947): 144. "Group
Outlines Films Program," *Los Angeles Times*, March 17, 1949, PCA
NCC—BFC.

28. Hollywood Office Annual Report, September 1950; Report of the West Coast
Office of the Protestant Film Commission, Meeting of the Administrative

Committee, June 29, 1949, PHS RG 16, box 3, folder 31; "Picture of the Month," *Christian Herald*, February 1950, 62; "The Picture of the Year," *Christian Herald*, March 1951, 91.

29. Shurlock quoted in Wall, *Oral History with Geoffrey Shurlock*, 316. On "The Gauntlet" production, see correspondence in PCA The Gauntlet File and PHS RG 18, box 15, folder 2.

30. Hopper quoted in Richard Merryman, *Mank: The Wit, World, and Life of Herman Mankiewicz* (New York: William Morrow and Company, 1978), 313. Quotations drawn from correspondence between Oren Evans, Breen, Shurlock, Chevigny, Mankiewicz, Mrs. Harjie Likins (Riverside Church), and Rolf K. McPherson between March and July 1950 in PCA Woman of the Rock File; Annual Report of the Hollywood Office, September 1950, PHS RG 16, box 3, folder 31.

31. Ray Stark to Breen, July 21, 1950; Breen to Sidney Schreiber, July 21, 1950; Breen to Harmon, July 25, 1950; Breen Memo, August 8, 1950, PCA Woman of the Rock File.

32. Barnes to Harmon, August 14, 1950, PHS RG 18, box 15, folder 2.

33. Shurlock to Robert A. Franklyn (Vanessa Productions), January 13, 1956; Franklyn to Shurlock, January 12, 1956, PCA Woman of the Rock File.

CHAPTER 8

1. William P. Clancy, "The Catholic as Philistine," *Commonweal*, March 16, 1951, 567; "'The Miracle' and Related Matters," *Commonweal*, March 2, 1951, 507–508. See Daniel Poling, "Something Worse Than 'The Miracle'," *Christian Herald*, April 1951, 16; "Ban 'Miracle' Film as 'Sacrilegious'," *Christian Century*, March 5, 1951, 309.

2. See Garth Jowett, "'A Significant Medium for the Communication of Ideas': The *Miracle* Decision and the Decline of Motion Picture Censorship, 1952–1968," in *Movie Censorship and American Culture*, ed. Francis G. Couvares (Washington, DC: Smithsonian Institution Press, 1996), 258–276.

3. "A Basis for Union Between the Protestant Radio Commission and the Protestant Film Commission, Feb–March 1950, n.d., PHS RG 16, box 1, folder 17. See "The Use of Audio-Visual Aids in the Work of the Broadcasting and Film Commission of the National Council of Churches of Christ in the U.S.A.," *Film News* (1955–1956): 6–7.

4. Paul Heard resigned in 1951 and became an independent producer of religious films; Ronald Bridges served as the BFC's executive director until February 1954. Three-year Report (1951–1954), Executive Director Ronald Bridges; BFC Annual Report, 1952; Annual Report, March 2–3, 1954, WCO, PHS RG 16, box 1, folder 4. Murray Schumach, *The Face on the Cutting Room Floor: The Story of Movie and Television Censorship* (New York: William Morrow, 1964), 98. On Shurlock's views, see his "The Motion Picture Production Code," *Annals of the*

American Academy of Political and Social Science 254 (1947): 140–146. Heimrich retained a law firm and demanded compensation, but was not successful when it was shown that the United Church Canvas had developed its program strategy and materials much earlier. See correspondence between November 1949 and September 1950 in Heimrich, George A., November. 1949–September. 1950, PHS RG 18, box 10, folder 25.

5. F. Thomas Trotter, Personal Interview, June 23 2004; Ken Wales, Personal Interview, June 13 2004.

6. Memo Trotti to Zanuck, July 28, 1952, TCF-USC A Man Called Peter, folder 1 of 4; Note attached to script (May 12, 1954) to Zanuck, July 27, 1954; Breen to McCarthy, August 12, 1954, TCF-USC A Man Called Peter, folder 3 of 4; Annual Report, WCO, March 6–7, 1956, PHS RG 16, box 1, folder 5; "A Man Called Peter," *Christian Herald*, March 1956, 90.

7. Evans to Reginald LeBorg, May 13, 1953, PCA Sins of Jezebel File; Oren Evans to Finlay McDermid, February 12, 1953, PCA Gown of Glory File; Moriarity to Heimrich, June 11, 1958, PCA The Remarkable Mr. Pennypacker; WCO Report, BFC Annual Report, March 2–3, 1954, PHS RG 16, box 1, folder 4.

8. Evans to Foreman, August 29, 1951, PCA High Noon File; Barbara Hall, *An Oral History with Albert E. Van Schmus* (Beverly Hills, CA: Margaret Herrick Library, Academy of Motion Picture Arts and Sciences, 1993), 198. On Catholic advising, see correspondence in PCA The Keys of the Kingdom File; AALA LOD #57, Material for AER Article and John J. Devlin Correspondence Files, box 59; "How the Catholic Church Supervises the Movies," *Christian Century*, February 7, 1945, 164–165.

9. Gregory quoted in Simon Callow, *The Night of the Hunter* (London: BFI Publishing, 2000), 25; Hall, *An Oral History with Albert E. Van Schmus*, 199.

10. Heimrich to Breen, September 16, 1954; Mack to Shurlock, December 21, 1954; Shurlock to Mack, December 21, 1954, PCA The Night of the Hunter File.

11. John McCarten, "Back in West Virginia," *New Yorker*, October 8, 1955, 159–160. For representative reviews see "The Night of the Hunter," *Time*, August 1, 1955, 58; "Mood by Laughton," *Newsweek*, August 29, 1955, 78; Robert Hatch, "Films," *The Nation*, October 15, 1955, 329.

12. Annual Report, March 1–2, 1955, PHS RG 16, box 1, folder 5; Annual Report, WCO, March 6–7, 1956; West Coast Committee Analysis of West Coast Office Functions, PHS RG 16, box 1, folder 5.

13. Annual Report, March 1–2, 1955, PHS RG 16, box 1, folder 5.

14. "New Picture," *Time*, December 24, 1956, 61; "Old Movie Taboos Eased in New Code for Film Industry," *New York Times*, December 12, 1956, 21, 51. Spellman quoted in "Cardinal Scores 'Baby Doll' Film," *New York Times*, December 17, 1956, 28; Pike quoted in "Joint Fight Urged on Immoral Films," *New York Times*, January 27, 1958, 18. Nathan A. Scott, "The Baby Doll Furor," *Christian Century*, January 23, 1957, 110–112. The PMPC labeled it Objectionable. "Baby Doll," *Christian Herald*, March 1957, 84.

15. Bosley Crowther, "Changing the Script," *New York Times*, December 16, 1956, 3.

16. "Films Fairness Attested to by Protestants," *Los Angeles Times*, March 23, 1957; Report of the WCO, BFC to the Executive Committee, May 27, 1958, PHS RG 16, box 2, folder 32; "Interview on Church of the Air," February 3, 1963, 7, GSC, box 162, File #1732, Greatest Story, George Heimrich; "Even Some Film Scripts by Protestant Ministers Can't Pass Prod'n Code," *Daily Variety*, March 13, 1957; also "Protestants Avoid Clash with Catholicism over Which Gets Biggest H'wood Buildup," *Daily Variety*, March 13, 1957, PCA, Moral and Religious Aspects (1941–1966).

17. "Interview on Church of the Air," 2–4; Annual Report to the Board of Managers, BFC, February 17–19, 1959, PHS RG 16, box 1, folder 6.

18. Shurlock to Kenneth Clark, July 21, 1959; Shurlock Memo, August 13, 1959; also Heimrich to Shurlock, May 21, 1959, PCA Elmer Gantry File; Mack to Smith, July 28, 1959; Mack to Lancaster, n.d., RBC Elmer Gantry—Protests (Protestant) #231.

19. Quoted material in Heimrich to Henry Blanke, July 17, October 1, August 20, 1959, PCA The Sins of Rachel Cade File.

20. "The Nun's Story—Filmed," *America*, May 23, 1959, 356. James M. Wall, *Oral History with Geoffrey Shurlock* (Los Angeles: Louis B. Mayer Library, American Film Institute, 1970), 312–313. See Philip T. Hartung, "The Screen: Nuns Fret Not," *Commonweal*, July 17, 1959, 374; Moira Walsh, "The Nun's Story," *Catholic World*, July 1959, 315.

21. "The National Council and the Entertainment Film Industry: Another Point of View on Protestantism and Hollywood Films," Order of the Day Discussion, Executive Committee Meeting, October 6, 1959, PHS RG 16, box 2, folder 32. This document was prepared for the BFC Executive Committee as a summary of events beginning with Heimrich's statement in Hollywood. "Film Morals Worry Protestants," *Daily Variety*, August 24, 1959, 1, 4; "Protestants Now in Anti-Code Mood; 'Some Kind of Action' Threatened," *Variety*, August 26, 1959, 5, 22. There were almost 67 million Protestants and about 42 million Catholics at the time; the National Council's constituency numbered 40 million. Benson Y. Landis, ed., *Yearbook of American Churches* (New York: National Council of Churches, 1961).

22. Heimrich quoted in Murray Schumach, "Film Aide Replies to Church Critic," *New York Times*, August 27, 1959, 24; Mack in "Protestants Disavow Pix Rap," *Hollywood Reporter*, September 8, 1959, 1, 8. See also Schumach, "Protestant Unit Criticizes Films," *New York Times*, August 25, 1959, 35. The West Coast Office reportedly reviewed 30 scripts in 1958–1959 and found 10 offensive. Bruce L. Williams, "Southern California," *Christian Century*, September 30, 1959, 1126–1167.

23. MPAA Press Release, n.d. [August 27, 1959], PHS RG 16, box 4, folder 22; "MPAA Turns Counter-Battery Fire on Protestant Council's Artillery," *Hollywood Reporter*, August 28, 1959, 4. Murray Schumach, "Hollywood Issue:

Industry Is Disturbed by Protestant Group's Criticism of Some Movies," *New York Times*, August 30, 1959, 7.

24. Johnston to Spike, September 2, 1959; Spike to Johnston, September 3, 1959, PCA Elmer Gantry File; Robert W. Spike, "Another Point of View on Protestantism and Hollywood Films," Executive Committee Meeting, October 6, 1959, PHS RG 16, box 2, folder 32; John Wicklein, "Churches Decry Attack on Films," *New York Times*, September 6, 1959, 57; "Fire & Fall Back," *Time*, September 7, 1959, 50. Some producers were quite contemptuous of Protestant criticism, if also rather limited in their understanding of Protestantism. See Phil M. Daly, "Along the Rialto," *The Film Daily*, June 7, 1960, 5, 8, PHS RG 16, box 2, folder 16.

25. "Protestants Disavow Pix Rap," 1; "Rifts among Protestant Groups K.O. New Pressures Against Hollywood," *Variety*, September 9, 1959, 1, 63; "Protestants Disclaim Raps," *Film Daily*, September 8, 1959, 1, 6; Schumach, "Hollywood Issue," 7.

26. Mack to Kennedy, September 21, 1959; Mack to Segerhammar, October 14, 1959, PHS RG 16, box 4, folder 22.

27. Jack Vizzard Memo, August 20, 1959; Shurlock to Jack L. Warner, September 18, 1959, PCA The Sins of Rachel Cade File.

28. Heimrich to Blanke, October 1, 1959; Jack A. Vizzard Memo, November 30, 1959, PCA The Sins of Rachel Cade File.

29. Executive Committee Minutes, October 6, 1959: Order of the Day, Protestants and the Film Industry, PHS RG 16, box 2, folder 32.

30. Methodist News Press Release, September 20, 1960; Leon Robertson to Robert Selig, September 30, 1960; Inter-Office Memo, Ken Clark to Clarke H. Wales, October 11, 1960. See also Wales to Clark, October 6, 1960; Wales to Selig, October 6, 1960; Mack to Clark, September 29, 1960; Mack to Murray Stedman, September 26, 1960, PCA Association of Motion Picture and Television Producers (AMPTP), H—Miscellaneous.

31. Proposal for a Study Commission on the Role of Radio, Television and Films in Religion, PHS RG 16, box 2, folder 31; Study Commission on the Role of Radio, Television and Films in Religion, Precis of Fourth Meeting, Union Theological Seminary, October 16–17, 1959, RG 16, box 4, folder 16. Study of the Role of Radio, Television and Films in Religion, Correspondence, March 1958–June 1960, PHS RG 16, box 4, folder 14.

32. Engel quoted in Thomas M. Pryor, "Hollywood Trials: Industry Reacts Favorably to Revised Code but Is Unsettled by Tax Plan," *New York Times*, December 16, 1956, 7; Report of the WCO, BFC to the Executive Committee, May 27, 1958, PHS RG 16, box 2, folder 32.

33. "Interview on Church of the Air," February 3, 1963; "Cleric Warns of Protestant Legion," *Hollywood Reporter*, September 16, 1949, 1, 15; "Film Censorship Urged," *New York Times*, September 17, 1949, 11; Friedrich to Mrs. Theodore Wedel, August 28, 1959, PHS RG 16, box 4, folder 22; Wales, Personal Interview.

34. Heimrich, Driver, and Mack are quoted in Study Commission on the Role of Radio, Television and Films in Religion, Precis of Fourth Meeting, Union Theological Seminary, October 16–17, 1959, PHS RG 16, box 4, folder 16. See also John Wicklein, "Sex and Crime on Screen Assailed in Church Report," *New York Times,* June 2, 1960, 1, 23. A sidebar, "Excerpts of Church Study of Mass Media," summarizes the key conclusions and recommendations (23).

35. Everett C. Parker, "Christian Perspective on Mass Communication," *Social Action* 24, no. 8 (1958): 8; Reinhold Niebuhr, *Introduction,* ed. Wilbur Schramm, *Responsibility in Mass Communication* (New York: Harper & Row, 1957), xii. Parker directed a BFC-sponsored Communications Research Project, started in 1951, that resulted in publication of Everett C. Parker, David W. Berry, and Dallas W. Smythe, *The Television-Radio Audience and Religion* (New York: Harper, 1955). See also Everett C. Parker, *Religious Television: What to Do and How* (New York: Harper, 1961), 205. Niebuhr was a member of the Commission on Freedom of the Press that resulted in the report by Ruth Inglis, *Freedom of the Movies.* Schramm investigates theories of the press in the study referred to here, which originated with the Federal Council in 1949. Wilbur Schramm, *Responsibility in Mass Communication* (New York: Harper & Brothers, 1957).

36. "Fire & Fall Back," 50; Bosley Crowther, "One Man's Opinion," *New York Times,* September 27, 1959, 1; "'Adult' Films: (a) Sex, (b) Crude," *Variety,* October 7, 1959, 1, 21. See William K. Zinsser, "The Bold and Risky World of 'Adult' Movies," *Life,* February 29, 1960, 79–86, 89; Jack Hamilton, "Hollywood Bypasses the Production Code," *Look,* September 29, 1959, 80, 83–84.

37. Vincent Canby, "Johnston Relents Re 'Classification'; Questioned by Cannes Press Mob on MPEA Slants on Festivals," *Variety,* May 17, 1961, 4, 17; "Johnston Joins Film Censor Talk," *New York Times,* October 6, 1959, 45. For industry views on classification see "Hollywood in 'Adult' Hot-Seat," *Variety,* September 16, 1959, 1, 18; "Kids, Sex, Films & Tomorrow," *Variety,* September 23, 1959, 3, 86. Schumach outlines the major arguments for and against classification at the time and identifies these organizations as in favor of age classification: the BFC, Episcopal Committee on Motion Pictures, Radio and Television, American Jewish Committee, General Federation of Women's Clubs, National Congress of Parents and Teachers, and American Library Association. Schumach, *The Face on the Cutting Room Floor,* 256–257.

CHAPTER 9

1. David Zeitlin, "A Lovely Audrey in Religious Role," *Life,* June 8, 1959, 141; Moira Walsh, "The Sins of Rachel Cade," *America,* April 8, 1961, 134.

2. John D. Morris, "Interfaith Drive on Films Urged," *New York Times,* November 25, 1959, 30.

3. Almost 82 million people—about 54 percent of the population—were listed on church rolls in 1950. Protestants made up about 59 percent of the total, Catholics about 33 percent, Jews about 6 percent. The number would peak at over 63 percent around 1960. Clarence W. Hall, "The State of the Church," *Christian Herald*, July 1950, 26; *Yearbook of American and Canadian Churches* (Nashville: Abingdon Press, 1961).

4. Thurston N. Davis, editor of *America*, quoted in "Joint Fight Urged on Immoral Films," *New York Times*, January 27, 1958, 18; *Variety*, *The New Yorker*, and *Time* are referenced in "'Martin Luther'—The Story of a Film," *Christian Century*, October 21, 1953, 1195–1198; "Picture of the Year: Martin Luther," *Christian Herald*, March 1954, 99.

5. "Luther Film Makes Belated Television Debut," *Christian Century*, March 13, 1957, 317. The petition is cited in "150,000 Protest Ban on 'Martin Luther' Film," *Presbyterian Outlook*, February 11, 1957, 4.

6. Salvatore Trozzo, "Education for the Movies," *The Catholic Mind*, September-October 1958, 395. "'Avoid Film Evaluation,'" *Christian Advocate*, April 26, 1962, 24. See Press Release, Episcopal Committee for Motion Pictures, Radio and Television, December 3–4, 1960, AANY S/C—37, folder 3 (Microfilm); NCWC, Bureau of Information, Rev. John E. Kelly, November 25, 1959, AALA LOD #56, LOD—1956–1959; Quigley to Spellman, July 30, 1956, QP box 1, folder 44.

7. Masterson to Ready, January 23, 1953, QP box 1, folder 14; Sullivan to Quigley, September 20, 1957, an essay on Censorship, QP box 1, folder 41; John Courtney Murray, "Literature and Censorship," *Books on Trial* 14 (1956): 393–395, 444–446. The Supreme Court joined two cases, *Roth v. United States* and *Alberts v. California*, and made the test for obscenity whether "to the average person, applying contemporary community standards, the dominant theme of the material taken as a whole appeals to the prurient interests."

8. "The Free Screen Censored: Statement of the Motion Picture Association of America Before a Committee of the United States Congress," February 2, 1960, 2–3, 6–8, PHS RG 16, box 3, folder 5.

9. J. D. Nicola, an editor of *Information*, a national Catholic monthly, quoted in "Beware 'Generalized Raps'," *Variety*, February 24, 1960, 7; Mack quoted in "Protestants View: Edicts Bad," *Variety*, February 17, 1960, 7, 16. See "Decency Legion in Bid to All Faith," *Variety*, November 25, 1959, 22.

10. Walter MacEwen to Steve Trilling, March 2, 1960, WBA Sins of Rachel Cade, box 1, folder 2204B (1/3); "Motion Picture Reviews," *Christian Herald*, July 1960, 16. The title change coincides with the *Herald*'s review. Bill L. Hendricks to J. L. Warner, July 11, 1960, WBA Sins of Rachel Cade, box 1, folder 1016A.

11. Study Commission on the Role of Radio, Television and Films in Religion, June 1, 1960, 2–4, PHS RG 16, box 1, folder 19; "The Church and the Mass Media of Communication," June 7–8, 1962, PHS RG 303.2, 16, 16; S. Franklin Mack, Executive

Director's Report: Progress, Problems and Promise, 1, PHS RG 16, box 1, folder 7; Executive Committee Minutes, May 7, 1962, 4, PHS RG 16, box 3, folder 1.

12. William F. Fore, Personal Interview, May 9, 2001.

13. "Protestants Term Sex & Gore 'Worse'," *Variety*, July 6, 1960, 1, 25; Clark to Mack, July 8, 1960, PHS RG 16, box 2, folder 16; Shurlock to Mack, June 17, 1960; Ross to Mack, June 21, 1960; Briefing Memorandum, Church-Industry Consultation, June 24, 1960, PHS RG 16, box 2, folder 16. I could find no record of Heimrich's attendance, and also of note, that of invited guest, Richard Brooks. Ross to Brooks, May 24, 1960, RBC, Elmer Gantry—Correspondence #216. See also "Protestants Give Views on Media Rue 'Weak' Code," *Variety*, June 8, 1960, 2, 13.

14. This summary is drawn from a book by Richard Dyer MacCann, *Hollywood in Transition* (Boston: Houghton Mifflin, 1962), which made the rounds in the BFC. Minutes, WCO Committee, January 3, 1963, PHS RG 16, box 4, folder 22. See Annual Report, BFC Board of Managers, February 7–9, 1961, PHS RG 16, box 1, folder 7; "The Bible Against Itself," *The Christian Century*, October 28, 1959, 1235.

15. Howard Whitman, "Sick Sex—A Public Plague," *Christian Herald*, July 1960, 12, 36; Shurlock to Mack, July 21, 1960, PHS RG 16, box 2, folder 16.

16. Quoted in "'Elmer Gantry' Carries Religious Sensitivity Disclaimer for Kids," *Variety*, June 8, 1960, 2.

17. "'Elmer Gantry' and U. S. Sinners," *Variety*, June 15, 1960, 7, 10; "Elmer Gantry Review," *Christian Herald*, September 1960, 26. "'Gantry' and the Catholics," *Variety*, June 29 1960, 4; "Protestants More Consulted Today but Catholic Influence Greater," *Variety*, July 6, 1960, 19; "'Gantry' Director Accepts Criticisms," *Variety*, June 23, 1960, 20.

18. "Elmer Gantry," *Variety*, June 29, 1960, 8; "Methodist Bishop as Critic," *Variety*, July 6, 1960, 19; F. Thomas Trotter, "The Return of Elmer Gantry," *Christian Advocate*, October 27, 1960, 8; Robert Hatch, "Elmer Gantry Review," *The Nation*, August 6, 1960, 78. See, for example, "Elmer Gantry," *America*, July 16, 1960, 463; "Elmer Gantry," *Time*, July 18, 1960, 76; A. H. Weiler, "Elmer Gantry," *New York Times*, July 8, 1960, 16; "The Moral—None at All," *Newsweek*, July 11, 1960, 90–91.

19. Murray Schumach, "The Censor as Movie Director," *New York Times Magazine*, February 12, 1961, 38; David Chute, "Wages of Sin: An Interview with David F. Friedman," *Film Comment* 22, no. 4 (1986): 32; William K. Zinsser, "The Bold and Risky World of 'Adult' Movies," *Life*, February 29, 1960, 84.

20. Press Release of the Episcopal Committee for Motion Pictures, Radio and Television, December 3–4, 1960, AANY S/C—37, folder 3 (Microfilm); Daniel Poling, "We Do Agree," *Christian Herald*, February 1961, 23; "Film Trend Stirs Catholic Attack," 31.

21. Heimrich to Earl Bright, May 5, 1958; Robert C. Moriarty to Heimrich, June 11, 1958, (also Frank McCarthy to Charles Brackett, June 18, 1958), PCA The Remarkable Mr. Pennypacker File; Report of the WCO, BFC to the Executive

Committee, May 27, 1958, PHS RG 16, box 2, folder 32; Annual Report, WCO, February 18–20, 1958, PHS RG 16, box 1, folder 6. Shurlock to Kramer, October 15, 1959; PCA Memo, November 18, 1959, PCA Inherit the Wind File.

22. Annual Report, BFC Board of Managers, February 7–9, 1961, PHS RG 16, box 1, folder 7; Annual Report, WCO, February 18–20, 1958, PHS RG 16, box 1, folder 6; BFC Executive Committee, Minutes, May 1958–May 1961, PHS RG 16, box 2, folder 32.

23. As it was, BFC operations on both coasts were under some financial strain, with staff unable to "maintain much more than a holding operation for its Protestant-Orthodox constituency at the present time." BFC Annual Report, February 18–20, 1958, PHS RG 16, box 1, folder 6.

24. Kennedy to Mack, September 23, 1959 (also Carl Segerhammar to Mack, October 5, 1959), PHS RG 16, box 4, folder 22; Annual Report, BFC Board of Managers, February 7–9, 1961, PHS RG 16, box 1, folder 7.

25. Annual Report, WCO, February 7–9, 1961, PHS RG 16, box 1, folder 7.

26. Thomas F. Driver, "Muzzling Hollywood," *Christianity and Crisis*, March 6, 1961, 23; William Fore, Personal Interview, May 9, 2001; Executive Committee, Correspondence, June 1953–December 1961, PHS RG 16, box 2, folder 28. The proposed categories were: Family, Children, Over 12, Adults and mature young people, Adults only over 18, and Totally Objectionable.

27. Council official quoted in John Wicklein, "Churchmen Wary on Rating Films," *New York Times*, February 10, 1961, 23; Driver, "Muzzling Hollywood," 23. On the press coverage, see John Wicklein, "Protestant Unit Seeks Film Shift," *New York Times*, February 8, 1961, 24; "Protestants Map Films Screening," *New York Times*, February 9, 1961, 37; "Eyeing Hollywood," *Christianity Today*, February 27, 1961, 34; "Protestants' Film Schism," *Variety*, February 15, 1961, 3, 19; "Heimrich's Script O.O. Project," *Variety*, February 15, 1961, 19.

28. Notes on the meeting between representatives of the NCC and representatives of the Motion Picture Association, March 22, 1961, PHS RG 16, box 2, folder 16.

29. Committee to Study the WCO, "Study and Recommendations Regarding the BFC's West Coast Office," February 6–8, 1962, WFF-PP; S. Franklin Mack, "Statement to WCO Committee," November 6, 1961; Minutes, Committee of the WCO, November 6, 1961, PHS RG 16, box 4, folder 22; Report of the WCO, Annual Report to the Board of Managers, BFC, February 6–7, 1964, PHS RG 16, box 1, folder 8.

30. WCO Minutes, October 8, 1962, FTT-PP WCO folder; West Coast Office Meeting, May 31, 1962, PHS RG 16, box 4, folder 22. Of note, Mrs. H. H. (Ruth) Kodani of the United Church Women appears to be the first woman to serve on the WCO Committee.

31. "Advisory Film-Classification, A Contemporary Obligation of Society: A Statement of the Roman Catholic Episcopal Committee for Motion Pictures, Radio and Television," December 7, 1962, PHS RG 16, box 1, folder 20. Kennedy quoted in Minutes, WCO Committee, January 3, 1963, PHS RG 16, box 4, folder 24.

32. "Crunch at the Council," *Time*, December 12, 1969, 70.

33. "Protestants' 1st Official Pix 'Sex & Violence' Slam Via Chi Lutheran NCC Member," *Daily Variety*, October 19, 1959, 1, 4; "Protestants View: Edicts Bad," 7, 16; Press Release, Hollywood Ministerial Association, September 15, 1959, PHS RG 16, box 4, folder 22; Vance Hayes, "Storm over Hollywood," *Worship and Arts*, October-November 1959, 1, 10. See "H'wood Protestant Toppers Back Up Heimrich Pix Slap," *Variety*, September 16, 1959, PCA, NCC—BFC; "Lutheran Group Whacks 'Morality Downtrend' of Hollywood Product, Fume over Sinclair Lewis' 'Gantry'," *Variety*, October 31, 1959, 13.

34. Minutes, WCO Committee, January 3, 1963, PHS RG 16, box 4, folder 24; "Protestants View: Edicts Bad," 7, 16.

CHAPTER 10

1. H. K. Rasbach chaired this committee for "selection of Protestant pictures to receive awards," with members Carroll Shuster, Clifton Moore, Fred Essex, and George Heimrich (ex officio). Report and Recommendations of the Awards Committee, October 8, 1962, FTT-PP WCO folder; Report of the Awards Committee, Revised, Adopted by the BFC Board of Managers, October 8, 1963, WFF-PP; Minutes, Awards Committee Meeting, April 15, 1964, FTT-PP BFC Film Nominations Panel.

2. William F. Fore, Personal Interview, May 9, 2001. Fore testified before government committees in support of the Public Broadcasting Bill (1967) and was involved in filing an *amicus* brief on the constitutionality of the Fairness Doctrine regarding *Red Lion Broadcasting Co. v. Federal Communications Commission* (1969).

3. Trotter to Fore, January 8, 1964, FTT-PP WCO folder; F. Thomas Trotter, Personal Interview, June 23 2004; Remarks by Dr. Robert E. Lee to the BFC Board of Managers, February 6, 1964, 5–6, FTT-PP WCO folder. Lee co-wrote the play, a fictionalized account of the 1925 Scopes Trial that was adapted for the screen by director Stanley Kramer, *Inherit the Wind* (1960).

4. Policy Statement of the Executive Director to the West Coast Committee, September 11, 1964, 6–7; also BFC Executive Director, Report to the BFC Board of Managers, September 23–24, 1965, WFF-PP.

5. Paul Tillich, *Theology of Culture*, ed. Robert C. Kimbal (New York: Oxford University Press, 1959), 7–8, 42.

6. William F. Fore, Address to BFC Board of Managers Luncheon, February 6, 1964, 9, WFF-PP. These four issues are taken directly from "William F. Fore, Keynote Address, "Our Tasks as Christian Communicators," BFC Council Cooperation Conference, June 29, 1966," 6–8, WFF-PP.

7. James M. Wall, Personal Interview, March 16, 2001; Thomas F. Trotter, "The Church Moves toward Film Discrimination," *Religion in Life* (1969): 265.

8. Mack to Espy, August 2, 1963, PHS RG 16, box 4, folder 23; Heimrich to Mack, September 30, 1963, PHS RG 303.2, 16, 16.

9. Stevens quoted in "Stevens Tells of 'Story' Production, *Hollywood Citizen-News*; also "'Great Artists' Casting Plan for 'Greatest Story,'" *Hollywood Reporter*, August 25, 1960; Jack Hirshberg, "$20 Million Film Gamble," *Los Angeles Times*, January 10, 1965,GSC The Greatest Story Ever Told, Clippings File. On the production research, see materials in GSC box 202, file 2499 and file 2448. An informative summary of production and marketing of the film is Sheldon Hall, "Selling Religion: How to Market a Biblical Epic," *Film History* 14, no. 2 (2002): 170–185.

10. Stevens's staff remark in Memo, Re: Telephone Call TVR to George Heimrich, January 30, 1962, GSC box 162, file 1732; Heimrich quoted in WCO Report, February 7–8, 1963, PHS RG 16, box 1, folder 7. On the WCO and DeMille, see correspondence in DMA box 993, folders 6 and 16; box 990, folder 16; box 994, folder 28.

11. Press Release, Episcopal Committee for Motion Pictures, Radio and Television, December 4, 1964, AALA Legion of Decency #56, Legion of Decency—1962–1970; "Churches to Give Prizes for Films," *New York Times*, December 5, 1964, 26. Anhalt quoted in Trotter, "The Church Moves Toward Film Discrimination," 269. On the first awards luncheon, see Minutes, WCO Meeting, May 17, 1965, FTT-PP WCO folder. Anhalt won an Oscar for *Panic in the Streets* (1950), directed by the acclaimed Elia Kazan, and would pick up another for *Becket*.

12. Malcolm Boyd, "Who Speaks for the Church?," *Christian Century*, April 21, 1965, 493–495; John W. Bachman, "Who Speaks?," *Christian Century*, June 23, 1965, 815; Gerald Kennedy, "Who Speaks?," *Christian Century*, June 23, 1965, 815.

13. "Calendar Christ," *Time*, February 26, 1965, 96; Moira Walsh, "The Night of the Hunter," *America*, October 8, 1955, 296; Fred Myers, "We Kid You Not!," *The Christian Century*, April 21, 1965, 492. Thomas Trotter, Personal Interview, June 23, 2004.

14. *The Greatest Story* did not appear on *Variety*'s top films of 1965 because United Artists refused to release rental figures, a sure sign "that its business was disappointing," according to the trade magazine. James M. Wall, "BFC Film Awards Signal Change," *Christian Advocate*, March 10, 1966, 16–17.

15. Leonard J. Leff, "Hollywood and the Holocaust: Remembering the Pawnbroker," *American Jewish History* 84, no. 4 (1996): 353–376.

16. Ely Landau to Shurlock, January 29, 1965; Shurlock to Alfred Markim, December 31, 1964; Shurlock to Landau, February 2, 1965, PCA Pawnbroker File.

17. James M. Wall, "Classification Is Essential," *Christian Advocate*, June 18, 1964, 2; Wall, "Dirty Joke," *Christian Century*, February 3, 1965, 144–145. Wall furnished the author with details of the Shurlock meeting. James M. Wall, Personal Interview, December 17, 1999; Wall, E-mail, March 16, 2001; Wall, Personal Interview, March 16, 2001.

18. James M. Wall, "Toward Christian Film Criteria," *Christian Century*, June 16, 1965, 777. Balaban to Hetzel, March 29, 1965, PCA Pawnbroker File.

"'Pawnbroker' Nude Scenes Stay, Even If Seal Refused: Landau," *Variety*, March 10, 1965, 4.

19. Pike statement in PCA Pawnbroker File. Bosley Crowther, "Screen: 'The Pawnbroker' Opens at 3 Theaters," *New York Times* April 21, 1965, 51; Richard Oulahan, "Hot Bargain in a Pawnshop," *Life*, April 2 1965, 16; "A Jew in Harlem," *Time*, April 23 1965, Andrew Sarris, "Films," *Village Voice*, July 15, 1965, 11; "Life in Pawn," *Newsweek*, April 26, 1965, 96–97.

20. Trotter, Personal Interview, June 23, 2004. Members of the Film Awards Nomination Panel (1966) were: Thomas Trotter (chair), Malcolm Boyd, Charles Brackbill, Jr., Leonidas Contos, Frederick L. Essex, Don Hall, Philip A. Johnson, Arthur Knight, Clifton E. Moore, H. K. Rasbach, Philip K. Scheuer (Motion Picture Editor, *Los Angeles Times*), and James Wall. Minutes, Film Nominations Panel Committee, October 14, 1965, FTT-PP BFC folder 1.

21. James M. Wall, "Christian Criteria for Film Criticism," Unpublished Paper, JMW-PP; Executive Committee Minutes, September 1961–May 1966, PHS RG 16, box 3, folder 1; James M. Wall, "1968 BFC Film Awards," *Christian Advocate*, April 17, 1969, 13.

22. *The Pawnbroker* received eight votes; Essex and Philip Johnson abstained, Cliff Moore and H. K. Rasbach voted against it. Boyd, Charles Brackbill, Knight, Don Hall, Wall, and Trotter voted against *Greatest Story*; Essex, Leonidas Contos, Moore, Rasbach, and Philip Scheuer for it, with Philip Johnson, who had not seen the film, abstaining. (Panel members were asked to abstain from voting on films they have not seen.) Film Nominations Panel Minutes of Conference Call, January 28, 1966; RE: 1965 Film Awards Committee Nominations, n.d.; Report of the Film Awards Nominations Panel to the Board of Managers of the BFC, February 3, 1966, FTT-PP BFC folder 2.

23. Fore to Shuster, March 11, 1966, PHS RG 16, box 3, folder 5; American Baptist New Service, February 3, 1966, GSC Personal Files, 1966, NCC; Fore "security check" quoted in RNS, "Baptist Executive Says Panel Knew of His Interest in "Greatest Story," February 17, 1966, PHS RG 16, box 3, folder 5. RNS, "Protesting Film Panel Member Had Interest in 'Greatest Story,'" February 4, 1966 PHS RG 16, box 3, folder 5. On Essex's promotional activity, see Forrest Weir to Mueller and Espy, April 6, 1966, PHS RG 16, box 3, folder 5. Trotter, Fore, and Wall provided accounts of these events. Trotter, E-mail, February 6, 2004; Trotter, E-mail February 12, 2004; Trotter, Personal Interview, June 23, 2004; Fore, Personal Interview, May 9, 2001; Fore, E-mail, February 10, 2004; Wall, Personal Interview, February 26, 2004. On the press coverage, see "Row Erupts over Omission of 'Greatest Story' from Protestant Awards," *Daily Variety*, February 4, 1966, 1, 30; "Protestants Skip UA's 'Greatest Story' in Bestowing Awards for 1965," *Variety*, February 9, 1966, 15.

24. Morry Roth, "Member of Nat'l Council of Churches' Awards Committee Reveals Why 'Greatest Story' Got the Brush-Off," *Daily Variety*, February 23, 1966, 4;

Segerhamar to Stevens, February 25, 1966, GSC Personal Files, 1966, National Council of Churches.

25. "Film's Failure to Win Council Prize Deplored," *Los Angeles Times*, March 26, 1966, 6. "Statement of the Concerned," March 10, 1966, PHS RG 16, box 3, folder 5. Carroll Shuster, Forrest Weir, Carl Segehammar, H. K. Rashbach, and Clifton Moore put out the statement. Clifton E. Moore, Radio Program, KFAC, March 27, 1966, GSC Personal Files, 1966, NCC (Ann Del Valle). On the Los Angeles Council of Churches award, see "Council of Churches Will Present Award to George Stevens," *Los Angeles Herald-Examiner*, Saturday, February 19, 1966, A9.

26. Gerald Kennedy, "What About the Code?," *Journal of the Screen Producers Guild*, March 1965, 6; Trotter to Carroll Shuster, March 15, 1966, FTT-PP BFC Awards 1965; Kennedy to Trotter, March 22, 1966, FTT-PP BFC folder 2. Kennedy, Shurlock, and Louis Greenspan, editor of *The Journal of the Screen Producers Guild*, occasionally had lunch together. James M. Wall, *Oral History with Geoffrey Shurlock* (Los Angeles: Louis B. Mayer Library, American Film Institute, 1970), 328–330.

27. Fore to Carroll L. Shuster, March 11, 1966, PHS RG 16, box 3, folder 5; John Wicklein, "Church Demands Proof in Charges," *New York Times*, May 2, 1961, 23; Jeffrey K. Hadden, "Clergy Involvement in Civil Rights," *Annals of the American Academy of Political and Social Science* 387 (1970): 118–127; Robert N. Bellah et al., eds., *Habits of the Heart: Individualism and Commitment in American Life* (Berkeley: University of California, 1985), 238.

28. Press Release, LOD, December 8, 1965, AALA LOD #56, LOD—1962–1970; "The Changing Legion of Decency," *Time*, December 3, 1965, 77–78. Fore E-mail, February 10, 2004.

29. Fore quoted in "Churches: Excitement on the Tube," *Time*, January 28, 1966, 70; BFC Executive Director, Report to the Board of Managers, September 22–23, 1966; also Annual Report to the Board of Managers, BFC, February 3–4, 1966, WFF-PP. "Attendance Decline in Young Adults," *Presbyterian Outlook*, February 27, 1967, 7; William F. Fore, "A Short History of Religious Broadcasting," Unpublished Paper, National Council of Churches, 1968, 8.

30. Fore Handwritten Notes, Meeting January 4–5, 1966; Fore Typewritten Notes, Meeting with Wall, January 10, 1966, WFF-PP; Fore to Wall, February 18, 1966, JMW-PP. For financial details related to the WCO, see correspondence between Fore, Heimrich, and Kennedy from May to September, 1966, PHS RG 16, box 4, folder 24; Fore to WCO Committee, September 29, 1966, FTT-PP BFC folder 1. On the WCO closing, see NCC Press Release, September 27, 1966, PHS RG 16, box 4, folder 24; "NCC Shutters Office Here," *Daily Variety*, September 26, 1966; "Council of Churches to Close Hollywood Office in January 1," *Hollywood Reporter*, September 30, 1966, PCA, NCC—BFC.

31. Heimrich quoted in Tape Transcription, WCO Committee Meeting, November 1, 1966; Minutes, WCO Committee Meeting, November 1, 1966, PHS RG 16,

box 4, folder 24; William F. Fore, Personal Interview, May 9, 2001; Arthur Knight, "Knight at the Movies," *The Hollywood Reporter*, April 3, 1972, 7; Fore E-mail, November 26, 2003. WCO Committee member Clifton Moore (Director of Radio and Television, United Presbyterian Church) transcribed the minutes from a tape recording, which Fore described as "quite accurate and rather pungent." William F. Fore, Report of the November 1966 Meeting of the WCO Committee, January 20, 1967, PHS RG 16, box 4, folder 24.

32. Archbishop John J. Krol, chair of the U.S. Episcopal Committee on Motion Pictures, quoted in Ronald Gold, "Catholics' 10-Year Switch from Film Censorship to Sympathy," *Variety*, February 9, 1966, 15. Fore Personal Interview, May 9, 2001; Wall, Personal Interview, March 16, 2001.

33. Quoted in Ronald Gold, "Clergy in Romance with Pix," *Variety*, March 13, 1968, 1.

CHAPTER 11

1. Jack Valenti, Letter, May 19, 2005; Valenti, Personal Interview, May 16, 2005; Peter Bart, "Valenti Presents Film-Talent Plan," *New York Times*, June 21, 1966, 36. Bosley Crowther, "A New Responsibility for Films," *New York Times*, August 28, 1966, 1, 14. Ralph Hetzel had served as interim president of the MPAA after Eric Johnston's death in August 1963.

2. William F. Fore, "The Church and Motion Pictures," *The Journal of the Screen Producers Guild*, December 1966, 12. BFC Executive Director, Report to the BFC Executive Committee, May 5, 1966; BFC Executive Director, Report to the Board of Managers, September 22–23, 1966, WFF-PP; Fore to Trotter, December 31, 1968, FTT-PP BFC folder 3.

3. Quoted in Vincent Canby, "A New Movie Code Ends Some Taboos," *New York Times*, September 21, 1966, 1, 42. The appeals board was reconstituted to include MPAA members, producers, and exhibitors. Vincent Canby, "New Production Code for Films Endorsed by Theater Owners," *New York Times*, October 1, 1966, 34. NATO was formed by the merger of the Theater Owners of America and the Allied States Association.

4. William Tusher, "Gov't Control Asked by Coast Churchman," *Variety*, September 26, 1966, 1, 4; Gerald Kennedy, "The New Code," *The Journal of the Screen Producers Guild*, December 1966, 4–5; Fore quoted in "NCC Official Qualifies Movie Code Approval," *Presbyterian Outlook*, October 17, 1966, 11. Vincent Canby, "Bishops Applaud Eased Film Code," *New York Times*, September 28, 1966, 40.

5. The two cases were *Ginsberg v. New York* and *Interstate Circuit v. Dallas*. The court established the principle of "variable obscenity" as a way to deny minors access to adult material. Richard F. Hixson, *Pornography and the Justices: The Supreme Court and the Intractable Obscenity Problem* (Carbondale: Southern Illinois University Press, 1996), 75–78.

6. Barbara Stones, "Julian Rifkin: Oral History Interview," (Duxbury, MA, 1991), 18; Executive Committee Minutes, May 8, 1968, PHS RG 16, box 3, folder 2; Vincent Canby, "Plan to Classify Movies Debated," *New York Times*, June 12, 1966, 36; "Senate Mulls Classifying Pix," *Daily Variety*, May 28, 1968, 1; "Harry Lando, "Film-Rating Row in the Senate," *Film and Television Daily*, June 12, 1968, 1, 3.

7. "It's More Revolution Than Noted: 'Classification' Only Recently MPAA's Idea of a Hideous Trade Solution," *Variety*, July 3, 1968, 5, 20; Connie Bruck, "The Personal Touch," *New Yorker*, August 13, 2001, 42–48, 50–54, 56–59.

8. Wall to Ralph D. Churchill, April 30, 1968; Churchill to Wall, May 3 and 4, 1968; Wall to Churchill, May 7, 1968, JMW-PP.

9. Wall quoted in "NATO Exec Comm. Votes for Exhib Pix Ratings Via Code," *Film and Television Daily*, July 19, 1968, 1, 7; "NATO Executives Okay National Rating System," *Boxoffice*, July 22, 1968, 9; "Plan Exhibitor—Church Dialogue," *Motion Picture Daily*, July 19, 1968, 1–2. On these events see correspondence between Wall, Rifkin, and London from June to August 1968, JMW-PP.

10. Rifkin quoted in Stones, "Julian Rifkin: Oral History Interview," 19; Clarke H. Wales to Wall, March 9, 1970, JMW-PP; Valenti, Personal Interview, May 16, 2005. Fore, E-mail, November 25 2003; Fore, Personal Interview, May 9, 2001. Valenti also consulted with leaders of Jewish organizations, although "they were not as structured" as the Protestant and Catholic ones. National Council constituents numbered 38.6 million in 1968; the Catholic figure was 47.4 million. Lauris B. Whitman, ed., *Yearbook of American Churches*, vol. 37 (New York: Council Press, 1969).

11. "Church Backs Rating System," *Hollywood Reporter*, October 2, 1968, 1, 7; Wall, Personal Interview, March 16, 2001. BFC Board of Managers Minutes, September 26, 1968, 6, PHS RG 16, box 1, folder 27.

12. BFC-NCOMP Press Release, October 9, 1968, JMW-PP; Fore, Personal Interview, May 9, 2001. MPAA Press Release, October 7, 1968, JMW-PP; "Churches Hail New MPAA Code," *Daily Variety*, October 9, 1968, 27; Vincent Canby, "Catholic and Protestant Groups Back Movie Classification Plan," *New York Times*, October 9, 1968, 43.

13. Rifkin quoted in Thomas M. Pryor, "Youth with 'Em, Exhibs Grin," *Variety*, November 13, 1968, 1, 23.

14. James M. Wall, "Film Protection for All," *Christian Advocate*, August 8, 1968, 2; London to Wall, August 5, 1968, JMW-PP. "Which Films Are OK for Our Children?," *Together*, February 1969, 44–47. See Wall to Twyman, May 15, 1969; also correspondence between Wall, London, Rifkin, and Twyman from August 1968 to January 1971; "Churchman Urges Theater Owner-Clergy Truce," *Detroit Free Press*, April 5, 1969; *NATO Flash News Bulletin*, December 29, 1971, JMW-PP.

15. James M. Wall, "Toward Christian Film Criteria," *Christian Century*, June 16, 1965, 778; Wall to Valenti, April 18, 1969, JMW-PP; Wall, "Movie Ratings: A Hedge Against Repression," *The Christian Science Monitor*, August 14, 1971, 16.

16. Rifkin to Wall, August 25, 1969, JMW-PP.

17. Rick Setlowe, "Is MPAA Code Working? Views Vary Vastly Outside Industry," *Daily Variety*, December 3, 1969, 12; James M. Wall, "A Film Critic Looks at the Rating System," *The Journal of the Screen Producers Guild* (1969): 15; Wall to Valenti, April 18, 1969; Valenti to Wall, May 2, 1969; Wall to McCutcheon, September 30, 1968; Wall to Rifkin, November 1, 1968, JMW-PP. "Movies—G, M, R, X," *Newsweek*, October 21, 1968, 98–99.

18. Edward Lipton, "Ratings: Seeing the Flaws," *Film and Television Daily*, December 2, 1969, 1, 5; "Women's Fed Prez Blasts Code," *Daily Variety*, January 13, 1969, 1, 18; "ACLU Attacks MPAA Ratings," *Daily Variety*, April 11, 1969, 1, 6; "AFL Film Council Raps Code," *Daily Variety*, July 14 1969, 1; MPAA Memo, January 20, 1970, JMW-PP. The M rating was changed twice, first to GP (Parental Guidance Suggested), which was not much of an improvement, and then to PG (Parental Guidance Suggested, film contains material that may not be suitable for pre-teenagers).

19. Report by National Church Film Offices on the Code and Rating Program of the Motion Picture Association of America, May 14, 1970, PHS RG 16, box 3, folder 2; James M. Wall, "A Film Critic Looks at the Rating System," 15.

20. Ben Kaufman, "Church Groups Blast Code," *Hollywood Reporter*, May 20, 1970, 1, 11; Charles Champlin, "Churches Challenge Film-Rating System," *Los Angeles Times*, May 23, 1970, 8; Philip C. Rule, "Film Ratings: 1934 Revisited," *America*, May 29, 1971, 571–572. "Cleric to Enlist Religious Groups In Fight on Screen 'Contamination,'" *Motion Picture Daily*, JMW-PP. See "Churches Say Code Ratings Are in 'Danger',", *Variety*, May 20, 1970, 1, 8; Howard Thompson, "Film Rating System Attacked by Two Major Church Groups," *New York Times*, May 30, 1970, 12; Jack Valenti, "The Public Votes 'Yes' for the Rating System," Speech delivered at the NATO Convention, November 3, 1970; Highlights of Opinion Research Corporation 1970 Survey on Code and Rating System, MPAA Press Release, November 4, 1970, JMW-PP.

21. Wall to Valenti, April 18, 1969; Wall to Twyman, December 10, 1970; Twyman to Wall, December 8, 1970; Wall to Twyman, December 28, 1970, JMW-PP. James M. Wall, "Those Fragile Ratings," *Christian Advocate*, January 7, 1971, 18. See Thomas Thompson, "Film Ratings Flunk Out," *Life*, August 20, 1971, 50B, 54–57; A. H. Weiler, "2 Church Groups Disavow 'Unreliable' Film Rating," *New York Times*, May 19, 1971, 1; Ronald Gold, "Attack & Defend 'Appeals'," *Variety*, May 26, 1971, 5, 18.

22. Fore, Personal Interview, May 9, 2001. Wall to Rifkin, November 18, 1971; Wall to Twyman, June 8, 1971, JMW-PP; Fore, E-mail, November 4, 2007.

23. BFC/NCOMP Joint Press Release, May 18, 1971, WFF-PP; "Jack Valenti's Blanket Repudiation," *Variety*, May 19, 1971, 78; "Churches Give Film Code an 'X'," *Variety*, May 19, 1971, 1, 78; MPAA, "The Film Rating Program," Unpublished Paper, June 1971, 2, PCA, Files—General, Ratings; "Valenti Charges Clergy

Seeks Film Censorship," *New York Times*, May 20, 1971, 83. See "Valenti Hits Church Agencies' Decision to Withdraw Endorsement of Film Ratings," RNS, May 18, 1971, JMW-PP; "Low-Rating the Ratings," *Newsweek*, May 31, 1971, 50.

24. MPAA, "The Film Rating Program," Attachment No. 2, "Legislative Summary 1971"; Wall to Sullivan, July 30, 1971, JMW-PP; Fore, Personal Interview, May 9, 2001.

25. "Rating the Rating System," *Time*, May 31, 1971, 72; Thompson, "Film Ratings Flunk Out," 50B. MGM's James Aubrey and CARA intern Stephen Farber are quoted in the *Time* article.

26. Thompson, "Film Ratings Flunk Out," 54, 57; "Psychiatrist to Head MPAA Code, Ratings," *Daily Variety*, June 24, 1971, 9; Minutes, Tri-Faith Film Meeting, April 25, 1972, JMW-PP; "Set MPAA Code Revision Goals: (1) Sharpen Public Comprehension, (2) Guide Producers, (3) Alter Appeals," *Variety*, July 7, 1971, 3. See Wall to Stern, August 26, 1971, JMW-PP; James M. Wall, "Man in the Middle of the Ratings Game," *Together*, October 1972, 54–57; Wall, "MPAA Ratings," *Film Information* 3, no. 5 (1972): 4; Ronald Gold, "Quiet Changes in Movie Code," *Variety*, December 15, 1971, 1, 60.

27. A. D. Murphy, "As Code Ratings Begin Third Year, Some Interesting Comparison Emerge," *Variety*, November 20 1970, 1, 26. See Highlights of Opinion Research Corporation 1970 Survey on Code and Rating System, JMW-PP. The estimates on ratings and earnings come from Thompson, "Film Ratings Flunk Out," 54. In the second year, films rated G and GP dropped from 71 to 55 percent, the number of R-rated films increased from 23 to 37 percent, making the GP and R categories almost equal in numbers. On newspapers, see Bob Thomas, "Film Rating System Celebrates Third Birthday—Is It Working?" *Los Angeles Herald Examiner*, December 24, 1971, PCA, Files—General, Ratings.

28. Ben Shlyen, "A Problem Seeking Solution," *Boxoffice*, October 11, 1971, PCA, Files—General, Ratings. See correspondence between Wall, Twyman, Rifkin, and Valenti, June–November 1971, JMW-PP. Twyman told Wall his plan to revise the GP and X ratings was consistent "with the general direction things here seem to be taking," and assured him that although the MPAA may not do exactly what he recommended, "our goals are identical" (Twyman to Wall, July 27, 1971). The idea to add "good citizens" to the Appeals Board also had solid support among the MPAA staff. For Wall's editorial on the matter see "Films," *Christian Advocate*, June 24, 1971, 17–18. On the panel see "Religious Reps, NATO to Discuss Rating System," *Daily Variety*, September 29, 1971, 1, 8; Gene Arneel, "United Front vs. Pic Censorship," *Daily Variety*, October 28, 1971, PCA, Files—General, Ratings.

29. Valenti quoted in Ronald Gold, "Rating System Toughens under Religious Pressure," *Daily Variety*, December 15 1971, 1, 8; Jack Valenti, *Address at the North American Branch of the World Association of Christians in Communications (NABSWAAC)* (1995), Videocassette; Fore, Personal Interview May 9, 2001.

The author received additional information on these events from Wall and Fore. Wall, E-mails, April 16, 2004, and November 4, 2007; Fore, E-mail, November 4, 2007. Fore and Sullivan initially represented the BFC and NCOMP; Wall and Henry Herx later replaced them. At this writing, Wall, a self-described "humble, movie-loving, politically-obsessed blogger from Illinois," continues to attend appeals hearings in Los Angeles. James M. Wall, "Finding Shared Communities in the Academy's Final Ten Films," Wallwritings (Chicago 2010).

30. Annual Report to the Board of Managers of the Broadcasting and Film Commission, February 3–4, 1966, PHS RG 16, box 1, folder 8; BFC Press Release, February 13, 1973, WFF-PP.

31. George Dugan, "Baptists Say Films Are Lacking in Social Value," *New York Times*, June 8, 1972, 50. Nixon quoted in "Pornography Goes Public," *Newsweek*, December 21, 1970, 26. In response to a Southern Baptist protest, CBS reportedly pledged not to broadcast R- or X-rated movies without cutting objectionable material. "Religion in Transit," *Christianity Today*, November 10, 1972, 64.

CHAPTER 12

1. Ralph Blumenthal, "Porno Chic: 'Hard-Core' Grows Fashionable—and Very Profitable," *New York Times Magazine*, January 21, 1973, 28, 30, 32–34; Robert L. Cleath, "Pornography: Purulent Infection," *Christianity Today*, October 10, 1975, 21–22.

2. "Excerpts from Pornography Opinions," *New York Times*, June 22, 1973, 42. See "Pornography Goes Public," *Newsweek*, December 21, 1970, 26–32; Paul Bender, "The Obscenity Muddle," *Harper's*, February 1973, 46, 50–52; James M. Wall, "Pornography and Court Presuppositions," *Christian Century*, July 18, 1973, 747–748.

3. Jack Valenti, "To Rate a Film Is Not to Censor It," *New York Times*, December 9, 1973, 15, 25. For responses to the *Miller* ruling, including one from Valenti, see "Has the Supreme Court Saved Us from Obscenity?," *New York Times*, August 5, 1973, 1, 11, 16; "The Outer Limits of Free Speech," *Christian Century*, May 2, 1973, 500.

4. Rifkin quoted in James M. Wall, "MPAA Ratings," *Film Information* 5, no. 3 (1974): 4; BFC Annual Report, 1973, PHS RG 16, box 1, folder 10. See BFC Board of Managers Minutes, February 8–9, 1974, PHS RG 16, box 1, folder 27.

5. BFC Press Release, February 12, 1974, WFF-PP; James M. Wall, "A Cinema-Church Political Standoff," *Christian Century*, February 20, 1974, 198–199; Wall to Paul Roth, NATO, February 11, 1974, JMW-PP. See Wall, "Church Clout at the Box Office," *Christian Century*, January 16, 1974, 35–36. Stern's eventual replacement, Richard Heffner, came to favor a "blue ribbon" appeals board as "another layer of honest rating judgments." Philip C. Rule, "Film Ratings: 1934 Revisited," *America*, May 29, 1971, 571–572.

6. "Protestants Needed by MPAA," *Variety*, March 6, 1974, 3; BFC Press Release, February 12, 1974, WFF-PP. See also "Protestant Churches Re-Eye Anti-Pic Rating Code Stance," *Daily Variety*, March 7, 1974, 1, 16, PCA, NCC—BFC.

7. NCC, BFC Press Release, February 28, 1974, WFF-PP; James M. Wall, "Pornography and Court Presuppositions," *Christian Century*, July 18, 1973, 747.

8. "Protestants Partly Mollified Re MPAA, but Irked by Exhibitors," *Variety*, September 17, 1975, 4. See "MPAA, Religious, Industry Figures Discuss Possible Pic-Rating Changes," *Daily Variety*, May 12, 1976, 1; "Protestants New Slant on R Rating," *Variety*, April 13, 1977, 30; MPAA Press Release, "A New Rating, PG-13, Inserted Between the PG and the R, Is Added to the Motion Picture Industry's Voluntary Rating System," June 28, 1984. Fore and Wall continued to press for brief descriptions, "information tag lines," to be appended to the ratings. Fore to Valenti, July 14, 1978; Rifkin to Fore, July 21, 1978; Fore to Sullivan, September 28, 1978; Wall to Valenti, July 30, 1982, WFF-PP.

9. James M. Wall, "Fighting the Media's Eroticizing of Violence," *Christian Century*, October 3, 1984, 892; Communication Commission, "Violence and Sexual Violence in Film, Television, Cable and Home Video," (New York: National Council of Churches, 1985), 12; Richard Corliss, "Backing into the Future," *Time*, February 3, 1986, 65; Corliss, "Turned On? Turn It Off," *Time*, July 6, 1987, 72; Jefferson Graham, "A Hot Market for X-Rated Videos," *USA Today*, June 22, 1987, 1D; Richard Corliss, "Binge and Purge at the B.O.," *Time*, January 20, 1992, 59; Peter M. Nichols, "Home Video," *New York Times*, July 30, 1993, B8; Andy Marx, "Technology Is Sexy Biz," *Variety*, September 12–18, 1994, 33.

10. Communication Commission, "Violence and Sexual Violence in Film, Television, Cable and Home Video," 12; David A. Cook, *Lost Illusions: American Cinema in the Shadow of Watergate and Vietnam 1970–1980*, ed. Charles Harpole, vol. 9, *History of the American Cinema* (Berkeley: University of California Press, 2000), 209; Jon Lewis, *American Film: A History* (New York: W. W. Norton, 2008), 355–356.

11. Wall, "Fighting the Media's Eroticizing of Violence," *Christian Century*, October 3, 1984, 891–892.

12. See William F. Fore, "Where Do You Draw the Line?," *Media & Values*, no. 33 (1985): 6–8, 10–11; Report of the Assistant General Secretary to the Board of Managers, Communication Commission, September 17, 1981, WFF-PP; Fore, "Truth, Lies and the Media," *Christian Century*, November 29, 2003, 10–11. For Wall's summary of the commission's report and a Protestant critical response see Wall, "Out-of-Control Media Hear Harsh Criticism," *Christian Century*, October 9, 1985, 883–884; Gerald E. Forshey and Jeffery Mahan, "Critique of Media Lacks Imagination," *Christian Century*, January 1–8, 1986, 20–21.

13. "Panel Urges TV Controls," 22; "TV Protest," *Time*, September 30, 1985, 72. In July 1986, Attorney General Edwin Meese's Commission on Pornography reversed the conclusion of the 1970 Commission's findings. Although

committee members could not reach a consensus on whether depictions of nonviolent sexual activities were harmful, a majority report maintained that sexually violent pornography was nonetheless harmful. See Stephen Prince, *A New Pot of Gold: Hollywood under the Electronic Rainbow, 1980–1989* (New York: Charles Scribner's Sons, 2000), 359–360.

14. "Religion: Counting Souls," *Time*, October 4, 1976, 75; A. James Reichley, *Religion in American Public Life* (Washington, DC: Brookings Institutions, 1985), 278–279; Report of the Assistant General Secretary to the Communication Commission, September 21, 1984, WFF-PP. The NCC represented 31 Protestant and Orthodox denominations in North America in 1974 and nearly 41 million people. BFC Brochure, March 1974, WFF-PP; *Yearbook of American and Canadian Churches* (Nashville: Abingdon, 1974). On the "new evangelicalism," see "Fundamentalists, Evangelicals, and New Evangelicals," in George M. Marsden, *Reforming Fundamentalism: Fuller Seminary and the New Evangelicalism* (Grand Rapids: Eerdmans, 1987), 1–11. Evangelicalism is not a monolithic movement, but a broad coalition that includes denominations like the Southern Baptist Convention, nondenominational churches, Pentecostal, Lutheran, Reformed, and other groups, and parachurch organizations. Depending on how they are identified, evangelicals are just over 26 percent of the overall adult population and roughly one-half of all Protestants. "The Religious Composition of the United States," The Pew Forum on Religion & Public Life, http://religions. pewforum.org/pdf/report-religious-landscape-study-chapter-1.pdf.

15. Les Brown, "TV: 4 Church Units Plan to Fight 'Soap'," *New York Times*, August 31, 1977, 63; Mark Fackler, "Religious Watchdog Groups and Prime-Time Programming," in *Channels of Belief: Religion and American Commercial Television*, ed. John P. Ferré (Ames, Iowa: Iowa State University Press, 1990), 99–116; William F. Fore, "A Manual for the People: Deprogramming Television," *Christianity and Crisis*, May 2, 1977, 93–96; Report of the Assistant General Secretary to the Board of Managers, Communication Commission, September 22, 1977, WFF-PP.

16. Fackler, "Religious Watchdog Groups and Prime-Time Programming." In defense of the American family and "traditional" values, Wildmon organized boycotts of 7-Eleven convenience stores for selling *Playboy* and *Penthouse*, Holiday Inns for showing pornographic movies, and protested the National Endowment for the Arts for funding immoral art. His organization in need of a facelift, Wildmon renamed it the American Family Association around 1987.

17. James M. Wall, "Attack on Pornography Misses the Mark," *Christian Century*, September 30, 1987, 811–812.

18. James M. Wall, "Like Crying Fire?: Erotic Violence Stretches Right to Free Speech," *Media & Values* 33 (1985): 14.

19. "Arresting the Restless Ones," *Christianity Today*, April 1, 1966, 46; D. Bruce Lockerbie, "The Theater of Deceit," *Christianity Today*, July 3, 1970, 6. A 1984

survey revealed that only 7 percent of respondents watched "Christian" films exclusively; just over half went to secular movies. "How Much Do Christian Like Movies?," *Christianity Today*, September 21, 1984, 23. Sex was the biggest turn-off, followed by profanity and violence. The majority of *CT* readers preferred films based on history, book classics, and those featuring religious conversions.

20. Tom Minnery, "*Chariots of Fire* Hits the Heights," *Christianity Today*, March 19, 1982, 34–35; Lloyd and Kent Hughes Billingsley, "*Chariots of Fire*: 'Muscular Christianity' in Conflict," *Christianity Today*, January 22, 1982, 41.

21. Scorsese quoted in Steve Rabey, "Producer Tries to Dim Fears over Movie," *Christianity Today*, March 4, 1988, 43; Script quotation in Charles Lyons, *The New Censors: Movies and the Culture Wars* (Philadelphia: Temple University Press, 1997), 161; Penland quoted in "Publicist Quits Film Project," *Christianity Today*, July 15, 1988, 51–52; MPAA statement cited in Aljean Harmetz, "Top Studios Support 'Christ' Film," *New York Times*, July 25, 1988, C18. See Harmetz, "New Scorsese Film Shown to Religious Leaders," *New York Times*, July 15, 1988, C30; Patrick Goldstein, "Controversial Films: The Temptation to Apply Media Heat," *Los Angeles Times Calendar*, August 7, 1988, 26, 28, PCA, Moral and Religious Aspects (1985–1992).

22. Wildmon quoted in Charles Lyons, "The Paradox of Protest: American Film, 1980–1992," in *Movie Censorship and American Culture*, ed. Francis G. Couvares (Washington, DC: Smithsonian Institution Press, 1996), 307. Falwell quoted in Aljean Harmetz, "Film on Christ Brings out Pickets and Archbishop Predicts Censure," *New York Times*, July 21, 1988, C19. See David Ansen, "Wrestling with 'Temptation'," *Newsweek*, August 15, 1988, 56; John Leo, "A Holy Furor," *Time*, August 15, 1988, 34–36.

23. Billy A. Melvin quoted in "*E. T.* Boycotted," *Christian Century*, November 2, 1988, 977. Some evangelicals working in film and television thought the strong arm tactics these religious leaders relied on were not successful and only fueled antagonism between conservative Christians and entertainment executives and producers. See Ken Sidey, "Last Temptation Boycott Gets Mixed Reviews," *Christianity Today*, April 21, 1989, 36–37; "Why Hollywood Doesn't Like You," *Christianity Today*, August 10, 1998, 64.

24. David Neff, "Scorsese's Christ," *Christianity Today*, October 7, 1988, 12–14; Brian Bird, "Film Protesters Vow Long War on Universal," *Christianity Today*, September 16, 1988, 41–42.

25. Falwell quoted in Bird, "Film Protesters Vow Long War on Universal," 41–42. Falwell was joined by James Dobson's Focus on the Family, Donald Wildmon's American Family Association, and Bill Bright's Campus Crusade for Christ. Patrick Buchanan, "Hollywood Gleefully Assaults Christianity in 'Last Temptation of Christ,'" *Los Angeles Herald-Examiner*, July 27, 1988, PCA, Moral and Religious Aspects (1985–1992).

26. James M. Wall, *"The Last Temptation*: A Lifeless Jesus," *Christian Century,* August 17–24, 1988, 723. Fore quoted in Harmetz, "New Scorsese Film Shown to Religious Leaders," C30 and RNS, "NCC's BFC Discontinues Annual "Best Films" Awards," *Tempo Newsletter: An Ecumenical Publication of the National Council of Churches,* February 1974.

27. John E. Fitzgerald, "Joint Film Awards," *The Catholic News,* April 1, 1971, JMW-PP; Arthur Knight, "Knight at the Movies," *The Hollywood Reporter,* April 3 1972, 7; "Three Faith Groups Give Awards to Three Films," *Boxoffice,* April 10, 1972, PCA, NCC—BFC; Ronald Gold, "Clergy in Romance with Pix," *Variety,* March 13, 1968, 21. On *Film Information,* see BFC Film Review Service: Report of the Sub-Committee, June 6, 1968, FTT-PP BFC folder 3; "Nat'l Council of Churches Film Bulletin to Fill Void Left by Green Sheet Demise," *Daily Variety,* December 18, 1969, 1, 32; Annual Report, 1973, BFC, PHS RG 16, box 1, folder 10; NCC Government and Industry, Film Committee Report, September 20, 1979, JMW-PP. The Catholic counterpart was *Catholic Film Newsletter.* On the Catholic office closing, see "Film Office Closed," *Christian Century,* October 15, 1980, 960; Richard N. Ostling, "A Scrupulous Monitor Closes Shop," *Newsweek,* October 6, 1980, 70–71.

28. Remarks of William F. Fore, Communication Commission, NCC, Annual Meeting, February 23, 1989, WFF-PP.

CHAPTER 13

1. James M. Wall, "NC-17 Rating Removes Restraints on Filmmakers," *Christian Century,* October 10 1990, 891; Wall, "Discriminating Movies for Discriminating Adults," *Christian Century,* July 11–18, 1990, 659.

2. Fore and Valenti quoted in "Readers' Response: Mixed Reviews for NC-17," *Christian Century,* January 2–9 1991, 24–27; James M. Wall, "Movies and Censorship: Who Will Protect Freedom?," *Christian Century,* March 18–25, 1987, 277. The National Council and National Conference of Catholic Bishops both denounced the new NC-17 rating.

3. David J. Fox, "Religious Leaders Decry Movies, TV," *Los Angeles Times,* February 28, 1991, F3, PCA, Moral and Religious Aspects (1985–1992). See Anti-Christian Bigotry?," *Christianity Today,* April 29, 1991, 40; Doug LeBlanc, "MPAA: Alphabet Soup," *Christianity Today,* November 5, 1990, 71–72.

4. Ted Baehr, *Hollywood's Reel of Fortune* (Ft. Lauderdale, FL: Coral Ridge Ministries, n.d.), 55, 61; Baehr, "Called to Be Salt and Light," *Religious Broadcasting,* February 1993, 64, 66. Baehr routinely gave this historical account, which he apparently drew in part from an unpublished manuscript by George Heimrich, who bequeathed the West Coast Office files to him. See Baehr, *The Media-Wise Family* (Colorado Springs: Chariot Victor Publishing, 1998), 228–244; "New Film Code Sought," *Christianity Today,* April 5, 1993, 74.

5. "Help Re-Establish the Church's Presence in Movies and Television," *Movieguide*, April 24, 1992, 17; Ted Baehr, "Movie & Television Studios Presented with 145,000 Pledges," *Movieguide*, October 16, 1992, 5, 20; Baehr, *Hollywood's Reel of Fortune*, 20–21. On the CFTVC, see James Young Trammell, "The Power of Religious Media Criticism: An Analysis of the Christian Film and Television Commission, 1985–2005" (University of Iowa, 2007).

6. Valenti quoted in Amy Wallace, "Mahony Urges Film Industry to Accept Code," *Los Angeles Times*, February 2, 1992, A1. Mahony quoted in Donna Parker, "Mahony Offers H'wood Guide for 'Human Values,'" *Hollywood Reporter*, October 1, 1992, 1, 19, PCA, Moral and Religious Aspects (1985–1992); John Leo, "One Poke over the Line," *U.S. News & World Report*, October 26, 1992, 34. On Wasserman, see Larry B. Stammer and David J. Fox, "Mahony Urges 'Human Values' in Films, TV," *Los Angeles Times*, October 1, 1992, 1; Aljean Harmetz, "Film on Christ Brings out Pickets and Archbishop Predicts Censure," *New York Times*, July 21, 1988, C19. See Paul Likoudia, "Fired Anti-Porn Chairman Claims Cardinal Was Pressured to Abandon Call for Film Code," *Movieguide*, October 16, 1992, 21–22; Stephen Vaughn, *Freedom and Entertainment: Rating the Movies in an Age of New Media* (Cambridge: Cambridge University Press, 2006), 224–229.

7. Michael Medved, "A Sickness of the Soul Replaces the Tinsel," *Los Angeles Times*, February 6, 1992, B7; Medved, *Hollywood vs. America: Popular Culture and the War on Traditional Values* (New York: HarperCollins, 1992), 3; "The Thorn in Hollywood's Side," *Christianity Today*, April 27, 1992, 40.

8. Rolfe quoted in "Family Films Rake in Cash for Studios," Dove Foundation Press Release, January 27, 1999. Medved, *Hollywood vs. America*, 286–291; "Profitability Study of MPAA Rated Movies Relased During 1988–1997," Grand Rapids, MI: Dove Foundation, 1999. See Arthur De Vany and W. David Walls, "Does Hollywood Make Too Many R-Rated Movies? Risk, Stochastic Dominance, and the Illusion of Expectation," *Journal of Business* 75, no. 3 (2002): 425–451.

9. Jack Valenti, Personal Interview, May 16, 2005; Medved, *Hollywood vs. America*, 324–225.

10. Jack Mathews, "Mark Canton's Wrongheaded Chant," *Los Angeles Times/ Calendar*, April 18, 1993, 24; Peter Bart, "Relling in 'R' Pix," *Variety*, March 22, 1992, 5, 7; MPAA, Incidence of Motion Picture Attendance among the Adult and Teenage Public, July 1994.

11. Robert C. Allen, "Home Alone Together: Hollywood and the 'Family Film,'" in *Identifying Hollywood's Audiences: Cultural Identity and the Movies*, eds. Melvyn Stokes and Richard Maltby (London: British Film Institute, 1999), 118–119. As expected, only a small number of family-oriented films were enormously profitable; most were only moderately successful or simply failed. See William D. Romanowski, *Pop Culture Wars: Religion and the Role of Entertainment in American Life* (Downers Grove, IL: InterVarsity Press, 1996), 270–275.

12. Dick Rolfe, "Give Families Choice of Editing Movies," *Grand Rapids Press*, June 14, 1993, A11. While it was generally accepted that about 40 percent of the U.S. population attended church weekly, sociological studies indicate actual church attendance is perhaps half that. C. Kirk Hadaway, Penny Long Marler, and Mark Chaves, "What the Polls Don't Show: A Closer Look at U.S. Church Attendance," *American Sociological Review* 58 (1993): 741–752; Penny Long Marler and C. Kirk Hadaway, "Testing the Attendance Gap in a Conservative Church," *Sociology of Religion* 60, no. 2 (1999): 3–11.

13. See Francis G. Couvares, "Introduction," *Movie Censorship and American Culture*, ed. Francis G. Couvares (Washington, DC: Smithsonian Institution Press, 1996), 10–11; Charles Lyons, *The New Censors: Movies and the Culture Wars* (Philadelphia: Temple, 1997).

14. Donohue quoted in "Release of Movie Delayed after Protest," *Christian Century*, April 19, 1995, 415–416. Not all Catholics agreed; David Toolan, a Jesuit priest and editor of *America*, did not think *Priest* was "an anti-Catholic film, or Catholic-bashing." At least one Southern Baptist faulted the denomination for failing to recognize that America is a "pluralistic, post-Christian society" and yearning "for the informal or even formal establishment of Christianity as the national religion." David P. Gushee, "The Speck in Mickey's Eye," *Christianity Today*, August 11, 1997, 13; "Groups Protest R-Rated Priest," *Christianity Today*, May 15, 1995, 52.

15. SBC delegate Rick Markham quoted in Jim Jones, "SBC Approves Disney Boycott," *Christianity Today*, July 14, 1997, 72. Eisner quoted in "Disney Executive Reacts to SBC Boycott," *Christian Century*, December 10, 1997, 1150. Examples of what the SBC called Disney's "Christian-bashing agenda" included movies like *Pocahontas* and *Priest*, and television shows like *Ellen* and *Nothing Sacred*. Gayle White, "Disney Boycott Gathers Steam," *Christianity Today*, October 6, 1997, 84. See Dale D. Buss, "Holding Corporate America Accountable," *Christianity Today*, October 28, 1996, 76–79.

16. Laurie Goodstein, "Some Christians See 'Passion' as Evangelism Tool," *New York Times*, February 5, 2004, A18; David Neff, "Mel, Mary, and Mothers," *Christianity Today*, March 2004, 34.

17. Anschutz quoted in Dave McNary, "Walden Brings Arsenal to Kid-Pic Wars," *Variety*, October 8–14, 2007, 1; James Russell, "Narnia as a Site of National Struggle: Marketing, Christianity, and National Purpose in *the Chronicles of Narnia: The Lion, the Wich and the Wardrobe*," *Cinema Journal* 48, no. 4 (2009): 59–76.

18. SBC delegate Lisa Kenney quoted in Jones, "SBC Approves Disney Boycott," 72; Russell, "Narnia as a Site of National Struggle," 73. See Andrew Hindes, "Will Baptists Break Mouse House Walls," Variety, June 23–29, 1977, 5, 16; Josh Rottenberg, "Movies, Money & God," *Entertainment Weekly*, May 15, 2009, 30.

19. Daniel and Gillian Flynn Fierman, "The Greatest Story Ever Sold," *Entertainment Weekly*, December 3, 1999, 55.

20. Desson Howe, "'Left Behind': Heaven Help Us," *Washington Post*, Online Edition, http://www.washingtonpost.com/wp-srv/entertainment/movies/reviews/leftbehindhowe.htm; Terry Mattingly, "Did Religious Content in 'Giants' Affect Rating?," *Grand Rapids Press*, July 29, 2006, D5.

21. The MarketCast survey and executive are cited in Sharon Waxman, "The Passion of the Marketers," *New York Times*, July 18, 2005, C3.

22. David S. Cohen, "Execs Say Prayers for Next 'Passion'," *Variety* Online Edition, April 2, 2007; Rottenberg, "Movies, Money & God," 31.

23. Grace Hill Media, About Us, http://www.gracehillmedia.com/aboutus/; Andrew Hampp, "How a Faith-Based Strategy Pushed 'Blind Side' to No. 1 at the Box Office," *Advertising Age Online*, December 8, 2009.

24. Ronald Gold, "Catholics' 10-Year Switch from Film Censorship to Sympathy," *Variety*, February 9, 1966, 15.

25. See James Davison Hunter, *To Change the World: The Irony, Tragedy, and Possibility of Christianity in the Late Modern World* (New York: Oxford, 2010); Michael O. Emerson and Christian Smith, *Divided by Faith: Evangelical Religion and the Problem of Race in America* (New York: Oxford, 2000).

CONCLUSION

1. William F. Fore, "The Church and Motion Pictures," *The Journal of the Screen Producers Guild*, December 1966, 11.

2. Robert N. Bellah et al., ed. *Habits of the Heart: Individualism and Commitment in American Life* (Berkeley: University of California, 1985), 224. Mark Chaves, "Secularization as Declining Religious Authority," *Social Forces* 72, no. 3 (1994): 749–774; P. C. Kemeny, "Banned in Boston: Commercial Culture and the Politics of Moral Reform in Boston During the 1920s," in *Faith in the Market: Religion and the Rise of Urban Commercial Culture*, eds. John M. and Diane Winston Giggie (New Brunswick: Rutgers, 2002): 133–152; Richard Wightman Fox, "The Discipline of Amusement," in *Inventing Times Square: Commerce and Culture at the Crossroads of the World*, ed. William R. Taylor (New York: Russell Sage Foundation, 1991): 83–98.

3. Jack Valenti, *Address at the North American Branch of the World Association of Christians in Communications (Nabswaac)* (1995), Videocassette. Howard S. Becker, *Art Worlds* (Berkeley: University of California Press, 1982); Calvin Seerveld, *Bearing Fresh Olive Leaves: Alternative Steps in Understanding Art* (Carlisle and Toronto: Piquant and Toronto Tuppence Press, 2000), 12–14.

4. See "The Digital Future" in Stephen Vaughn, *Freedom and Entertainment: Rating the Movies in an Age of New Media* (Cambridge: Cambridge University Press, 2006), 251–265.

5. Gabriel Snyder, "Don't Give Me an 'R'," *Variety*, February 21–27, 2005, 8, 45.

6. Quoted in Snyder, "Don't Give Me an 'R'. Sharon Waxman, "Study Finds Film Ratings Are Growing More Lenient," *New York Times*, July 14, 2004, E1; Julie

Salamon, "The Rating Says PG, But Is That Guidance Enough?," *New York Times*, January 7, 2005, E28; Jack Valenti, Personal Interview, May 16, 2005; Harvard School of Public Health Press Release, Study Finds "Ratings Creep": Movie Ratings Categories Contain More Violence, Sex, Profanity Than Decade Ago, July 13, 2004. On new media and culture, see Henry Jenkins, *Convergence Culture: Where Old and New Media Collide* (New York: New York University Press, 2006).

Index